Stamp Duty Land Tax: a practical guide for lawyers (second edition)

by

Ann L Humphrey and

Philip Freedman

Published by

Spiramus Press, 102 Blandford Street, London, W1U 8AG.

November 2007

ISBN 978 1904905 24 0

British Library Cataloguing-in-Publication Data.

A catalogue record for this book is available from the British Library.

Disclaimer: This publication is intended to assist you in identifying issues which you should know about and about which you may need to seek specific advice. It is not intended to be an exhaustive statement of the law or a substitute for seeking specific advice. Neither this book nor any part of it constitutes, nor is a substitute for, legal advice which should still always be sought on any particular issue or in respect of any proposed activity or use and neither the authors nor the contributors accept responsibility or liability for the accuracy of the same or any loss or damage howsoever sustained by any person acting or placing reliance on the same or otherwise arising therefrom.

This publication is based upon the law and HMRC practice as at 20 July 2007.

All references are to the Finance Act 2003 unless otherwise stated.

Typeset by: Spiramus Press Ltd

Printed in Great Britain by: Biddles, UK

How to use this book

This book is divided into six sections, each written to help the practitioner in different ways, moving from an explanation of the law to applying it in transactions:

Part One is an introduction to stamp duty land tax, giving an overview of how the tax works, and what the main changes have been since its introduction.

Part Two provides a detailed analysis of the legislation and regulations which dictate the scope, calculation and administration of the tax. It also covers the reliefs available, and the anti-avoidance measures in place. Where possible, we have included examples in the text to help illustrate how the law works.

Part Three covers the practical mechanics of completing the forms and calculating the tax charge. In this new edition, we include information explaining how the online service works and highlighting differences between the paper- and online processes.

Part Four illustrates how SDLT works by providing a number of scenarios from straightforward purchase of a freehold to more complex cases such as sale and leaseback arrangements, so that the reader can see how SDLT works in practice.

Part Five is a glossary of the key terms used in the legislation and the text of this book.

Part Six contains the main forms used for SDLT transactions. We have not included the guidance notes in this edition because HMRC now updates these regularly online, and the practitioner is advised to refer to the HMRC website.

Acknowledgements

The authors and publisher would like to thank Gerald Moran of Hunters Solicitors, and Jill Hallpike for reading and commenting on the text, and helping us to improve this publication. Any errors which remain are ours.

Contents

Abbreviations

EC	European Community (citations for directives and regulations after 1992)
EEC	European Economic Community (citations for directives and regulations before 1992)
FA	Finance Act
ICTA 1988	Income and Corporation Taxes Act 1988
IHTA 1984	Inheritance Tax Act 1984
NI	Northern Ireland
NLPG	National Land and Property Gazette Unique Property
UPRN	Reference Number
NPV	Net Present Value
PFI	Private Finance Initiative
PIF	Property Investment Fund
REIT	Real Estate Investment Trust
RRV	Relevant Rental Value
SDLT	Stamp Duty Land Tax
SDLTM	Stamp Duty Land Tax Manual
SI	Statutory Instrument
SP	Statement of Practice
TCGA1992	Taxation of Chargeable Gains Act 1992
TMA 1970	Taxes Management Act 1970
TRN	Transaction Reference Number
UK	United Kingdom
VAT	Value Added Tax

References

AC……………………………………………Law Reports, Appeal Cases
All ER ……………………………………All England Law Reports
Ch.……………………………Law Reports, Chancery Division (1891 -)
KB…………………………………………Law Reports, King's Bench
LT………………………………………………Law Times Reports
PCR…………………………………Property and Compensation Report
SC………………………………………………Court of Session Cases
STC………………………………………………Simon's Tax Cases

Tables of Authorities

Cases

Statutes

PART ONE

SDLT: AN OVERVIEW

Key features of the SDLT regime

- SDLT is chargeable whether or not the land transaction is effected by an instrument.
- If there is an instrument, SDLT is chargeable whether or not that instrument is executed in the UK.
- SDLT applies regardless of whether or not any party is present or resident in the UK.
- A certificate replaces the old duty 'stamp'.
- SDLT is not voluntary – a land transaction return must be filed together with a cheque or penalties and interest are incurred.
- The land transaction return must be signed by the purchaser or his attorney.
- SDLT on leases is based on the net present value of any rent (charged at a rate of 1%) as well as any premium (charged at rates between 1% and 4%) once the nil rate band is exceeded.
- Original documents are no longer sent for stamping.
- No adjudication – self assessment applies.

Main changes since first edition

- Introduction of full online submission process ('e-filing');
- Removal of requirement to submit payment at same time as SDLT return;
- Updating of the land transaction form and guidance notes;
- Simplification measures to remove certain transactions from the scope of SDLT;
- New rules to deal with the transfer of land into and out of partnerships;
- The introduction of a range of anti-avoidance measures to prevent exploitation of the rules.

Introduction

It is now nearly four years since SDLT was introduced, bringing in an entirely new system of charging tax on UK land transactions. Around £10 billion a year is now collected. SDLT is self-assessed. There is no equivalent to the stamp duty adjudication procedure whereby a case could be presented to the Stamp Office for a definitive ruling.

Since 1 December 2003, while practitioners and officers of HM Revenue & Customs (the combined body of the former Inland Revenue and HM Customs & Excise) have been familiarising themselves with the operation of SDLT, there have been a number of changes, both to the underlying legislation and to the administration of the tax; many of these resulting in a smoother process for the actual transmission of the land tax return through the sorting out of some procedural quirks. Other changes have resulted in the closure of loopholes in the law which were being exploited to gain SDLT advantages (or to avoid payment of SDLT altogether).

Key changes since the publication of the first edition of this book include:

- Removal of disadvantaged areas relief except in very limited circumstances;
- Increase in exempt threshold for residential transactions;
- Introduction of full online submission process ('e-filing');
- Updating of the land transaction form and guidance notes;
- Simplification measures to remove certain transactions from the scope of SDLT and to clarify the application of SDLT to particular transactions e.g. the transfer of an interest in a land-owning UK trading partnership;
- Introduction of anti-avoidance measures to counter exploitation of the group relief rules, the use of lease variations in return for the payment of a capital sum, and the ending of the exemption for transfers to unit trusts;
- Requirement to disclose to HMRC details of high value commercial property transactions which have SDLT avoidance as their main (or one of their main) purpose(s);
- Removal of requirement to submit payment at same time as SDLT return (FA 2007);
- New rules to deal with the transfer of land into and out of partnerships (FA 2007);
- Introduction of a general anti-avoidance rule to disregard certain stages of a transaction which have produced a lower SDLT charge than a straightforward disposal and acquisition (FA 2007).

The key features of the regime remain the same, however, and are set out below (and in the box opposite).

An Overview of SDLT

SDLT is payable on UK land transactions. Land transactions caught by SDLT include the conveyance of a freehold and the assignment of a lease. The grant, surrender or variation of a lease may also attract SDLT and if a person acquires the benefit of any obligation, restriction or condition that affects the value of any interest in land (for example, the grant of an easement or the release of a restrictive covenant) this may also constitute a land transaction for SDLT purposes. The grant of an option or of a pre-emption right is a land transaction.

SDLT only applies if there is chargeable consideration for the transaction. If there is no chargeable consideration, the transaction is normally exempt provided the parties are unconnected. There are other exemptions, for instance, the grant of a licence and the acquisition of a security interest or charge over UK land. Some transactions must be notified to HMRC even though a relief is available. Reliefs are claimed in the land transaction return.

In most cases the chargeable consideration is any consideration in money or money's worth given directly or indirectly by the purchaser or someone connected with him. The categories of chargeable consideration for SDLT are wider than those which applied for stamp duty purposes and include, in some cases, an undertaking to carry out works or provide services. A reverse premium is not chargeable consideration. Special rules apply to treatment of deferred, contingent or uncertain consideration.

The rate of SDLT on purchase prices and lease premiums varies depending on the amount of chargeable consideration for the transaction, with the highest rate of 4% applying to transactions with a chargeable consideration of more than £500,000. The threshold for residential property is £125,000 and for non-residential or mixed property, £150,000. On the grant of a lease, SDLT is charged, once the relevant threshold is exceeded, at the rate of 1% on the net present value of the rents payable throughout the lease term, discounted at an annual rate of 3.5%. There are complex rules for determining the SDLT charge on leases with variable rent, such as turnover leases and leases with market value rent reviews.

SDLT must be paid within 30 days of the effective date of the relevant transaction which in most cases will be the date of completion. SDLT may be due before completion if the contract is substantially performed before that date (including where the purchaser has taken possession and where a substantial amount of the consideration is paid). If this is the case, the effective date of the transaction is the date when the contract is substantially performed.

The purchaser is obliged to deliver a land transaction return to HMRC within 30 days of the effective date of the transaction. SDLT due must also be paid within 30 days of the effective date if interest and penalties are to be avoided, but payment does not necessarily have to be made at the same time as the return (from March 2007). Then if the land transaction return has been filled in satisfactorily and the right amount of SDLT has been paid, HMRC will issue a certificate to the purchaser. Without the certificate, or a self-certificate if no land transaction return is required, the land transaction cannot be registered at the Land Registry.

PART TWO

THE SDLT REGIME IN DETAIL

1. Scope of SDLT

Section 42(1) sets out the SDLT charge and reads as follows:

'A tax (to be known as 'stamp duty land tax') shall be charged in accordance with this Part on land transactions'.

Payment of SDLT is an obligation of the purchaser.[1]

1.1. Land transactions – the trigger

SDLT is levied on 'land transactions'. This is deceptively simple.

A 'land transaction' is defined in section 43 as the 'acquisition' of a 'chargeable interest'.

1.1.1. Chargeable interests

(Section 48)

A chargeable interest is defined in section 48 as:

- any estate, interest, right or power in or over land situated in the UK
- the benefit of any obligation, restriction or condition which affects the value of such an estate, interest, right or power

A chargeable interest includes an equitable interest as well as a legal interest in land. A commonhold interest is a chargeable interest[2] as is a power of appointment over land. Chargeable interests also include interests, rights or powers in or over land as well as estates in or over land, such as easements, profits à prendre and rentcharges. Wayleaves (the right to put pipes or cables over another's land) are contractual rights and not interests in land. Common examples of easements are rights of way, rights of light, and rights of support. Examples of profits à prendre are pasture rights and rights to hunt or fish.

A rentcharge is a sum of money, payable either annually or biannually, which is a charge on land. A rentcharge is usually created in a conveyance or transfer. The party selling the land reserves an annual rent payable to him and his successors in title, which is charged on the land sold. A rentcharge is usually perpetual but can also be for a term of years (terminable). A rentcharge can affect freehold or leasehold estates. If it affects a leasehold estate it will always

---

[1] Section 43(4) provides that references to the 'purchaser', in relation to a land transaction, are to 'the person acquiring ... the subject-matter of the transaction'. This applies even if there is no consideration for a transaction but a person cannot be a purchaser unless he has given consideration for a transaction or is a 'party to' it (section 43(5)).

[2] See SDLTM00285

be terminable[3]. The assignment of rentcharges is common in financing transactions and joint ventures.

Where a major interest in land is acquired together with an interest or right pertaining to it, then that is treated as one land transaction.[4] The acquisition of freehold land with the benefit of a right of way over the seller's adjoining land would be an example of this.

'Land' includes buildings and structures and land covered by water.[5]

The 'UK' means England, Wales, Scotland and Northern Ireland.[6] The boundary of 'land situated in the UK' is the low-water mark of the coastline of the UK.[7] It does not cover the bed of the territorial sea but piers, jetties and similar structures attached to the UK as defined are part of the UK for this purpose.[8]

The benefit of an obligation, restriction or condition is a chargeable interest provided that it affects the value of an estate, interest, right or power in or over land in the UK. Hence the grant, assignment, variation or release of such an obligation, restriction or condition for consideration is a land transaction. An example would be the grant or release of a covenant even if it did not amount to an equitable interest in land because it did not bind the land of the covenantor in equity.

Certain interests are exempted from being chargeable interests by section 48(2). Currently these are:

- a security interest[9]
- a tenancy at will[10]

---

[3] See Land Registry Practice Guide 56 at paragraph 2.1

[4] Section 43(6) A 'major interest' is defined in section 117(2) (in relation to England and Wales) as a fee simple absolute or a term of years absolute at law or in equity. The definitions applying to Scotland and Northern Ireland are in section 117(3) and (4) respectively.

[5] Section 121

[6] Schedule 1 Interpretation Act 1978.

[7] *Argyll & Bute DC v. Secretary of State for Scotland* [1976] S.C. 248

[8] See judgment of Technology and Construction Court in *Staveley Industries t/a EI WHS v. Odebrecht Oil and Gas Services* (2001) in which it was held that structures which are, or are to be founded in the seabed below the low water mark are not structures forming part of the land.

[9] Defined as any interest or right (other than a rentcharge) held for the purpose of securing the payment of money or the performance of any other obligation (section 48(3)).

[10] Paragraph 1 Schedule 17A (introduced by FA 2004) includes a tenancy at will in the definition of 'lease' however the express exclusion in section 48(2)(c)(i) should override this and keep tenancies at will outside the SDLT regime.

- an advowson[11], franchise[12] or manor[13]
- a licence to use or occupy land[14]

FA 2007 provides[15] that where a financial institution has provided an alternative property finance product falling within the scope of sections 71A, 72 or 72A any subsequent dealing in the interest held by the institution or in any interest derived from it, will be exempt from SDLT. The new provision will apply where the effective date of the dealing is on or after 22 March 2007.

The Treasury has a general power to make regulations exempting other interests from being chargeable interests.[16]

1.1.2. What is meant by the 'acquisition' of a chargeable interest?

If an interest is not a chargeable interest there is no obligation to make a land transaction return in respect of its acquisition. Where a chargeable interest is acquired, there is a land transaction for SDLT purposes.[17]

Section 43(2) provides that there will be a land transaction however the acquisition is effected - whether by act of the parties, court order or operation of law. This means that the acquisition need not be contractual or involve formal documentation – the surrender of a lease by operation of law would be an 'acquisition' for this purpose.

Her Majesty's Revenue & Customs (HMRC) have confirmed that the vesting of property on registration of a society under the Industrial and Provident Societies Act 1965[18] is not a land transaction and so no SDLT is chargeable.[19]

Section 43(3) provides that 'acquisition' includes the creation, surrender, release or variation of a chargeable interest, with the person who benefits from

---

[11] An advowson is the right in perpetuity to present a new vicar to a parish.

[12] A franchise is defined as a grant from the Crown, such as the right to hold a market or fair or take tolls (section 48(3)).

[13] A manor is the interest held by a lord of the manor.

[14] But allowing entry onto land pursuant to a licence may amount to 'substantial performance' of a contract and trigger a charge to SDLT under section 44 –see 1.3 below.

[15] By inserting section 73B (Exempt interests) in FA 2003 with effect from 22 March 2007.

[16] No regulations have been made to date.

[17] A deed of rectification may result in the acquisition of a chargeable interest by a party to it – see examples at SDLTM00305.

[18] On registration any property previously vested in any person on trust for the society becomes vested in the society.

[19] SDLTM31610

the creation, surrender,[20] release or variation being the person making the acquisition and the other party being the person making the disposal. This ties in with section 43(4) which provides that references to the 'purchaser' and 'vendor', in relation to a land transaction, are to 'the person acquiring and the person disposing of the subject-matter of the transaction'.[21]

So the grant of a right of way or entry into a restrictive covenant will be the creation of a chargeable interest and in such a case the SDLT charge will fall on the person entitled to the interest created. The release of a restrictive covenant (resulting in an owner of land being able to do something which the covenant would have prohibited) will give rise to the acquisition of a chargeable interest and the SDLT charge will fall on the person who benefits from the release.

SDLTM00270 confirms that 'acquisition' does not include the case where an interest is reserved or excepted from a conveyance to a third party by the transferor[22], even where a reservation operates, for conveyancing purposes, as a re-grant.

The variation of a lease is treated as an acquisition and disposal where it takes effect as, or is treated for SDLT purposes as, the grant of a new lease or the provisions of paragraph 15A Schedule 17A apply.[23] If the lease was varied within the first five years to increase the rent (which would be treated as the grant of a new lease by reason of paragraph 13 Schedule 17A) or to extend the term or increase the extent of the premises (which takes effect in law as a surrender and re-grant) this variation could therefore give rise to an SDLT charge. Paragraph 15A applies to treat reductions in rent or term and any other variation of a lease for consideration (other than an increase in rent) as acquisitions of chargeable interests.

---

[20] The 'purchaser' would be the landlord (as he is acquiring the chargeable interest which is the subject of the land transaction) even when he is paid by the tenant to accept the surrender. In the case of a reverse premium paid on surrender there will be no 'chargeable consideration' so no SDLT will be due. The reverse surrender will fall within paragraph 1 Schedule 3 and will not be notifiable.

[21] These expressions apply even if there is no consideration for a transaction but a person cannot be a purchaser unless he has given consideration for a transaction or is a 'party to' it (section 43(5)).

[22] For example, the reservation of easements or covenants on a sale of the freehold.

[23] Section 43(d) as amended by section 297(2) FA 2004 in relation to transactions with an effective date on or after 22 July 2004.

The exercise of a break clause in a lease is not the acquisition of a chargeable interest because it does not cause a surrender or release of the interest[24].

1.1.3. Effective date

(Section 119[25])

The effective date of a transaction is important as it is the date from which the rate of tax applicable to the transaction is to be determined as well as the date at which the applicability of various of the reliefs from SDLT is tested.

The 'effective date' of a transaction is determined in accordance with section 44 and is normally the date that the land transaction is completed. There are exceptions to this:

- Where a contract has been made and is 'substantially performed' without being completed the effective date is the date on which the contract is substantially performed.[26]
- Where a land transaction consists of the grant of an option or a right of pre-emption the effective date is the date on which such rights are acquired, not when they are exercised;[27] and

There are special rules for the effective date in:

- section 44A (3) (contract providing for conveyance to third party)
- section 45A(8) (contract providing for conveyance to third party: effect of transfer of rights)
- paragraph 12A(2) Schedule 17A (agreement for lease substantially performed without being completed)
- paragraph 12B(3) Schedule 17A (assignment of agreement for lease occurring after agreement substantially performed), and paragraph 19(3) Schedule 17A (missives of let etc in Scotland followed by substantial performance).

1.2. SDLT on conveyancing contracts and completions

While an SDLT charge will arise whether or not the acquisition is effected by an instrument, section 44 makes special provision for the application of SDLT

---

[24] *Pennel v Payne CA* [1995] 2 All ER 592 as expressly approved in *Barrett v Morgan* HL [2000] 2 AC 264

[25] As amended by F(No.2)A 2005 to allow HMRC to prescribe an alternative date to completion by regulations.

[26] Section 44(4)

[27] Section 46(3)

where there is a contract[28] which is to be completed by a conveyance[29] to effect the land transaction.

A land transaction in which exchange of contracts is followed by completion by conveyance is taxed as a single land transaction, with the 'effective date' being completion (section 44(3)). In such a case, entering into the contract is not regarded as entering into a land transaction (section 44(2)).

1.3. Substantial performance – the charge to SDLT – no more 'resting on contract'

(Section 44 and paragraph 12A Schedule 17A)

Where there is an exchange of contracts under which a land transaction is to be completed by a conveyance and the contract is 'substantially performed' without at that time being completed,[30] the contract is treated as if it were the land transaction provided for in the contract with the date of substantial performance as the effective date (section 44(4)). There are therefore potentially two land transactions in such a case – the first being substantial performance and the second being the conveyance. This rule also applies to conditional contracts.

The inclusion of substantial performance as the trigger for a deemed land transaction in these circumstances is intended to prevent a form of avoidance common under the old stamp duty regime, known as 'resting on contract', where parties would exchange contracts, the purchaser taking possession under the contract, and defer completion for a long period thus avoiding stamp duty until such time as completion occurred. In the period between contract and completion the vendor would hold the legal title as trustee for the buyer and often the legal title would end up directly or indirectly under the purchaser's control. Resting on contract for stamp duty purposes no longer achieved savings with effect from 25 July 2002 in cases where the consideration exceeded £10 million as it was counteracted by section 115 FA 2002, yet the device continued in a variety of different forms.

'Substantially performed' means that either the purchaser or a person 'connected with' the purchaser[31] 'takes possession' of the whole or substantially

---

[28] 'Contract' for the purposes of section 44 includes any agreement (section 44(10)).

[29] 'Conveyance' for the purposes of section 44 includes any instrument (section 44(10)).

[30] 'Completion' for the purposes of section 44 means 'completion of the land transaction proposed, between the same parties, in substantial conformity with the contract' (section 49(10)).

[31] Section 44(5)(a) as amended by paragraph 1 of the Schedule to the Stamp Duty and Stamp Duty Land Tax (Variation of the Finance Act 2003) (No. 2) Regulations 2003 (SI 2003/2816) The Stamp

the whole of the 'subject matter' of the contract (the 'taking possession test') or a 'substantial amount' of the consideration is paid or provided (the 'payment test').[32] The 'subject-matter' of the contract is not defined however section 43(6) provides that references to the subject matter of a land transaction are references to the chargeable interest acquired together with any interest or right appurtenant or pertaining to it that is acquired with it.

Suppose that a contract is substantially performed before it is completed by a conveyance. Substantial performance would be a notifiable transaction which will trigger the liability both to submit a land transaction return and to pay any SDLT due. The contract is subsequently completed. It may be thought that there are no further compliance obligations, especially if no further consideration is paid. However, both the contract and completion of it are notifiable transactions, although SDLT is due on completion only to the extent (if any) that the SDLT chargeable on completion exceeds the SDLT paid on the contract (section 44(8)).

It should therefore not be assumed that where no further consideration is due (and no more SDLT payable) there are no more compliance obligations. A land transaction return must nevertheless be delivered or the penalty provisions for failure to submit a return may bite.

If the contract is substantially performed before completion and there is a subsequent conveyance, SDLT is payable on the conveyance only to the extent that it exceeds the SDLT on the contract – in other words, SDLT is chargeable only once on the same consideration[33]. As section 44(4) deems the contract which is substantially performed to be the transaction provided for in the contract, the charge on substantial performance will always be on the entire consideration payable under the contract leaving nothing further to be charged on completion, unless the purchaser gives additional consideration not provided for in the contract, or the conditions for a relief are fulfilled at the time of substantial performance but not at completion.

Notification: substantial performance followed by completion

There are different HMRC practices for dealing with cases where a further land transaction return needs to be made because an agreement or contract that has

---

Duty and Stamp Duty Land Tax (Variation of the Finance Act 2003) (No. 2) Regulations 2003 were revoked by paragraph 14(2) Schedule 39 FA 2004 and in this respect replaced in the same form by Part 2 Schedule 39 with effect for any transaction of which the effective date is on or after 22 July 2004. The section 839 ICTA 1988 definition of 'connected' applies (see SDLT Glossary in Part Five).

[32] Section 44(5)(b) (based on the wording in section 115 FA 2002 which referred to 'the whole, or substantially the whole, of the intended consideration [having] been paid or transferred').

[33] Section 44(8)(b)

been previously notified on substantial performance needs to be notified again on completion[34].

If the agreement is for the transfer of a freehold or the assignment of an existing lease, the completion land transaction return (form SDLT1) should be sent to Birmingham Stamp Office with a covering letter and a copy of the original land transaction return relating to substantial performance.

If the agreement is for the grant of a new lease, the grant of the new lease is treated as a completely separate transaction from the notional lease (notification on substantial performance), using the surrender and re-grant mechanism with overlap relief. A Code L SDLT1 and SDLT4 need to be submitted in the normal way; either by submitting online or if using paper forms, to the Rapid Data Capture Centre, Netherton.

If overlap relief resulted in nil rent being entered on the grant of lease, and there was no additional premium over and above what had been notified in the notional lease, there would be the grant of a lease for no chargeable consideration. This means a SDLT60 could be used for the grant.

1.3.1. Substantial performance – the taking possession test

It is not clear whether 'possession' for the purposes of deciding whether there has been substantial performance (and a resulting land transaction) bears its technical land law meaning (extended where necessary by the specific provisions of the SDLT legislation) or its every day meaning. On balance, giving 'possession' a technical meaning would seem the more appropriate; in the words of Lord Hoffmann in *MacNiven v. Westmoreland Investments Limited*,[35] it "is a purely legal concept – a commercial man, asked what it means, would say 'You had better ask a lawyer'." However, subsequent decisions of the courts, notably *Barclays Mercantile Business Finance v. Mawson* and *Scottish Provident Institution v. Revenue and Customs Commissioners* have moved away from Lord Hoffman's 'legal/commercial' dichotomy as a valuable distinction in giving words a meaning.

'Taking possession' is obviously not the same as having an entitlement to possession nor is it the same as being 'in possession'.[36] Whether a person has taken possession will be a question of fact. In *Marsden v. Miller and Others*

---

[34] See 'Where to send your SDLT paper work' available at http://www.hmrc.gov.uk/so/mctu.htm

[35] [2001] UKHL 6, [2001] 1 AC 311

[36] In *Wallrock v. Equity and Law Life Assurance Society* [1941] 2 KB 82 the Court of Appeal remarked that 'in the absence of a clear context, the words 'take possession' are suitable only to the case of physical things.'

[1992], a case which turned on whether the plaintiff had ever had possession of certain disputed land, the Court of Appeal expressed the test in the following way:

> "It is well-established that in order to obtain or retain possession of land both a mental element and a factual element are requisite. The factual element must involve an appropriate degree of physical control. The mental element, the so-called animus possidendi, must consist of an intention to take possession to the exclusion of all others."[37]

If the landowner retains control over the premises in a manner inconsistent with the purchaser's right to possession (for example, by requiring a purchaser to make detailed access arrangements with the landlord's building contractor, who is still carrying on works elsewhere in the building) the purchaser's presence in the premises would not amount to 'possession' and consequently would not be substantial performance.

If the purchaser is already in possession before the date of the contract, for example, as a sitting tenant or licensee, then he does not 'take' possession under that contract so this would not amount to substantial performance of the contract.[38]

To amount to substantial performance possession must be taken of 'the whole or substantially the whole' of the 'subject-matter' of the contract. The subject-matter of the land transaction is defined in section 43(6) as the chargeable interest acquired (the 'main subject matter') together with any interest or right appurtenant or pertaining to it that is acquired with it and it is possession of this interest (and not the land subject to it) which must be taken by the purchaser or a person connected with him to constitute substantial performance.

Simply going onto the land would not amount to taking possession for this purpose. However, section 44(6) provides that it is immaterial whether possession is taken under the contract or under a lease or licence of a temporary nature. To trigger a charge, the possession taken must still be of the chargeable interest which is to be acquired under the contract. A purchaser of, say, a 21 year lease of vacant land who enters onto that land for the purpose of carrying out fitting-out works pursuant to a licence would not normally be regarded as having taken 'possession' of the leasehold interest as his possession in such a case is not to the exclusion of the rights of the legal owner,

---

[37] 64 PCR [1992] at page 242-3

[38] See SDLTM07900

rather it is pursuant to the licence. The effect of section 44(6) is therefore unclear, although HMRC seem to take a simplistic view of its operation.[39]

'Possession' includes the receipt of rents and profits or the right to receive them.[40] Therefore in the case of a land transaction involving the reversion to a tenancy, an entitlement to receive rent before completion, provided that it related to the whole or substantially the whole of the interest acquired, would amount to possession. In this respect condition 5.2.2(e) of the Standard Conditions of Sale[41] may give rise to a problem as it is in the following terms:

Occupation by buyer

5.2. The buyer is a licensee and not a tenant. The terms of the licence are that the buyer:...
5.2.2....
(e) is entitled to any rents and profits from any part of the property which he does not occupy."

Conversely, the payment of rent before completion of the contract would, in the case of a land transaction which consisted of the grant of a lease,[42] trigger a charge to SDLT under the payment test of substantial performance (see below). This is distinct from the taking possession test, for example, where an agreement for lease allowed the tenant to enter the property before the grant of the lease under a licence but required him to pay a licence fee. This may amount to substantial performance under the taking possession test if it amounts to taking possession of the leasehold interest.

The example given in the HMRC Stamp Duty Land Tax Manual ('SDLTM') is not particularly illuminating:[43]

"Contracts and substantial performance: Purchaser takes possession FA03/S44(5)(a)
A contract will be substantially performed where the purchaser obtains 'the keys to the door' and is entitled to occupy the property (however this is documented) or when the purchaser of a building that is let becomes entitled to receive the rents. "

---

[39] See SDLTM17900 - 'Where premises are entered into for fitting out that will count as possession'

[40] This wording follows the wording of section 205(1)(xix) Law of Property Act 1925.

[41] 4th Edition

[42] i.e. in a case where the rent was all or part of the 'chargeable consideration' for the land transaction (which in the case of an assignment it would not be).

[43] SDLTM07900

1.3.2. Substantial performance – the payment test

A 'substantial amount of the consideration is paid or provided':

- if none of the consideration is rent, where the whole or substantially the whole of the consideration is paid or provided;
- if rent is the only consideration, when the first payment of rent is made;
- if the consideration includes both rent and other consideration, when the whole or substantially the whole of the consideration other than rent is paid or provided or the first payment of rent is made.

(section 44(7))

SDLTM07950 gives HMRC's view of what 'the whole or substantially the whole' means for the purposes of section 44(7):

> 'Substantially the whole means an amount equal to or greater than 90% of the total consideration due under the contract unless the circumstances of the transaction are such that in substance the whole of the consideration has been paid or provided.
>
> Such a case might be an arrangement where a contract dated January 2004 provides for the purchase of a property with a market value of £10 million and provides for payment of £15 million with £10 million payable now and the balance in 2099'.

The intention is, in part, to prevent the payment of a deposit which is normally 10% of the purchase price in the case of a residential transaction, triggering a charge on the contract.

1.3.3. Substantial performance – the charge

If the provisions of section 44(4) and (5) are read together with the associated definitions, the charging provision in relation to a contract which is performed before it is completed is as follows:

"If before a contract or agreement for the land transaction has been completed between the same parties and in substantial conformity with its terms:

- the purchaser or any person connected with the purchaser takes possession of the whole or substantially the whole of the chargeable interest to be acquired by that contract or agreement; or
- in a case where none of the consideration for the land transaction is rent, the whole or substantially the whole of the consideration is paid or provided; or
- in a case where rent is the only consideration, the first payment of rent is made; or
- in a case where the consideration includes both rent and other consideration:

- the whole or substantially the whole of the consideration other than rent is paid or provided; or
- the first payment of rent is made,

  whichever happens first,

then the contract or agreement is treated for SDLT purposes as if it were the land transaction provided for in the contract."

Substantial performance - effective date

The effective date of the transaction is the date when the contract is substantially performed and this may result in an obligation to file a land transaction return and pay any SDLT before the date of completion.

Where the contract is later completed, both the contract which has been substantially performed and the subsequent conveyance are 'notifiable', and further SDLT may be payable to the extent that the SDLT chargeable on completion is greater than that paid on the earlier effective date (section 44(8)). This rule also applies where there is a part subsale, in relation to the part which is not sub-sold, as if that part were the subject of a separate contract.

Where an exchange takes place and is taxed under section 44(4) as a result of substantial performance, but the contract is rescinded or annulled or its terms are not, for any other reason, carried into effect then the appropriate proportion of any SDLT levied is to be refunded (section 44(9)). In order to obtain the refund it is necessary to make a claim by amending the land transaction return made in respect of the substantial performance of the contract. However, this can only be done within 13 months of the effective date.

1.3.4. Substantial performance – agreement for lease

(Paragraph 12A Schedule 17A):

An agreement for lease does not give rise to a charge to SDLT unless the agreement is substantially performed before the lease is granted. Similar rules to those in section 44 apply to prevent 'resting on contract' in the case of agreements for lease.

Where an agreement for lease is entered into and is 'substantially performed'[44] without at that time being completed, a notional lease is deemed to have been granted, in accordance with the agreement, for a term beginning on the date on which the agreement for lease was substantially performed. The end of the term of the notional lease is the date when the actual lease will end, if that is known. If the term of the actual lease is unknown (for example, because it will

---

[44] This has the same meaning as in section 44.

be ten years from the date of completion of the actual lease), then the notional lease is to be treated as a lease for an indefinite term and the rules in paragraph 4 of Schedule 17A will apply[45]. The deemed grant may give rise to an obligation to submit a land transaction return.

Where a lease is later granted in pursuance of the agreement which has earlier been substantially performed, this is treated for the purposes of paragraph 9 Schedule 17A (overlap relief on surrender and re-grant) as a surrender and re-grant and overlap relief is available[46]. From 19 July 2006[47], the agreement for lease and the lease executed pursuant to it are not within the successive linked leases provisions[48].

On the grant of an actual lease pursuant to a substantially performed agreement for lease, Box 17 on the land transaction return ('start date as specified in lease') should show the start date of the actual lease. Box 20 ('annual starting rent') should show the full rent payable under the actual lease and not simply the amount left after deducting the rent declared on the land transaction return for the notional lease. As neither Box 17 nor Box 20 is used to compute the NPV'[49] this will not affect the charge to SDLT which will take into account overlap relief.

The question arises whether any premium for the lease might be taxed twice – once as a premium for the notional lease and again as a premium for the actual lease. The lease chapter of the SDLT Manual (April 2007 version) states[50]:

> "In cases where a premium is payable, the premium is only subject to tax once. It is a question of fact whether the premium was paid as consideration for entering into the agreement or as consideration for the lease being granted. The purchaser must report the transaction accordingly."

There are provisions similar to those in section 44(9) to deal with annulments and rescissions of the agreement for lease.

---

45 See 2.6.18 below

46 See 1.8 below and see also examples in the lease chapter of the SDLT Manual (April 2007) at SDLTM17015 and SDLTM17020.

47 The date from which the provision (in section 12A(3) Schedule 17A) was amended by paragraph 4 Schedule 25 FA 2006.

48 In paragraph 5 Schedule 17A – see 2.6.4 below.

49 The NPV (Net Present Value) calculation is considered in detail at 2.6.9 below. Broadly, the rent payable under a lease is taxed by reference to the NPV of each yearly amount of rent that will become payable under the lease if it runs its full course.

50 At SDLTM17010

1.3.5. Contract providing for conveyance to a third party: development and building joint ventures

(Section 44A)[51]

The charge to SDLT extends to transactions where a purchaser, typically a developer, enters into a contract requiring the vendor to convey the property to a third party at the purchaser's direction. If there is substantial performance of that contract before it is completed then a charge to SDLT arises and the original purchaser is liable for the tax. Section 44A will catch some development and building joint ventures. To avoid a liability for SDLT under section 44A, a developer must ensure that the contract is a genuine building contract and that he is not entitled or committed to direct the landowner to sell to nominated third parties. In practice this may be difficult, as landowners will want the developer to have the responsibility for finding purchasers and may want the developer to undertake to buy the development or any part of it which is unsold after a specified time.

Background to introduction of section 44A

A 'building licence' structure was a fairly standard arrangement in contracts to sell commercial property and was seen as avoidance by HMRC. The explanatory notes to the Finance Bill 2004 set out the purpose behind what became section 44A as follows:

> "Paragraph 4 makes provision for where a contract (a 'section 44A contract') is entered into whereby one party to the contract (B) has the right to direct a conveyance to himself or to a third party (C). An example is a development agreement where the developer has the right to enter on the land and build on it and then direct the conveyance of the completed plots. The new provisions put it beyond doubt that such a contract is charged to SDLT when it is substantially performed (in the same way as a contract which is to be completed by a conveyance to B (a 'section 44 contract')). They also ensure that it is the consideration that is given or is to be given by B that is charged to SDLT once substantial performance occurs."

The Financial Secretary to the Treasury made the following statement during the Finance Bill 2004 Committee Stage debate in the House of Commons on 26 April 2004[52]:

---

[51] Inserted by paragraph 4 Schedule 39 FA 2004 and applies in relation to any contract entered into after 17 March 2004.

[52] Hansard 28 April 2004 : Cols 915 to 916

> "... new section 44A is there to ensure that SDLT is not avoided, especially in commercial transactions, by disguising what is in substance the purchase of land for development as a non-land transaction, often described as a 'building licence' ...
>
> Concern has been expressed about the interaction between new section 44A and existing section 44, dealing with contracts to be completed by a conveyance. I reassure the hon. Gentleman that section 44 remains the primary charging section where contracts for land transactions are substantially performed. In particular, the fact that a normal contract for sale includes a provision permitting the contracting purchaser to nominate someone else to take the conveyance does not take the contract out of section 44 into section 44A.
>
> The hon. Gentleman mentioned the fact that section 44A may catch a contractor. I believe that it will not. It should not catch a person who genuinely acts only as an agent. "

Before the introduction of SDLT, a typical transaction between a developer and a landowner would be carried out pursuant to a development agreement under which the developer had the right to enter on the land and develop it (as licensee) and then have the completed development conveyed to himself or as he directed. The price payable to the landowner would normally include a share of the developer's profit. The land was developed and once a purchaser was found the developer directed the landowner to transfer the land direct to the purchaser. Stamp duty was chargeable on the price paid by the purchaser.

After the introduction of SDLT the above structure would give rise to a double charge to tax – the developer would be liable for SDLT on the price paid to the landowner and the purchaser would be liable for SDLT on the price he paid for the acquisition of the completed development.[53] To avoid this result, and in the absence of section 44A, the transaction could have been restructured as the grant by the landowner of a non-exclusive licence to the developer to go onto land to construct a development for £x (the developer's profit) – this would not be a land transaction for SDLT purposes so £x would not be chargeable to SDLT. The landowner would then sell to a purchaser found by the developer (or the developer would sell as the landowner's agent) and SDLT would be payable on the sale price. A double charge to SDLT on £x would have been avoided and SDLT deferred until the development was sold.

---

[53] Subsale relief is not available as the developer substantially performed the contract before the transfer of the land to the purchaser – see 1.4 below.

By inserting section 44A HMRC wished to eliminate a grey area where building agreements could have been outside the scope of SDLT, so section 44A imposes a charge where section 44 would not (or might not). The Minister's reassurance set out above can be taken to mean that where section 44 and section 44A might both apply, section 44 will take precedence.

The detail of section 44A

Section 44A provides:

1) Where a contract is entered into under which one party (A) is to convey a chargeable interest 'at the direction or request' of the other party (B) to:
   (a) a third party (C) or
   (b) either to B or C
   (a 'section 44A contract'); and
2) that section 44A contract is substantially performed,

then B is treated as having acquired a chargeable interest and, accordingly, as having entered into a land transaction, the effective date of which is the date the section 44A contract is substantially performed.

A section 44A contract is not in itself a land transaction but is charged to SDLT only when it is substantially performed (in the same way as a contract which is to be completed by a conveyance to B). Entry onto the land by B pursuant to the section 44A contract would amount to substantial performance. It is the consideration given or to be given by B that is charged to SDLT once substantial performance occurs.

The substantial performance rule in section 44 is disapplied (except for the purposes of determining *when* substantial performance has occurred[54]) in relation to a section 44A contract unless that contract is completed by a conveyance to B (and not by a conveyance direct to C at the direction of B)[55]. In practice the disapplication of section 44 in such a case makes no difference as the charge under section 44A operates in the same way. Unlike section 44, section 44A continues to apply if the contract provides for A to grant leases and is not affected by paragraph 12A of Schedule 17A.[56]

If all or part of the land is in fact conveyed to B under the section 44A contract, section 44 applies so that a charge to SDLT arises on the earlier of substantial

---

[54] Section 44A(5)

[55] Section 44A (4)-(6)

[56] See 1.3.4 above

performance or completion[57]. Section 44 also applies to a contract between B and C which is to be completed by a conveyance from A to C.

There are provisions (similar to those in section 44(9)) dealing with repayment of SDLT in a case when a section 44A contract is rescinded or annulled after substantial performance has taken place.

'Contract' and 'conveyance' are defined in the same manner as in section 44.

Substantial performance of a section 44A contract gives rise to a duty to notify the land transaction.

Examples:

1) A contracts with B that B will build a residential development on land owned by A and market the development. A agrees to transfer the residential units to purchasers found by B in exchange for consideration of £1 million. B pays a deposit of £100,000 to A. B goes into possession of the land and begins the development. At this point, B will be chargeable to SDLT on £1 million, being the amount payable to A. Once the development is completed A transfers the residential units to the purchasers nominated by B. Each residential purchaser to whom A makes a transfer will also be liable for SDLT on his acquisition.
2) A contracts with B that B will build a residential development on land owned by A and receive a fee equal to his development costs plus a profit share. A is to market the development and transfer the completed units to the purchasers it identifies. B is not liable for SDLT on his fee as he is merely acting as contractor. Each purchaser to whom A makes a transfer will be liable for SDLT on his acquisition.

Relief on assignment or subsale of a section 44A contract

Section 45A gives relief from a double charge to SDLT where a section 44A contract is the subject of a transfer of rights before it is substantially performed. Section 45A is dealt with at 1.4.4 below.

1.4. Subsales and assignments of rights under contracts

(Sections 44, 45 and 45A)

A subsale is where there is a contract for the sale of land but, before the contract is completed, the same land is sold on (possibly more than once) and the land is transferred by the original vendor directly to a sub-purchaser or to

[57] Section 44A(6)

the ultimate sub-purchaser. The same result can be achieved by the purchaser assigning his rights under the original contract to a third party.[58]

Under the old stamp duty regime, duty was charged on a subsale by reference only to the price paid by the sub-purchaser or ultimate sub-purchaser who took a conveyance.[59] Under the SDLT regime, all the transactions in a subsale chain are in principle chargeable. However provided that the original contract is not substantially performed or completed other than as part of the subsale the relieving provisions of section 45 (which are discussed in detail below) apply.

The basic rule for SDLT purposes is that if A contracts to sell land to B, and B contracts by way of subsale with (or assigns his contract with A to) C then, provided that the A/B contract has not been substantially performed, the transfer to C is the only land transaction for SDLT purposes, and SDLT is payable by C by reference to the consideration paid by C to A and/or B.

Where the A/B transaction is relieved there is no need to file a land transaction return (and claim relief) in respect of it – it is only necessary to file a land transaction return for the transfer to C. This is borne out by the Land Registry internal guidance[60]:

> "2.10 Subsales
>
> If you are processing a subsale, you need not concern yourself with the intervening transaction.
>
> For example, [A] enters into a contract to sell land to [B]; the contract is not substantially performed and [B] either assigns the benefit of that contract to [C] or enters into a sub-contract to sell the land to [C]. On completion, the land is transferred from [A] to [C]. There is only need for one SDLT certificate (which, in this example, could show either [A] or [B] as the vendor, with [C] being shown as the purchaser).
>
> The position is the same if the first contract is for the grant of the lease and the second is for the assignment of that lease.
>
> It is not essential that only one transfer be used (in the example above, the parties being [A] and [C]). Two transfers, or a lease and transfer, can be used, provided they take effect at the same time."

---

58 In such a case, the original contract remains in existence and the original purchaser retains the burden of it vis-à-vis the original seller.

59 By reason of section 58(4) and 58(5) Stamp Act 1891 unless the consideration under the contract exceeded £10 million (section 115 FA 2002).

60 NP6

HMRC have confirmed that a double conveyance structure can also qualify for relief under section 45[61] (and therefore generate only one charge to SDLT[62]), where the A/B contract is completed by the transfer to B, followed immediately[63] by the completion of the B/C contract by the transfer to C, provided that there is no prior act of substantial performance by B[64]. This might be of use where B does not wish A to know the price at which he has sold on to C or that he has sold on to C at all.

Where a subsale is effected by a double conveyance C will need to submit the SDLT certificate (in respect of the transfer to him) to the Land Registry together with the two transfers and confirm that the conditions for relief under section 45 apply (i.e. that the sale and subsale were completed 'simultaneously'). The Land Registry accepts applications on this basis.

1.4.1. Subsales and assignments of rights: the provisions in detail

Section 45 applies where:

(1) a contract [65] for a land transaction (the 'original contract') is entered into which is to be completed by a conveyance;[66]

(2) there is an assignment, subsale or other transaction (a 'transfer of rights') which relates to all or part of the subject matter of the original contract as a result of which a person other than the original purchaser becomes entitled to call for a conveyance to him; and

(3) paragraph 12B of Schedule 17A (assignment of agreement for lease) does not apply.[67]

Where these conditions are satisfied, the 'transferee'[68] is not regarded as entering into a land transaction by reason of the transfer of rights but section 44 has effect in accordance with section 45. Section 45(3) provides that section 44

[61] In spite of the fact that section 45(1)(b) requires that a person other than the original purchaser (C) 'becomes entitled to call for a conveyance to him'.

[62] This would not have been the case under the old stamp duty regime when completion by an intermediate purchaser would have been fatal to a claim for subsale relief.

[63] Section 45(3) requires the original contract to be completed 'at the same time as and in connection with' the substantial performance or completion of the secondary contract.

[64] See SDLTM1080.

[65] 'Contract' for the purposes of section 45 includes any agreement (section 45(7)).

[66] 'Conveyance' for the purposes of section 45 includes any instrument (section 45(7).

[67] See1.4.5 below.

[68] There is no definition of 'transferee' in the provisions but it is taken to mean the person to whom a 'transfer of rights' (as defined) is made – there may, therefore, be more than one transferee.

is to apply as if there were a contract for a land transaction (a 'secondary contract') under which:

1) the transferee is the purchaser; and
2) the consideration for the transaction is:
    - so much of the consideration under the original contract as is referable to the subject-matter of the transfer of rights and is to be given (directly or indirectly) by the transferee or a person 'connected' with him,[69] and
    - the consideration given for the transfer of rights.

The actual contract giving rise to the transfer of rights (the B/C contract) is then ignored as it is superseded by the deemed secondary contact.

Where section 45(3) applies, substantial performance or completion of the original contract (the A/B contract) 'at the same time as, and in connection with', the substantial performance or completion of the deemed secondary contract will be disregarded – in such a case, the provision is a relieving one. However, if, before completion or substantial performance of the transfer of rights, the original contract is substantially performed (for example, by the original purchaser (B) going into possession) then SDLT is chargeable in respect of the original contract (and the transfer of rights) and no relief is available. The relief can also apply where there is a chain of subsales or assignments.[70]

Although section 45(3) deems there to be a secondary contract under which the transferee is the purchaser it does not identify the vendor under that contract.[71] For the purposes of the relief for transfer between associated companies *only*[72] the vendor under the secondary contract is deemed to be the original purchaser (A) but for all other purposes, references to the vendor mean either the vendor under the original contract or the transferor.[73]

The provision[74] that the consideration for the deemed acquisition by the sub-purchaser includes not only the consideration given by him but also any consideration under the original contract given by a person connected with

---

[69] The definition in section 839 ICTA 1988 applies – the section is reproduced in full in Part Five.

[70] Section 45(4)

[71] It would therefore seem open to the transferee to show either A or B as the seller on the land transaction return and it is Land Registry practice to accept this.

[72] See 1.4.3 below

[73] Section 45(5A)(b)

[74] In section 45(3)(b)(i)

him prevents the avoidance of SDLT through the subsale by the original purchaser at a loss to a connected person (see Example 3 below).

Examples - subsale:[75]

1) A contracts to sell land to B for £650,000 and B pays A a deposit of £65,000. B contracts by way of subsale with (or assigns his contract with A to) C, an unconnected third party, for £680,000 and receives a deposit of £68,000. C then completes the original contract in B's place and pays A the balance of £585,000 due under that contract and B the balance of £27,000 due to him. A conveys the land to C. The acquisition by C is the only land transaction for SDLT purposes, and SDLT is payable by C by reference to the consideration paid by C, £680,000.
2) A contracts to sell land to B for £650,000 and B pays A a deposit of £65,000. The property market weakens and B runs into financial difficulties forcing him to sub-sell the land at a loss to C, an unconnected third party, for £600,000. C pays B a deposit of £60,000. C then pays B the balance of £540,000 and A conveys the land to C (after B has paid A the outstanding sum of £585,000 pursuant to the A/B contract). The acquisition by C is the only land transaction for SDLT purposes, and SDLT is payable by C by reference to the consideration paid by C, £600,000, notwithstanding that A has received £650,000.
3) A contracts to sell his house to B for £650,000. On completion B pays £600,000 to A and directs A to convey the house to his daughter, C, who pays A the balance of £50,000. The acquisition by C is the only land transaction for SDLT purposes, and SDLT is payable by C by reference to the consideration given by B and C, to A, £650,000 since B and C are connected.

Section 45(3) was amended by F(No. 2)A 2005[76] to except from its relieving effect any case where the secondary contract gives rise to a transaction that is exempt from SDLT by virtue of section 73(3) (alternative property finance: land sold to financial institution and resold to individual).

Where there are successive transfer of rights, the provisions of section 45(3) apply to each such transfer and the substantial performance or completion of the secondary contract arising from an earlier transfer of rights at the same time as and in connection with the substantial performance or completion of the secondary contract arising from a subsequent transfer of rights will be disregarded.

---

[75] There are other examples of the operation of the rules at SDLTM01090aand SDLTM01110a.

[76] Section 49 and paragraph 2 Schedule 10 with effect for any transaction with an effective date after 19 May 2005.

1.4.2. Subsale of part

Section 45(3) applies where there is a contract for the sale of land between A and B, B sub-sells or assigns to C and the sale to C is completed by a transfer from A without earlier substantial performance of the contract between A and B. In such a case there is no charge to SDLT on the A/B transaction. Section 45(5)[77] clarifies how this relief works when only part of the land subject to the A/B contract is transferred to C (after subsale or assignment by B) by deeming there to be two separate A/B contracts, one relating to the part transferred to C and one to the balance of the subject matter of the original contract. The price due under the original contract is then apportioned between the sub-sold part and the balance of the land subject to the original contract and the relief applies where appropriate. No basis for the apportionment is laid down but the examples in SDLTM01110a apportion the original price on the basis of area.

The rule in section 44(8) which prevents a further charge on the later completion of a contract which has been substantially performed (except to the extent that the tax chargeable on completion exceeds the tax chargeable on substantial performance) can also apply where there is a partial subsale. In such a case, section 45(5)(a) provides that section 44(8)(b) applies as if the reference to the amount of tax chargeable on the contract was a reference to an 'appropriate proportion' of that amount[78]. This is an anti-avoidance provision designed to stop the exploitation of subsale relief in respect of part of the land by allocating a disproportionate amount of the consideration to the sub-sold portion of the land and not completing in relation to the balance.

Example – subsale of part[79]:

A contracts to sell 10 acres of land to B for £650,000 and B pays A a deposit of £65,000. B contracts to sub-sell 2.5 acres of the land to C, an unconnected third party, for £250,000 and receives a deposit of £25,000. C then pays B the balance of £225,000 due to him, and B pays A the balance of £585,000 due under the original contract. A conveys the land directly to B as to the 7.5 acres and to C as to the 2.5 acres. The original contract between A and B is treated as two A/B contracts, one in relation to 7.5 acres at a price of £487,500 and the second in relation to 2.5 acres at a price of £162,500. SDLT is payable by B by reference to the price paid by B for 7.5 acres, £487,500

[77] As amended by paragraph 5 Schedule 39 FA 2004 with effect for any transfer of rights occurring after 17 March 2004.

[78] 'Appropriate proportion' is not defined but apportioning the tax on the basis of area would be consistent with the approach taken by HMRC in other cases where the phrase is used but not defined – see examples at SDLTM01110a.

[79] There are other examples of the operation of the rules at SDLTM01110a.

and by C by reference to the consideration paid by C for 2.5 acres, £250,000. The linked transactions rules[80] do not apply as B and C are not connected.

1.4.3. Subsales within corporate groups

Where the parties to a transfer of rights are part of the same corporate group then the sub-purchaser or assignee (C) cannot claim group relief[81] in respect of that transaction.

The reason for not allowing group relief in this situation (on the B/C transaction) is that the transfer of rights provisions would present an avoidance opportunity where B and C were members of the same group, enabling the land to be transferred from A into the B/C group without payment of SDLT. The intra group transfer from B to C could have been used as a way of 'franking' the tax on the first leg of the transaction with the result that there would have been no SDLT charge for B, as the completion of the A/B contract by means of the transfer from A and B's payment of the outstanding purchase price would be disregarded by virtue of section 45(3). There would be no SDLT for C because group relief was claimed on the basis that the 'vendor' was B and not A.

Section 45(5A) therefore provides that, for the purposes of group relief, references to the 'vendor' are to be read as references to the vendor under the original contract (A) and not the selling group member (B).[82]

Examples – subsales involving group companies:

1) A contracts to sell land to B Limited for £650,000 and B Limited pays A a deposit of £65,000. B Limited contracts by way of subsale with (or assigns his contract with A to) C Limited, a company in the B Limited group, for £680,000 and receives a deposit of £68,000. C Limited then completes the original contract in B Limited's place and pays A the balance of £585,000 due under that contract and B Limited the balance of £27,000. A conveys the land to C Limited. The acquisition by C Limited is the only land transaction for SDLT purposes, and SDLT is payable by C Limited by reference to the consideration paid by C Limited, £680,000.
2) The facts are as in Example 1 but B Limited enters into possession of the land before completion in order to begin work on the land. One month later A transfers the land direct to C Limited and C Limited pays. In this

80 See 2.1.1 below

81 Section 45 (5A) inserted by paragraph 5 Schedule 39 FA 2004 with effect for any transfer of rights occurring after 17 March 2004.

82 Inserted by paragraph 5(4) Schedule 39 FA 2004 with effect for any transfer of rights occurring after 17 March 2004.

case there will be a two SDLT charges – the first on the A/B Limited transaction (as the A/B contract will have been substantially performed other than by a conveyance to C Limited) and the second on the B Limited/C Limited transaction (which will be deemed to take place at market value[83] and which will not benefit from group relief[84]). The double charge could have been avoided by B Limited completing the original contract and then transferring the land to C Limited (as C Limited could then claim group relief) or by B Limited delaying entry onto the land until after A had transferred the land to C Limited (when subsale relief would be available).

1.4.4. Contract providing for conveyance to third party: effect of transfer of rights

(Section 45A[85])

Where there is a 'section 44A contract'[86] and there is an assignment or other transaction in respect of all or part of the subject matter of that contract (the 'transfer of rights') with the result that another person (D) becomes entitled to exercise any of B's rights under the original contract, the transfer of rights (the B/D transaction) is not, of itself, chargeable. Section 44A applies in such a case as if:

(1) D had entered into a contract with A (the 'secondary contract') in the same terms as the A/B contract; and

(2) the consideration under the secondary contract were:

    a. so much of the consideration under the original contract as is referable to the transfer of rights and is to be given by D (or a person connected with D); and

    b. the consideration for the transfer of rights.

The substantial performance of the A/B contract is disregarded if it occurs 'at the same time as and in connection' with substantial performance of the secondary contract or it occurs after the transfer of rights.

In contrast to section 45, the definition of 'transfer of rights' in section 45A does not expressly include a subsale. However the Explanatory Notes to the Finance Bill 2004 state that section 45A is intended to make 'provision similar to that for

---

[83] As B Limited and C Limited are connected companies and section 53 applies.

[84] Because of section 45(5A).

[85] Inserted by paragraph 5 Schedule 39 FA 2004 with effect for any transfer of rights taking place after 17 March 2004.

[86] A section 44A contract is one under which one party (A) is to convey a chargeable interest 'at the direction or request' of the other party (B) to a third party (C) or either to B or C – see 1.3.5 above.

section 44 contracts in section 45' and there seems to be no reason in principle why subsales of section 44A contracts should be excluded.

As with section 44A, section 45A applies to successive transfers of rights in relation to all or part of the original subject matter. There are similar provisions relating a transfer of rights in relation to part of the land[87] and also preventing D claiming group relief in respect of the B/D transaction.[88]

Example of the operation of section 45A:

A contracts with B under which B will build a residential development on land owned by A and market the development. A agrees to transfer the homes to purchasers found by B in exchange for consideration of £1 million. B pays a deposit of £100,000 to A. Before the A/B contract is substantially completed B assigns his rights under it to C Limited, a development company, for £200,000. C Limited goes into possession and begins the development. C Limited will be chargeable to SDLT on £1.1 million, being the £200,000 paid to B and the £900,000 paid to A. No SDLT is payable by B. Each purchaser (to whom A makes a transfer) will also be liable for SDLT on his acquisition.

1.4.5. Assignment of agreement for lease

(Paragraph 12B Schedule 17A)

Paragraph 12B applies to the exclusion of section 45 where the interest of a lessee under an agreement for lease is assigned. The effect is however the same as if section 45 applied.

If the assignment occurs before 'substantial performance' of the agreement for lease (see 1.3.1 and 1.3.4 above) then section 44 has effect as if the contract (the agreement for lease) were with the assignee and not the assignor (the 'notional contract'). Any consideration for entering into the assignment will be treated as consideration for the notional contract in addition to the consideration due under the agreement for lease.

If the assignment occurs after substantial performance (which would itself have triggered an effective date for an SDLT charge) then the assignment is treated as a separate land transaction, that is to say, it is treated as an assignment of a notional lease, the effective date of which is the date of the assignment. The grant of the lease to the assignee will then be treated as the

[87] In section 45A(7)

[88] In section 45A(9)

surrender by the assignee of the notional lease in exchange for the grant of the actual lease which is treated as a re-grant for SDLT purposes.[89]

Paragraph 12B applies to each assignment where there are successive assignments.

1.5. Assignment of lease treated as grant of lease

(Paragraph 11 Schedule 17A)[90]

If the grant of a lease is exempt from charge as a result of certain specified provisions (listed below) then the first assignment of that lease that is not exempt under any of the same provisions and in relation to which the assignee does not acquire the lease as bare trustee of the assignor is treated for SDLT purposes as if it were the grant of a lease by the assignor. This is an anti-avoidance rule intended to prevent reliefs being used as a conduit to pass the lease on tax-free to a purchaser who would not be entitled to the relief if the lease were granted to him directly.

The specified provisions are:

(a) section 57A (sale and leaseback arrangements – see 3.2 below);
(b) Part 1 or 2 Schedule 7 (group relief or reconstruction or acquisition relief – see 3.4-3.6 below);
(c) section 66 (transfers involving public bodies – see 3.14 below);
(d) Schedule 8 (charities relief – see 3.7 below);
(e) any such regulations as are mentioned in section 123(3) (regulations reproducing in relation to SDLT the effect of enactments providing for exemption from stamp duty).[91]

Paragraph 11 does not apply where the lease was exempted from stamp duty by equivalent provisions under the old stamp duty regime.

Where paragraph 11 applies, the first assignment is treated for SDLT purposes as a grant of a lease to the assignee for a term equal to the unexpired term of the actual lease, and on the same terms as those on which the assignee holds that lease after the assignment. Tax is then payable by the assignee in the normal way on the deemed grant (in addition to the charge on any actual consideration given for the assignment). The provisions of paragraph 12 of

---

[89] See 1.3.4 above.

[90] As re-enacted in amended form by Part 2 Schedule 39 to FA 2004 with effect for transactions with an effective date on or after 22 July 2004 and as amended by F(No.2)A 2005 with effect from 20 May 2005 (subject to transitional provisions).

[91] No regulations have been made to date.

Schedule 17A (assignment of lease: responsibility of assignee for returns etc.) dealt with at 7.22 below will not apply.

The provision does not apply where the relief in question is group relief, reconstruction or acquisition relief or charities relief and the relief is withdrawn as a result of a disqualifying event occurring before the effective date of the assignment of the original lease, as SDLT will have been paid on the original grant before the assignment takes place.

A 'disqualifying event' means:

(a) in relation to the withdrawal of group relief, the purchaser ceasing to be a member of the same group as the vendor within the meaning of paragraph 3(1)(a) Schedule 7[92];

(b) in relation to the withdrawal of reconstruction or acquisition relief, the change of control of the acquiring company mentioned in paragraph 9(1)(*a*) Schedule 7 or the event mentioned in paragraph 11(1)(*a*) or (2)(*a*) Schedule 7;

(c) in relation to the withdrawal of charities relief, a disqualifying event as defined in paragraph 2(3) Schedule 8.

As there is no time limit on the application of paragraph 11 it could cause problems for an unwary assignee where the chargeable assignment is a long time after the original transaction on which relief was claimed. As a result standard pre-contract enquiries now commonly ask whether the lease being sold was previously the subject of relief from SDLT.

1.6. Chargeable transactions

(Section 49 and Schedule 3).

Every land transaction is a chargeable transaction unless it is exempted from charge. Identifying chargeable transactions is important because the SDLT charge bites on the chargeable consideration for a chargeable transaction.

Schedule 3 exempts from charge (subject to certain conditions):

- transactions where there is no chargeable consideration,
- grants of leases by housing associations,
- transactions in connection with divorce,
- assents and appropriations by personal representatives, and
- the variation of testamentary dispositions.

---

[92] Taking into account the effect , if any, of paragraph 4A Schedule 7 – see paragraph 11(5)(a) as amended by F(No.2)A 2005 where the effective date of the relevant transaction (within the meaning of paragraphs 3 or 4A Schedule 7) is after 19 May 2005.

Each of these is discussed in more detail at 1.6.1 to 1.6.5 below. The Treasury has power to add further exemptions by regulation. Certain other transactions are not subject to SDLT by virtue of the provisions relating to reliefs.[93]

Where the transaction is exempted from charge under Schedule 3 it does not have to be notified on a land transaction return but self-certification is required (see 7.3.2 below). The exemptions from charge in Schedule 3 mirror some of the categories for exemption from fixed duty by certification set out in the Stamp Duty (Exempt Instruments) Regulations 1987.[94] There are no fixed duties under SDLT.

1.6.1. Transactions for no chargeable consideration

(Paragraph 1 Schedule 3)

Land transactions for which there is no chargeable consideration are exempt from SDLT. Gifts, dispositions of property to beneficiaries under a trust in accordance with the terms of that trust, and most acquisitions by operation of law are exempt from the charge to SDLT pursuant to this provision. Distributions in specie fall within this provision provided that there is no consideration (such as the giving of an indemnity)[95].

Where the disposition is deemed to be for a consideration equal to the market value of the interest acquired, the exemption in paragraph 1 Schedule 3 is disapplied.[96] The exemption is also disapplied where the provisions of paragraphs 10, 14, 17 and 18 of Schedule 15 apply.[97]

---

[93] See Chapter 3 below

[94] SI 1985/7516

[95] See *Laird Group v. IRC* [2003] STC 1358 per Lord Millett at paragraph 37:
"[37] Once realised the assets of a company in liquidation are a distributable fund in the hands of the liquidator, who no longer needs funds with which to carry on its undertaking. After the creditors have been paid and the amounts credited as paid up on the shares have been repaid, the balance is distributable to the ordinary shareholders because it belongs to them, subject only to the liquidator's discretion to retain sufficient funds in his hands to enable him to complete the winding up. The distribution of the undistributed profits of a company in liquidation to its shareholders is not a transaction relating to securities because neither the shares themselves nor the rights attached to them are affected by a payment which merely gives effect to the shareholders' rights; they receive only what is already theirs. Distributions are made to shareholders in respect of the shares, but the shares of the individual shareholder are nothing more than the measure of the proportion of the total which is due to him."

[96] Section 53 (4)

[97] Paragraph 25 Schedule 15. These provisions apply to partnership transactions – see Chapter 4 below.

1.6.2. Grants of certain leases by registered social landlords

(Paragraph 2 Schedule 3)

Where a 'registered social landlord' grants a lease which is either an indefinite term or terminable by notice of a month or less to one or more individuals, that transaction is exempt from the charge to SDLT. The exemption only applies if the lease is granted pursuant to arrangements entered into between the registered social landlord and a housing authority whereby the landlord provides accommodation for individuals nominated by the authority.

A 'registered social landlord' is defined in section 121 as:

- in England and Wales, a body registered as a social landlord in a register maintained under section 1(1) of the Housing Act 1996;
- in Scotland, a body registered in the register maintained under section 57 of the Housing (Scotland) Act 2001;
- in Northern Ireland, a housing association registered in the register maintained under article 14 of the Housing (Northern Ireland) Order 1992.[98]

Housing authority is defined [99]as:

(a) in England and Wales, a principal council within the meaning of the Local Government Act 1972 or the Common Council of the City of London
(b) in Scotland, a council constituted under section 2 of the Local Government etc. (Scotland) Act 1994
(c) in Northern Ireland, the Department for Social Development in Northern Ireland, or the Northern Ireland Housing Executive

1.6.3. Transactions in connection with divorce

(Paragraph 3 Schedule 3)

A transaction between one party to a marriage and the other is exempt from the charge to SDLT if it is effected:

(1) in pursuance of an order of a court made on granting in respect of the parties a decree of divorce, nullity of marriage or judicial separation;
(2) in pursuance of an order of a court made in connection with the dissolution or annulment of the marriage, or the parties' judicial separation, at any time after the granting of such a decree;
(3) in pursuance of:
    a. an order of a court made at any time under section 22A, 23A or 24A of the Matrimonial Causes Act 1973 or

[98] SI 1992/1725 (NI 15)

[99] Paragraph 2(3) Schedule 3

b. an incidental order of a court made under section 8(2) of the Family Law (Scotland) Act 1985 by virtue of section 14(1) of that Act; or

(4) at any time in pursuance of an agreement of the parties made in contemplation or otherwise in connection with the dissolution or annulment of the marriage, their judicial separation or the making of a separation order in respect of them.

With effect from 5 December 2005 this exemption was extended to include transfers between civil partners in connection with the dissolution or annulment of a civil partnership or the legal separation of the civil partners.[100]

1.6.4. Assents and appropriations by personal representatives

(Paragraph 3A Schedule 3)[101]

The acquisition of property by a person in or towards satisfaction of his entitlement under or in relation to the will of a deceased person or on intestacy is exempt from the charge to SDLT. The exemption applies even if consideration is given by a beneficiary in the form of the assumption of 'secured debt'.

'Secured debt' is defined in paragraph 3A(4) as debt which was secured on the property immediately after the death of the deceased (for example, a mortgage not paid off on death). 'Debt' means an obligation whether certain or contingent, to pay a sum of money either immediately or at a future date.

Where the beneficiary gives any other form of consideration, then the transaction is both notifiable and chargeable. In such a case, the chargeable consideration is to be determined without including any secured debt assumed.[102]

SDLT and inheritance tax planning schemes

There is a potential charge to SDLT which could affect planning strategies currently used to minimise inheritance tax on the death of a surviving spouse. The schemes work by the surviving spouse providing 'funds' to set up a nil-rate band discretionary trust in the deceased spouse's estate, in return for receiving the deceased's share of the family home. The 'funds' are provided by the surviving spouse giving an IOU equal to the amount of the nil-rate band (the 'debt scheme') or by the executors creating a charge (the 'charge scheme')

---

[100] A new paragraph 3A was included in Schedule 3 by regulation 174 Tax and Civil Partnership Regulations 2005 (SI 2005/3229).

[101] Inserted by section 300 FA 2004 and deemed always to have had effect.

[102] Paragraph 8A(1) Schedule 4 as inserted by section 301(2), 301(5) and 301(7) FA 2004 and deemed always to have had effect.

over the assets in the residuary estate, including the share in the family home, in return for payment on demand from the surviving spouse of a sum equal to the nil-rate band for inheritance tax purposes.

Paragraph 3A does not apply to exempt a land transaction if the person acquiring the property gives any consideration for it, other than the assumption of secured debt. Whether the exemption applies would depend, for the debt scheme, on whether the IOU by the surviving spouse represented the assumption of secured debt. If not, SDLT could arise on an assent by the executors vesting the deceased spouse's interest in the family home in the surviving spouse.

Under paragraph 8 Schedule 4, the assumption of a personal liability by a person to whom land is transferred is chargeable consideration for SDLT purposes. HMRC's view is that it is not legally possible for a surviving spouse to receive the interest in the family home which is subject to the charge, without assuming personal liability for the debt secured by the charge. If so, in the case of the charge scheme, the assent would be chargeable to SDLT, unless it could be argued that the secured debt exemption applied. The difficulty is that in most cases, the charge is not secured immediately after the death of the deceased.

HMRC's views on the SDLT treatment of the commonest examples of such schemes are set out at SDLTM04045 and are as follows:

1) The nil-rate band discretionary trustees accept the surviving spouse's or civil partner's promise to pay in satisfaction of the pecuniary legacy and in consideration of that promise land is transferred to the surviving spouse or civil partner.

   The promise to pay is chargeable consideration for SDLT purposes.

2) The nil-rate band discretionary trustees accept the personal representatives' promise to pay in satisfaction of the pecuniary legacy and land is transferred to the surviving spouse or civil partner in consideration of the spouse or civil partner accepting liability for the promise.

   The acceptance of liability for the promise is chargeable consideration for SDLT purposes. The amount of chargeable consideration is the amount promised, not exceeding the market value of the land transferred.

3) Land is transferred to the surviving spouse or civil partner and the spouse or civil partner charges the property with payment of the amount of the pecuniary legacy. The nil-rate band discretionary trustees accept this charge in satisfaction of the pecuniary legacy.

The charge is money's worth and so is chargeable consideration for SDLT purposes

4) The personal representatives charge land with the payment of the pecuniary legacy. The personal representatives and nil-rate band discretionary trustees also agree that the trustees have no right to enforce payment of the amount of the legacy personally against the owner of the land for the time being. The nil-rate band discretionary trustees accept this charge in satisfaction of the legacy. The property is transferred to the surviving spouse or civil partner subject to the charge.

   There is no chargeable consideration for SDLT purposes provided that there is no change in the rights or liabilities of any person in relation to the debt secured by the charge.

1.6.5. Variations of testamentary dispositions etc.

(Paragraph 4 Schedule 3)[103]

A transaction following a person's death which varies a disposition (whether effected by will, under the law relating to intestacy, or otherwise) of property of which the deceased was competent to dispose, is exempt from the charge to SDLT if the following conditions are met:

1) the transaction is carried out within the period of two years after a person's death;
2) no consideration in money or money's worth other than the making of a variation of another such disposition is given for it.

This means that both the variation and the vesting of the deceased's asset in the substituted beneficiary are exempt from the charge to SDLT. Where any other form of consideration is given the transaction is both notifiable and chargeable. In such a case, the chargeable consideration is to be determined without including any consideration consisting of the making of a variation of another such disposition.[104]

This exemption mirrors the relief from inheritance tax in section 142(3) IHTA 1984.

Where no consideration is given the transaction will be exempt under paragraph 1 Schedule 3.

1.7. Chargeable consideration

(Section 50 and Schedule 4)

---

[103] As amended by section 301(1) and 301(7) FA 2004 and deemed always to have had effect.

[104] Paragraph 8A(2) Schedule 4 as inserted by section 301(2), 301(5) and 301(7) FA 2004 and deemed always to have had effect.

Unless the deemed market value rule applies (see section 1.7.12 below), the chargeable consideration is:

- the consideration given[105] by the purchaser or a person 'connected with' the purchaser
- directly or indirectly
- in money or money's worth
- for the 'subject-matter' of the land transaction

and is inclusive of any VAT chargeable in respect of the land transaction.[106]

There are special rules in Schedules 5 and 17A which apply to determine the SDLT charge where the chargeable consideration consists of or includes rent (see 2.6.8 below).

A peppercorn is not regarded as chargeable consideration (either as rent or premium).[107]

The payment by the buyer, or a person connected with him, of the vendor's costs would normally be chargeable consideration.[108]

The 'subject-matter' of a land transaction is defined in section 43(6) as the chargeable interest acquired together with any interest or right appurtenant or pertaining to it that is acquired with it.

The definition of chargeable consideration is important as SDLT is payable on the full amount of the chargeable consideration even if payment of all or part of it is to be made at a later date (paragraph 3 Schedule 4).

1.7.1. Consideration - effect of VAT[109]

(Paragraph 2 Schedule 4)

Chargeable consideration includes any VAT payable in respect of a land transaction.[110] Where an election to waive the exemption from VAT takes effect after the effective date of a transaction, any VAT that subsequently becomes payable does not constitute chargeable consideration.

---

105 'Consideration' involves the principle of reciprocity or mutuality of contractual obligations (*Glenrothes Development Corporation v. IRC* [1994] STC 74).

106 Paragraphs 1 and 2 Schedule 4. The definition of 'connected' in section 839 ICTA 1988 applies.

107 SDLTM11010 (April 2007 draft)

108 Unless one of the exclusions discussed at 1.7.9 below applies or a separate supply to the buyer is arranged – for example, considering or supplying draft documentation, especially if undertaking given to pay costs whether or not the transaction does proceed.

109 See SDLTM03800

110 This means that the effective ate of SDLT is increased even where the VAT is recoverable – for example the 4% rate increases to an effective rate of 4.7%.

VAT payable in respect of rent but which is not reserved as rent will not be rent for SDLT purposes but, as for stamp duty, will be taxed as consideration other than rent. Accordingly, the total VAT payable over the term of the lease will be chargeable, except where the lease exceeds 12 years, when the amount charge will be limited to the total of the 12 highest annual payments by reason of section 52[111].

If, following an HMRC ruling, it is confirmed that VAT is chargeable in respect of a land transaction and the purchaser has not included the VAT element of the purchase price in their SDLT1, the purchaser will be required to amend their land transaction return under the provisions of paragraph 6 Schedule 10. Any additional SDLT due on the VAT element should be accounted for with their amendment.

Alternatively if as a result of HMRC's ruling it is confirmed that VAT is not chargeable in respect of a transaction and the purchaser had included the VAT element of the purchase price in his SDLT1, the purchaser will be required to amend their land transaction return under the provisions of paragraph 6 Schedule 10 and request a refund of the overpaid SDLT.

1.7.2. Apportionment of consideration to chattels, crops etc.

(Paragraph 4 Schedule 4)

The legislation allows for an apportionment to be made on a 'just and reasonable' basis where consideration is attributable:

- to two or more land transactions
- in part to a land transaction and in part to another matter
- in part to matters making it chargeable and in part in part to matters that are not (such as chattels).

Where there is, in substance, one bargain, any consideration given is to be treated as attributable to all elements of the bargain even in a case where separate consideration has been given for different elements or where there are separate transactions in respect of different elements of the bargain.

Fixtures and chattels

The same general legal principles which applied in relation to chattels for stamp duty purposes also apply to SDLT. For an item to be regarded as a fixture or part of the land (chargeable to SDLT), as opposed to a chattel or personal property (not chargeable), the item must, normally, be annexed to the property. The issue then turns on the degree and purpose of the annexation, with greater emphasis being placed (in the more recent cases) on purpose.

---

[111] See 1.7.11 below

Where a purchaser agrees to buy a property for a price which includes an amount properly attributed to chattels, that amount will not be charged to SDLT.

A sale of growing crops may be a sale of either an interest in land or of chattels. If the sale is of the crop when growing, it may nevertheless be a sale of chattels if the crop is cultivated (*fructus industriales*), whether the crops are in a state of maturity or not.[112]

Where a price is paid partly for a land transaction and partly for a non-land transaction such as the purchase of chattels, and the price is apportioned on a just and reasonable basis, as provided for in Schedule 4 paragraph 4, the apportionment of the purchase price may well be one of the aspects of the SDLT1 into which HMRC will make enquiries. They may also make enquiries into cases where a deduction has been made for chattels to confirm that those items properly fall within the definition of chattels.[113]

The following are, however, confirmed as being items that will normally be regarded as chattels:[114]

- carpets (fitted or otherwise)
- curtains and blinds
- free standing furniture
- kitchen white goods
- electric and gas fires (provided that they can be removed by disconnection from the power supply without causing damage to the property)
- light shades and fittings (unless recessed).

On the other hand, the following will not normally be regarded as chattels:

- fitted kitchen units, cupboards and sinks
- Agas and wall mounted ovens
- fitted bathroom sanitary ware
- central heating systems
- intruder alarm systems.

Externally any plants, shrubs or trees growing in the soil form part of the land and are not regarded as chattels. A deduction would, however, be possible for amounts properly apportioned to any plants growing in pots or containers.

---

[112] *Duppa v Mayo* (1669) 1 Wms Saunders 275; *Marshall v Green* (1875) 1CPD 35. See Halsbury's Laws Vol 1(2) at paragraph 706

[113] SDLTM4010

[114] SDLTM4010

The same principles apply when considering the purchase of industrial or commercial property where the sale may also involve the acquisition of plant, machinery or equipment. An apportionment for capital allowances will not necessarily be acceptable for SDLT purposes.

Goodwill

The exclusion of goodwill from the charge to stamp duty by section 116 FA 2002 does not apply to SDLT, so if the goodwill is an inherent part of a land transaction it will be chargeable. In other cases the goodwill will not and an apportionment will be necessary.

In *Whiteman Smith Motor Co. Ltd v. Chaplin*[115] Maugham LJ described inherent goodwill as follows:[116]

> "The only kind of goodwill which can be in addition to the value of the premises in the hands of the landlord is that kind which has become attached to the premises, irrespective of their position, and which would naturally be reflected in a higher rent payable by a person carrying on a similar business. It may be greatly diminished if the tenant is able to obtain premises in the neighbourhood .... Whilst it is obvious that profits due to the reputation of the proprietor or to the personal skill or ability of the persons or the assistants employed in the business must be excluded, it should be pointed out that there is not necessarily any such goodwill as that referred to in the last paragraph, even if the personal goodwill is excluded, since that which surveyors and referees sometimes call adherent goodwill ... may be largely or wholly due to the custom of persons who come to the premises simply because of their proximity, or because they lie on a line of route which the customers frequent. If the term 'adherent goodwill' is used, it is essential to define it. I shall use the phrase, 'net adherent goodwill' as meaning the goodwill, if any, which will remain attached to the premises, not including the 'site goodwill', that is irrespective of customers who would come to a new tenant, starting a new business, simply because of their convenient situation. In a sentence it is important not to confuse site goodwill, which is inherent, with net adherent goodwill."

The SDLTM[117] refers to the classification of goodwill into three categories set out in HMRC's Capital Gains Manual.[118] However, this classification was

---

115 [1934] 2 KB 34

116 At page 38

117 At SDLTM04005

118 At CG60803 to CG68046

criticised by the Special Commissioner in *Balloon Promotions Ltd and Others v. Wilson*[119] as 'over-analytical'. Issues relating to the categorisation of goodwill, or the valuation of goodwill where an apportionment is required, should be referred to the Valuation Office Agency.[120]

Goodwill which is sold as part of a business sale is likely to be outside the SDLT charge as it will attach to the business rather than the land. However in *Morvic Pty Ltd and Another v Commissioner of State Revenue*[121] the taxpayer entered into two contracts to purchase a motel business. One contract was in respect of the land and improvements and the other was for the acquisition of the business, including the goodwill. It was held that the benefit of almost all the goodwill of the business was necessarily transferred upon acquisition of the land leaving the business sale contract was largely redundant. Hence the goodwill under the sale of business contract was assessable together with the conveyance of the land.

Goodwill: completing the SDLT forms

The guidance notes on completing the SDLT forms read as follows[122]:

> "A payment for goodwill that is part of the land is part of the chargeable consideration for SDLT purposes. The price paid for this goodwill should be included in the figure shown at question 10 of the SDLT1 where code A, F or O has been entered at question 2."

Where the land transaction is part of the sale of a business, non-chargeable goodwill should be indicated on form SDLT4 in Box 1 and the amount of the consideration for the sale of the business apportioned to it entered.

1.7.3. Exchanges

(Paragraph 5 Schedule 4)

The legislation specifies how chargeable consideration is to be calculated where land has been exchanged (see 1.9.3 below).

1.7.4. Partition or division

(Paragraph 6 Schedule 4)

Where there is a partition or division of a jointly owned land, the share of the interest held by the purchaser immediately before the partition or division does not count as chargeable consideration for the interest received as a result

---

119 SPC 524, [2006] STC (SCD) 167

120 See SDLTM04005

121 [2002] ATC 4459 (an Australian case)

122 SDLT6 (Online version - updated to September 2007) at page 34

of the partition[123]. In effect, the SDLT charge is limited to an balancing payment[124].

1.7.5. Consideration - release or assumption of a debt[125]

(Paragraph 8 Schedule 4)

Where there is the release or assumption of a debt (or the transfer of a property subject to a debt) the debt can constitute chargeable consideration. However a mere increase in the borrowing secured on a property will not have SDLT consequences. There is no assumption of a debt in a case where the debt is inherent in or runs with the property, such as a liability for chancel repairs.

Where the chargeable consideration for a land transaction consists in whole or in part of:

1) the satisfaction or release of debt due to the purchaser or owed by the vendor (paragraph 8(1)(a)); or
2) the assumption of 'existing debt' by the purchaser (paragraph 8(1)(b)),

the amount of debt satisfied, released or assumed is taken to be the whole or, as the case may be, part of the chargeable consideration for the transaction.

This provision will not apply in the case of the transfer of property subject to a mortgage only if there is neither a release of the vendor (falling within paragraph 8(1)(a)) nor an assumption of liability by the purchaser (falling within paragraph 8(1)(b)).

If the effect of determining chargeable consideration in this way would be that the amount of the consideration exceeded the market value of the subject-matter of the transaction, the amount of the consideration is treated as limited to that value. This is a change from the position under the stamp duty rules.

'Debt' means an obligation, whether certain or contingent, to pay a sum of money either immediately or at a future date.

'Existing debt' means debt created or arising before the effective date of, and otherwise than in connection with, the transaction. The taking on of new debt by the purchaser, for the purpose of funding the transaction, is not consideration.

References to the amount of a debt are to the principal amount payable or, as the case may be, to the total of the principal amounts payable, together with the amount of any interest that has accrued due on or before the effective date

---

[123] This is discussed in more detail at 1.9.2 below

[124] See example at SDLTM04030a

[125] See SDLTM04040 and SDLTM04040a

of the transaction. Any principal or interest that has been paid off at the effective date, however, is not 'payable' at that date.

Where:

1) debt is secured on the property immediately before and after the land transaction; and
2) the rights or liabilities of any party in relation to that debt are changed as a result of or in connection with the transaction,

there is taken to be an assumption of debt by the purchaser falling within paragraph 8(1)(b).[126] This is an anti-avoidance provision intended to prevent parties temporarily paying off secured debt before property is transferred and reinstating it immediately afterwards.

If there are two or more purchasers or vendors with undivided shares in the property the amount of secured debt treated as assumed is determined on the basis that the proportion of the amount owed by a person corresponds to the share that they own in the property subject to the debt.[127] For this purpose tenants in common are treated as owning the property in equal shares.[128]

The statutory rules apply even where lenders have required joint and several liability for existing debt.[129]

Examples – release or assumption of a debt:

1) Property is transferred by A to the ownership of A and B in equal shares subject to a subsisting mortgage and B assumes liability for all or part of the debt. Notwithstanding B's actual liability B is treated as assuming debt equal to 50% of the amount owing (because he is treated as owing none before the transaction and 50% after it).[130]
2) Property is owned by A and B in 70:30 shares and is transferred to the sole ownership of B subject to a subsisting mortgage. Assuming A is released from the debt or B agrees to indemnify A there is an assumption of debt by B, B is treated as assuming debt equal to 70% of the amount owing (because he is treated as owing 30% before the transfer and 100% after it).[131]

---

[126] Paragraph 8(1A) Schedule 4 (introduced by section 301 FA 2004 with effect for any transaction the effective date of which is on or after 22 July 2004).

[127] Paragraph 8(1B) Schedule 4 (introduced by section 301 FA 2004 with effect for any transaction the effective date of which is on or after 22 July 2004).

[128] Paragraph 8(1C) Schedule 4 (introduced by section 301 FA 2004 with effect for any transaction the effective date of which is on or after 22 July 2004).

[129] Confirmed at SDLTM04040

[130] Paragraph 8(1B) Schedule 4

[131] Ibid

Although the rules in paragraph 8(1A) to 8(1C) were said to be introduced (in FA 2004) to mirror the law and practice for stamp duty[132], they are much wider. The legislation provides that there is an assumption of debt by the purchaser when the 'rights or liabilities' of any party to the transaction in relation to the debt are changed as a result of or in connection with the land transaction. The provision could apply not only where B gives a personal covenant but also where A is released from his personal covenant to creditors, or where B agrees to indemnify A for any liability (other than in respect of a breach of an obligation owed by the vendor to a third party in relation to the subject-matter of the transaction[133]). This could give rise to problems as it could apply in cases where the lender requires commercial changes to a secured loan on the arm's length transfer of the property to which it relates.

The acquisition of property by the beneficiary of a will, or a person entitled under intestacy, including a case where consideration is given by a beneficiary in the form of the assumption of 'secured debt', is exempt from SDLT.[134]

1.7.6. Consideration - carrying out of works

(Paragraph 10 Schedule 4)

The general rule is that if the carrying out of any works to enhance the value of land (not necessarily the land being acquired) forms part of the consideration for a land transaction, an amount equal to the open market value of those works is taken into account as chargeable consideration for SDLT purposes. This will not apply where the obligation to do the works is inherent in the property acquired, such as an obligation to carry out works pursuant to a planning obligation.

The works need not be carried out on the land which is being sold so, for example, infrastructure works carried out by the purchaser on the seller's land, even if necessary for construction work on the land sold, could give rise to an increased SDLT charge if those works were consideration. Another example where the value of the works would be caught would be where a developer acquires land from a local authority for development and agrees to construct a building on other land owned by the local authority.

---

[132] See Revenue Press Release of 13 July 2004, 'Stamp Duty Land Tax – transfers of property subject to a debt and variations of testamentary dispositions' for background to the changes.

[133] Specifically excluded from chargeable consideration by paragraph 16 Schedule 4

[134] Section 49 and Schedule 3 – see 1.6.4 above

Relief for certain works not carried out by the vendor

Paragraph 10 Schedule 4 disapplies the general rule (and so the works are not chargeable consideration) to the extent that three conditions are met. It gives relief in respect of work done pursuant to building leases and certain other works.

The first condition is that the works are carried out after the 'effective date'. This condition prevents relief being available for works carried out before the earlier of substantial performance or completion.

Where there are two notifiable transactions in relation to a land transaction (the first being the contract or agreement and the second being the transaction effected on completion or the grant or execution of a lease), the first condition is treated as met in relation to the second transaction if it was met in relation to the first.[135] An example of this would be where there is a contract for the sale of land to a developer to be completed on satisfactory completion of works by the developer, and the developer takes possession before he carries out the works. In such a case, the subsequent completion of the sale after the date the works have been completed is also a notifiable transaction by virtue of section 44(8).

The second condition is that the works are carried out on land acquired or to be acquired under the land transaction or on other land held by the purchaser[136] or a person connected with him. For this purpose a major interest in the land must be acquired.[137] This condition will be fulfilled in the case of a building lease but will create difficulties where developers merely have the right to direct the conveyance to third parties and never themselves acquire a major interest in the land which is developed by agreement between the vendor and the developer. Works done on the vendor's or a third party's land are excluded from the relief by this condition.

The third requirement is that it is not a condition of the transaction that the works are carried out by the vendor or a person connected with him. This condition excludes sale-and-build contracts from relief under paragraph 10 but

---

[135] Paragraph 10(2A) Schedule 4

[136] Section 43(4) provides that references to the 'purchaser' and 'vendor', in relation to a land transaction, are to 'the person acquiring and the person disposing of the subject-matter of the transaction'. These expressions apply even if there is no consideration for a transaction but a person cannot be a purchaser unless he has given consideration for a transaction or is a 'party to' it (section 43(5)).

[137] Paragraph 10(3)(a) Schedule 4. A 'major interest' is defined in section 117(2) (in relation to England and Wales) as a fee simple absolute or a term of years absolute at law or in equity. The definitions applying to Scotland and Northern Ireland are in section 117(3) and (4) respectively.

does not mean that works under such contacts will necessarily be chargeable consideration for a land transaction (see below).

The provisions of paragraph 10 are subject to the rules in paragraph 17 Schedule 4 in relation to PFI transactions (see 3.20 below).

Works carried out by the vendor – sale-and-build

The SDLT legislation does not deal specifically with the case where a landowner enters into an agreement to sell land and also agrees to build on that land at the purchaser's expense.

The question to be determined is whether the transaction is a single contract for the sale of land with a completed building on it or two separate contracts, one for a sale of the land and the other for the carrying-out of the works. If it is the latter, the price paid for the building works[138] is not subject to SDLT as it is not consideration for a land transaction. If it is the former, the total amount paid will be chargeable consideration for a single land transaction (land with completed building). The provisions of paragraph 10 Schedule 4 will not affect the position in either case as the paragraph applies only where the whole or part of the consideration for a land transaction 'consists of' the carrying out of works.

The treatment of sale-and-build contracts for stamp duty purposes was considered in the *Prudential Case*[139] and the principles established in that case apply for SDLT purposes. The facts were that Prudential entered into a sale agreement with two companies (the developers) whereby Prudential agreed to buy a freehold interest in certain land from the developers. On the same day, Prudential and the developers entered into a development agreement. The terms of that agreement provided for the development of offices on the property by the developers in return for which Prudential agreed to pay the developers certain specified building costs. By a deed of transfer of the same date the developers transferred to Prudential the land agreed to be sold. At the date of the transfer, a substantial part of the construction work had already been carried out but there was a considerable amount still to be done.

The sale agreement and the development agreement were negotiated together and were executed simultaneously. There was no intention on the part of either party that one agreement should be entered into unless both were entered into, nor was there any practical possibility of this happening.

---

[138] Arrived where necessary at by apportionment of the consideration for both contracts on a just and reasonable basis as required by paragraph 4 Schedule 4.

[139] *Prudential Assurance Co. Ltd v. IRC* [1992] STC 863

HMRC assessed Prudential to stamp duty by reference to the total amount of consideration payable for the sale of the land and all the building works, whether completed or uncompleted at the date of the transfer. They contended that there was a single contract of sale contained in two instruments (the sale agreement and the development agreement) by which Prudential agreed to buy from the developers the land together with the completed office development.

Prudential appealed against that assessment contending that there were two separate contracts, one relating to the sale of land and the other to the building works, and that stamp duty was payable only in respect of the consideration for the sale of the land and the building works completed at the date of the deed of transfer.

The question before the court was to identify the subject-matter of the sale. HMRC's argument in this regard was rejected by the court:

> "In the present case the sale agreement and the development agreement and, indeed, the transfer were all part of one transaction in the sense that together they comprised a single package or bargain. ...Clearly the end result intended by the parties was that the land, previously belonging to the developers, would become the property of the taxpayer company together with the new buildings being constructed by the developers. The commercial object of the transaction was that the taxpayer company would acquire a development being carried out for it by the developers with funds provided by the taxpayer company.
>
> ... I am unable to characterise the transaction by which that end result was sought to be achieved as a sale of the land with finished buildings thereon...
>
> Let me take a simple analogy. A builder agrees to sell an empty plot of land, with immediate completion. At the same time and as part of the same transaction the builder agrees to construct a house on the land for the buyer over the next few months. The Crown's argument involves the proposition that such a transaction is to be characterised as a sale of land and a completed house. That cannot be correct. In many cases a builder will not be prepared to part with title to the land until he has been paid in full both for the land and for the house he has agreed to erect, and the buyer will not be prepared to pay for the land until the house has been finished. Then the conveyance, which will be of the completed house, will attract stamp duty on the overall price. But the transaction negotiated and agreed may be a different one. The builder may be prepared, or may want, to sell and convey the land outright to the buyer before he has carried out the building work and been paid for it; the buyer may be prepared, or may

> want, to complete his purchase of the land at once and for the future rely on the builder's agreement to build the house. If the transaction takes that form it cannot accurately be described as a sale of a completed house. It is a sale of a plot of land, coupled with an agreement to build. The rights of the parties, and the remedies available to them, are different in the two cases. In the latter case, although commercially there is only one transaction, the price payable for the building works is not properly attributable to the sale of the land. The two contracts form part of one transaction at their inception, but in their performance they are independent of each other. Completion of the sale of the land is not dependent on, or geared to, the due completion of the building works. The sale is of the plot of land at the agreed price, and the consideration payable by the buyer for the subsequent building work is in return for those works and not for the sale of the land.
>
> In my view the present case stands on all fours with the latter example."[140]

Based on the reasoning in the *Prudential Case* it is not necessary that there are two different documents for the cost of the works to escape a charge to SDLT provided that it is clear that there are two independent contracts, one for the sale of the land and the other for the building works.

However HMRC's published view on the matter is as follows:[141]

> "SDLT—sale of land with associated construction, &c, contract
>
> We have been asked how to determine the chargeable consideration for Stamp Duty Land Tax purposes where V agrees to sell land to P and V also agrees to carry out work (commonly works of construction, improvement or repair) on the land sold. Our view is that the decision in *Prudential Assurance Co Ltd v. IRC* applies for the purposes of Stamp Duty Land Tax as it does for stamp duty. This is because the basis of the decision was the identification of the subject matter of the transaction and this is as relevant for Stamp Duty Land Tax as it is for stamp duty.
>
> It follows that SP8/93 will be applied for Stamp Duty Land Tax as it was for stamp duty. The paragraphs on 'contracts already entered into' and 'procedure for submitting documents' are, however, not relevant to Stamp Duty Land Tax.

---

[140] Nicholls V-C at pages 868 to 869

[141] On 5 April 2004

> Where, however, the sale of land and the construction, &c, contract are in substance one bargain (as they were in the Prudential case) there must be a just and reasonable apportionment of the total consideration given for all elements of the bargain in order to arrive at the chargeable consideration for Stamp Duty Land Tax purposes."[142]

This view is now reflected at SDLTM04015.

The relevant parts of SP8/93[143] provide:

> "1.Two Transactions/Two Contracts
>
> Where the purchaser or lessee is entitled under the terms of a contract to a conveyance or lease of land alone in consideration of the purchase price or rent of the site and a second genuine contract for building works is entered into as a separate transaction, the ad valorem duty on the conveyance or lease will be determined by the amount of the purchase price or rent which the purchaser or lessee is obliged to pay under the terms of the first contract. In these circumstances it does not matter whether any building work has commenced at the date of the conveyance or lease. The consideration chargeable to ad valorem duty will still be only that passing for the land.
>
> 2. One Transaction/Two Contracts
>
> Where there is one transaction between the parties but this is implemented by two contracts, one for the sale or lease of the building plot and one for the building works themselves, the amount of ad valorem duty charged on the instrument will depend on the amount of the consideration, which in turn will depend on whether those contracts can be shown to be genuinely independent of each other.
>
> i. If the two contracts are so interlocked that they cannot be said to be genuinely capable of independent completion (and in particular where if default occurs on either contract, the other is then not enforceable) ad valorem duty will be charged on the total consideration for the land and buildings, whether completed or not, as if the parties had entered into only one contract.
>
> ii. If the two contracts are shown to be genuinely independent of each other, ad valorem duty will be charged by reference to the consideration paid or payable for the land and any building works on that land at the

---

[142] This is HMRC's gloss on the *Prudential decision* – in that case the apportionment made by the parties in the two agreements was accepted by the court. HMRC are referring to the provisions of paragraph 4(3) Schedule 4 which provide for an apportionment on a just and reasonable basis where there is one 'bargain'.

[143] 12 July 1993

date of execution of the instrument. It follows that, where the instrument is executed after the building works are completed, ad valorem duty will be charged on the consideration for the land and the completed building(s)."

1.7.7. Consideration - provision of services

(Paragraph 11 Schedule 4)

If the provision of services by or on behalf of the purchaser (other than carrying out of works under the conditions outlined above) forms all or part of the consideration for a land transaction, those services constitute chargeable consideration. The value of that consideration is taken to be the amount that would have to be paid in the open market to obtain the services.

In PFI transactions the provisions of paragraph 11 are subject to the rules in paragraph 17 Schedule 4 (see 3.20 below).

1.7.8. Land transaction entered into by reason of employment

(Paragraph 12 Schedule 4)

If an employer provides an employee with accommodation, the SDLT treatment will depend on the income tax status of the transaction. The legislation is not helpfully drafted, referring to a 'purchaser' whereas in fact there will be no actual 'purchase' at all, but an arrangement where an employee pays a rent below the market rate (or pays nothing) for accommodation provided by his employer[144]. The provisions do not apply where an employee occupies by reason of a licence (not a lease) as giving an employee a licence to occupy is not a land transaction.

Taxable benefit under ITEPA 2003

The legislation states that where a land transaction is entered into by reason of the purchaser's employment, or that of a person 'connected with' him,[145] and gives rise to a charge to income tax as a taxable benefit under Part 3 of Chapter 5 of ITEPA 2003, and either:

- no rent is payable, or
- any rent payable is less than the cash equivalent of the benefit,

---

[144] See section 43(4) which provides that references to the 'purchaser' and 'vendor', in relation to a land transaction, are to 'the person acquiring and the person disposing of the subject-matter of the transaction'. These expressions apply even if there is no consideration for the transaction but a person is not treated as a 'purchaser' unless he has given consideration for or is a party to the transaction.

[145] For example, a transfer to an employee's pension fund. The test of 'connected' is that in section 839 ICTA 1988.

then the purchaser is treated as paying rent equal to the 'cash equivalent' for the purpose of the SDLT charge.

A charge to income tax arises under Part 3 of Chapter 5 of ITEPA 2003, broadly, where any living accommodation is provided for any period during or comprising a tax year to an employee, or to members of his family or household, by his employer. The 'cash equivalent' is treated as earnings for that year unless it is provided in the normal course of domestic, family and personal relationships, or by a local authority under its usual terms for council tenants who are not employees.

A charge to income tax similarly arises where the accommodation is provided by someone other than the employer but 'by reason of' the employment.

The 'cash equivalent' of the provision of accommodation for a period is the 'rental value' of the accommodation for that period less any sum made good by the employee to the person at whose cost the accommodation is provided (normally the employer) and attributable to that provision. The 'rental value' is calculated by reference to an annual rent equal to the annual value of the property ascertained under section 110 ITEPA 2003, which for UK property is equivalent to the gross rateable value. Alternatively, if the person at whose cost the accommodation is provided pays actual rent for the whole or part of the period at an annual rate greater than the annual value, then that actual rent is the rental value for the period (or part).

No taxable benefit under ITEPA 2003

If the transaction would give rise to a charge to income tax but for the provisions of section 99 ITEPA 2003 (accommodation provided is necessary for the proper performance of duties e.g. a flat on-site for a school caretaker), the consideration for SDLT purposes is the actual consideration (if any).

In any other case, (that is, where the land transaction is entered into 'by reason of the purchaser's employment' but the provisions of Chapter 5 of ITEPA 2003 do not give rise to a charge (other than by reason of section 99 ITEPA 2003)), for example, where the employee pays rent equal to or in excess of the cash equivalent of the benefit, the land transaction in question will be treated as taking place at market value at the effective date.

1.7.9. Exclusions from chargeable consideration

The following are specifically excluded from chargeable consideration:

(a) the giving of an indemnity by the purchaser to the vendor in respect of a breach of an obligation owed by the vendor to a third party in relation to the subject-matter of the transaction - for example, an indemnity against restrictive covenants on the title to the land - and any payment made under such an indemnity (paragraph 16 Schedule 4);

(b) the liability for, or agreement to pay, or payment of, inheritance tax by the purchaser in respect of a land transaction that is a transfer of value within section 3 IHTA 1984 or is a disposition, effected by will or under the law of intestacy, of a chargeable interest comprised in the estate of a person immediately before his death (paragraph 16A Schedule 4[146]);

(c) the liability for, or agreement to pay, or payment of, CGT by the purchaser in respect of a land transaction under which the chargeable interest is acquired otherwise than by a bargain made at arm's length, or is treated by section 18 TCGA 1992[147] as so acquired, unless, disregarding that liability or payment, there is chargeable consideration for the transaction (paragraph 16B Schedule 4[148]);

(d) costs borne by the purchaser under section 9(4) of the Leasehold Reform Act 1967 or section 33 of the Leasehold Reform, Housing and Urban Development Act 1993 (costs of enfranchisement) (paragraph 16C Schedule 4[149]);

(e) a reverse premium on the grant, assignment or surrender of a lease (paragraph 18 Schedule 17A);

(f) the assumption by an assignee of a lease of the obligation to pay rent or to perform the tenant's covenants under that lease (paragraph 17 Schedule 17A);

(g) covenants by a tenant on the grant of a lease to:

   1. repair, maintain or insure the demised premises (paragraph 10(1)(a) Schedule 17A)
   2. pay any amount in respect of services, repairs, maintenance, insurance or the landlord's costs of management (paragraph 10(1)(b) Schedule 17A);

(h) any obligation undertaken by a tenant on the grant of a lease that is not such as to affect the rent that a tenant would be prepared to pay in the open market – i.e. ordinary tenant's covenants in a lease (paragraph 10(1)(c) Schedule 17A);

(i) any guarantee of the payment of rent or the performance of any other obligation of the tenant under the lease (paragraph 10(1)(d) Schedule 17A);

---

146 Inserted by the SDLT (Amendment to the Finance Act 2003) Regulations 2006 (SI 2006/875) in relation to land transactions with an effective date on or after 12 April 2006.

147 Section 18 TCGA 1992 applies where there are transactions between connected persons.

148 See footnote 146.

149 See footnote 146.

(j) any penal rent or increased rent in the nature of a penal rent payable in respect of any breach of the obligations of a tenant under the lease (paragraph 10(1)(e) Schedule 17A;

(k) any liability of the tenant for costs under section 14(2) of the Leasehold Reform Act 1967 or section 60 of the Leasehold Reform, Housing and Urban Development Act 1993 (costs to be borne by person exercising statutory right to be granted lease) (paragraph10(1)(f) Schedule 17A[150]);

(l) any other obligation of the tenant to bear the landlord's reasonable costs or expenses of or incidental to the grant of a lease (paragraph 10(1)(g) Schedule 17A[151]);

(m) any obligation under the lease to transfer to the landlord, on the termination of the lease, payment entitlements granted to the tenant under the single payment scheme[152] in respect of land subject to the lease (paragraph 10(h) Schedule 17A[153]);

(n) any payment made to discharge any of the obligations referred to in (g) to (m) above (paragraph 10(2) Schedule 17A). This would cover compensation for breach of covenant, such as a dilapidations payment;

(o) the release of any obligation referred to in (c) to (h) above in relation to the surrender of a lease (paragraph 10(3) Schedule 17A); and

(p) where the trustees of a settlement reallocate trust property which consists of chargeable interests, the fact that the beneficiary gives consent to the reallocation does not mean that there is chargeable consideration for the acquisition by him (paragraph 8 Schedule 16[154]).

SDLTM03710 indicates that costs under section 23 Compulsory Purchase Act 1965 and compensation for disturbance and other matters not directly based on the value of land under section 5(6) Land Compensation Act 1961 are not chargeable consideration.

---

[150] Inserted by the SDLT (Amendment to the Finance Act 2003) Regulations 2006 (SI 2006/875) in relation to land transactions with an effective date on or after 12 April 2006.

[151] See footnote 150

[152] Support for farmers in pursuance of Title III of Council Regulation No 1782/2003.

[153] See footnote 150

[154] Inserted by section 165 FA 2006 in relation to any acquisition the effective date of which is on or after 19 July 2006 – see 7.18.4 below

1.7.10. Consideration - contingencies, uncertain or unascertained consideration and adjustments

(Sections 51 and 80)

Where some or all of the consideration for a transaction is contingent[155], for example, a sum which is payable only if planning permission is obtained within a stated period, section 51 provides that the consideration for SDLT purposes is calculated on the assumption that the outcome of the contingency will be that the consideration is payable or does not cease to be payable, as the case may be. The amount of chargeable consideration is to be determined without any discount for the postponement of the right to receive it.[156]

An adjustment is made (under section 80) if the contingency occurs or it becomes clear that it will not occur. In addition, if the contingent element is or may be payable more than six months after the effective date, an application can be made to defer payment of the SDLT on the contingent element of the consideration.[157]

Section 51 further provides that where the consideration is uncertain or unascertained[158] at the date of the transaction, for example, where there is an uplift to the consideration based on future increases in the market value of the land (commonly called 'overage'), a 'reasonable estimate' must be made and SDLT paid on that basis.[159] If it were not for section 51, SDLT could be avoided or deferred by ensuring that the consideration cannot be calculated at the time of the land transaction.

Consideration is 'uncertain', as distinct from 'unascertained', where its amount or value is dependent on 'uncertain future events'[160]. This would cover an amount which is to be paid only if a future event occurs and which is to be calculated by reference to that event. As the amount is unascertainable at the effective date the consideration is uncertain (and not contingent) for the purposes of section 51.

---

[155] Defined in section 51(3) as to be paid (or provided) or to cease to be paid (or provided) if some uncertain future event occurs.

[156] Paragraph 3 Schedule 4

[157] Pursuant to section 90 - for deferral applications see 7.8 below.

[158] i.e. the amount can be established in theory but this has not yet been done, for example, a price linked to completion accounts which have yet to be drawn up or to acreage which has not yet been measured.

[159] The obtaining of a professional valuation supporting the estimate may be advisable where the costs of doing do would not be disproportionate.

[160] Section 51(3).

If the uncertain element of the consideration is, or may be, payable more than six months after the effective date, an application can be made to defer payment of the SDLT on that element of the consideration. No deferral is possible where the consideration is unascertained or contingent, rather than uncertain.

When the contingency occurs (or it becomes clear that the contingency will not occur) or the amount payable becomes known, the SDLT consequences of the transaction must be reconsidered.[161] This liability remains even where the original purchaser has disposed of the land.[162]

If the effect of the reconsideration is that the transaction becomes notifiable or chargeable or SDLT or additional SDLT is payable then the purchaser must file a land transaction return within 30 days. Interest will run from the effective date of the transaction under section 87 so if the original estimate was an under-estimate, interest will be due.

In accordance with the legislation in force until 19 July 2007 the return had to be accompanied by any tax payable. Legislation was introduced in FA 2007 (taking effect from Royal Assent) amending section 80 so that payment of any SDLT due no longer has to accompany the land transaction return[163]. The tax is still payable by the filing date for the return.

Where a land transaction return was submitted in respect of the transaction, a further return should be made, in the form of a letter which should state the amendment required to the original land transaction return[164]. The further return and any payment of tax, which should previously have been sent to the Complex Transaction Unit[165], should now be sent to the Birmingham Stamp Office.

If the effect of the reconsideration is that SDLT has been overpaid it is repaid on a claim being made either by an amendment of the land transaction return or, if more than 12 months from the filing date have elapsed, by making a claim to HMRC.[166] The amended return or letter of claim should be sent to

---

[161] Section 80(1)

[162] Unless the original purchaser is no longer liable to pay the contingent consideration in such circumstances.

[163] Section 80(2)(d) repealed by section 80 FA 2007 with effect from 19 July 2007.

[164] See SDLTM50300

[165] See 8.3.2 below.

[166] Section 80(4) as amended by section 299(4) FA 2004 with effect from 22 July 2004.

Customer Service Office
Birmingham Stamp Office
9th Floor City Centre House
30 Union Street
Birmingham
B2 4AR
DX: 15001 Birmingham 1
The envelope and any letter should be marked 'SDLT'.

Interest may be payable by HMRC, subject to the terms of any successful deferral application.

F(No.2)A 2005 introduced changes to the rules on contingent consideration where there is consideration for the grant or assignment of a lease in the form of a loan or deposit.[167] Sub-paragraph (4A) was inserted in section 80[168] precluding claims for adjustment of the consideration under section 80(4) where:

- there is full or partial repayment of any loan or deposit treated as consideration under paragraph 18A; or
- there is any refund of the consideration for the grant of a lease or assignment of a lease and that refund is contingent on the determination or assignment of the lease or on the grant of a chargeable interest out of the lease.

Variable or uncertain rent[169]

Paragraph 7 Schedule 17A deals with cases where rent is variable or uncertain. Where the rent is contingent, uncertain or unascertained, paragraph 7 applies section 51(1) and 51(2) to determine the amount brought into the charge as rent. The provisions of section 80 (adjustment where contingency ceases or consideration is ascertained) do not apply to consideration in the form of rent - similar provisions in paragraph 8 Schedule 17A apply instead.

1.7.11. Chargeable consideration - annuities

(Section 52)

Where a land transaction is entered into in return for an annuity of a particular type, section 52 provides that the first 12 years of payments only are aggregated and SDLT calculated by reference to that amount.

---

[167] See 2.6.6 below

[168] By paragraph 15 Schedule 10 F(No. 2)A 2005 in relation to transactions with an effective date after 19 May 2005, subject to transitional provisions in paragraph 16(7) Schedule 10.

[169] See 2.6.12 below

'Annuity' for the purposes of section 52 includes any consideration (other than rent) which is paid or provided periodically[170]. The section applies to an annuity which is:

- payable for life
- payable in perpetuity
- payable for an indefinite period
- payable for a definite period exceeding 12 years.

Where payments under such an annuity vary, the 12 highest annual payments are taken. Adjustments by reference to the retail price index ('RPI') are ignored.

Where necessary the amount of any payment is determined by reference to section 51 (contingent, uncertain or unascertained consideration[171]) but no adjustment can be made under section 80 when a contingency or uncertain consideration becomes known. Deferral of tax under section 90 is not available[172].

Section 52 would, for example, apply to determine the consideration in the case of an equity release scheme where an individual sells property to a life insurance company in exchange for the right to live in the property until his death and an annuity for life.

VAT payable in respect of rent but which is not reserved as rent will not be rent for SDLT purposes and, as for stamp duty, will be taxed as consideration other than rent. Accordingly, where the lease exceeds 12 years, section 52 will apply to limit the amount chargeable to the total of the 12 highest annual payments.

1.7.12. Chargeable consideration - deemed market value rule[173]

(Sections 53 and 54)

Section 53 provides that where the purchaser[174] is a company[175] and either:

---

[170] For the meaning of periodically see *Blendett v IRC, Quietlece v IRC* [1984] STC 95 (CA)

[171] See 1.7.10 above

[172] See 7.8 below

[173] A similar rule applied for stamp duty purposes – see section 119 FA 2000.

[174] Section 43(4) provides that references to the 'purchaser' and 'vendor', in relation to a land transaction, are to 'the person acquiring and the person disposing of the subject-matter of the transaction'. These expressions apply even if there is no consideration for a transaction but a person cannot be a purchaser unless he has given consideration for a transaction or is a party to it (section 43(5)).

[175] 'Company' means any body corporate (section 53(3)) and a unit trust scheme is treated as a company for this purpose.

(1) the vendor is treated as 'connected' with the purchaser for SDLT purposes (using the test of connection in section 839 ICTA 1988),[176] or
(2) some or all of the consideration for the land transaction consists of the issue of shares, stock or securities in a company with which the vendor is connected,

then the land transaction will be treated as having taken place for not less than the market value of the property transferred (or, in the case of an acquisition which is the grant of a lease at a rent, the rent)[177] even if there would otherwise be no chargeable consideration.[178] Section 53 therefore operates to increase the chargeable consideration in such a case and would take the transaction outside the scope of the exemption in paragraph 1 Schedule 3 (transactions where there is no chargeable consideration - see section 1.6.1 above). Other exemptions or reliefs may nevertheless apply to eliminate or reduce the SDLT charge.

The reason for the deemed market value rule is to prevent avoidance of SDLT by the transfer of property to a connected company for no consideration or at an under-value and then selling the shares in that company to the purchaser, incurring a liability to stamp duty or SDLT of 0.5% (which could be avoided altogether if a foreign company was used) rather than a charge to SDLT at up to 4%. However, the rule can apply to ordinary commercial transactions, such as the incorporation of a business.

'Market value' is to be determined in accordance with the capital gains tax rules in sections 272 to 274 TCGA 1992[179] and is, broadly, the price that might be expected to be obtained on a sale on the open market. There is no indication in the legislation of whether or how encumbrances (which would reduce the value of the interest transferred) should be taken into account.

The deemed market value rule is subject to three exceptions laid down in section 54. The exceptions are:
(1) where the transferee company holds the property as trustee as part of a trust management business; or
(2) where the transferee company holds the property as trustee and the vendor is connected to the company only in his capacity as trustee of a settlement; or

---

[176] See SDLT Glossary in Part Five for the full text of section 839.

[177] Section 53(1A) inserted by section 297(4) FA 2004 in relation to transactions of which the effective date is on or after 22 July 2004.

[178] Section 53(4)

[179] Section 118

(3) where the vendor is a company transferring the property by way of a distribution of the assets of the company (whether as part of a winding up or not), but this exception does not apply if the 'subject matter of the transaction'[180] or an interest from which that interest is derived has been the subject of a claim by the vendor for group relief in the three years immediately preceding the effective date of the acquisition by the transferee company.

On an exchange of non-major interests in land involving a company connected with the vendor it is HMRC's view that the rules in section 53 override the provisions of paragraph 5(4) Schedule 4(which provide that the amount of the consideration for each transaction is taken to be only any consideration other than the disposal or disposals given in exchange for the acquisition (for example, any equality money)).[181]

It is HMRC's intention that the third exception above (set out in section 54(4)) should still apply where a group relief claim was made by the vendor but that relief was clawed back under paragraph 3 of Schedule 7 either at the time of or before the effective date of the transaction to which the market value rule would otherwise apply.[182] Broadly, the clawback under paragraph 3 of Schedule 7 applies where the purchaser company leaves the group within three years of an intra-group transaction to which group relief applied.

The exclusion from the third exception is aimed at preventing a type of 'envelope' trick which could otherwise be used to avoid the SDLT charge. If any of the exceptions apply SDLT will only be charged on the actual chargeable consideration, if any.

Transfers of legal title to corporate nominees are not excluded from the deemed market value rule. The stamp duty exceptions in relation to the transfer of land to connected companies where one party was a bare nominee for the other[183] have not been reproduced for SDLT purposes, however it is understood that HMRC accept that the market value of such an interest is nominal and a transfer of the bare legal title will therefore fall within the nil-rate band. Such a transaction will be notifiable pursuant to section 77.

Where a lease is granted to a nominee, paragraph 3 of Schedule 16 provides that the nominee is to be treated as the purchaser of the whole interest. The

---

[180] Defined in section 43(6) as a reference to the chargeable interest acquired together with any interest or right appurtenant or pertaining to it that is acquired with it.

[181] See Tax Journal Issue No. 862 (20 November 2006) at page 19.

[182] See SDLTM30220

[183] Section 120 FA 2000

deemed market value rule is, in principle, applicable in such a case if the vendor and nominee are connected and the nominee is a body corporate (even if the nominor is neither a body corporate nor connected with the vendor).

1.8. Surrender and re-grant

(Paragraphs 9 and 16 Schedule 17A)[184]

The old stamp duty relief on the surrender and re-grant of leases is carried over for SDLT purposes in paragraph 16 Schedule 17A. The surrender of a lease is not treated as chargeable consideration for the grant of the new lease between the same parties. Accordingly, the charge to SDLT is calculated on the consideration (premium and/or rent) under the new lease, ignoring the value of the lease that is surrendered. Where the relief applies, the SDLT provisions relating to exchanges (discussed at 1.9 below) are disapplied[185].

HMRC have confirmed their view that the relief can apply to part.[186]

Care should be taken to ensure that the re-grant is not to a nominee (even where the nominee has surrendered the old lease) as, in such a case, the provisions of paragraph 3(3) Schedule 16 will apply and the re-grant will be treated for SDLT purposes as made to the nominee and not to the party who has surrendered the lease, so the relief would not be available.

1.8.1. Overlap relief[187]

In addition 'overlap relief' is given in relation to the rent under the new lease in any of the following circumstances:

(1) the new lease is of 'the same or substantially the same' premises as the old lease[188]; or
(2) the tenant under a lease of premises to which Part 2 of the Landlord and Tenant Act 1954 applies makes a request for a new tenancy which is duly executed; or
(3) on termination of a head lease a sub-tenant is granted a new lease of the same or substantially the same premises in pursuance of an order of the

---

[184] As amended by paragraph 11 Schedule 39 FA 2004 in relation to transactions the effective date of which is after 17 March 2004.

[185] By paragraph 16 Schedule 17A

[186] See Tax Journal Issue 862 (20 November 2006) at page 20.

[187] Paragraph 9 Schedule 17A as amended.

[188] It is understood that HMRC interpret this to allow overlap relief where the leaseback is of premises which *include* the same or substantially the same premises and that SDLTM will be amended to reflect this interpretation.

court on a claim for relief against re-entry on forfeiture or in pursuance of a contractual entitlement in the event of the head lease being terminated; or

(4) a person who has guaranteed the obligations of the lessee under a lease is granted a lease of the same or substantially the same premises in pursuance of the guarantee.

There are five factual examples of the operation of the overlap relief rules in the lease chapter of the SDLT Manual (April 2007) starting at SDLTM16015.

A specific relief (similar to overlap relief) is available where a backdated lease is granted to a tenant who is holding over after his lease has terminated[189].

Claiming overlap relief

Overlap relief is not a relief which is claimed by checking yes in Box 4 ('Are you claiming relief') on the land transaction return (form SDLT1)[190]. The starting rent inserted in Box 20 should be the actual starting rent for the new lease without reduction then for the purposes of calculating the NPV[191], to be included in Box 23 the rent under the new lease in respect of any 'overlap period' is treated as reduced by the amount of the rent payable under the old lease in respect of the same period. The 'overlap period' is the period between the date of grant of the new lease and what would have been the expiry date of the term of the old lease had it not been terminated. The rent payable under the old lease is the amount that was taken into account in determining the SDLT chargeable in respect of the grant of the old lease. There is therefore no overlap relief for stamp duty paid under the old regime nor is there overlap relief if the rent under the first lease was relieved from SDLT.

If the effect of applying the relief in respect of the overlap period is to reduce the taxable rent under the lease to nil, no land transaction return is required. If the lease requires registration at the Land Registry it can be self-certified on form SDLT60 as a lease made for no chargeable consideration.

1.9. Exchange relief abolished

(Section 47 and paragraph 5 Schedule 4))

Under the old stamp duty regime, where properties were exchanged and equality money paid, stamp duty was chargeable only by reference to the value

---

[189] Paragraph 9A Schedule 17A discussed at *'Backdated lease granted to tenant holding over'* in section 2.6.17 below.

[190] See SDLTM17015 in the lease chapter of the SDLT Manual (April 2007)

[191] The NPV (Net Present Value) calculation is considered in detail at 2.6.9 below. Broadly, the rent payable under the lease is taxed by reference to the NPV of each yearly amount of rent that will become payable under the lease if it runs its full course.

of the more expensive property and was paid by the person acquiring the more expensive property.[192] This relief was not carried over into SDLT and the general rule is that tax is charged on each leg of an exchange as a separate transaction.

The only vestige of the stamp duty exchange relief is in paragraphs 1 and 2 of Schedule 6A which provide relief for various exchanges involving residential property. For the details of this relief see section 3.8.1 below.

1.9.1. Exchanges – the provisions in detail

Section 47 provides that where a land transaction is entered into by a purchaser (alone or jointly) wholly or partly 'in consideration of' another land transaction being entered into by him (alone or jointly) as vendor, each transaction is taxed as if it were distinct and separate from the other. Each purchaser must complete a separate land transaction return for his transaction. Merely reserving or excepting right or interests from a transfer or a lease does not turn a sale or grant into an exchange[193].

Section 47(2) provides that a transaction is treated as entered into by the purchaser wholly or partly in consideration of another land transaction being entered into by him as vendor (and thus being an exchange) in any case where an obligation to give consideration for a land transaction that a person enters into as purchaser is met wholly or partly by way of that person entering into another transaction as vendor. This catches the case where an exchange is structured as a sale.

HMRC's view of the operation of the provisions is extremely wide.[194] Section 47 can apply even though the parties are not identical and its application should be considered wherever parties to a transaction each acquire interests in or rights over land. Exchanges are always governed by section 47 even where additional consideration other than the entering into another land transaction is present.

---

[192] For stamp duty purposes a transaction could often be structured as a sale of the more expensive property for a consideration consisting of the other property plus a cash amount. Where a transaction was properly documented as a single sale in that way, section 241 FA 1994 did not apply and the transfer of the consideration property was chargeable only to £5 fixed duty as a 'conveyance of any other kind'. This was because there was no 'sale' of the consideration property.

[193] See SDLTM00270

[194] See article in HMRC SDLT Technical News Issue 5 (August 2007) which is to be incorporated in SDLTM and which gives guidance on HMRC's interpretation of 'in consideration of' in section 45

Although each leg of an exchange is treated as a separate land transaction by reason of section 47(1), HMRC's view[195] was that they were linked transactions where the parties were 'connected' with each other so that the values had to be aggregated in order to ascertain the appropriate rate of SDLT[196]. For example, if land worth £220,000 was exchanged between connected parties for land worth £330,000, SDLT would be due at 4% on £520,000.

Legislation was introduced in FA 2007 to provide that where an exchange of property takes place between connected persons, the two legs are not linked with each other for determining the rate of SDLT. The provision[197] applies to any land transaction which is part of an exchange taking place on or 19 July 2007.[198] This change means that, if land worth £220,000 is exchanged between connected parties for land worth £330,000 the two properties are treated separately, so SDLT is due at 1% on the property worth £220,000 and 3% on the other.

Section 47 would cover a surrender and re-grant and, in a case where the relief provided by paragraph 16 of Schedule 17[199] is not available, the transaction will be taxed as an exchange.

The exchange provisions do not apply where an exchange or a sale and leaseback takes place which involves certain public bodies[200].

Conversion of a lease into a commonhold unit under section 9(3)(f) of the Commonhold and Leasehold Reform Act 2002 is not an exchange because the lease is extinguished by operation of law - the lease is not exchanged for the commonhold unit.[201]

1.9.2. Exchanges – application of the rules to partitions[202]

(Paragraph 6 Schedule 4)

In principle section 47 also covers partitions. A partition involves jointly owned land where there is the acquisition of a chargeable interest in exchange for the giving up of another. However SDLT will not be chargeable on a simple partition where property is divided according to the parties' existing

---

195 See Example 3 at SDLTM04020a

196 By reason of section 108 – see 2.1.1 below.

197 Section 76(1) and (3) FA 2007 amending section 47(1) with effect from 19 July 2007

198 The date of Royal Assent to FA 2007

199 See 1.8 above

200 Paragraph 17 Schedule 4 - see 3.20 below

201 See SDLTM00285 for guidance on the SDLT treatment of commonholds.

202 See example at SDLTM04030a

entitlements because of the rule in paragraph 6 of Schedule 4 that 'the share of the interest held by the purchaser before the partition or division does not count as chargeable consideration'.

The reason for this provision was explained by the Chief Secretary to the Treasury as follows:

> "A and B are joint owners of two properties. They agree to split ownership, so that A is left as sole owner of one property and B sole owner of the other. That is an example of partition and will be familiar to a number of Committee members opposite and behind me. Paragraph 6 is a relieving provision that operates in such a situation, since paragraph 5 on exchanges, ... could lead to a higher charge[203]."

The terms of paragraph 6 of Schedule 4 are unclear but the intention appears to be to leave out of account the interest given up by each party to the partition (rather than merely excluding it as consideration) so that the acquisition resulting from the partition is not 'in consequence of' a disposal and the exchanges rules therefore do not apply. In effect the charge to SDLT is limited to any balancing payment.

1.9.3. Exchanges – chargeable consideration

(Paragraph 5 Schedule 4)

These special rules determining the chargeable consideration on an exchange are expressly disapplied in relation to partitions (to which paragraph 6 of Schedule 4 applies) by paragraph 5(6). The linked transactions rules do not apply to exchanges[204].

Exchange involving a major interest in land

If either leg of the exchange involves a 'major interest'[205] the amount of the consideration for each transaction is taken to be the market value of the subject matter acquired by the purchaser and, if the acquisition is the grant of a lease at a rent, the rent payable.[206]

---

[203] Hansard, Standing Committee B, 5 June 2003 am, Col 374.

[204] Section 47(1) as amended by FA2007 with effect in relation to a set of land transactions if the effective date of any of them is on or after 19 July 2007.

[205] Defined in section 117(2) (in relation to England and Wales) as a fee simple absolute or a term of years absolute at law or in equity. The definitions applying to Scotland and Northern Ireland are in section 117(3) and (4) respectively.

[206] Paragraph 5(3) Schedule 4

Exchange not involving a major interest in land
In the case of exchanges where neither leg involves a major interest, the amount of the consideration for each transaction is taken to be only any consideration other than the disposal or disposals given in exchange for the acquisition (for example, any equality money).[207] On an exchange of non-major interests in land involving a connected company it is HMRC's view that the rules in section 53 override the provisions of paragraph 5(4) Schedule 4.[208]

The following examples are taken from SDLTM04020a:

Example One:

Mr. Blue has a house with a market value of £600,000. Mrs. White has a house with a market value of £700,000. They exchange with Mr Blue paying Mrs. White £100,000.

The chargeable consideration on the acquisition by Mr Blue is £700,000.

The chargeable consideration on the acquisition by Mrs. White is £600,000.

Example Two:

Mr Brown has a piece of freehold land with a market value of £500,000. He exchanges this with Mrs. Green who grants him a 50 year lease over office premises at an annual rent. No premium is paid.

The chargeable consideration on the acquisition by Mr Brown is the NPV of the rent payable under the 50 year lease.

The chargeable consideration on the acquisition by Mrs. Green is £500,000.

1.10. Options and rights of pre-emption

(Section 46)

One stamp duty avoidance scheme provided for the majority of the value of land, and, thus, the majority of the consideration, to be allocated to a payment for the option, while the balance was paid for the land subject to the option on its exercise. Stamp duty was not paid on the consideration for the option as, although the option document was liable to stamp duty, under that scheme it would be executed and held offshore.

Section 46 prevents avoidance of SDLT through the use of options. It is only necessary to consider the provisions of section 46 where the grant of an option or right of pre-emption would not otherwise be chargeable.

---

[207] Paragraph 5(4) and 5(5) Schedule 4

[208] See Tax Journal Issue No. 862 (20 November 2006) at page 19.

Section 46(1)(a) provides that the acquisition[209] of an option binding the grantor to enter into a land transaction[210] is itself a land transaction distinct from any land transaction resulting from the exercise of the option. Therefore, both the grant and exercise of such an option may be chargeable to SDLT.

The effective date of the transaction constituted by the acquisition[211] of the option is the date on which the option or right is acquired, as opposed to when it becomes exercisable.[212] Where the option is exercised between the original parties to the grant (or parties connected with them), the exercise and grant of the option will form a series of transactions to which section 108 (linked transactions) will apply, meaning that the grant and exercise of the option are treated as a single transaction in determining the rate of SDLT applicable to the consideration for the acquisition of the land, and any SDLT or additional SDLT payable in respect of the earlier grant.[213]

In determining the rate of SDLT on the price paid for the option, any sum payable on its later exercise will not be taken into account as until exercise there will be no series of transactions to bring section 108 in point. SDLT on the land transaction that would arise on the option being exercised is chargeable if and when the option is exercised.

Once granted, the option is itself a chargeable interest and SDLT may therefore arise on its assignment, variation or release.

Example:[214]

On 1 January 2005, Mr Smith is granted an option by Mrs Jones to buy her house for £200,000 on or before 31 December 2005. Mr Smith paid Mrs Jones £70,000 for the grant of the option. Mr Smith exercises the option on 1 December 2005.

Although the purchase of the option by Mr Smith is a land transaction in its own right as the consideration is below the 1% threshold for SDLT, a land transaction return is not required on the grant of the option. The exercise of the

[209] An 'acquisition' includes a 'grant' but for SDLT purposes the transaction is considered from the point of view of the acquirer who is liable for the tax.

[210] Including a case where the grantor must either enter a land transaction or discharge his obligations under the option 'in some other way' – section 46(2).

[211] Or 'grant' – see footnote 209

[212] Section 46(3)

[213] A return or an additional return may be due in respect of the grant – section 81A (see 7.1.1 below).

[214] Taken from SDLTM1300a

option on 1 December 2005 constitutes a separate land transaction from the grant of the option. Once the option is exercised, Mr Smith must lodge two land transaction returns, one for the grant of the option[215] and one for the exercise of the option.[216] The effective date of both these land transactions is the date of completion of the sale of the house to Mr Smith or, if earlier, the date of substantial performance.

Section 46(1)(b) provides that the acquisition of a right of pre-emption over land (preventing the grantor from entering into, or restricting the right of the grantor to enter into, a land transaction with another party) is itself a land transaction. Once granted the right of pre-emption is a chargeable interest and SDLT may therefore arise on its assignment, variation or release. The effective date of the transaction constituted by the acquisition of a right of pre-emption is the date on which the right is acquired and not when it becomes exercisable.[217]

An option or pre-emption right is not a 'major interest[218]' so the acquisition is not notifiable unless tax is chargeable or would be chargeable but for a relief.[219] The fact that the acquisition and the exercise are linked may mean that the acquisition becomes notifiable at the time of exercise.

Section 46(4) provides that section 46 does not apply 'to so much of an option or right of pre-emption as constitutes or forms part of a land transaction apart from this section'. The special rules in section 46 therefore only apply where the general SDLT charging provisions do not. A call option in relation to land is an interest in land and is a chargeable interest within the meaning of section 48. However, as a put option relating to land is a personal right against the grantor it would not be a chargeable interest and would therefore not within the charge to SDLT in the absence of section 46.

---

[215] Showing £70,000 at Box 10, £270,000 at Box 13 and £2100 (SDLT at 3% rate) at Box 14.

[216] Showing £200,000 at Box 10, £270,000 at Box 13 and £6000 (SDLT at 3% rate) at Box 14.

[217] Section 46(2)

[218] A 'major interest' is defined in section 117(2) (in relation to England and Wales) as a fee simple absolute or a term of years absolute at law or in equity. The definitions applying to Scotland and Northern Ireland are in section 117(3) and (4) respectively.

[219] Section 79(4)

2. Calculating the charge to SDLT

2.1. Consideration (other than rent)

SDLT, other than where it is charged on rent (see 2.6.7 below), is a threshold based tax in the same way as stamp duty was. The charge is set out in section 55(1) and is a percentage of the 'relevant consideration'. The 'relevant consideration' is the 'chargeable consideration' modified in the following way:

1) If the transaction is one of a series of 'linked transactions' the relevant consideration is the total chargeable consideration for all those transactions (section 55(4)(b)).
2) Where the provisions of section 74 (collective enfranchisement by leaseholders – see 2.2 below) and section 75 (crofting community right to buy – see 0 below) apply the chargeable consideration is reduced by the appropriate fraction (section 55(5)).

The amount of the SDLT is rounded down to the nearest pound. Consideration paid in foreign currency is converted into sterling on the effective date of the transaction unless the parties use a different rate for the transaction.[220] The rate to be used is the London closing exchange rate.

2.1.1. Linked transactions – consideration (other than rent)

(Section 108)

The linked transactions rule is an anti-avoidance rule intended to prevent transactions being fragmented to save tax. Transactions are 'linked' for the purposes of SDLT if they 'form part of a single scheme, arrangement or series of transactions between the same vendor and the same purchaser, or, in either case, persons connected with them (section 108(1)).[221] The 'connected persons' test in section 839 ICTA 1988 applies.[222] The vendor and purchaser must be acting in the same capacity in relation to each transaction. Legislation was

---

[220] Paragraph 9 Schedule 4

[221] Section 43(4) provides that references to the 'purchaser' and 'vendor', in relation to a land transaction, are to 'the person acquiring and the person disposing of the subject-matter of the transaction'. The expressions apply even if there is no consideration for a transaction but in such a case a person cannot be treated as a purchaser unless he is a party to the transaction (section 43(5)).

[222] For full text of section 839 see SDLT Glossary in Part Five. With effect from 5 December 2005 civil partners are 'connected persons' within the meaning of section 839, so that purchases by civil partners from the same vendor can be linked transactions (regulation 100 Tax and Civil Partnership Regulations 2005 (SI 2005/3229).

introduced in FA 2007 to provide expressly that where an exchange of land takes place between connected persons, the two legs are not linked[223].

The equivalent for stamp duty purposes was that a transaction had to be part of a 'larger transaction or series of transactions' in order to be aggregated. The SDLT rule is wider than the aggregation provision for stamp duty purposes and is intended to ensure that transactions carried out at the same time between the same vendor and purchaser are treated as linked even if they are documented independently. *A.G. v Cohen*[224], a case under the old stamp duty rules, illustrates the difference between the two sets of provisions.

The facts in *Cohen* were that 12 houses were offered by auction in 12 separate lots. Six were bought by one purchaser as they were put up for sale and six deposits were paid. It was held that each of the six transfers did not effect a transaction which was part of a larger transaction or series, because the relationship between the transactions was fortuitous, casual and coincidental. The sales were not under a single contract or interdependent or integral (some broader legal nexus). In *Cohen* Greene LJ gave as examples of a series of transactions the vesting in a purchaser of different parts of a property by successive orders of a court in the same action and the acquisition of plots by a builder developing an estate who has, under one contract, options which provide for the purchase of different plots at different times.

Had the facts in Cohen arisen under the SDLT regime, the acquisition by one purchaser of six of the 12 lots would be linked as they would be a series of transactions between the same vendor and purchaser. Contemporaneous transactions between the same parties will fall outside the linked transactions rule if, as a matter of fact, they are not part of a single scheme, arrangement or series of transactions. There is a single scheme where the transactions form part of some pre-agreed plan. A series of transactions exists where the transactions are entered into sequentially between the parties and there is a connection or interdependence between them[225].

Where transactions are linked, section 55(4) provides for the rate of tax to be determined by reference to the aggregate chargeable consideration for all of those transactions. Consideration that is not chargeable (such as that attributable to chattels) is not aggregated. Where a linked transaction is a lease

[223] Section 108(4) inserted by FA 2007 with effect in relation to a set of land transactions if the effective date of any of them is on or after 19 July 2007.

[224] [1937] 1 KB 478, CA

[225] Ibid per Greene LJ

under which rent is payable, no account is taken of the rent in determining the relevant consideration[226] but special rules apply in taxing the rent under such leases.[227] Relief from aggregation is given to certain transactions in relation to collective enfranchisement by leaseholders and crofting community right to buy schemes.

The fact that transactions are between the same vendor and purchaser (or persons connected with them) does not always mean that they are linked (if the parties are not the same the transactions cannot be linked). For example, A buys two separate farms from B - the two sales are negotiated together but documented separately. Provided that A would have bought either farm, irrespective of the other and the price for each would not have changed, the sales will not be linked.[228] In such a case, contemporaneous evidence should be retained to support the fact that Box 13 on form SDLT1[229] has been checked to show that the transaction in question is not linked with another and the declaration at the end of the form completed.

It should be borne in mind that transactions can be linked through persons connected with either vendor or purchaser. Transactions may need to be reviewed to establish whether they are linked to a later transaction, in which case a second land transaction return may need to be filed and the SDLT on the earlier transaction recalculated.[230] The SDLTM gives the example of the purchase of a house with gardens which is structured in such a way that a husband buys the house and his wife buys the gardens. The two transactions will be linked and the rate of tax will be determined by the sum of the chargeable considerations paid for both house and gardens.[231]

Where there are linked transactions with the same effective date, the purchaser, or all the purchasers if more than one, may make a single land transaction return as if all those linked transactions that are 'notifiable' were a single notifiable transaction (section 108(2)). Where a single return is made in these circumstances, the provisions relating to joint purchasers in section 103[232] apply

---

[226] Paragraph 9(5) Schedule 5

[227] Paragraph 2(5) and 2(6) Schedule 4 – see 0 below

[228] However if the two farms were only viable as one business or if there was a discount for purchasing both the linked transactions rule would apply.

[229] See Appendix for the SDLT forms

[230] Section 81A

[231] SDLTM30100.

[232] See 7.17 below

as if the transactions were a single transaction and the purchasers were acting jointly. The single return is not mandatory.

2.2. Relief from aggregation for collective enfranchisement by leaseholders

(Section 74)

Note: this relief cannot yet be claimed

Section 4A of the Leasehold Reform, Housing and Urban Development Act 1993 had not been brought into force at the date the text of this book was finalised[233] and as it is by virtue of this legislation that an RTE company can be formed (see below). Relief under section 74 is not yet available.

Collective enfranchisement by leaseholders is where a group of leaseholders acts together in order to purchase the freehold of the property under certain statutory provisions which are referred to below. The SDLT relief only applies if, in pursuance of a 'right of collective enfranchisement', leaseholders act together through a company known as an 'RTE company'. Section 74 determines the rate at which SDLT is charged on the purchase by allowing relief from the aggregation of the consideration.

The rate of tax chargeable is determined by the total payment for the freehold being purchased divided by the number of leasehold interests involved. That figure is used as consideration, but only for determining the rate of tax chargeable. That rate of tax is then applied to the total consideration for the transaction. The intended effect is that the rate of tax paid is in line with that which would have been due if the leaseholders had each bought their share of the freehold separately. The following example of how the relief works is taken from SDLTM28505a:

> An RTE company purchases the freehold of eight flats and some communal areas (for example halls, stairs communal garden etc.) for £600,000. The rate of tax applicable to this transaction without relief would be 4%.
>
> The relief works by determining the rate of tax for the fractional proportion of the relevant consideration. As there are eight flats being purchased, the fractional proportion of the relevant consideration is £600,000/8 (£75,000) and the rate of tax is 1% and that rate is applied to the whole of the consideration.
>
> SDLT of £600,000 x 1% (£6,000) is due after relief. The SDLT legislation gives no rules for how this amount is to be divided between the tenants. The RTE company is liable for the SDLT.

---

[233] 20 July 2007

Often collective enfranchisement includes, after the freehold purchase, the grant of extension leases to each participating tenant for a premium equal to his contribution to the cost of buying the freehold. The normal SDLT rules would apply to these transactions.

Relevant definitions[234]

'RTE company' (a 'Right to Enfranchise' company) has the meaning given by section 4A of the Leasehold Reform, Housing and Urban Development Act 1993. A company is a RTE company in relation to premises if:

(a) it is a private company limited by guarantee; and
(b) its memorandum of association states that its object, or one of its objects, is the exercise of the right to collective enfranchisement with respect to the premises.

A company is not a RTE company if it is a commonhold association (within the meaning of Part 1 of the Commonhold and Leasehold Reform Act 2002) and a company is not a RTE company in relation to premises if another company which is a RTE company in relation to the premises, or any premises containing or contained in the premises, has given a notice under section 13 Leasehold Reform, Housing and Urban Development Act 1993 with respect to the premises, or any premises containing or contained in the premises, and the notice continues in force in accordance with subsection (11) of that section.

'Right of collective enfranchisement' means the right exercisable by an RTE company under Part 1 of the Landlord and Tenant Act 1987 or Chapter 1 of Part 1 of the Leasehold Reform, Housing and Urban Development Act 1993.

2.2.1. Claiming the relief

The RTE company is liable for the SDLT payable and must claim the relief. Relief is claimed by completing the land transaction return (form SDLT1), checking Box 9 to show that a relief is being claimed and inserting code 25.

---

[234] Section 74(3)

2.3. Relief from aggregation for transactions entered into in pursuance of the crofting community right to buy

(Section 75)

Where a chargeable transaction is entered into in pursuance of the crofting community right to buy and two or more crofts are being bought under that transaction, the rate of SDLT is determined by reference to the fraction of the relevant consideration produced by dividing the total amount of that consideration by the number of crofts being bought. The tax chargeable is then determined by applying that rate to the amount of the chargeable consideration for the transaction in question. This is intended to avoid a detriment to the crofters by the aggregation of consideration a, in order to exercise their right to buy under the relevant legislation, the crofters must act in concert.

'Crofting community right to buy' means the right exercisable by a crofting community body under Part 3 of the Land Reform (Scotland) Act 2003.[235]

2.3.1. Claiming the relief

Relief is claimed by completing the land transaction return (form SDLT1), checking Box 9 to show that a relief is being claimed and inserting code 26.

2.4. Rate of SDLT on residential property - consideration (other than rent)

Section 55(2) provides that SDLT is charged in relation to a land transaction relating to residential property on a percentage of the chargeable consideration for the transaction (other than rent) as follows:

Relevant consideration	SDLT Percentage
Not more than £125,000[236]	0%
More than £125,000 but not more than £250,000	1%
More than £250,000 but not more than £500,000	3%
More than £500,000	4%

The 'slab' principle applies so that once the consideration exceeds a particular threshold the whole of the consideration is taxed at the rate appropriate to the band in which the excess falls.

---

[235] Section 75(4)

[236] The threshold for residential property was increased from £60,000 to £120,000 for transactions with an effective date after 16 March 2005 by section 95 FA 2005 and was further increased to £125,000 for transactions with an effective date after 22 March 2006 by section 162 FA 2006.

Tax on any rent is calculated separately under different rules. However where there is consideration other than rent (for example, a lease is granted at a premium below the £125,000 threshold), but the 'annual rent' is greater than £600, paragraph 9 Schedule 5 disapplies the 0% band in the table at section 55(2) in relation to that other consideration and any case that would have fallen within that band is treated as falling within the 1% band. This is to prevent the nil-rate band applying more than once in respect of the same lease.

The charge to SDLT on rent is dealt with in detail in section 2.6.8 below.

2.4.1. Residential/non-residential property

To determine whether the relevant land is residential it is necessary to apply the tests set out in section 116 at the effective date of the land transaction.[237]

> "Where a building is in use at the [effective date], it will be a question of fact whether and to what extent it is used as a dwelling. Use at the [effective date] overrides any past or intended future uses for this purpose."[238]

The tests can be applied to a part of a building (section 116(6)).

'Residential property' means:

(a) a building that is:
  i. used as a dwelling, or
  ii. suitable for use as a dwelling, or
  iii. in the process of being constructed or adapted for such use, and

(b) land that is or forms part of the garden or grounds of a building within paragraph (a) (including any building or structure on such land), or

(c) an interest in or right over land (such as a restrictive covenant) that subsists for the benefit of a building within paragraph (a) or of land within paragraph (b)

(section 116(1)).

The suitability test in (a)(ii) above applies to 'the state of the building at the [effective date], having regard to the facilities available and any history of

---

[237] The wording of section 116 is identical to the wording of section 92B FA 2001 which applied for stamp duty purposes therefore the HMRC commentary on the old provision in SP1/2003 'Stamp duty - Disadvantaged areas relief' (April 2003) on whether or not property is "residential" will apply equally to the SDLT provisions. Certain of that guidance is reproduced in SP1/2004 'Stamp Duty Land Tax: Disadvantaged Area Relief'.
Paragraph 5 of SP1/2004 states:
"In most cases there will be no difficulty in practice in establishing whether or not a property is 'residential'. This statement sets out in more detail the Stamp Office's approach to borderline cases and gives guidance on the practical application of the legislation."

[238] Paragraph 11 SP1/2004

use'.[239] Whether a building is suitable for use as a dwelling will depend upon the precise facts and circumstances. The simple removal of, for example, a bathroom suite or kitchen facilities will not be regarded by HMRC as rendering a building unsuitable for use as a dwelling. Where it is claimed that a previously residential property is no longer suitable for use as a dwelling, the claimant will need to provide evidence that this is the case.[240] HMRC will not regard an office block as 'suitable for use as a dwelling', but a house which has been used as an office without particular adaptation may well be so.[241]

If a building is not in use at the effective date but its last use was as a dwelling, it will be taken to be 'suitable for use as a dwelling' and treated as residential property for the purposes of the relief, unless evidence is produced to the contrary.[242]

Undeveloped land will be residential property for SDLT purposes if a residential building is being built on it at the effective date. Where an existing building is being adapted for domestic use, it is residential property. The process of construction or adaptation is taken as commencing when the builders first start work.[243]

In applying the test in (b) above in relation to a garden or grounds, HMRC will have regard to the similar test that is applied for the purposes of the capital gains tax relief for main residences contained in section 222(3) TCGA 1992.[244] The land will include that which is needed for the reasonable enjoyment of the dwelling having regard to the size and nature of the dwelling.

The test in (c) above means that the treatment of interests in, or rights over, land or buildings follow that of the land or buildings to which they relate.

Section 116 also sets out particular building uses that are specifically included in, or specifically excluded from, the definition of residential property.

Section 116(2) states that a building used for any of the following purposes is 'used as a dwelling' for the purposes of section 116(1) and therefore is residential property:

(a) residential accommodation for school pupils;

---

239 Paragraph 15 SP1/2004

240 Paragraph 17 SP1/2004.

241 Paragraph 15 SP1/2004.

242 Paragraph 16 SP1/2004.

243 Paragraph 34 SP1/2004.

244 Paragraph 35 SP1/2004.

(b) residential accommodation for students, other than accommodation falling with subsection (3)(b);
(c) residential accommodation for members of the armed forces;
(d) an institution that is the sole or main residence of at least 90% of its residents and does not fall within any of paragraphs (a) to (f) of subsection (3).

A building used for any of the following purposes is not 'used as a dwelling' for SDLT purposes and therefore is non-residential property:
(a) a home or other institution providing residential accommodation for children;
(b) a hall of residence for students in further or higher education;
(c) a home or other institution providing residential accommodation with personal care for persons in need of personal care by reason of old age, disablement, past or present dependence on alcohol or drugs or past or present mental disorder;
(d) a hospital or hospice;
(e) a prison or similar establishment;
(f) a hotel or inn or similar establishment.
(Section 116(3))

Where a building is actually being used for a purpose specified in subsection (3), and is, therefore, not being used as a dwelling, the building's suitability for any other use is to be ignored (section 116(4)).

Where a building not in use at the effective date is suitable for one or more of the qualifying purposes specified in subsection (2) and is also suitable for one or more of the non-qualifying purposes specified in subsection (3), then if there is one of those uses for which the building is most suitable, or if the multiple uses for which it is most suitable are all listed in the same sub-paragraph, no account is to be taken for the purposes of subsection (1)(*a*) of its suitability for any other use – this is referred to by HMRC as the 'tie-breaker provision' and is set out in section 116(5). Whether or not a vacant building has one or more uses for which it is most suitable is a question of fact. Evidence supporting such uses should be provided with the claim for relief.

In any other case, the building is to be treated as suitable for use as a dwelling.

Where six or more separate dwellings are the subject of a single land transaction involving the transfer of a 'major interest'[245] in, or the grant of a

---

[245] Defined in section 117(2) (in relation to England and Wales) as a fee simple absolute or a term of years absolute at law or in equity. The definitions applying to Scotland and Northern Ireland are in section 117(3) and (4) respectively.

lease over them, then, for SDLT purposes, those dwellings are treated as not being residential property (section 116(7)) For example, this provision would apply to a sale of a block of more than six flats to a single purchaser and would mean that the higher threshold for non-residential property set out below would apply. In order to qualify as non-residential property under this provision, the dwellings must be self-contained and part of a single transaction.

There is a flowchart available on HMRC website which provides a quick guide for simpler cases as to whether property constitutes residential property.[246]

HMRC has also produced an intelligent decision-maker[247] which is reproduced on the next two pages.

[246] www.hmrc.gov.uk/so/resprop/a3.htm

[247] Available at http://www.hmrc.gov.uk/so/decisionmaker2.pdf

Flow chart to determine whether property is or is not 'residential property'

Is the subject of the conveyance/transfer/lease…

(A)

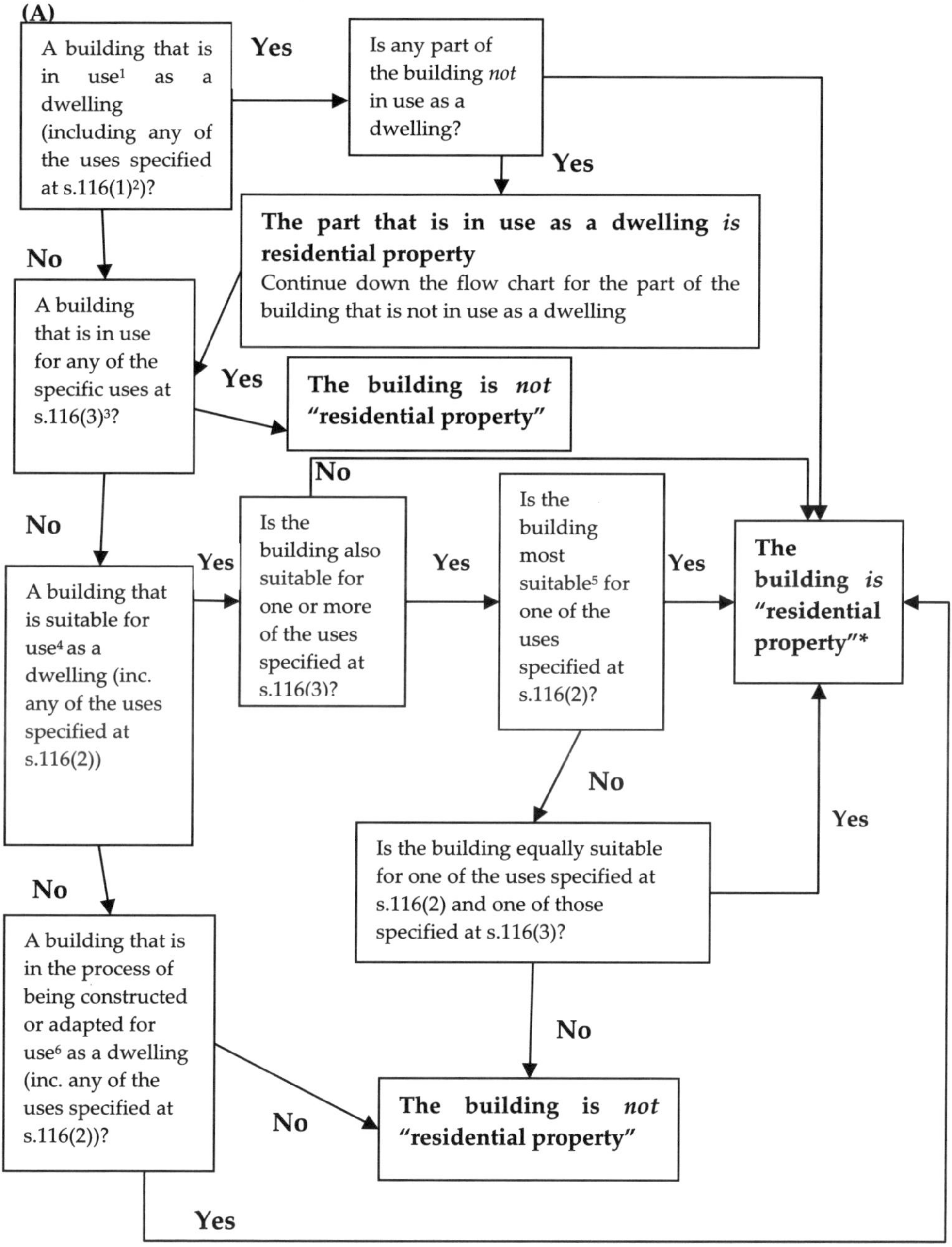

*unless the conveyance, transfer or lease comprises or includes six or more separate dwellings[7] made pursuant to a single transaction, in which circumstances none of the land will be 'residential property'

Is the subject of the conveyance/transfer/lease…

(B)

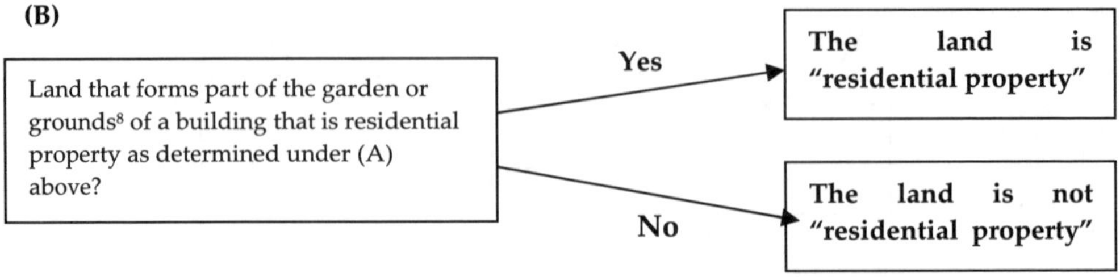

(C)

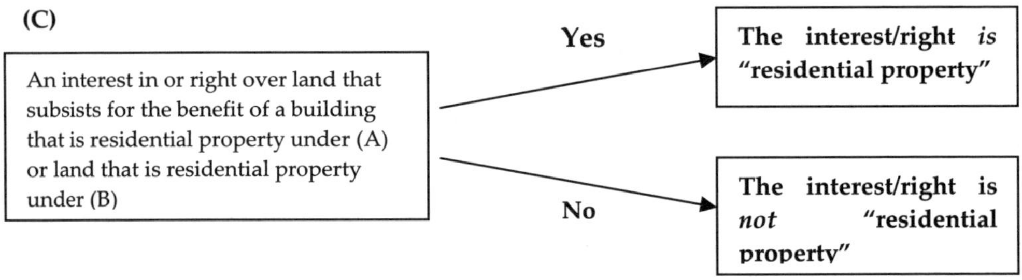

Footnotes to flow charts

1. See paragraphs 11 to 14 of SP1/2004
2. See paragraph 22 of SP1/2004
3. See paragraph 23 of SP1/2004
4. See paragraphs 15 to 18 of SP1/2004
5. See paragraph 29 of SP1/2004
6. See paragraphs 33 to 34 of SP1/2004
7. See paragraphs 40 to 44 of SP1/2004
8. See paragraph 35 of SP1/2004

2.5. Rate of SDLT for non-residential or mixed property - consideration other than rent

Non-residential property is defined by exclusion – anything which is not residential property is non-residential property.[248]

For land transactions where the relevant land is either non-residential property or does not entirely consist of residential property,[249] no SDLT is payable unless the consideration exceeds £150,000. Thereafter, the bands are:

Relevant consideration	SDLT Percentage
More than £150,000 but not more than £250,000	1%
More than £250,000 but not more than £500,000	3%
More than £500,000	4%

The 'slab' principle applies so that once the consideration exceeds a particular threshold the whole of the consideration is taxed at the rate appropriate to the band in which the excess falls.

Tax on any rent is calculated separately under different rules[250]. However where there is consideration other than rent (for example, a lease is granted at a premium below the £150,000 threshold), but the 'annual rent' is greater than £600, paragraph 9 Schedule 5 disapplies the 0% band in the table at section 55(2) in relation to that other consideration and any case that would have fallen within that band is treated as falling within the 1% band. This is to prevent the 0% band applying more than once in respect of the same lease.

The charge to SDLT on rent is dealt with in detail in section 2.6.8 below.

2.6. The charge to SDLT on leases

In the first year of SDLT approximately 29% of all transactions dealt with under the new regime were leasehold transactions - 9% in relation to new leases and 20% assignments of existing leases. Of the 20% relating to assignments, three quarters were residential and one quarter commercial.[251] HMRC data indicated that most commercial leases were for 35 years or less.

---

[248] Section 116(1).

[249] In the case of mixed property there is no provision for an apportionment as there is for disadvantaged areas relief - see 3.2 below.

[250] Dealt with at 2.6.8 below.

[251] See HMRC SDLT Practitioners' Newsletter Issue 2 (21 July 2004).

2.6.1. SDLT on new leases – overview

When a lease is granted,[252] the SDLT due on it depends on the premium payable (if any), the rent reserved by the lease and the term of the lease. Both rent and any premium will, in principle, be taxable and the SDLT due will be the total of the tax due in respect of the premium and the tax due in respect of the rental stream over the term of the lease.

A lease is defined for SDLT purposes as:[253]

(a) an interest or right in or over land for a term of years (whether fixed or periodic), or

(b) a tenancy at will or other interest or right in or over land terminable by notice at any time.[254]

The amount on which tax is charged is the 'net present value' ('NPV') of the rent payable over the term of the lease. The SDLT due in relation to rent is charged at a fixed rate of 1% once a threshold is crossed. In most cases the SDLT charge on a lease will be higher than the stamp duty charge would have been. The detailed rules for calculating the SDLT charge are set out below.

SDLT on a lease is normally payable by the lessee (tenant) and not by the lessor (landlord) although where a landlord pays a tenant to vary a lease he may be a 'purchaser' for SDLT purposes in respect of the variation. However, a landlord is not considered to be a 'purchaser' under section 43 merely by reason of his consent to an assignment.[255]

On an assignment any monetary consideration premium paid for the assignment is taxable. The rent element is not chargeable unless the grant of the lease benefited from an exemption such as group relief or charities relief (see 3.7 below).

---

[252] Including a deemed grant and a grant which is 'treated as' taking place.

[253] By paragraph 1 Schedule 17A

[254] Note: a tenancy at will is not a chargeable interest by reason of section 48(2)(c)(i)

[255] See Hansard, 3 June 2003, Cols. 305 to 306. Section 43(4) provides that references to the 'purchaser' in relation to a land transaction, are to 'the person acquiring … the subject-matter of the transaction'. The expression applies even if there is no consideration for a transaction but a person cannot be a purchaser unless he has given consideration for a transaction or is a party to it (section 43(5)).

2.6.2. Pre-implementation leases[256]

Only a lease that is granted, or, for SDLT purposes, deemed to be granted[257] on or after 1 December 2003 are within the SDLT regime. This brings into charge to SDLT renewals and extensions of pre-implementation leases on or after 1 December 2003 and variations of such leases which amount to a surrender and re-grant. It does not include those pre-1 December 2003 leases which continue after that date by operation of law (for example, under the Landlord and Tenant Act 1954), statutory periodic leases (for example, assured shorthold tenancies which continue after the expiry of the fixed term) or other forms of holding-over.

2.6.3. Linked transactions where consideration is or includes rent

(Paragraphs 2(5) and 2(6) Schedule 6)

If a lease is one of a number of 'linked transactions'[258] but there are not 'successive linked leases' then special rules apply in calculating the tax charge on the rent. The formula for calculating the SDLT charge in respect of each lease is set out in paragraphs 2(5) and 2(6) of Schedule 6.

Where an earlier transaction to which a later transaction is linked is not an 'SDLT transaction', the special rules are varied as set out in paragraph 7(1) Schedule 19.[259] These special rules are considered at 2.6.7 below

Where the leases are 'successive linked leases' (see 2.6.4 below) the provisions of paragraph 5 Schedule 17A apply in calculating the charge to SDLT.

2.6.4. Successive linked leases and options to renew

(Paragraph 5 Schedule 17A)

If successive leases of the same or substantially the same premises are granted or treated as granted (whether at the same time or at different times) and the 'grants' are 'linked transactions'[260] the SDLT provisions apply as if the series of leases were a single lease granted at the same time as the grant of the first lease for a term equal to the aggregate of all the terms in the series and in

[256] SDLTM13000

[257] For example certain lease variations can give rise to a deemed grant for SDLT purposes – see paragraph 15A Schedule 17A (discussed at 2.6.22 below).

[258] Applying the test in section 108 (for linked transactions see 2.1.1 above).

[259] The rules are applied as if references to 'chargeable consideration' in relation to a transaction which was not an SDLT transaction were references to the amount by reference to which *ad valorem* stamp duty was payable in respect of the instrument which effected the transaction.

[260] Applying the test in section 108 - for linked transactions see 2.1.1 above.

consideration of the rent payable under all the leases I the series. Tax will then be charged on that basis and credit given for any SDLT previously paid.

Where a lease is granted in pursuance of the agreement which has earlier been substantially performed, this is treated for the purposes of paragraph 9 Schedule 17A (overlap relief on surrender and re-grant) as a surrender of a deemed lease and a re-grant[261]. From 19 July 2006[262], the agreement for lease and the lease executed pursuant to it in such circumstances are not within the successive linked leases provisions.

'Linked' is widely defined in section 108. Transactions are 'linked' for the purposes of SDLT if they 'form part of a single scheme, arrangement or series of transactions between the same vendor and the same purchaser, or, in either case, persons connected with them.'

HMRC's views on successive linked leases are set out at SDLTM17035[263]:

> "A series of leases will often exist between the same parties, for example where a short lease is renewed between the same tenant and landlord. A renewal lease will be treated as linked with the original lease if, for example, the rent was fixed under the terms of the original lease or is stated to be the same as that payable under the original lease.
>
> However, the renewal of a lease will not be treated as linked with the original lease at all for SDLT purposes if it can be shown (with appropriate evidence) to have been negotiated at arm's length, for example if the original or earlier lease:
>
> - expired naturally
> - contained no right or compulsion of either party to renew, and/ or
> - was renewed following entirely new negotiations, as would apply to a new tenant.
>
> Otherwise, where leases of the same premises are granted:
>
> - between the same or connected parties
> - to take effect one immediately after the other
> - whether at the same time or not
>
> these are successive linked leases for SDLT purposes".

(see example at SDLTM17045[264]).

---

[261] See 1.8 above

[262] The date from which the provision (in section 12A(3) Schedule 17A) was amended by paragraph 4 Schedule 25 FA 2006.

[263] Lease chapter (April 2007)

[264] See footnote 263

Where a tenant is granted a new lease pursuant to the provisions of the Landlord and Tenant Act 1954, the right to the new lease is conferred by operation of law. Such leases will not be 'linked' for SDLT purposes unless either the landlord or the tenant or both have an express contractual option for a new lease (which would be unusual).

Where the linked leases in a series are granted at the outset, a land transaction return is required for the deemed aggregate lease. Where the leases are granted in succession and are linked, for example, by way of options to renew, a return or further return is required in relation to the later linked transaction if the aggregation of the series to that point means that the lease becomes notifiable or tax or additional tax becomes payable, and any (or additional) SDLT must then be paid. In such a case, both the earlier transaction and the later transaction must be specified in the land transaction return. However, the effective date for the purposes of the later return is still the effective date of the later transaction or transactions and the 30 day filing period runs from then.[265]

For the purposes of paragraph 5 Schedule 17A no account is to be taken of any transaction that is not an 'SDLT transaction',[266] broadly, a transaction where the effective date was before 1 December 2003[267].

Planning points

In some cases, such as where the rent under the later lease increases[268], the linked leases rule will result in a lower charge to SDLT than if the leases were taxed separately. A tenant will never be worse off by taking two short leases rather than one longer one and SDLT on the second lease can be, in effect, deferred.

Example One[269]:

On 1 January 2005 A granted a ten year lease of business premises to B at an annual rent of £700,000 with an option to renew for a further ten years at an increased rent of £900,000.

If the leases are not successive linked leases the total SDLT payable would be: £56,716 (original lease) + £73,349 (renewal lease) = £130,065

Applying the rule for successive linked leases the total SDLT payable is £97,986, a saving of £32,079

265 Paragraph 5(3) Schedule 17A and section 81A

266 For 'SDLT transaction' see 6.2.1 below

267 Paragraph 7(4) Schedule 19 (inserted by FA 2004)

268 Other than by an abnormal amount – see 2.6.15

269 See 2.6.8 below for the detail of how to calculate the charge to SDLT on rent.

As there is no interest penalty, a tenant who takes a shorter lease with an option to renew will be able to defer payment of SDLT on the lease resulting from the renewal, making him better off than if he had taken a longer lease[270] at the outset. If the lease is not renewed, there is a saving of the SDLT on the additional term.

Where the rent is likely to reduce after the fifth year structuring the transaction as two 'unlinked' leases would be beneficial if this result could be achieved.

Example Two[271]:

On 1 January 2005 A granted a 15 year lease to B at an annual rent of £700,000 for the first ten years with a reduced rent of £250,000 for the balance of the term. The SDLT payable would be £79,121.

If there were two leases, the first for ten years at an annual rent of £700,000 and a subsequent lease for a five year term at a rent of £250,000, and the leases were not successive linked leases the total SDLT payable would be:
£56,716 (first lease) + £9,787 (second lease) = £57,694 giving a saving of £21,427

Applying the rule for successive linked leases the total SDLT payable would be £79,121 (the same as if a single lease for a 15 year term had been granted).

2.6.5. Leases – specific SDLT provisions in relation to chargeable consideration

The following specific exclusions from chargeable consideration are relevant to leases[272]:

(a) costs borne by the purchaser under section 9(4) of the Leasehold Reform Act 1967 or section 33 of the Leasehold Reform, Housing and Urban Development Act 1993 (costs of enfranchisement) (paragraph 16C Schedule 4[273]);

(b) a reverse premium on the grant, assignment or surrender of a lease (paragraph 18 Schedule 17A);

(c) the assumption by an assignee of a lease of the obligation to pay rent or to perform the tenant's covenants under that lease (paragraph 17 Schedule 17A);

(d) covenants by a tenant on the grant of a lease to:

---

[270] Or a lease with a break clause as the break clause is ignored for SDLT purposes with no refund of SDLT paid if the break clause is employed.

[271] See 2.6.8 below for the detail of how to calculate the charge to SDLT on rent.

[272] The exclusions relevant to leases are repeated her for ease of reference. See 1.7.9 (*Exclusions from chargeable consideration*) above for a list of all the specific exclusions.

[273] See footnote 146.

ii. repair, maintain or insure the demised premises (paragraph 10(1)(a) Schedule 17A)

iii. pay any amount in respect of services, repairs, maintenance, insurance or the landlord's costs of management (paragraph 10(1)(b) Schedule 17A);

(e) any obligation undertaken by a tenant on the grant of a lease that is not such as to affect the rent that a tenant would be prepared to pay in the open market – i.e. ordinary tenant's covenants in a lease (paragraph 10(1)(c) Schedule 17A);

(f) any guarantee of the payment of rent or the performance of any other obligation of the tenant under the lease (paragraph 10(1)(d) Schedule 17A);

(g) any penal rent or increased rent in the nature of a penal rent payable in respect of any breach of the obligations of a tenant under the lease (paragraph 10(1)(e) Schedule 17A;

(h) any liability of the tenant for costs under section 14(2) of the Leasehold Reform Act 1967 or section 60 of the Leasehold Reform, Housing and Urban Development Act 1993 (costs to be borne by person exercising statutory right to be granted lease) (paragraph10(1)(f) Schedule 17A[274]);

(i) any other obligation of the tenant to bear the landlord's reasonable costs or expenses of or incidental to the grant of a lease (paragraph 10(1)(g) Schedule 17A[275]);

(j) any obligation under the lease to transfer to the landlord, on the termination of the lease, payment entitlements granted to the tenant under the single payment scheme[276] in respect of land subject to the lease (paragraph10(1)(h) Schedule 17A[277]);

(k) any payment made to discharge any of the obligations referred to in (d) to (j) above (paragraph 10(2) Schedule 17A). This would cover compensation for breach of covenant, such as a dilapidations payment; and

(l) the release of any obligation referred to in (a) to (e) above in relation to the surrender of a lease (paragraph 10(3) Schedule 17A).

There is a relief for surrenders and re-grants (see 2.1.8 above).

---

[274] Inserted by the SDLT (Amendment to the Finance Act 2003) Regulations 2006 (SI 2006/875) in relation to land transactions with an effective date on or after 12 April 2006.

[275] See footnote 150

[276] Support for farmers in pursuance of Title III of Council Regulation No 1782/2003.

[277] See footnote 150

2.6.6. Leases - loans and deposits in connection with grant or assignment

Paragraph 18A(1) of Schedule 17A is an anti-avoidance provision inserted by F(No.2)A 2005[278] and intended to prevent the disguising of chargeable consideration as a potentially repayable loan or deposit.

The provision applies where, under arrangements made in connection with the grant of a lease, the lessee (or any person connected[279] with him or acting on his behalf) pays a deposit or makes a loan to any person (in practice likely to be the lessor, a person connected with him or a bank), and the repayment of the deposit or loan is contingent on anything done or omitted to be done by the lessee or on the death of the lessee. In such a case, the amount of the deposit or loan (disregarding any repayment) is taken to be consideration other than rent given for the grant of the lease. Paragraph 18A(2) makes similar provision in connection with assignments of leases.

Paragraph 18A(3) disapplies sub-paragraph (1) where the loan or deposit does not exceed twice 'the relevant maximum rent'. The 'relevant maximum rent' is the highest amount of rent payable (determined in accordance with paragraph 7(3) of Schedule 17A) in respect of any consecutive twelve month period in the first five years of the term in the case of a grant or in the first five years of the term remaining as at the date of the assignment in the case of an assignment.[280] This may still leave a potential problem in relation to loans or deposits to secure dilapidations or other expenses exceeding this de minimis limit.

In determining the charge the rule in paragraph 9(5) of Schedule 5, which excludes the 0% band for consideration other than rent where rent exceeds £600, is disapplied.[281] Thus there is no charge under paragraph 18A unless the 'loan' or 'deposit', together with any consideration other than rent for any linked transaction, exceeds £150,000 for non-residential or mixed property or residential property in a disadvantaged area or £125,000 for residential property not in a disadvantaged area.

To avoid claims that the making of a loan or the payment of a deposit was contingent consideration such that when repayment occurred, part of the SDLT paid pursuant to paragraph 18A should be refunded, section 80 was

---

[278] By paragraph 14 Schedule 10 F(No. 2)A 2005 in relation to transactions with an effective date after 19 May 2005, subject to transitional provisions in paragraph 16(7) Schedule 10.

[279] Section 839 ICTA 1988 applies

[280] Paragraph 18A(4) Schedule 17A

[281] By paragraph 18A(5) Schedule 17A

amended.[282] A sub-paragraph (4A) was inserted in section 80 precluding claims for adjustment of the consideration under section 80(4) where:

- there is full or partial repayment of any loan or deposit treated as consideration under paragraph 18A; or
- there is any refund of the consideration for the grant of a lease or assignment of a lease and that refund is contingent on the determination or assignment of the lease or on the grant of a chargeable interest out of the lease.

2.6.7. SDLT on rent - introduction

(Section 56 and Schedules 5 and 17A)

Under the stamp duty regime, the duty on a lease depended on the premium paid, the yearly or average rent payable and the length of the term of the lease. Paragraph 12 Schedule 13 FA 1999 provided for the most common type of lease duty. It applied to leases for a definite term of a year or more, or for any indefinite term. Stamp duty was charged on the average annual rent at one of four rates of duty depending on the length of the term of the lease.

The charge to SDLT where the consideration for a land transaction consists wholly or partly of rent is set out in Schedules 5 and 17A. Under the SDLT regime, the rent payable under the lease is taxed by reference to the NPV of each yearly amount of rent that will become payable under the lease if it runs its full course. The total of those NPVs is referred to as the 'relevant rental value'[283] ('RRV').

SDLT on the rental element of a lease is charged at the rate of 1% where the RRV is over £125,000 for 'residential property'[284] and over £150,000 for 'non-residential' or mixed property. The 'slab' principle does not apply to the rental element of leases (as it does for other consideration). Instead, there is a 'slice' system. This means that SDLT is chargeable only on the excess over the relevant threshold.

The amount of the SDLT is rounded down to the nearest pound. Consideration paid in foreign currency is converted into sterling on the effective date of the

---

[282] By paragraph 15 Schedule 10 F(No. 2)A 2005 in relation to transactions with an effective date after 19 May 2005, subject to transitional provisions in paragraph 16(7) Schedule 10.

[283] Paragraph 2(4) Schedule 5

[284] The threshold for residential property was increased from £60,000 to £120,000 for transactions with an effective date after 16 March 2005 by section 95 FA 2005 and was further increased to £125,000 for transactions with an effective date after 22 March 2006 by section 162 FA 2006.

transaction unless the parties use a different rate for the transaction.[285] The rate to be used is the London closing exchange rate.

2.6.8. The detail of Schedules 5 and 17A[286]

'Tax is chargeable under this Schedule in respect of so much of the chargeable consideration as consists of rent.'[287]

The tax is calculated by taking the 'relevant percentage' of the RRV of the 'relevant land' as falls within each rate band (paragraph 2(2) Schedule 5 as amended). The 'relevant percentages' and the rate bands are set out in paragraph 2(3) Schedule 5 and are as follows:

TABLE A: RESIDENTIAL

Rate Bands	Percentage
£0 to £125,000[288]	0%
Over £125,000[289]	1%

TABLE B: NON-RESIDENTIAL OR MIXED

Rate Bands	Percentage
£0 to £150,000	0%
Over £150,000	1%

Tax is chargeable on each slice of the RRV at either the nil or 1% rate as appropriate, ensuring that the nil rate is applied to the first £125,000 or £150,000 where the RRV exceeds this figure.

For the purposes of the SDLT calculation the 'relevant land' is the land that is the subject of the lease and the RRV is the total NPV of the rent payable over the term of the lease. If the lease is one of a number of linked transactions for which the chargeable consideration consists of or includes rent, the 'relevant

---

[285] Paragraph 9 Schedule 4

[286] Schedule 17A and a new section 120 were inserted in FA 2003 by paragraph 8 of the Schedule to Stamp Duty and Stamp Duty Land Tax (Variation of the Finance Act 2003) (No. 2) Regulations 2003 (SI 2003/2816). The Stamp Duty and Stamp Duty Land Tax (Variation of the Finance Act 2003) (No. 2) Regulations 2003 were revoked by paragraph 14(2) Schedule 39 FA 2004 and replaced in amended form by Part 2 Schedule 39 with effect for any transaction of which the effective date is on or after 22 July 2004.

[287] Paragraph 2(1) Schedule 5

[288] The threshold for residential property was increased from £60,000 to £120,000 for transactions with an effective date after 16 March 2005 by section 95 FA 2005 and was further increased to £125,000 for transactions with an effective date after 22 March 2006 by section 162 FA 2006.

[289]See footnote 288 above

land' is any land that is the subject of any of those leases and the RRV is the total of the NPVs of the rent payable over the terms of those leases.[290]

Once the RRV has been calculated the SDLT due can be determined. In order to calculate the RRV in relation to a lease it is necessary to establish the 'rent' and the 'term'.

2.6.9. NPV – the calculation

(Paragraph 3 Schedule 5)

The NPV of the rent payable over the term of a lease is calculated by applying the formula

$$v = \sum_{i=1}^{n} \frac{r_i}{(1+T)^i}$$

where:

v	is the net present value
r_i	is the 'rent' payable in respect of[291] year i
i	is the first, second, third etc year of the term
n	is the 'term' of the lease
T	is the 'temporal discount rate'[292]

Thus, the NPV of the lease rentals is the total of the NPVs of the rents payable in each year of the term of the lease, and is not affected by the fact that the rent may be payable by quarterly, monthly or other instalments. Where a lease is for part of a year, for example, 7.5 years, that figure is used to calculate NPV rather than rounding up to 8 and a full year's discounting is given for the final part-year.

A tool is available on the Stamp Office website at:
http://ldcalculator.inlandrevenue.gov.uk
to assist in the calculation of the amount of SDLT due on a lease.[293] A print-out for each transaction should be kept on file.

---

[290] Paragraph 2(4) Schedule 5

[291] Changed from 'in year i' by FA 2006 so as to bring the wording into line with that in paragraph 7 Schedule 17A

[292] The temporal discount rate is set by the Treasury and is currently 3.5% (the figure to be used in the NPV formula is 0.035)

[293] See 1.1 below

2.6.10. NPV: example of manual calculation[294]

A lease has a fixed term of five years and the rent payable in each year is as follows:

Year 1 - £4000
Year 2 - £5000
Year 3 - £6000
Year 4 - £7000
Year 5 - £8000

The NPV of the rental over this period is calculated as follows:

Year 1:
4,000/(1+0.035)
=£3,864.73

Year 2:
5,000/[(1+0.035) x (1+0.035)]
=£4,667.55

Year 3:
6,000/[(1+0.035) x (1+0.035) x (1+0.035)]
=£5,411.65

Year 4:
7,000/[(1+0.035) x (1+0.035) x (1+0.035) x (1+0.035)]
=£6,100.09

Year 5:
8,000/[(1+0.035) x (1+0.035) x (1+0.035) x (1+0.035) x (1+0.035)]
=£6,735.78

The total NPV of the lease rentals (and therefore, the RRV of the lease for SDLT purposes) is the sum of the calculated values, £26,779, rather than the £30,000 actually due.

No SDLT will be chargeable on the grant of this lease as the RRV is less than the threshold

Term of lease: planning point

The SDLT regime favours very short and very long leases and taxes most heavily leases in the 15 to 35 year range. It can be seen from the following table that it may sometimes (but not always) be better from an SDLT point of view to take a number of shorter leases (assuming that the application of the rules in

[294] There is an example of a manual calculation at SDLTM13080 (lease chapter April 2007)

relation to linked transactions can be avoided) or to take a short lease with an option to renew rather than a long lease with a break clause.

Acquisitions of chargeable interest

The exercise of a break clause in a lease is not the acquisition of a chargeable interest because it does not cause a surrender or release of the interest[295].

TABLE - LEASE OF NON-RESIDENTIAL OR MIXED PROPERTY[296]

Term	Annual rent	SDLT
5 years	£100,000	£3,015
10 years	£100,000	£6,816
15 years	£100,000	£10,017
20 years	£100,000	£12,712
25 years	£100,000	£14,987
30 years	£100,000	£16,892
35 years	£100,000	£18,500
40 years	£100,000	£19,855
45 years	£100,000	£20,995
50 years	£100,000	£21,955

2.6.11. The charge on rent – what is rent?

Rent is not defined for SDLT purposes. It was once thought that payments which were not reserved out of the land were not rent.[297] However, the concept of rent is no longer confined to an amount in respect of which the remedy of distress is available. In *United Scientific Holdings v. Burnley Borough Council*[298] (which was concerned with the meaning of rent for rent review purposes) Lord Diplock stated:

> "My Lords, the mediaeval concept of rent as a service rendered by the tenant to the landlord has been displaced by the modern concept of a payment which a tenant is bound by his contract to pay to the landlord for the use of his land."

The fact that the parties have described a payment as rent is not conclusive.[299]

---

[295] *Pennel v Payne CA* [1995] 2 All ER 592 as expressly approved in *Barrett v Morgan* HL [2000] 2 AC 264

[296] No applicable reliefs and no premium

[297] See *Hill v. Booth* [1930] 1 KB 381; *British Electric Traction Co v. IRC* (1901) 84 LT 84

[298] [1978] AC 904

[299] See *Donellan v. Read* (1832) 3 B & Ad 899

For the purposes of Schedule 17A a *single* sum expressed to be payable in respect of:

(1) rent or

(2) rent and other matters (where the sum is not apportioned between rent and the other matters)

is treated entirely as rent.

(paragraph 6 Schedule 17A)

This means that where the rent, insurance premium and service charge are reserved as a single sum, SDLT may be payable on the service charge and insurance premium elements, as well as on the true rent. Service charges 'recoverable' as rent are not rent for SDLT purposes.

Where separate sums are expressed to be payable in respect of rent and other matters, the 'just and reasonable' apportionment rules in paragraph 4 Schedule 4 apply.

In spite of paragraph 6 the HMRC view is that reserving a service charge in the lease as rent does not make it rent for SDLT purposes and that service charges expressed in the lease as part of an inclusive rent payment and apportioned on a just and reasonable basis are not chargeable consideration for SDLT purposes.[300]

'Rent', for SDLT purposes, does not include any chargeable consideration for the grant of a lease payable in respect of a period before the grant of a lease.[301] Such an amount is not, however, excluded from the definition of chargeable consideration altogether and may still be subject to SDLT.[302]

Effect of VAT on Rent[303]
(Paragraph 2 Schedule 4)

Where VAT is chargeable on the rent payable under the lease as at the 'effective date' of the lease and is reserved as rent, VAT is added to the rent for the purposes of calculating the SDLT payable on the rent. VAT payable in respect

---

300 See SDLTM11015 (lease chapter – April 2007)

301 Paragraph 1A Schedule 5

302 It is, in principle, taxable as a premium for the grant unless the backdated grant is to a tenant who is holding-over under an old lease or unless the provisions of paragraph 9A Schedule 17A apply – see *'Backdated lease granted to tenant holding-over'* in 2.6.17 below.

303 See SDLTM03800

of rent but which is not reserved as rent will not be rent for SDLT purposes but, as for stamp duty, will be taxed as consideration other than rent.[304].

Where the lessor has not opted to waive VAT exemption for the property as at the 'effective date', VAT is not taken into account at that time, nor is it taken into account if the option is later exercised.[305] It also follows that in these circumstances VAT is not treated as a contingency. This is a change from the old stamp duty rules under which VAT was added to the rent for the purposes of calculating the duty unless the lease prevented the lessor from opting to waive VAT exemption for the property in the future.

2.6.12. Leases with variable or uncertain rent (including turnover leases and leases with an equity rent)

(Paragraphs 7 and 8 Schedule 17A)

These provisions cover cases where the terms of a lease provide for variation in the amount of the rent (such as a rent review provision or a stepped rent) or the amount of the rent is 'contingent, uncertain or unascertained' (such as a lease where the rent is based on turnover or a rent-sharing lease). Broadly, the rules provide that variations in the amount of the rent after five years are not taken into account (subject to the anti-avoidance provisions in paragraphs 14 and 15 Schedule 17A) but variations up to the end of the fifth year are. The detailed rules are set out below.

Paragraph 7(4A)[306] provides that for the purposes of paragraph 7 and paragraph 8, the cases where the amount of rent payable under a lease is uncertain or unascertained include cases where there is a possibility of that amount being varied under:

- section 12, 13 or 33 of the Agricultural Holdings Act 1986
- Part 2 of the Agricultural Tenancies Act 1995
- section 13, 14, 15 or 31 of the Agricultural Holdings (Scotland) Act 1991
- section 9, 10 or 11 of the Agricultural Holdings (Scotland) Act 2003

---

[304] See 1.7.1 above

[305] VAT chargeable on a premium paid on any later assignment of the lessor's interest would however be included in the chargeable consideration for that assignment but the charge on the rent would remain undisturbed.

[306] Inserted by paragraph 2(1) Schedule 25 FA 2006 in relation to any lease granted or treated as granted on or after 19 July 2006 but having effect from 1 December 2003 as the same insertion was made by the Stamp Duty land Tax (Variation of the Finance Act 2003) (No. 2) Regulations 2003 (SI 2003/2816).

2.6.13. Fluctuations or uncertainty in rent up to end of fifth year

(Paragraph 7(2) Schedule 17A)

Where a lease provides for fluctuations in the rent before the end of the fifth year of the lease, the provisions for determining chargeable consideration apply in the same way as they apply in relation to consideration other then rent. Where the rent during that period is contingent, uncertain or unascertained, section 51 applies to determine the annual rent for the first five years for the purposes of calculating the SDLT due. The measurement of the five year period is explained at 2.6.16 below (*'The term of the lease'*).

No account is to be taken of any provision for rent to be adjusted in line with the RPI[307] and, in such a case, the rent to be included in the SDLT calculation is the rent provided for in the lease before any RPI adjustment. It is understood that where adjustments are to be made to rent in accordance with a formula incorporating RPI but not 'in line with' it, for example, where an RPI increase is subject to a maximum or minimum, HMRC take the view that the provisions of paragraph 7(2) apply and the RPI increases are not disregarded.

If the lease continues after five years, the rules set out in 2.6.14 below (Fluctuations or uncertainty in rent after the end of the fifth year) will apply to determine the rent for the balance of the term.

The application of section 51 means that where the rent payable in respect of any period before the end of the fifth year of the term of the lease is uncertain or unascertained at the 'effective date', a 'reasonable estimate' of the amount of SDLT must be made and paid.[308] Where there is a contingency, the rent for that period will, for SDLT purposes, be calculated on the assumption that the outcome of the contingency will be that the consideration is payable or does not cease to be payable.

A reconsideration of the SDLT consequences of the transaction is required at the end of the five year period or earlier if the actual rent becomes certain.[309] The SDLT payable will, in a case where the rent has not become certain by the end of the five year period, be based on the rent payable in the first five years. Any SDLT which has been charged in relation to rent for the balance of the term (see below) may also need adjustment (upwards or downwards) to take

---

[307] Paragraph 7(5) Schedule 17A

[308] Royalty payments in relation to extraction of minerals represent payments for the use of or right over land and are treated in the same way as rent. As the amount payable is not known a reasonable estimate of the amount payable should be included for the first five years in calculating the NPV – see SDLTM11500.

[309] Paragraph 8(3) Schedule 17A

into account the highest rent actually paid in any consecutive twelve month period in the first five years of the term.

If the effect of the reconsideration is that the transaction becomes notifiable or chargeable or tax or additional tax is payable then the purchaser must file a land transaction return within 30 days. Any SDLT due will be calculated on the basis of the rates in force at the effective date of the transaction.

If the reconsideration results in SDLT having been overpaid, the overpaid tax can be reclaimed, either by amending the land transaction return (which must be done within 12 months of the filing date)[310] or by making a claim to HMRC[311].

Example One:

A lease is entered into which provides for a single rent review to open market rent after eighteen months. The lease is for a three year term.

The rent initially paid is £25,000 per annum. At the date of grant it is expected that, after the rent review, the rent will increase to £30,000 per annum.

The figure to be taken for annual rent as from the review date until the end of the term is the expected figure of £30,000 (section 51). The SDLT charge on grant will be calculated on that basis and would be adjusted after the rent review has taken place.

Example Two:

A projected VAT inclusive rent based on a percentage of turnover in respect of commercial premises is £100,000 a year for a 25 year term. There is no other chargeable consideration and no reliefs apply. The SDLT payable is £14,981.

The actual rent in the first four years is £100,000 for the first four years then turnover improves to give turnover rent of £150,000 in year five. The SDLT payable is recalculated at £21,385. Therefore a further return is required together with payment of an additional £6,404.

Special rule: first rent review in final quarter of fifth year

An adjustment to the rent arising in the final three months of year five is ignored where[312]:

---

[310] Paragraph 6 Schedule 10

[311] Birmingham Stamp Office, 9th Floor, City Centre House, 30 Union Street, Birmingham B2 4AR
Tel: 0845 603 0135 Fax: 0121 643 8381
When writing, mark the envelope and the letter 'SDLT'.

[312] Paragraph 7A Schedule 17A inserted by paragraphs 11 and 22 Schedule 39 FA 2004 in relation to any transaction the effective date of which is after 17 March 2004.

- the lease contains a provision under which rent may be adjusted;
- it is the first or only such adjustment under that provision;
- the adjustment is 'to an amount' that before the adjustment was uncertain;[313]
- the review date is expressed as falling five years after a specified date;
- the specified date falls within three months before the beginning of the term of the lease.

This rule recognises the fact that landlords and tenants commonly agree rent review dates at intervals of five years calculated from a date shortly before the beginning of the lease term. There are a number of reasons for this, including synchronising review dates for different units in the same building, changing the rent on a rent payment date for ease of calculation, or running the rent review pattern from the date the tenant was first allowed to start fitting out the premises.

The legislation refers to a 'specified date' and so, strictly, only applies where the five-year review is provided for in the terms of the lease. However in practice HMRC accept that the provision applies to any reviews falling within the last three months of the fifth year of the lease[314].

The 'concession' in paragraph 7A Schedule 17A (summarised above) does not apply if the lease in question was granted between 24 and 28 September since a term starting on the previous quarter day (24 June) would have been more than three months earlier than the start of the lease.

For the purposes of paragraph 7A the beginning of the term of the lease means the date of substantial performance of an agreement for lease where this is treated as the grant of a lease by reason of paragraph 12A Schedule 17A. The same applies where other provisions result in a 'deemed' lease.

2.6.14. Fluctuations or uncertainty in rent after end of fifth year

(Paragraph 7(3) Schedule 17A[315])

Where the lease provides for fluctuations in the rent after the end of the fifth year of the term of the lease (for example, as a result of a provision for stepped rent) or the rent after that date is contingent, uncertain or unascertained, then for the purposes of the SDLT calculation:

---

[313] The phrase 'to an amount' in paragraph 7A is ambiguous but can be taken to mean that the effect of the adjustment is uncertain in advance of its application i.e. it is a formula and not merely a fixed increase or decrease.

[314] SDLTM13165 (lease chapter April 2007 version)

[315] As amended by FA 2006 with effect from 19 July 2006

- the possibility of an adjustment or fluctuation in rent is to be disregarded; and
- the annual rent for the balance of the term is assumed to be equal to the highest rent payable in any consecutive twelve month period in the first five years of the term, taking into account (if necessary) any amounts determined under section 51(1) and (2) if the amount is contingent, uncertain or unascertained and disregarding any relief given under paragraphs 9(2) (overlap relief) and 9A(3) (backdated lease granted to tenant holding-over) of Schedule 17A (which in certain circumstances result in a deemed reduction of rent for a period during which rents overlap).

However, if, after the five year point when rent changes are not taken into account in calculating the NPV, the rent rises by more than 20% annually (an 'abnormal rent'), this rent increase is deemed to be the grant of a new lease (see 2.6.15 below).

For the purposes of paragraph 7(3) the beginning of the term of the lease means the date of substantial performance of an agreement for lease where this is treated as the grant of a lease by reason of paragraph 12A Schedule 17A. The same applies where other provisions result in a 'deemed' lease.

Example One:

A lease of commercial property is granted on 25 December 2003 for 10 years. No reliefs apply. The rent is a turnover rent, with no payments on account. The basic rent of £100,000 is payable quarterly in advance and three months after the end of each year a turnover calculation is done and a top-up payment is made as follows:

Year 1 – no top-up
Year 2 – top up of £10,000 (paid in Year 3)
Year 3 – top-up of £20,000 (paid in Year 4)
Year 4 – top-up of £30,000 (paid in Year 5)
Year 5 – top-up of £40,000 (paid in Year 6)
The land transaction return to be delivered in respect of the grant of the lease has to be based on a reasonable estimate of the turnover element of the rent. This estimate is that it will be equal to 20% of basic rent.

NPV calculation in respect of grant:
Year 1 rent - £100,000.
Years 2 to 5 Assumed rent of £120,000
Years 6 to 10 Assumed rent of £120,000 (highest rent in first five years)
RRV £978,668 giving SDLT payable of £8,286.

The uncertainty in relation to the amount of rent payable in respect of the first five years of the term does not end before the end of the fifth year, so a second land transaction return needs to be made within 30 days of the end of the fifth year. By then, however, the top-up payment in respect of the fifth year will not be known.

NPV calculation at the end of the fifth year:
Rent payable in respect of Year 1 - £100,000
Rent payable in respect of Year 2 - £110,000 (includes the £10,000 top-up payment made in Year 3)
Rent payable in respect of Year 3 - £120,000 (includes the £20,000 top-up payment made in Year 4)
Rent payable in respect of Year 4 - £130,000 (includes the £30,000 top-up payment made in Year 5)
Rent payable in respect of Year 5 – The rent for Year 5 is still uncertain at the end of Year 5 as the top-up not yet calculable so a reasonable estimate must be made. There is no provision for later adjustment of this estimate. The estimated top-up is £38,000 giving a rent of £138,000
Years 6 to 10 Assumed rent of £138,000

RRV £1,061,631 giving additional SDLT payable of £9,116 - £8,286 = £830

Example Two – rent review at intervals during term of lease:

A lease is entered into which provides for an upwards only rent review every 2 years. The lease is for 8 years.

The initial rent is £25,000 per annum. It is estimated that, after the first rent review, the rent will increase to £30,000 per annum.

The second review will take place at the end of year four – the rent payable after the second review must also be estimated at the date of grant. The third review will take place at the end of year six and is ignored.

The SDLT charge on grant will be calculated on the basis of the following rents:
Year One - £25,000
Year Two - £25,000
Year Three - £30,000
Year Four - £30,000
Year Five – £x (estimate for rent after second review)
Years Six to Eight - £x
and would be adjusted (if necessary) after the first and second rent reviews have taken place.

No account is to be taken of any provision for rent to be adjusted in line with the RPI (paragraph 7(5) Schedule 17A).

2.6.15. Abnormal increase in rent after fifth year

(Paragraphs 14 and 15 Schedule 17A[316])

Paragraph 14 deals with increases in rent after the end of the fifth year of the term of a lease (whether in pursuance of a provision in the lease or otherwise). It provides that where an increase in rent is 'abnormal' (as defined in paragraph 15) that increase is treated as the grant of a new lease for a new rent equal to the 'excess rent' which is the difference between the new rent and that previously 'previously taxed'. Paragraph 14 can apply more than once and there can, therefore, be multiple charges.

The rent 'previously taxed' is determined as follows[317]:

(1) Where paragraph 14 has not previously applied to an increase in the rent payable under the lease:
   a. if the amount of rent payable under the lease is determined under paragraph 7 of Schedule 17A (variable or uncertain rent), the rent previously taxed is the rent assumed to be payable after the fifth year of the term of the lease (in accordance with paragraph 7(3) Schedule 17A);
   b. if there has been a variation in the lease falling within paragraph 13 of Schedule 17A (increase of rent treated as grant of new lease: variation of lease in first five years), the rent previously taxed is the rent payable as a result of the variation (or, if there has been more than one such variation, the most recent one);
   c. in any other case, the rent previously taxed is the rent payable under the lease without the abnormal increase.

(2) Where paragraph 14 has previously applied to an increase in the rent, the rent previously taxed is the rent payable as a result of the last increase in relation to which the provision applied.

In applying these rules, paragraphs 9(2) and 9A(3) of Schedule 17A (which in certain circumstances result in a deemed reduction of rent for a period during which rents overlap) are to be disregarded[318].

The 'deemed' lease will be linked with the earlier actual lease (the 'original lease') and is treated as beginning on the date on which the increased rent first became payable and being for a term equal to the unexpired term of the original lease. The rules relating to the effect of later linked transactions will

---

[316] As amended by paragraph 7 Schedule 25 FA 2006 with effect from 19 July 2006.

[317] In paragraphs 14(4), (4A) and (4B) Schedule 17A

[318] The reliefs under paragraph 9(2) and 9A(3) are discussed at 1.8 and 2.6.17.

apply with the result that there may be an obligation to notify the deemed grant.

No abnormal increases falling within paragraph 14 can occur until 2008 as the provision applies only to rent increases under leases actually granted on or after the implementation date, 1 December 2003, or under deemed leases with an effective date on or after that date[319]. Any due diligence exercise will, however, need to take this possibility into account.

When is an increase in rent abnormal?

Paragraph 15 defines what is 'abnormal' for the purposes of paragraph 14. Broadly speaking, an 'abnormal' increase is one where the annualised increase in rent, calculated since the later of the grant of the lease or the last time the provisions of section 14 were applied, is greater than 20%.

Paragraph 15 sets out a three step calculation which needs to be done to establish whether a rent increase is abnormal.

Step One - Find the start date.

Where paragraph 14 has not previously applied to an increase in the rent payable under the lease:

- if the amount of rent payable under the lease is determined under paragraph 7 of Schedule 17A (variable or uncertain rent), the start date is the beginning of the period by reference to which the rent assumed to be payable after the fifth year of the term of the lease is determined (in accordance with paragraph 7(3) Schedule 17A);
- if there has been a variation in the lease falling within paragraph 13 of Schedule 17A (increase of rent treated as grant of new lease: variation of lease in first five years), the start date is the date of the variation (or, if there has been more than one such variation, the date of the most recent one);
- in any other case, the start date is the beginning of the term of the lease.

Where paragraph 14 has previously applied to an increase in the rent, the start date is the date of the last increase in relation to which that provision applied.

Step Two - Find the number of whole years in the period between the start date and the date on which the increased rent first becomes payable.

Step Three

The rent increase is regarded as abnormal if difference between the increased rent and the rent previously taxed (the 'excess rent') is greater than:

---

[319] See SDLTM13250 (lease chapter – April 2007 version).

$$\frac{R \times Y}{5}$$

where:

R is the rent previously taxed and
Y is the number of whole years found under Step Two

It is intended that in due course an abnormal rent calculator will be included on HMRC website. There is an example of a manual calculation in the lease chapter of the SDLTM at SDLTM13255.[320]

2.6.16. The term of the lease

The term of a lease was dealt with in paragraph 6(1) and 6(2) Schedule 5 as originally enacted but these sub- paragraphs were repealed by the Stamp Duty and Stamp Duty Land Tax (Variation of the Finance Act 2003)(No.2) Regulations 2003 and not replaced. It is understood that HMRC have indicated in correspondence that they nevertheless intend to apply the provisions of the repealed paragraph[321] and it is therefore reproduced below in full:

> "6—(1) For the purposes of this Schedule the term of a lease is determined as follows.
>
> (2) Subject to the following provisions of this paragraph, the term of a lease is:
>
> (*a*) the contractual term specified in the lease, or
>
> (*b*) if shorter, the period from the date of the grant of the lease until the end of the contractual term."

The provisions of repealed paragraph 6(2), in any event, did no more than state the position at common law which is that, although the parties to a lease can define the duration of the term by reference to a date earlier than that of the lease and can create obligations under the lease in respect of a prior period, the term of the lease cannot begin before the lease is executed.[322] Special SDLT rules apply for lease renewals (see 2.6.17 below).

Paragraph 12A Schedule 17A[323] provides that where an agreement for lease is entered into and is substantially performed without at that time having been completed, the agreement for lease is treated as if it were the grant of a lease in

---

320 April 2007

321 This is reflected at SDLTM10400 and SDLTM 14060 lease chapter (April 2007 version)

322 See *Bradshaw v. Pawley* [1980] 1 WLR 10

323 Inserted by paragraph 22(2) Schedule 39 FA 2004 with effect for any transaction of which the effective date is on or after 22 July 2004

accordance with the agreement, for a term beginning on the date of that substantial performance. Where a lease is subsequently granted in pursuance of the agreement for lease this is treated for SDLT purposes as a surrender and re-grant[324].

For SDLT purposes, no account is to be taken of any right of either party to determine the lease or to renew it (paragraph 2 Schedule 17A). In other words, the term of the lease is the term set out in the lease without taking account of the right of either party to end it early or extend it. There is no provision for repayment of SDLT if a lease is surrendered or forfeited during the term.

This means that tenants (who will be the purchasers for SDLT purposes) may prefer to take shorter leases with options to renew – a 15 year lease with a right to break at 10 years is taxed as a 15 year lease with no refund of SDLT if the break clause is exercised (unless a new lease is taken and the surrender and re-grant provisions apply) whereas a 10 year lease with a five year option to renew is taxed as a 10 year lease with SDLT payable on the additional five year term only if it is taken up. acquisitions of chargeable interests. The exercise of a break clause in a lease is not the acquisition of a chargeable interest because it does not cause a surrender or release of the interest[325].

2.6.17. Lease which continues after a fixed term

(Paragraph 3 Schedule 17A)

Where a lease is for a fixed term with provision to continue thereafter until determined by notice, or is a lease which may continue beyond the fixed term by operation of law (for example, under the Landlord and Tenant Act 1954), it is treated as follows for SDLT purposes:

1) in the first instance as if it were a lease for the original fixed term and no longer,
2) if the lease continues after the fixed term in (1), as if the lease had become a lease for a fixed term one year longer than the original fixed term
3) if the lease continues after the end of the extended term resulting from (2), as if it had become a lease for a fixed term two years longer than the original fixed term,

and so on.

This treatment continues until the tenant ceases to occupy the property or a new lease is granted.

---

[324] See 1.3.4 above ('*Substantial performance – agreement for lease*')

[325] *Pennel v Payne CA* [1995] 2 All ER 592 as expressly approved in *Barrett v Morgan* [2000] 2 AC 264 HL

HMRC have confirmed at SDLTM14100[326] that holding-over under a lease that was granted before 1 December 2003 does not bring the lease within the scope of SDLT. The SDLT legislation does not deal with this point expressly, although a pre-SDLT lease which continued after a fixed term and to which paragraph 3 applied would still have been granted before the SDLT regime began and would, therefore remain outside its scope. In any event, paragraph 3 does not apply to leases granted or treated as granted before 1 December 2003[327].

Paragraph 3 Schedule 17A would apply to a holding-over under Part II of the Landlord and Tenant Act 1954. Where the original lease was contracted out of the security of tenure provisions of the 1954 Act and the tenant remains in occupation after the expiry of the original term of the lease, the tenant will be treated as a tenant at will and paragraph 3 will not apply.

A lease to which paragraph 3 Schedule 17A applies is treated as a lease for its original fixed term (and not the lease term as extended by the operation of paragraph 3) for the purposes of notification.[328]

The operation of paragraph 3 Schedule 17A may increase the SDLT payable or cause it to be payable in a case where it was not payable before. In such a case a land transaction return or an additional return must be submitted within 30 days after the end of the original fixed term (and within 30 days of the start of each successive notional yearly extension of it).[329]

Example:

A tenant under a lease granted on 1 January 2004 holds-over at the end of a contractual term of 15 years. On the first day of the holding-over a lease for a term of 16 years from the original commencement date is treated as granted and a land transaction return must be delivered within 30 days if further SDLT is payable.

If the holding-over continues beyond a year, then a lease for 17 years from the original commencement date is treated as granted and a further land transaction return may need to be delivered on that basis and so on.

There may be an interim rent payable in respect of any lease extension, and this is usually settled retrospectively when the terms for the renewal lease are

---

[326] Lease chapter (April 2007 version)

[327] SDLTM14100 lease chapter –(April 2007)

[328] Paragraph 3(5) Schedule 17A inserted by paragraph 22 Schedule 39 FA 2004 with effect from 22 July 2004. For the rules on notification see 7.1 below

[329] Paragraph 3(3) Schedule 17A. The return or additional return should be sent to the Birmingham Stamp Office.

negotiated (or by order of the court). Any interim rent is taxed under the lease extension rules in paragraph 3 Schedule 17A. If the holding-over period ends part way through the period for which the lease is treated as extended under paragraph 3 (without the grant of a new lease[330]) there is no provision for adjustment of any SDLT paid.

Where the interim rent is more than the 'old' rent, the increase may be deemed to be the grant of a lease pursuant to paragraph 13 Schedule 17A. [331]

Backdated lease granted to tenant holding over
(Paragraph 9A Schedule 17A[332])

Where:
(1) a tenant remains in occupation after the date a lease terminates in accordance with its terms;[333] and
(2) a new lease is granted to him of the same or substantially the same premises; and
(3) the new lease is expressed to begin on or immediately after the termination date of the old lease

relief is given for any rent payable under the new lease in respect of the period between the termination date of the old lease and the date of grant of the new lease. This is necessary because the rent paid in respect of that holding-over period may already have been taxed under the rules set out in paragraph 3 of Schedule 17A[334].

The relief is given by reducing the rent brought into charge in calculating the SDLT payable on the new lease by the amount of rent paid in respect of the period between the termination date of the old lease and the date on which the new lease is granted (where this rent has been subject to SDLT[335]). However, there can, in certain circumstances, be a double charge on rent as shown below.

---

[330] Where a new lease is granted there may be a partial credit – see below

[331] See 2.6.21 below

[332] Inserted by paragraph 3 Schedule 25 FA 2006 and applies where the old lease was liable to SDLT and the new lease was granted on or after 19 July 2006.

[333] In other words, the lease expires – it is not terminated

[334] See above

[335] Paragraph 9A(4) Schedule 17A

Example:

On 1 January 2009 a tenant holds-over at the end of a contractual term of five years. The original lease incurred a charge to SDLT. On the first day of the holding-over (1 January 2009) a new lease for a term of six years from the original commencement date is treated as granted[336] and a land transaction return must be delivered within 30 days. The additional rent for the period of one year from 1 January to 31 December 2009 is taxed.

On 1 July 2009 a new five-year lease is granted with the rent backdated to 1 January 2009. The new lease will be taxed on the rent for the period from 1 January 2009 to 31 December 2014 with credit for the tax paid on the rent for the period from 1 January 2009 to 30 June 2009 (the period between the termination date of the old lease and the date of grant of the new lease). The rent for the period from 1 July to 31 December 2009 will therefore be taxed twice.

The reduction in the rent payable for SDLT purposes under the new lease to reflect rent paid in respect of the interim period is only available where the new lease is of 'the same or substantially the same premises'[337] and where the term of the new lease is expressed to being on or immediately after the expiration of the old. If the tenant has previously sub-let part of its original holding then the landlord can only be required to grant the new lease over that part of the premises actually occupied by the tenant for its business (not the whole premises originally let to the tenant[338]). Where the landlord elects to so limit the new lease and the difference is significant, credit for the interim rent may not be available.

The term of the new lease is treated for SDLT purposes as beginning on the date on which it is expressed to begin[339].

Where paragraph 9A applies, the earlier start date should be entered as the effective date when using the HMRC lease calculator[340]. When completing the land transaction return (form SDLT1), the date the new lease was granted should be entered at Box 4.

---

[336] Under the rules in paragraph 3 Schedule 17A – see above

[337] Paragraph 9A(1)(b) Schedule 17A - it is understood that HMRC interpret this to allow relief where the new lease is of premises which *include* the same or substantially the same premises.

[338] Sections 23(3) and 32(2) Landlord and Tenant Act 1954

[339] The rule in *Bradshaw v. Pawley* [1980] 1 WLR 10 does not apply

[340] Available at: http://ldcalculator.inlandrevenue.gov.uk

2.6.18. Treatment of lease for an indefinite term

(Paragraph 4 Schedule 17A)

A lease for an indefinite term is treated in the first instance (on grant) as if it were a lease for a fixed term of one year beginning on the date of grant. If the lease continues after the end of that notional term of one year (resulting from the application of paragraph 4) it is then treated as if it were a lease for a fixed term of two years from the date of grant and so on until the lease determines.

The operation of paragraph 4 Schedule 17A may increase the SDLT payable or cause a charge to arise where it did not before. For example, rent of £30,000 per annum would lead to an SDLT liability from year six onwards.

For the purposes of section 77 (notification), a lease for an indefinite term is treated as a lease for a term of less than seven years[341] (however long it continues) and so the grant or assignment of it is only notifiable if (and when) there is a charge to SDLT or would be but for a relief[342].

In such a case a land transaction return or an additional return must be submitted within 30 days of the commencement of the deemed fixed term in respect of which SDLT (or increased SDLT) is payable.

In particular, the provisions of paragraph 4 apply to:

- a periodic tenancy
- a lease for life
- a tenancy at will[343]
- any other interest or right terminable by notice at any time.

2.6.19. Reversionary lease[344]

A reversionary lease is a lease whose term commences at some time after the grant. It should be distinguished from an agreement to grant a lease in the future.

The effective date of a reversionary lease is the date of grant although the start date of the term is used for the NPV calculation. The HMRC automated process is unable to deal with reversionary leases. The land transaction return should be completed and sent to the Birmingham Stamp Office with a covering letter.

---

[341] Paragraph 4(1) Schedule 17A

[342] See 7.1 'Notifiable transactions' below

[343] Although a tenancy at will is not a chargeable interest by reason of section 48(2)(c)(i)

[344] See SDLTM17070 (lease chapter - April 2007 version)

2.6.20. Lease varied to extend the term

In England, Wales, and Northern Ireland, the express grant of an extension to the term of a lease (unless brought into effect by the grant of a reversionary lease[345]) amounts to a surrender and re-grant by operation of law. This applies even where the document purports to 'vary' the lease by extending its term. By contrast, there is no surrender and re-grant where an option to extend the term of an existing lease under a provision of the lease is exercised.

For SDLT purposes the extension of the term is treated as the grant of a new lease, the term of which starts on the date the extension is granted, in exchange for the surrender of the original lease[346]. This treatment will apply even where the original lease was not within the scope of SDLT. 'Overlap' relief will be available where the surrendered lease was subject to SDLT (not stamp duty) when it was granted.[347]

2.6.21. Lease varied in first five years to increase rent

(Paragraph 13 Schedule 17A[348])

Where a lease is varied to increase the amount of the rent from a date before the end of the fifth year of the term of the lease, the variation is treated as if it were the grant of a lease in consideration of the additional rent made payable by it. The term of the lease is measured using the rules set out in 2.6.16 above.

Paragraph 13 does not apply where the rent is increased as a result of a provision in a lease. Accordingly, the normal implementation of a rent review clause in accordance with its terms will not be treated as a variation of the lease, but an agreement which falls outside those terms (for example, agreeing stepped increases where the review clause contemplates a single increase at the review date) may constitute a variation for this purpose.

In addition the provision does not apply where there is an increase in rent pursuant to any of the following provisions[349]:

- section 12, 13 or 33 of the Agricultural Holdings Act 1986
- Part 2 of the Agricultural Tenancies Act 1995
- section 13, 14, 15 or 31 of the Agricultural Holdings (Scotland) Act 1991
- section 9, 10 or 11 of the Agricultural Holdings (Scotland) Act 2003

---

[345] See 2.6.19 above.

[346] See 'Surrender and re-grant' at 1.8 above

[347] See 1.8 above

[348] As amended by FA 2006 with effect from 19 July 2006

[349] Paragraph 13(2)(b) inserted by paragraph 2(1) Schedule 25 FA 2006 with effect in relation to any lease granted or treated as granted on or after 19 July 2006.

Paragraph 7(4A) provides that for the purposes of paragraph 7, the cases where the amount of rent payable under a lease is uncertain include cases where there is a possibility of that amount being varied under:

This provision can apply where the grant or assignment of the lease was not within the scope of SDLT.

2.6.22. Lease varied to reduce rent

(Paragraph 15A(1) Schedule 17A)[350]

Where a lease is varied to reduce the amount of the rent, the variation is treated as if it were the acquisition of a chargeable interest by the lessee and if there is chargeable consideration for the variation, an SDLT charge may arise. This provision would apply even where the lease itself was not within the scope of SDLT.

Paragraph 15A(1) is an anti-avoidance rule introduced to prevent a scheme to avoid SDLT along the lines of an old stamp duty avoidance scheme. The scheme was based on the grant of a 999 year lease at a market rent, followed by a variation of the lease to reduce the rent to a peppercorn in return for a substantial payment to the landlord which would not have been subject to SDLT. The worthless freehold was then sold to the tenant for a price which merely reflected any capital allowances available.

Where there is a 'genuine' rent reduction in consideration of a tenant agreeing to vary other provisions in the lease that reduction may give rise to an SDLT charge (on the tenant) as the tenant will have given money's worth for the variation.

2.6.23. Lease varied to reduce term

(Paragraph 15A(2) Schedule 17A)[351]

Where a landlord pays a tenant a sum in consideration of the surrender by the tenant of its leasehold interest, the landlord acquires a chargeable interest and SDLT may be due on the sum paid. If, instead, the landlord paid a sum to induce the tenant to enter into a variation of a lease, the effect of which was to reduce the term of the lease and effect a 'surrender' of part of the term, such a variation would not have amounted to the acquisition of a chargeable interest since it did not take effect as the grant of a new lease. This scheme has now been stopped by a provision deeming the variation of a lease which reduces

---

[350] Inserted by paragraph 22 Schedule 39 FA 2004 in relation to any transaction the effective date of which is on or after 22 July 2004.

[351] See footnote 350

the term to be the acquisition of a chargeable interest by the lessor. It follows that any payment given by the lessor as consideration for such a variation is potentially within the charge to SDLT.

This provision applies even where the lease which was varied was not within the scope of SDLT.

2.6.24. Leases - other variations made for consideration

(Paragraph 15A(1A) Schedule 17A)[352]

Paragraph 15A(1A) applies to treat a lessee who has given consideration in money or money's worth (other than an increase in rent)[353] for a variation of a lease (other than a variation which reduces the rent or the term which are already dealt with by paragraph 15A(1) and 15A(2) respectively) as if the lessee had acquired a chargeable interest in land as a result of the variation. This means that all lease variations where the lessee pays (or gives chargeable consideration) for the variation, such as where a payment is made to remove a restrictive covenant or to insert a break clause, are potentially liable to SDLT.

2.6.25. Leases - tax chargeable in respect of consideration other than rent

The SDLT chargeable in respect of lease rentals under Schedule 5 is in addition to any SDLT chargeable under section 55 in respect of consideration other than rent.[354] Both rent and other chargeable consideration are taxable (the rental element by virtue of Schedule 5 and the other consideration by virtue of section 55).

Where a land transaction involves the payment of rent and there is other chargeable consideration (for example, a premium) paragraph 9 Schedule 5 applies to determine the rate of SDLT applicable to that other consideration.

Where the 'relevant rental figure' is greater than £600, paragraph 9 disapplies the 0% band in the table at section 55(2) and any case that would have fallen within that band is treated as falling within the 1% band.[355] The effect of this is that where a premium is paid and there is a 'relevant rental figure' of more than £600, the whole of the premium is taxed at 1% rather than potentially

---

[352] Inserted by paragraph 13 Schedule 10 F(No. 2)A 2005 in relation to any transaction the effective date of which is after 19 May 2005 – subject to transitional provisions in paragraph 16(7) of Schedule 10 F(No. 2)A 2005.

[353] Dealt with by paragraph 13 Schedule 17A where the variation takes effect in the first five years

[354] Paragraph 9(4) Schedule 5

[355] As was the case under stamp duty

having the advantage of the 0% band. This provision prevents the nil-rate band applying more than once in respect of the same lease.

'The 'relevant rental figure' means the average annual rent over the term of the lease and in the case of 'linked' leases for which the consideration consists of or includes rent means the total of the average annual rents for those 'linked' leases.

Where different amounts of rent are payable for different parts of the term and those amounts (or any of them) are ascertainable at the effective date, the average annual rent is calculated over the period for which the highest rent is payable.[356] This is an anti-avoidance provision to prevent the 'weighting' of rental payments.

Only ascertainable rent is taken into account in the calculation of average annual rent. For example, if there was a lease rental based entirely on turnover with no minimum rent there would be no annual rent for this purpose. If there was a minimum rent payable, that minimum would be taken into account.

Where there are 'linked transactions' and one (or more) is a transaction where rent is due, no account is to be taken of that rent in determining the relevant consideration for the purposes of section 55.[357] This means that the rental element of the transaction is left out of account in taxing the other consideration, except for determining the rate of tax applicable to the consideration other than rent[358].

2.6.26. Linked leases where consideration is or includes rent[359]

(Paragraphs 2(5) and 2(6) Schedule 5)

If a lease is one of a number of 'linked transactions'[360] but the successive linked leases rules do not apply[361], then special rules apply in calculating the tax charge on the rent. The formula for calculating the SDLT charge in respect of each lease is set out in paragraphs 2(5) and 2(6) of Schedule 5.

---

[356] Paragraph 9(3) Schedule 5

[357] Paragraph 9(5) Schedule 5

[358] See also ''Linked transactions where consideration is or includes rent' at 2.6.7 above.

[359] See example at SDLTM17055 (lease chapter – April 2007).

[360] Applying the test in section 108 for linked transactions see 2.1.1 above.

[361] See 'Successive linked leases' at 2.6.4 above

Where an earlier transaction to which a later transaction is linked is not an 'SDLT transaction', the rules are varied as set out in paragraph 7(1) Schedule 19.[362]

The purpose of the rule on linked leases is to prevent the exploitation of the nil-rate band by the grant of a number of leases rather then a single lease. This is achieved by calculating the amount of tax that would be chargeable on the rent if the linked transactions were a single transaction and then apportioning that tax back to each lease in the proportion which the NPV of the rent payable under the relevant lease bears to the total of the NPVs of all the linked leases. The effect of this is to pro-rate the nil-rate band between the linked leases in proportion to their NPVs.

In detail, the rules operate as follows:

1) Calculate the total tax that would be chargeable if the linked transactions were a single transaction:
   (a) Calculate the NPV of the first lease ('NPV1')
   (b) Aggregate NPV1 with the NPV of the second lease ('NPV2') to give total NPV ('TNPV') of the rent payable over the terms of both leases. This is the RRV for the purposes of Schedule 5.
   (c) To arrive at the total tax chargeable on the first lease, apply TNPV to the threshold relevant at the date of grant of the first lease. Whether this is the residential or non-residential threshold will depend on the status of the total relevant land (all the land which is the subject of either lease).
2) Calculate the element of the total amount of tax which relates to the first lease by applying the fraction: $\frac{NPV1}{TNPV}$ to the figure for tax determined at (1)(c)
3) Calculate the total tax that would be chargeable on the second lease if the linked transactions were a single transaction:
   (a) Calculate NPV2
   (b) Aggregate NPV1 and NPV2 to give total TNPV of rent payable over the terms of both leases. This is the RRV for the purposes of Schedule 5.
   (c) To arrive at the total tax chargeable on the second lease, apply TNPV to the threshold relevant at the date of grant of the second lease. Whether this is the residential or non-residential threshold will depend on the status of the total relevant land (all the land which is the subject of either lease).

---

[362] The rules are applied as if references to 'chargeable consideration' in relation to a transaction which was not an SDLT transaction were references to the amount by reference to which *ad valorem* stamp duty was payable in respect of the instrument which effected the transaction.

4) Calculate the element of this total amount of tax which relates to the second lease by applying the fraction: $\frac{NPV2}{TNPV}$ to the figure of tax at (3)(c)

The chargeable consideration for each of the separate leases is aggregated to arrive at a figure of total tax which would have been payable had there been a single lease. However two separate tax calculations are needed to apply the SDLT rates and thresholds appropriate to each lease. The amount of tax in each case is then apportioned to arrive at a charge for each lease.

Example[363]:

On 1 January 2005 A granted a ten year lease of business premises to B at an annual rent of £700,000. At the same time A granted a separate lease of the adjacent car-park for ten years at an annual rent of £50,000.

If the leases were not linked the total SDLT payable would be:
£56,716 (premises) + £2,658 (car park) = £59,374

Applying the linked leases rule the total SDLT payable is £60,874 (an additional £1,500) which is apportioned as follows:
Lease of premises = £60,874 x (5,821,623/6,237,453)

=£56,816

Lease of car park = £60,874 x (415,830/6,237,453)
= £4,058

363 See 2.6.8 below for the detail of how to calculate the charge to SDLT on rent

3. Reliefs

(Sections 57 to 73 and Schedules 6 to 9, paragraph 17 Schedule 4)

3.1. Introduction to SDLT reliefs

The SDLT reliefs are largely based on those which previously existed for stamp duty, however, some are new and the reliefs that have been brought forward have been tightened.

Where a land transaction is relieved from SDLT it is not exempt from the SDLT regime; the transaction still needs to be notified under section 77. This means that in all such cases a land transaction return is required and the relief is claimed in the return.

In addition to the reliefs listed below there are two reliefs which apply in the calculation of the chargeable consideration (collective enfranchisement by leaseholders and crofting community right to buy) and these are dealt with at 2.2 and 2.3 above. Lease overlap relief is dealt with at 1.8.1 above.

The relief from treatment as exchanges of certain transactions carried out by public sector bodies (PPP and PFI projects) afforded by paragraph 17 Schedule 4 is considered in this section(at 3.20 below).

The reliefs dealt with in this section are:

1) Disadvantaged areas relief for residential property;
2) Sale and leaseback relief (exempts the leaseback element of a sale and leaseback arrangement from the charge to SDLT provided certain conditions are met);
3) Group relief (where a land transaction takes place between companies which at the effective date of that transaction are members of the same group);
4) Reconstruction relief (where a company acquires the whole or part of the undertaking of another target company in pursuance of a scheme for the reconstruction of the target company, and that acquisition involves a land transaction);
5) Acquisition relief (limits the SDLT charge to 0.5% where one company acquires the whole or part of the undertaking of another company and a land transaction is entered into for the purposes of or in connection with the transfer of the undertaking or part of the undertaking);
6) Charities relief (exempts a land transaction from charge if the purchaser is a charity and certain conditions are fulfilled);
7) Relief for certain acquisitions of residential property;
8) Relief for compulsory purchase facilitating development;
9) Relief for compliance with planning obligations;

10) Relief for demutualisation of insurance companies;
11) Relief for demutualisation of building societies;
12) Relief for incorporation of limited liability partnerships (prevents a charge to SDLT arising when a partnership converts into a limited liability partnership);
13) Relief for transfers involving public bodies;
14) Relief for transfer in consequence of reorganisation of parliamentary constituencies;
15) Relief for transactions involving museums and cultural organisations;
16) Relief for right to buy transactions, shared ownership leases, shared ownership trusts[364] etc;
17) Relief for certain acquisitions by registered social landlords;
18) Relief for alternative property finance: Sharia'a mortgages;
19) Relief for certain public bodies - PFI Projects; and
20) Relief for new zero-carbon homes.[365]

In addition, the stamp duty exemptions for diplomatic and consular premises are carried forward to SDLT (relief code 27 on the land transaction return (form SDLT1)).

3.1.1. Abolition of unit trust seeding relief

Following the introduction, in July 2004, of an SDLT charge for transfers of UK land into, within and out of partnerships, the limited partnership lost its appeal as a tax-efficient vehicle for holding UK property. From then on, the unit trust, usually located offshore (in Jersey or Guernsey), became the favourite vehicle for avoiding a charge on transfers of UK land because of the 'seeding relief' in section 64A. This relief was removed by FA 2006 (subject to transitional provisions) and the market value rules in section 53 now apply to transfers of chargeable interests to unit trusts (subject to the exceptions in section 54)[366].

Until 22 March 2006[367] the acquisition of a chargeable interest by trustees of a unit trust scheme was relieved from charge if three conditions were met. The conditions were that:

1) immediately before the seeding transfer no assets were held by the transferee trust and there were no units in issue;

---

[364] Introduced by FA 2007

[365] To be introduced from 1 October 2007 – see BN26 'Stamp Duty Land tax – Relief for new zero carbon homes' (21 March 2007) and sections 58B and 58C inserted by FA 2007.

[366] See 1.7.12 above

[367] Budget Day 2006

2) the only consideration for the acquisition was the issue of units in the scheme to the vendor; and
3) immediately after the acquisition by the transferee trust the vendor was the sole unit holder.

The ending of the seeding relief was subject to transitional provisions.[368]

Seeding relief continues to apply where the contribution of the property to the trustees of a unit trust is:

- pursuant to a contract entered into and 'substantially performed' before 2pm on 22 March 2006[369] (the 'relevant time'); or
- pursuant to any other contract entered into before the relevant time, provided that the contribution of the property is not an 'excluded transaction'.

A land transaction is an 'excluded transaction' if:[370]

1) any provision of the contract has effect by reference to a unit trust scheme and the scheme was not established before the relevant time;
2) the contract is varied by substituting a new purchaser, altering the subject matter of the land transaction or varying the consideration at or after the relevant time, in a way that significantly affects the land transaction;
3) the subject matter of the land transaction is not identified in the contract in a way that would have enabled its acquisition before the relevant time;
4) there is an assignment at or after the relevant time of rights under the contract;
5) the land transaction is effected as a result of the exercise of any option, right of pre-emption or similar right at or after the relevant time; or
6) there is an assignment, subsale or other transaction relating to the whole or part of the land as a result of which a person other than the purchaser under the contract becomes entitled to call for a conveyance to him.

No change was been made to bring transfers of units in a unit trust which owns UK land within the charge to SDLT so the offshore property unit trusts in existence remain tax efficient for SDLT purposes (as the units can still be sold free of SDLT).

Alternatively, as the exception to the market value rule in section 54(4) applies to unit trusts, unit trust seeding relief scheme can be unwound by winding-up the trust and making a distribution of the property in specie free of SDLT.

---

[368] Section 166(4)-(7) FA 2006

[369] See footnote 367 above

[370] Section 166(6)-(7) FA 2006

For the application of SDLT to unit trusts generally see 7.15 below.

3.2. Disadvantaged areas relief for residential property

(Section 57 and Schedule 6 as amended)[371]

Section 57 and Schedule 6 as originally enacted provided relief for land transactions where the property was situated in a disadvantaged area in substantially the same terms as the stamp duty relief as it existed immediately before the introduction of SDLT in 2003.

Disadvantaged areas relief completely exempted acquisitions of non-residential property situated in a disadvantaged area from SDLT. However, from 17 March 2005, the relief has been confined to residential property or that part of property that is residential. Transitional provisions (summarised below) broadly ensure that the removal of the relief from non-residential transactions does not apply to contracts entered into and substantially performed before 17 March 2005.

As the nil-rate threshold for residential transactions is £125,000 and disadvantaged areas relief is capped at £150,000 the relief is now of limited value.

Disadvantaged areas relief also applies to the transfer of an interest in a partnership that is a chargeable transaction by virtue of paragraph 14 or 17 Schedule 15 with the modifications set out in paragraph 27 of Schedule 15.

A 'disadvantaged area' means an area designated as such by the Stamp Duty (Disadvantaged Areas) Regulations 2001.[372]

There is a postcode search available on the HMRC website[373] to establish whether an area is disadvantaged. However, the results of such a search are 'indicative' only. The authoritative source is the Schedules to the Stamp Duty (Disadvantaged Areas) Regulations 2001, which contain Tables of designated areas listed by electoral ward. The ward boundaries are those at 7 May 1998 (for England).[374] Because 'disadvantage' for this purpose is determined by reference to household income in 1998, a number of surprising areas (such as Canary Wharf in London) benefit from the relief.

---

[371] By section 96 and Schedule 9 FA 2005 for transactions the effective date of which is after 16 March 2005.

[372] SI 2001/3747

[373] At www.hmrc.gov.uk/so/pcode_search.htm.

[374] www.neighbourhood.statistics.gov.uk

3.2.1. All land residential[375] and situated in a disadvantaged area

Where:

1) the consideration does not include rent and the 'relevant consideration'[376] does not exceed £150,000; or
2) the consideration for the transaction consists only of rent and the 'RRV'[377] does not exceed £150,000

the transaction is exempt.

Where the consideration for the transaction includes rent and the RRV does not exceed £150,000, the rent does not count as chargeable consideration.

If the consideration for the transaction includes consideration other than rent, provided that the 'annual rent'[378]does not exceed £600 and the relevant consideration does not exceed £150,000, the consideration other than rent does not count as chargeable consideration, so the transaction is exempt.

If the annual rent exceeds £600, the 0% band does not apply in relation to the consideration other than rent and any consideration that would have fallen within that band is treated as falling within the 1% band – this is the normal rule.

3.2.2. Mixed-use property situated in a disadvantaged area

Where the land is partly non-residential and partly residential, the consideration attributable to land that is non-residential is taxed in full in the normal way. The consideration attributable to residential property is dealt with in accordance with the rules which apply where all the land is residential. If the threshold for disadvantaged areas relief is exceeded the total consideration is taxed according to the normal rules.

The consideration for a sale of mixed-use property must be apportioned between the residential and non-residential elements on a just and reasonable basis. HMRC have expressed the following view on apportionment in SP1/2004:[379]

---

[375] The test for residential property is set out in section 116 – see 2.4.1 above.

[376] 'Relevant consideration' is the amount taken into account under section 55(2) in determining the rate of tax (paragraph 11(1) Schedule 4).

[377] RRV for this purpose is the amount taken into account for the purposes of paragraph 2(3) Schedule 5 (calculation of tax chargeable in respect of rent).

[378] 'Annual rent' is determined in accordance with paragraph 9(2) Schedule 5.

[379] At paragraph 20.

> "The 'just and reasonable' test is necessarily subjective, and each case will be considered on its merits. Apportionment might be on the basis of the percentage areas quoted in planning applications, where appropriate, or alternatively of floor space relating to the respective uses. Other methods of apportionment will be considered as part of a claim."

The provision for apportionment in relation to mixed-use property for the purposes of disadvantaged areas relief should be contrasted with the rule that applies in relation to determining the rate of tax (under section 55) where all mixed-use property is, in effect, treated as non-residential.

3.2.3. Land partly situated in a disadvantaged area

(Part 3 Schedule 6)

The consideration must be attributed between the part of the land situated in a disadvantaged area and the part not so situated on a just and reasonable basis.

If the whole of the part situated in the disadvantaged area is non-residential property, the consideration attributable to it is taxed in the normal way.

If the part of the land situated in the disadvantaged area is all residential, the consideration attributable to it is dealt with in accordance with the rules summarised above where all the land is residential. If the threshold for disadvantaged areas relief is exceeded, the total consideration is taxed according to the normal rules.

Where the part of the land situated in a disadvantaged area is partly non-residential and partly residential, the consideration attributable to land that is non-residential is taxed in the normal way. The consideration attributable to residential property is dealt with in accordance with the rules summarised above where all the land is residential. If the threshold for disadvantaged areas relief is exceeded the total consideration is taxed according to the normal rules.

3.2.4. Claiming the relief

Relief is claimed by completing the land transaction return (form SDLT1), checking Box 9 to show that a relief is being claimed and inserting code 05.

> "If partial relief is claimed on a mixed use property the payment due on the non-residential element should be submitted with the land transaction return. Before making a claim customers are advised to satisfy themselves that the relief is due and that the relevant conditions have been met. In

particular, customers should verify that the land is situated in a qualifying area and that the relevant consideration does not exceed £150,000."[380]

Removal of relief for non-residential property: transitional provisions[381]
The relief for non-residential property situated in a disadvantaged area remained available for transactions in pursuance of contracts entered into and substantially performed before 17 March 2005. Transactions in pursuance of contracts entered into before 17 March 2005 (but not substantially performed before that date) were also able to benefit from the relief provided that:

1) there was no variation of or assignment of rights under the contract after 16 March 2005;
2) the transaction was not effected in consequence of the exercise after 16 March 2005 of an option, right of pre-emption or similar right ; and
3) there was no assignment, subsale or other transaction after 16 March 2005 relating to all or part of the subject matter of the contract under which a person other than the purchaser under the contact becomes entitled to call for a conveyance.

Land transaction returns relating to transactions affected by the transitional provisions for non-residential property should be sent to Birmingham Stamp Office for processing. In these cases the effective date of the transaction at Box 4 is after 16 March 2005, but code 06 is claimed at Box 9.

3.3. Sale and leaseback relief

(Section 57A[382])

Provided certain conditions are met, the leaseback element of a sale and leaseback arrangement or lease and leaseback arrangement is exempted from the charge to SDLT by section 57A. The relief is only partial as the sale element of the transaction remains chargeable (as the transaction is, in effect, an exchange[383]) and the leaseback will be consideration for that sale.

The market value of the sale leg will depend upon whether there was an agreement, at the time of the sale, for the leaseback leg to be entered into. If there was, the market value of the sale leg should take this encumbrance into account

---

380 SDLTM20100

381 Paragraph 4 Schedule 9 FA 2005

382 As amended by FA 2004

383 Section 57A(4) as originally drafted expressly calculated market value as if the acquisition were not part of a sale and leaseback.

(and value any rent obtainable from the leaseback leg). If there is no such agreement, the market value of the sale leg should be the unencumbered value[384].

A 'sale and leaseback' arrangement is defined in section 57A(2) as an arrangement under which A transfers or grants to B a 'major interest'[385] in land (the 'sale'), and, out of that interest, B grants a lease to A (the 'leaseback'). The leaseback must therefore be to the person who sold the major interest. Relief will not therefore be available where, for example, one group company sells the major interest and another (C) takes the leaseback.[386]

The conditions are that:

(a) The sale is entered into wholly or partly in consideration of the leaseback.
This condition brings the transactions within the exchange provisions in section 47 and paragraph 5 Schedule 4 so that B will be charged to SDLT by reference to the market value of what he acquires.

(b) The only other consideration for the sale is the payment of money or the assumption, satisfaction or release of a debt (or both).
'Debt' means an obligation, whether certain or contingent, to pay a sum of money ether immediately or at a future date. 'Money' means money in sterling or another currency. In view of the lack of reference to 'existing debt[387]', this condition should be fulfilled even if monetary consideration is left outstanding.
In practice condition (b) restricts the relief to financing transactions as where the consideration for the sale also includes building works the relief is unavailable[388].

(c) The sale is not a transfer of rights within the meaning of section 45 or 45A.

(d) Where A and B are both bodies corporate at the effective date of the leaseback transaction, that they are not members of the same group for the purposes of group relief[389] (see 3.4 below) at that date.[390]

---

[384] See SDLTM16040 (lease chapter – April 2007)

[385] Defined in section 117(2) (in relation to England and Wales) as a fee simple absolute or a term of years absolute at law or in equity. The definitions applying to Scotland and Northern Ireland are in section 117(3) and (4) respectively

[386] In such a case an intra-group transfer from A to C before the sale and leaseback, (claiming group relief) would mean that sale and leaseback relief would apply on the leaseback

[387] As in paragraph 8(3) Schedule 4

[388] Even where those works do not count as chargeable consideration by reason of paragraph 10 Schedule 4

[389] Defined in paragraph 1 Schedule 7

[390] In such a case, group relief may be available

The provision applies to residential[391] and non-residential property alike and provides for relief where the first transaction is the grant of a lease rather than a sale or assignment and also where there is a leaseback of only part. Relief is not available where the leaseback includes additional premises.

Care should be taken to ensure that the leaseback is not to A's nominee as, in such a case, the provisions of paragraph 3(3) Schedule 16 will apply and the grant will be treated for SDLT purposes as made to the nominee and not to A.

3.3.1. Claiming sale and leaseback relief

Relief is claimed by completing the land transaction return (form SDLT1), checking Box 9 to show that a relief is being claimed and inserting code 28 ('Other relief').

3.3.2. Assignment of exempt lease[392]

If the grant of a lease is exempt from charge as a result of leaseback relief pursuant to section 57A, then the first assignment of that lease that is not itself exempt from charge under certain specified provisions[393] will be treated for SDLT purposes as a chargeable transaction comprising the notional grant of a new lease by the assignor (unless the assignee acquires the lease as bare trustee or nominee of the assignor). The grant is treated as being for a term equal to the unexpired term of the actual lease, and on the same terms as those on which the assignee holds that lease after the assignment.

For this reason, persons proposing to acquire existing leases should enquire whether any SDLT relief was claimed when the lease was granted.

---

[391] With effect for any transaction of which the effective date is on or after 22 July 2004.

[392] Paragraph 11 Schedule 17A as re-enacted in amended form by Part 2 Schedule 39 to FA 2004 with effect for transactions with an effective date on or after 22 July 2004.

[393] The specified provisions are:
(*a*) section 57A (sale and leaseback relief);
(*b*) Part 1 or 2 Schedule 7 (group relief or reconstruction or acquisition relief);
(*c*) section 66 (transfers involving public bodies);
(*d*) Schedule 8 (charities relief)
(*e*) any such regulations as are mentioned in section 123(3) (regulations reproducing in relation to SDLT the effect of enactments providing for exemption from stamp duty).

3.4. Group relief [394]

(Section 62 and Part 1 Schedule 7)

The old stamp duty 'group relief' under section 42 FA 1930 is broadly preserved for SDLT purposes. The restrictions which applied to section 42 relief are also carried over into SDLT in paragraphs 2 and 3 Schedule 7.

However, unlike stamp duty group relief which must be formally applied for and then adjudicated, SDLT group relief is self-assessed.[395]

The principle is that where a land transaction takes place between companies which at the effective date of the transaction are members of the same group[396] no SDLT will be chargeable. However the detailed rules, summarised below, are complex. Group relief also applies to the transfer of an interest in a partnership that is a chargeable transaction by virtue of paragraph 14 or 17 Schedule 15 with the modifications set out in paragraph 27 of Schedule 15.

Acquisitions (and disposals) of chargeable interests by a nominee or bare trustee (other than the grant of a lease) are treated as acquisitions (and disposals) by the beneficial owner,[397] so where, for example, a nominee acquires an interest from a company which is a member of a group, acquiring as nominee for another company which is a member of the same group as the transferor, group relief can apply.

The grant of a lease by or to a bare trustee or nominee is treated as a sale or purchase by him of the whole interest (legal and beneficial) which he holds.[398] In such a case, group relief could apply if the bare trustee and the transferor or transferee company are members of the same group.

Group relief can, in principle, apply where there is a transfer of a chargeable interest as a capital distribution between companies on a liquidation for consideration (for example, a transfer subject to a mortgage)[399].

---

[394] See Group Relief article in Issue 70 of the HMRC Tax Bulletin (April 2004) which now appears at SDLTM23011 to SDLTM23019.

[395] By making a claim in the land transaction return.

[396] The conditions for group membership are set out in paragraph 1 Schedule 7.

[397] Paragraph 3(1) Schedule 16.

[398] Paragraph 3(2) - 3(4) Schedule 16.

[399] On the assumption that the market value rule in section 53 would be disapplied by section 54(4) – see 1.7.12 above.

In the absence of group relief, a charge to SDLT may arise on a transfer between connected companies as a result of the operation of the deemed market value rule (see 1.7.12 above).

Group relief is not available if the transaction is a subsale or assignment of the benefit of a contract within the group.[400]

An interest in respect of the transfer of which paragraph 14 of Schedule 15 applies (Transfer of interest in a property-investment partnership[401]) is treated as a chargeable interest for group relief purposes to the extent that the relevant partnership property consists of a chargeable interest[402] This is to enable the group relief clawback provisions to apply to it.

3.4.1. General anti-avoidance test for group relief

Paragraph 2(4A) of Schedule 7[403] denies SDLT group relief where a transaction is either:

1) not effected for bona fide commercial reasons; or
2) forms part of 'arrangements' of which the main purpose or one of the main purposes is the avoidance of SDLT, stamp duty, corporation tax, income tax or capital gains tax.[404]

'Arrangements' is defined in paragraph 2(5) to include 'any scheme, arrangement or understanding, whether or not legally enforceable'.

The provision applies to land transactions with an effective date on or after 20 July 2005 with transitional relief.[405]

With effect from Royal Assent to FA 2007[406] businesses have an extended opportunity to seek clarification from HMRC of the SDLT treatment that will apply to a particular transaction[407] and the application of paragraph 2(4A) of

---

[400] Section 45(5A) provides that the vendor under the secondary contract which is deemed to take place under section 45(3) in such circumstances is the vendor under the original contract so unless the conditions for the application of group relief exist between original vendor and sub-purchaser the transfer to the sub-purchaser will be taxable – see 1.4.3 above.

[401] See section 4.5.3 below.

[402] Paragraph 14(9) Schedule 15 inserted by FA 2007 with effect for transfers occurring on or after 19 July 2007 subject to transitional provisions in section 72(14).

[403] Inserted by paragraph 19 Schedule 10 F(No. 2)A 2005 subject to transitional relief in paragraph 22(2) and 22(3) Schedule 10.

[404] VAT and inheritance tax are not in the list.

[405] In paragraph 22(2) and 22(3) Schedule 10 F(No. 2)A 2005

[406] 19 July 2007

[407] See HMRC 'Making a difference: review of links with large business' (March 2007).

Schedule 7 may be an area where such clarification is needed. The Code of Practice 10 ('COP10') procedure can currently only be used, broadly, in respect of legislation introduced in the last four Finance Acts, but from Royal Assent to FA 2007, in relation to SDLT, the procedure will be available without time limit where there is uncertainty over interpretation of the legislation. Requests for COP10 rulings should be addressed to the Birmingham Stamp Office.

The possibility of the denial of group relief may require additional tax due diligence (and additional indemnification by the seller) on purchases of corporate groups.

In *IRC v. Willoughby*[408] Lord Nolan expressed the following view on the motive test (which forms the second limb of the test in paragraph 2(4A)):

> "Tax avoidance was to be distinguished from tax mitigation. The hallmark of tax avoidance is that the taxpayer reduces his liability to tax without incurring the economic consequences that Parliament intended to be suffered by any taxpayer qualifying for such reduction in his tax liability. The hallmark of tax mitigation, on the other hand, is that the taxpayer takes advantage of a fiscally attractive option afforded to him by the tax legislation, and genuinely suffers the economic consequences that Parliament intended to be suffered by those taking advantage of the option. Where the taxpayer's chosen course is seen upon examination to involve tax avoidance (as opposed to tax mitigation), it follows that tax avoidance must be at least one of the taxpayer's purposes in adopting that course, whether or not the taxpayer has formed the subjective motive of avoiding tax."[409]

The introduction of paragraph 2(4A) was controversial principally because it was seen as introducing uncertainty into genuine commercial transactions, but also because HMRC had over the years been building a broad armoury in an attempt to prevent abuse in the area of group relief:[410]

- anti-avoidance provisions relating to the definition of a 75 per cent. corporate group;
- restrictions on the availability of relief if there are arrangements (at the time of the transaction) to de-group the transferee or for financing the transaction from outside the group;
- clawback of the relief within three years if the transferee was de-grouped (and F(No.2)A 2005 further extended the circumstances under which a clawback arose);

---

[408] [1997] 1 WLR 1071 (HL)

[409] Ibid at 1077

[410] Dealt with at 3.4.3 below

- a rule (in section 53) substituting market value for actual consideration (if greater) for transfers between connected companies.

From 1 August 2005 the direct tax disclosure rules for tax avoidance schemes were extended in modified form to certain SDLT schemes[411] and in December 2006 a general SDLT anti-avoidance rule was introduced[412]. These anti-avoidance provisions are covered in detail in Chapter 5.

The Economic Secretary to the Treasury gave the following clarification of the application of the two part avoidance test in paragraph 2(4A) during the Standing Committee debates:[413]

> "... the measure, ... will only stop claims to group relief where tax avoidance is the, or a, main purpose. The fact that a transaction gives rise to a tax benefit does not mean that avoidance is the main purpose.
>
> I was asked earlier for the definition of the term 'bona fide'. Successive Governments have used that term and most Committee members, and practitioners, understand its meaning to be 'genuine', which is a pretty straightforward understanding.
>
> The fact that a transaction gives rise to a tax benefit does not mean that avoidance is its main purpose. To take a specific example, a group may transfer a property into a special purpose vehicle so that after three years, the shares in that vehicle can be sold free of stamp duty and land tax. That is not tax avoidance, because the legislation specifically permits such transactions. On the other hand, if the property were transferred into the special purpose vehicle as part of arrangements whereby the property could leave the group in less than three years, that might be tax avoidance because it would go against the intention of Parliament."

The Economic Secretary also gave two further examples of planning which would not be caught:

1) Where property was transferred within a group to match chargeable gains with allowable losses or to match rental income with losses with rented property, provided that both the gains and losses arose from genuine economic activity and had not been artificially contrived.

---

[411] By the Stamp Duty Land Tax Avoidance Schemes (Prescribed Descriptions of Arrangements) Regulations 2005 (SI 2005/1868) and the Tax Avoidance Schemes (Information) (Amendment) Regulations 2005 (SI 2005/1869)

[412] In the form of a new section 75A which had effect from 6 December 2006.

[413] See Hansard Standing Committee B, 30 June 2005 p.m., Col 299.

2) Where normal commercial securitisations were carried out (securities were issued in the market and backed by a charge on assets held by the company).

HMRC have expanded on the list of transactions where it is accepted that group relief is not denied by the general anti-avoidance rule in paragraph 2 (4A). The complete 'white list' (last amended in April 2006) is as follows:[414]

1) The transfer of a freehold or the assignment of a lease to a group company having in mind the possibility that shares in that company might be sold more than three years after the date of transfer.
2) The transfer of a freehold or the assignment of a lease to a group company having in mind the possibility that shares in that company might be sold within three years of the date of transfer, with a consequent clawback of group relief, in order that any increase in value of the freehold or the assignment of a lease after the intra-group transfer might be sheltered from SDLT.
3) The transfer of a freehold or the assignment of a lease to a group company having in mind the possibility that either (1) or (2) might occur.
4) The transfer of a freehold or the assignment of a lease to a group company prior to the sale of shares in the transferor company, in order that the freehold or the assignment of a lease should not pass to the purchaser of the shares.
5) The transfer of a freehold or the assignment of a lease to a group company in order that commercially generated rental income[415] may be matched with commercially generated losses from a Schedule A business.
6) The transfer of a freehold or the assignment of a lease to a group company in order that commercially generated chargeable gains may be matched with commercially generated allowable losses.
7) The transfer of a freehold or the assignment of a lease to a non-resident group company, in the knowledge that future appreciation or depreciation in value will be outside the scope of corporation tax on chargeable gains.
8) Transactions undertaken as part of a normal commercial securitisation.
9) The transfer of the freehold reversion in a property to a group lessee in order to merge the freehold and the lease, and thus prevent the lease being subject to the wasting assets rules as respects corporation tax on chargeable gains.

---

[414] See SDLTM23040

[415] Including income, gains and losses which are generated intra-group on transactions which would have been commercial had they been entered into by unconnected third parties.

10) The transfer of a freehold or the assignment of a lease to a group company in order that interest payable on borrowings from a commercial lender on ordinary commercial terms may be set against commercially generated rental income.
11) Borrowings on ordinary commercial terms from a commercial lender, or intra-group in circumstances which would have been commercial had they arisen between unconnected third parties.

'Transfer' means the transfer of a freehold (in Scotland, ownership of land) or the assignment (in Scotland, assignation) of a lease. Cases involving the grant of a lease are to be considered 'on their facts'.

The list is subject to the following caveat:
"Note that the examples are intended only to give general guidance and do not use technical or statutory language, nor should they be interpreted as if they were a statute. They assume that the transactions described do not form part of any larger scheme or arrangement which might have tax consequences."[416]

3.4.2. Members of a group

Companies are members of the same group if either one is a '75% subsidiary' of another, or both are 75% subsidiaries of a third company.

'Company' means 'body corporate'. A unit trust is not treated as a company for this purpose.[417] In determining whether an entity qualifies as a body corporate HMRC will follow the guidelines for stamp duty set out at paragraph 6.124 of the Stamp Taxes Manual,[418] which contains a list of 'foreign bodies' (companies or corporations), for example, Delaware Limited Liability Corporations, which HMRC will regard as bodies corporate for these purposes.

There are three tests which must all be satisfied before a company ('Company A') is a 75% subsidiary of another ('Company B'). The tests are that Company B:

(a) is the beneficial owner of not less than 75% of the 'ordinary share capital'[419] of Company A; and

---

[416] HMRC Guidance Notes 'SDLT—Withdrawal of Group Relief: Guidance on FA 2003, Sch 7 Para 2(4a)' (10 February 2006)

[417] Section 101 (7)

[418] See Group Relief article in HMRC Tax Bulletin Issue 70 (April 2004) at paragraph 11- the list has been updated and expanded by Tax Bulletin Issue 83 (June 2006) which now appears at SDLTM23011 to SDLTM23019.

[419] 'Ordinary share capital' for this purpose means all the issued share capital other than share capital which gives the holders a right to a fixed rate dividend and no other rights to share in profits – paragraph 1(5) Schedule 7.

(b) is beneficially entitled to not less than 75% of the 'profits available for distribution' to 'equity holders' of Company A; and
(c) would be beneficially entitled to not less than 75% of any of the assets of Company A available for distribution to its equity holders on a winding up.

The meaning of 75% subsidiary is also relevant to the arrangements test in paragraph 2(2)(b) Schedule 7. These rules are complex, but it is worth setting them out in full so that you can judge whether they apply.

75% subsidiary – test (a) - determination of percentage of ownership of ordinary share capital

Ownership of share capital can be direct or indirect and the amount of share capital of Company A owned by Company B through another company or companies is determined by applying the rules in section 838(5) to (1) ICTA 1988. These rules are set out below:

(1) Where one body corporate directly owns ordinary share capital of the second and the second directly owns ordinary share capital of the third, then the first is deemed to own ordinary share capital of the third through the second, and, if the third directly owns ordinary share capital of a fourth, the first is deemed to own ordinary share capital of the fourth through the second and third, and in addition the second is deemed to own ordinary share capital of the fourth through the third; and so on.
(2) Any number of bodies corporate of which the first directly owns ordinary share capital of the next and the next directly owns ordinary share capital of the next but one, and so on, and, if they are more than three, any three or more of them, are referred to as 'a series'.
(3) In any series:
    a. that body corporate which owns ordinary share capital of another through the remainder is referred to as the 'first owner';
    b. that other body corporate the ordinary share capital of which is so owned is referred to as 'the last owned body corporate';
    c. the remainder, if one only, is referred to as 'an intermediary' and, if more than one, are referred to as 'a chain of intermediaries';
    d. a body corporate in a series which directly owns ordinary share capital of another body corporate in the series is referred to as 'an owner'; and
    e. any two bodies corporate in a series of which one owns ordinary share capital of the other directly, and not through one or more of the other bodies corporate in the series, are referred to as being directly related to one another.
(4) Where every owner in a series owns the whole of the ordinary share capital of the body corporate to which it is directly related, the first owner is

deemed to own through the intermediary or chain of intermediaries the whole of the ordinary share capital of the last owned body corporate.

(5) Where one of the owners in a series owns a fraction of the ordinary share capital of the body corporate to which it is directly related, and every other owner in the series owns the whole of the ordinary share capital of the body corporate to which it is directly related, the first owner is deemed to own that fraction of the ordinary share capital of the last owned body corporate through the intermediary or chain of intermediaries.

(6) Where:

   a. each of two or more of the owners in a series owns a fraction, and every other owner in the series owns the whole, of the ordinary share capital of the body corporate to which it is directly related; or
   b. every owner in a series owns a fraction of the ordinary share capital of the body corporate to which it is directly related;

(7) the first owner is deemed to own through the intermediary or chain of intermediaries such fraction of the ordinary share capital of the last owned body corporate as results from the multiplication of those fractions.

(8) Where the first owner in any series owns a fraction of the ordinary share capital of the last owned body corporate in that series through the intermediary or chain of intermediaries in that series, and also owns another fraction or other fractions of the ordinary share capital of the last owned body corporate, either:

   a. directly, or
   b. through an intermediary or intermediaries which is not a member or are not members of that series, or
   c. through a chain or chains of intermediaries of which one or some or all are not members of that series, or
   d. in a case where the series consists of more than three bodies corporate, through an intermediary or intermediaries which is a member or are members of the series, or through a chain or chains of intermediaries consisting of some but not all of the bodies corporate of which the chain of intermediaries in the series consists;

then, for the purpose of ascertaining the amount of the ordinary share capital of the last owned body corporate owned by the first owner, all those fractions are aggregated (notwithstanding the different chains of intermediaries) and the first owner is deemed to own the sum of those fractions.

75% subsidiary – tests (b) and (c)

Not only must Company B beneficially own 75% of the ordinary share capital of Company A but, in addition, both of the following tests must be satisfied:

(a) Company B must be beneficially entitled[420] to not less than 75% of the profits available for distribution to the equity holders of Company A, ('test (b)') and
(b) Company B must be beneficially entitled to not less than 75% of any assets of Company A available for distribution to its equity holders on a winding up ('test (c)').

The tests are determined in accordance with the rules set out in Schedule 18 ICTA 1988 with some modifications. These rules are extremely complicated – an overview is set out below but where the rules may be relevant it is necessary to undertake a detailed study of their application. HMRC's Company Tax Manual, at CTM80000, contains a commentary on the rules (which also apply for corporation tax group relief and certain other direct tax purposes) but that commentary does not take in the modifications which apply for SDLT purposes.[421]

In determining a company's beneficial interest in profit distributions or in a notional winding up, account should be taken of indirect equity holdings as well as direct equity holdings.[422]

The relevant accounting period for the purposes of the tests is the accounting period current at the time in question.[423]

Where the term 'security' appears in Schedule 18 ICTA 1988 it applies to all loans whether secured or unsecured.[424]

Test (b) - the profit distribution test

The percentage of profits available for distribution that is attributable to a company which is an equity holder of another company is determined by reference to:
(a) the total profits of the other company, and
(b) the amount of those profits to which the first-mentioned company would be beneficially entitled in the relevant accounting period[425] if all such profits were distributed.[426]

---

[420] Beneficial entitlement includes indirect entitlement through subsidiaries (paragraph 6 Schedule 18 ICTA 1988)

[421] Paragraphs 5(3) and 5B to 5E are omitted from Schedule 18 when applying it for SDLT purposes – see paragraph 1(6) Schedule 7

[422] Paragraph 6 Schedule 18 ICTA 1988

[423] Paragraph 7(1) Schedule 18 ICTA 1988

[424] Paragraph 7(2) Schedule 18 ICTA 1988

[425] As to the relevant accounting period, see paragraph 7(1) Schedule 18 ICTA 1988

'Total profits' for an accounting period means commercial profits, not tax profits. The amount is taken before any profits are distributed to equity holders as such but after deducting fixed rate preference dividends and commercial loan interest; no account is taken of prior year adjustments. Where there is no commercial profit, the calculation is based on notional profits of £100.[427]

Amounts to which an equity holder as such is entitled are to be treated as amounts to which the equity holder is entitled on a profit distribution. An exception is made for payments made by way of repayment of share capital or securities which would not constitute a distribution for corporation tax purposes.[428]

Test (c) - the notional winding-up test
There are complicated rules for determining the assets available for distribution.[429]

The percentage to which one company would be beneficially entitled of those assets of another company which would be available for distribution to its equity holders on a winding up is the percentage to which the first company would be so entitled on a notional winding up if, on that winding up, the value of the assets available for distribution to its equity holders were equal to the excess (if any) of—

(a) the total amount of the assets (at balance sheet values), over
(b) the total amount of the liabilities shown in the subsidiary's balance sheet at the end of the relevant accounting period.

If there is no excess, or the balance sheet is prepared to a different date, a notional £100 is taken for calculation purposes.[430]

Amounts to which an equity holder as such would be entitled on a notional winding up are to be treated as amounts to which he would be entitled on the distribution of assets;[431] but amounts distributable to equity holders which are equivalent to new consideration provided for shares or securities are left out of

---

[426] This is referred to in the legislation as 'the profit distribution'.

[427] Paragraph 2(1) Schedule 18 ICTA 1988

[428] Paragraph 2(2), (3) Schedule 18 ICTA 1988

[429] Paragraphs 3–5 Schedule 18 ICTA 1988

[430] Paragraph 3(1) and 3(2) Schedule 18 ICTA 1988

[431] Paragraph 3(3) Schedule 18 ICTA 1988

account in computing the total assets less liabilities and the amount available for distribution to any particular equity holder.[432]

Limited rights, variable rights and options attaching to ordinary shares

Despite the legislation described above it would still be possible to create an artificial group in one or more of the following ways by creating shares whose rights to participate in distributions or assets are severely limited so that the owner of them has little interest in the company issuing them or by creating shares whose rights may at some future time be reduced. Special provisions have been introduced to deal with each of these situations and with a combination of two or more of them.

Limited rights

A company may hold 75% of the ordinary share capital of another although its right to distributions or to assets on a winding-up may be restricted. Without further provisions, the first company could claim group relief for losses etc of the second company in a particular accounting period although its real interest in the profits and assets of the second company may be minimal. In such a case, in arriving at the first company's entitlement to distributions or assets, a notional calculation has to be made of the effect if the first company had waived its limited rights. The percentage of rights to distribution or assets is restricted to the lower of the actual percentage or the notional percentage.[433]

Variable rights

Shares may be issued with rights that may change from time to time. For the purpose of these provisions, shares have variable rights if, in a future accounting period, the entitlement to distribution of profits or to assets in a winding-up will be different from those in the current accounting period. In such a case, the percentage of the profits or assets for the current accounting period is the lower of:

(a) the percentage to which the parent company is entitled in the current accounting period, and
(b) the percentage to which it would be entitled in any later accounting period in which the rights had changed.[434]

Relevant definitions:

An 'equity holder' of a company is defined[435] as any person who—

---

[432] Paragraph 3(4) and 3(5) Schedule 18 ICTA 1988

[433] Paragraph 4 Schedule 18 ICTA 1988

[434] Paragraph 5(1), 5(2) and (4) Schedule 18 ICTA 1988

[435] Paragraph 1(1) Schedule 18 ICTA 1988

i. holds ordinary shares in the company; or
ii. is a loan creditor of the company in respect of a loan which is not a normal commercial loan.

In addition, if a person has directly or indirectly provided new consideration for any shares or securities in the company (including fixed rate preferential shares or normal commercial loans) and he (or a person connected with him) uses for the purposes of his trade assets belonging to the company on which the company has obtained capital allowances (for plant and machinery or research and development), then that person and no other is treated as being an equity holder in respect of those shares or securities and entitled to any distribution of profits or assets attributable to those shares or securities.[436] Where this applies, the interests of other equity holders in profits available for distribution or in assets available for distribution will be reduced. Where the new consideration in the form of a commercial loan has been provided by a bank, the bank will only be treated as an equity holder in respect of that part of the new consideration equal to the cost of the company's assets used by the bank.[437]

For the purposes of ascertaining who is an equity holder of a company, 'ordinary shares' include all shares other than fixed rate preference shares.[438]

'Fixed rate preference shares' are shares which:
i. are issued for consideration which is or includes new consideration; and
ii. do not carry rights of conversion into shares or securities of any other description or to the acquisition of any additional shares or securities. Conversion rights are disregarded for this purpose if they give rights to conversion only into shares or securities of the issuing company's quoted parent, or into other fixed rate preference shares or normal commercial loans (as defined below) which are not themselves convertible, except into shares or securities of the quoted parent;
iii. do not carry rights to dividends other than dividends which are limited to a fixed amount or at a fixed percentage of the nominal value of the shares representing no more than a reasonable commercial return on the new consideration received by the company in respect of the issue of the shares; and

---

[436] Paragraph 1(6), (8) Schedule 18 ICTA1988, 'New consideration' has the meaning given by section 254 ICTA and 'connected persons' has the meaning given by section 839 ICTA 1988.

[437] Paragraph 1(7) Schedule 18 ICTA 1988.

[438] Paragraph 1(2) Schedule 18 ICTA 1988.

iv. do not carry rights on redemption to an amount exceeding the new consideration (except to the extent that such rights are reasonable compared to other fixed-rate dividend shares listed on a recognised stock exchange).

One company is a 'quoted parent' of another for this purpose if:

i. the other is its 75% subsidiary;
ii. it is not itself a 75% subsidiary of any other company; and
iii. its ordinary shares (of each class, if more than one) are listed on a recognised stock exchange in the UK or overseas.[439]

A 'loan creditor' is defined[440] as a creditor in respect of any debt incurred by the company:

i. for any money borrowed or capital assets acquired by the company; or
ii. for any right to receive income created in favour of the company; or
iii. for consideration, the value of which to the company at the time the debt was incurred was substantially less than the amount of the debt (including any premium thereon); or
iv. in respect of any redeemable loan capital issued by the company.

The relaxation in the definition in the case of loans or debts from banks contained in section 417(9) ICTA 1988 is specifically excluded.[441]

A normal commercial loan is defined[442] as a loan:

- representing in whole or in part new consideration;[443] and
- which does not carry conversion rights into shares or securities of any other description or rights to the acquisition of additional shares or securities (there is a relaxation for certain rights of conversion);[444]
- the interest on which does not exceed a reasonable commercial rate and is not dependent on the results of a company's business or the value of its assets;[445] and

---

439 Paragraph 1(5C) Schedule 18 ICTA 1988

440 Section 417(7) ICTA 1988

441 Paragraph 1(4) Schedule 18 ICTA 1988

442 Paragraph 1(5), Schedule 18 ICTA 1988

443 Section 254(1) and paragraph 1(8) Schedule 18 ICTA 1988

444 See above under the definition of fixed-rate preference shares: paragraph 1(5)(*a*) and paragraph 1(5A) and (5B) Schedule 18 ICTA 1988.

445 The definition of a normal commercial loan has been relaxed to include a loan where the rate of interest reduces as the results of the business improve or the value of any of the assets increases, and it is also relaxed for cases where there is an increase in the rate of interest in the event of a

- in respect of which the loan creditor is entitled to no more than a reasonable premium on redemption based on the terms of issue of securities listed on a recognised stock exchange.

Where loans have been made to a company to facilitate the acquisition of land and the security for payments on the loan is restricted to the land which the loan is used to acquire, the interest payable on such a loan is not treated as dependent on the value of any of the company's assets solely because, under the terms of the loan, the only way the loan creditor can enforce payment of an amount due to him is by exercising rights by way of security over the land acquired. This relaxation only applies where:

- the whole of the loan is to be applied by the company in acquiring land or in meeting the incidental costs of obtaining the loan; and
- none of the land which the loan is used to acquire is acquired with a view to resale at a profit.[446]

3.4.3. Restrictions on availability of group relief

(Paragraph 2 Schedule 7)

In addition to the general anti-avoidance provision in paragraph 2(4A) discussed at section 3.4.1 above, paragraph 2 sets out more specific anti-avoidance rules which restrict the availability of group relief. These rules prevent relief being allowable in circumstances where certain types of 'arrangements' are in place at the effective date of a transaction.

Broadly, paragraph 2 updates the restrictions on stamp duty group relief (which are contained in section 27 FA 1967 and the proviso to section 42(2) FA 1930), and uses references to 'arrangements' throughout – rather than the reference to 'arrangement' in section 27 FA 1967.[447] It also does not replicate section 27(3)(b). Additionally, paragraph 2(2)(b) refers to the purchaser ceasing to be a 75 per cent subsidiary of the vendor or a third company, rather than ceasing to be associated with the vendor or a third body corporate.

'Arrangements' is defined in paragraph 2(5) to include 'any scheme, arrangement or understanding, whether or not legally enforceable'. This definition was used in section 76 (6A)(b) FA 1986[448] but 'arrangements' was not defined for the purposes of the equivalent stamp duty provisions in section 42(2) FA 1930 or section 27(2) FA 1967. Under the SDLT definition,

---

deterioration in the business (or part) or a diminution in the value of any of those assets (paragraph 1(5E) Schedule 18 ICTA 1988).

[446] Paragraph 1(5F) to 1(5I) Schedule 18 ICTA 1988

[447] Amplified by SP 3/98 'Stamp duty – group relief'.

[448] Inserted by section 112(6) FA 2002

'arrangements' include schemes, arrangements or understandings not in writing.

The first disqualifying circumstance – Arrangements for change of control of purchaser (but not of the vendor)
(Paragraph 2(1) Schedule 7)

Paragraph 2(1) prevents a claim to SDLT group relief if arrangements are in existence for a person (or persons together) to obtain control of the purchaser but not of the vendor. Arrangements under paragraph 2(1) have to be in existence at the effective date of the transaction and 'control' bears the same meaning as in section 840 ICTA 1988.[449] Paragraph 2(1) is intended to prevent avoidance of SDLT by passing property, or an economic interest in it, out of the group.

'Control' in relation to a body corporate in this context means the power of a person to secure:

(1) by means of the holding of shares or the possession of voting power in or in relation to that or any other body corporate; or
(2) by virtue of any powers conferred by the articles of association or other document regulating that or any other body corporate,

that the affairs of the first-mentioned body corporate are conducted in accordance with the wishes of that person.[450]

This is a tighter test than the 75% test for group relief itself as a more than 50% holding of shares can give control for section 840 purposes.

HMRC accept that the statements of the Economic Secretary during debate in Parliament on the stamp duty provision in FA 2000 are relevant to the SDLT equivalent:

> "I have received representations expressing concern about the blocking of relief for transfers from the company about to leave the group to another group member - in other words, when the company leaving the group is the transferor. I am persuaded that there are commercial situations in which an asset is transferred to another group company after arrangements are in place for the transferor company to leave the group. In a sense, therefore, the asset never leaves the original group. I am willing to make a concession for such cases, which will be useful to businesses, as their legal advisers have suggested.

---

[449] Paragraph 2(5) Schedule 7

[450] Section 840 ICTA 1988

I have some worry that it might be possible to construct avoidance devices from the concession, so I have asked the Stamp Office to monitor carefully the use of the relief. If the concession is abused, the Government will not hesitate to act swiftly".[451]

In view of this, HMRC have indicated that they will not contend that paragraph 2(1) denies group relief in cases where the transferor is to leave the group having transferred the land to another group member.[452]

Paragraph 2(1) does not apply to deny relief if the arrangements that are in place are for the acquisition of shares by a company (the 'acquiring company') pursuant to the reconstruction of another company as long as the conditions in paragraph 2(1)(a), (b) and (c) are met.[453] These conditions are that:

(1) Section 75 FA 1986 will apply to the acquisition and the conditions for relief under that section will be met; and
(2) after the acquisition the purchaser will be a member of the same group as the acquiring company.

Section 75 FA 1986 provides relief from stamp duty where a company acquires the whole or part of the undertaking of another company in pursuance of a scheme of reconstruction of that company, subject to two conditions[454].

The first condition for the application of section 75 FA 1986 is that the consideration for the acquisition:

(1) consists of or includes the issue of shares in the acquiring company to all the shareholders of the target company; and
(2) includes nothing else (if anything) but the assumption or discharge by the acquiring company of liabilities of the target company.[455]

The second condition for the application of section 75 FA 1986 is that:

(1) the acquisition is effected for bona fide commercial reasons and does not form part of a scheme or arrangement of which the main purpose, or one of the main purposes, is avoidance of liability to stamp duty, income tax, corporation tax or capital gains tax;
(2) after the acquisition has been made, each shareholder of each of the companies is a shareholder of the other; and

---

[451] See Hansard 18 July 2000, Col 253

[452] See Group Relief article in HMRC Tax Bulletin Issue 70 (April 2004) at paragraph 24.

[453] The stamp duty practice has been enacted in the SDLT legislation.

[454] Note: for SDLT reconstruction relief there is an additional condition – see 3.5.2 below.

[455] The requirement that that the registered office of the acquiring company be in the UK was removed with effect from Royal Assent, 19 July 2006, by section 169(2) FA 2006.

(3) after the acquisition has been made, the proportion of shares of one of the companies held by any shareholder is the same or as nearly as may be the same[456] as the proportion of shares of the other company held by that shareholder.

From Royal Assent to FA 2007[457], the rules governing reconstruction relief pursuant to section 75 FA 1986 have been changed, so that a company that has purchased its own shares is no longer be regarded as a shareholder in determining whether the conditions for relief have been met[458]. In practice this means it will no longer be necessary for such a company to cancel its own shares or accept shares in the acquiring company in order to qualify for the relief. This change arises from the fact that quoted companies can hold their own shares in treasury without the need to cancel them.

Paragraph 2(1) does not apply to deny relief where the offending arrangements are for the purpose of facilitating a transfer of the whole or part of the business of a company to another company which is intended to fall within section 96 Finance Act 1997 (stamp duty relief: demutualisation of insurance companies).[459]

Paragraph 2(2) provides rules for SDLT based on those which apply for stamp duty purposes (contained in section 27(3) FA 1967). Section 27(3)(b) FA 1967 (which applies to deny stamp duty group relief where the beneficial interest conveyed was previously conveyed by a person other than an associated body corporate) is not simply transposed into Schedule 7 because the problem it seeks to address, resting on contract, is not relevant to SDLT. It is not possible to 'rest on contract' to avoid SDLT because of the 'substantial' performance rule in section 44 (see 1.3 above).

The second disqualifying circumstance – arrangements for the provision of consideration by a third party
(Paragraph 2(2)(a) Schedule 7)

Paragraph 2(2)(a) denies SDLT group relief where there are arrangements under which consideration is to be provided or received (directly or indirectly) by a person other than a group company. Such an arrangement will exist if the vendor or the purchaser (or another group company, is to be enabled to

---

456 Inserted by section 169(2) FA 2006 with effect from Royal Assent, 19 July 2006.

457 19 July 2007

458 By section 74(1) and (4) FA 2007 inserting a new section75(5a) with effect from 19 July 2007.

459 Paragraph 2(3A) Schedule 7 inserted by section 167 FA 2006 with effect in relation to any transfer which took place (or was intended to take place) after 22 March 2006.

provide any of the consideration) or is to part with any of it, by or in consequence of the carrying out of a transaction or transactions involving, or any of them involving, a payment or other disposition by a person other than a group company.[460] In other words, the relief will not be available where a third party funds the purchase, either directly or indirectly.

'Group company' means a company that at the effective date of the transaction is a member of the same group as the vendor or the purchaser.[461]

'Consideration' is widely construed – for example, in relation to the equivalent stamp duty provision, the following arrangements would, in the Stamp Office's view, have been caught:

- where the consideration for the intra-group transfer was left outstanding and a third party guaranteed it or otherwise arranged to provide for it to be paid
- where the consideration was left outstanding and was financed by an onward sale of the relevant assets to a third party
- where the consideration for the intra-group transfer took the form of assets, as opposed to cash, and there was an arrangement to sell those assets
- where the consideration took the form of shares which as part of an arrangement were to be sold to a third party so the consideration was received by the third party
- where the transferee granted a long lease of the property to finance the purchase.

Where group relief is claimed HMRC will not interpret paragraph 2(2)(a) as denying relief unless the loan finance is provided as part of a scheme to save SDLT when the property or an interest in it leaves the group.[462]

HMRC has given the following as examples of situations where, in its view, it is unlikely that there will be arrangements falling within paragraph 2(2)(a):[463]

- if the group relief claim is not to be followed by a sale or underlease outside the group; or
- if the claim is followed by a sale or underlease outside the group but SDLT is to be paid by the purchaser outside the group on consideration close to market value (or there is deemed to be a grant of a lease under paragraph 11 Schedule 17A).

---

460 Paragraph 2(3) Schedule 7

461 Paragraph 2(4) Schedule 7

462 See Group Relief article in HMRC Tax Bulletin Issue 70 (April 2004) at paragraph 27.

463 Ibid at paragraph 28

Loans from commercial lenders on ordinary commercial terms to facilitate the transfer between group members will also not normally disqualify a claim by reason of the test in paragraph 2(2)(a). For example, HMRC have indicated that relief will not be disallowed by virtue of paragraph 2(2)(a) if:[464]

- a specific loan is taken for the purchase of the property, or
- the loan is secured on the property, or
- arrangements are made to replace or novate an existing charge on the property transferred.

Some examples of the type of circumstances which HMRC have indicated that they might want to examine in more detail during an enquiry are where the claim is part of (or is to be followed by):[465]

- the creation or transfer of loan stock or equity capital;
- a capital reorganisation of the transferee;
- a guarantee by a third party not associated with the group;
- the creation of a new charge or financial arrangement whereby title to the property is, or may be, vested in the lender otherwise than in satisfaction of all or part of the debt; or
- the assignment of the freehold reversion or the intra-group lease to a person outside the group.

Or where:

- all or part of the consideration for the transaction is to remain outstanding or is represented by intra-group debt (as the aim and effect may be to reduce the value of the transferee company on a possible future sale outside the group); or
- the existing shareholders of the transferee include shareholders outside the group and the transaction is to be followed by the declaration of a dividend in specie, or by the liquidation of the transferee.

The third disqualifying circumstance - arrangements for the purchaser to cease to be a member of the same group as the vendor
(Paragraph 2(2)(b) Schedule 7)

Group relief is not available where at the effective date of the transaction there are arrangements for the vendor and the purchaser to cease to be members of the same group by reason of the purchaser ceasing to be a 75% subsidiary of the vendor or a third company.

---

[464] Ibid at paragraph 29

[465] Ibid at paragraphs 31 and 32

Without this anti-avoidance rule, the property could be transferred intra-group and the transferee sold.

3.4.4. Claiming group relief

Relief is claimed by completing the land transaction return (form SDLT1), checking Box 9 to show that a relief is being claimed and inserting code 12. This means that companies claiming the relief must judge the admissibility of the claim themselves.

3.4.5. Clawback of group relief

(Paragraphs 3 and 4 Schedule 7)

Where a land transaction is relieved from SDLT because of group relief and:

(1) the purchaser in that relieved transaction ceases to be a member of the same group as the vendor:
(2) before the end of the period of three years beginning with the effective date of that transaction; or
(3) at any time in pursuance of or in connection with arrangements made before the end of that three year period; and
(4) at the time that the purchaser in the intra-group land transaction ceases to be a member of the group (the 'relevant time'), the purchaser or a 'relevant associated company' holds a chargeable interest:
    (a) that was acquired by the purchaser under the transaction relieved from SDLT; or
    (b) that is derived from a chargeable interest so acquired; and
    (c) that chargeable interest has not since the relived transaction been acquired at market value under a chargeable transaction for which group relief was available but was not claimed,

then (unless one of the four exclusions from clawback in paragraph 4 applies) SDLT is chargeable at the date of the disqualifying event (the event in (1) above) on the market value or the appropriate part of the market value of the interest transferred determined as at the date of the intra-group land transaction.

The amount of the clawback is the SDLT that would have been chargeable in respect of the relieved transaction (but for group relief) if the chargeable consideration had been equal to the market value of the subject-matter of the transaction or, in a case where the transaction was the grant of a lease at a rent, that rent.[466]

---

[466] Paragraph 3(2) Schedule 7 as substituted by paragraph 4 Schedule 10 F(No.2)A 2005 where the effective date of the transaction benefiting from relief under Part 1 of Schedule 7 is on or after 20 May 2005 (subject to the transitional relief in paragraph 16(7) Schedule 10 F(No.2)A 2005).

In some cases, only an appropriate proportion of the tax that would have been so chargeable is subject to clawback. 'An appropriate proportion' means an appropriate proportion having regard to the subject matter of the relevant transaction and what is held at the relevant time by the transferee company or by that company and its relevant associated companies (i.e. if part of the property in question has already been sold).

'Relevant associated company' in relation to the purchaser means:[467]

- a company that is a member of the same group as the purchaser immediately before the purchaser ceases to be a member of the same group as the vendor and
- that ceases to be a member of the same group as the vendor in consequence of the purchaser so ceasing.

The group relief clawback is aimed at making it harder for companies to transfer properties to a special purpose company and then sell the shares in that company to take advantage of the 0.5% duty on share transfers. The clawback does not operate if, when the purchaser leaves the group, it does not hold the chargeable interest and any company which leaves the group holding the chargeable interest is not a 'relevant associated company'.

The inclusion of 'relevant associated companies' is intended to prevent an initial intra-group property transfer on which group relief has been claimed escaping the clawback where the property is subsequently transferred to a third company which leaves the group together with the original purchaser (in a sub-group) (the 'double drop-down' or 'bungee jump'). For a company to be a relevant associated company it must leave the vendor's group 'in consequence of *the purchaser* so ceasing'.

'Arrangements' is defined in paragraph 3(4) of Schedule 7 in the same way as in paragraph 2(5).

HMRC will not assume, just because a purchaser company is transferred outside the group shortly after the end of the three year period, that the transfer is in accordance with arrangements made within the three year period.[468]

Paragraph 4 Schedule 7 excludes the following four cases from clawback:

(1) Where the vendor leaves the group by reason of a transaction relating to:
    a. shares in the vendor or

Therefore it does not alter the rules determining clawback where the effective date of the relieved transaction was before 20 May even if the event giving rise to clawback is on or after 20 May 2005.

[467] Paragraph 3(4) Schedule 7

[468] See Group Relief article in HMRC Tax Bulletin Issue 70 (April 2004) at paragraph 42

b. shares in another company that is 'above the vendor in the group structure' that as a result ceases to be a member of the same group as the purchaser.[469]

For this purpose a company is 'above the vendor in the group structure' if the vendor, or another company that is 'above the vendor in the group structure', is a 75% subsidiary of the company.[470]

(2) Where the purchaser ceases to be a member of the same group as the vendor by reason of anything done for the purposes of, or in the course of, winding up the vendor or another company that is 'above the vendor in the group structure'.

(3) Where the purchaser ceases to be a member of the same group as the vendor as a result of an acquisition of shares by another company ('the acquiring company') in relation to which stamp duty reconstruction relief under section 75 FA 1986 would apply and the purchaser is immediately after that acquisition a member of the same group as the acquiring company.

(4) Where the purchaser ceases to be a member of the same group as the vendor as a result of a transfer to which section 96 Finance Act 1997 (stamp duty relief: demutualisation of insurance companies) applies, of the whole or part of the vendor's business to another company (the acquiring company') provided that immediately after the transfer of business the purchaser is a member of the same group as the acquiring company.[471]

However, if, in a case falling within (3) or (4) above, the purchaser ceases to be a member of the same group as the acquiring company within three years of the effective date of the relevant transaction or leaves the group at any time in pursuance of or in connection with, arrangements made before the end of that period, and, at the time the purchaser ceases to be a member of the same group as the acquiring company, it, or a relevant associated company, holds a chargeable interest:

- that was acquired by the purchaser under the relevant transaction or that is derived from an interest so acquired, and

---

[469] Paragraph 4(3) Schedule 7 as amended by paragraph 5 Schedule 10 F(No. 2)A 2005 where the effective date of the transaction benefiting from relief under Part 1 of Schedule 7 is on or after 20 May 2005, (subject to transitional relief set out in paragraph 16(7) of Schedule 10 F(No. 2)A 2005). Therefore it does not alter the rules determining clawback where the effective date of the relieved transaction was before 20 May even if the event giving rise to clawback is on or after 20 May 2005.

[470] Paragraph 4(5) Schedule 7

[471] Paragraph 4(6A) Schedule 7 inserted by section 167 FA 2006 with effect in relation to any transfer which took place (or was intended to take place) after 22 March 2006.

- that has not subsequently been acquired at market value under a chargeable transaction for which group relief was available but was not claimed,

then the clawback provisions apply as if the purchaser had then ceased to be a member of the same group as the vendor.

For this purpose, 'relevant associated company', means a company that is a member of the same group as the purchaser that ceases to be a member of the same group as the acquiring company in consequence of the purchaser so ceasing.[472] 'Arrangements' is defined in the same way as for paragraph 2.

Where the clawback applies, a further land transaction return must be delivered by the purchaser within 30 days of the disqualifying event.[473] This return is not yet available from HMRC and, in the meantime, full details of the event requiring the return should be forwarded in a letter to Birmingham Stamp Office, attaching a copy of the original land transaction return and the appropriate payment[474].

Clawback of group relief: successive transactions
(Paragraph 4A Schedule 7)[475]

Paragraph 4A provides another trigger for the clawing-back of group relief and was introduced to counter avoidance:

> "The Government's intention has been clear ever since the clawback provisions were introduced in 2002. If group relief is claimed, and the transferee company leaves the group within three years, the relief should be clawed back. …
>
> …Although the Government's intention was clear, schemes aimed at frustrating it began to emerge almost as soon as the clawback provisions were published. The schemes work by interposing within the group transfers that have no commercial purpose but that stop the eventual clawback of group relief. Hence the need for [new paragraph 4A], which in effect causes the transfers to be disregarded, and which means that it is the relationship between the earliest transferor and the ultimate transferee in a three-year period that is considered. If, at the end of that period, those two

---

[472] Paragraph 4(8) Schedule 7

[473] Section 81

[474] See 'Where to send your SDLT paper work' available at http://www.hmrc.gov.uk/so/mctu.htm

[475] Inserted by paragraph 6 Schedule 10 F(No. 2)A 2005 where the effective date of the transaction benefiting from relief under Part 1 of Schedule 7 is on or after 20 May 2005 (subject to transitional relief set out in paragraph 16(7) of Schedule 10 F(No. 2)A 2005). Therefore it does not alter the rules determining clawback where the effective date of the relieved transaction was before 20 May even if the event giving rise to clawback is on or after 20 May 2005.

companies are no longer in the same group, then unless SDLT has been paid on one of the intermediate transactions, the relief is clawed back."[476]

One of the schemes to avoid clawback which are countered by paragraph 4A, the 'bungee' scheme, worked as follows. The interest in land which was ultimately to be sold outside the group was transferred from one group company to another. The purchaser in that first transaction was a wholly-owned subsidiary of a third company in the group and group relief was claimed on the transaction. The first purchaser then transferred the land to its parent which made a group relief claim. The parent company was later sold (within the three year clawback period) owning both the land and the shares in the first purchaser. Before paragraph 4A no clawback would have occurred in respect of either transaction. Although the parties to the first transaction would cease to be in the same group, the company holding the land at the time the purchaser in that transaction left the transferor's group, (the third company) was not a 'relevant associated company' as it did not leave the transferor's group 'as a result of the purchaser so ceasing' but because the shares in it were sold. The parties to the second transaction would remain grouped.

Paragraph 4A applies where:
(1) a transaction (the 'relevant transaction') is relieved from SDLT by the group relief provisions; and
(2) there is a 'change of control' of the purchaser either within three years of the effective date of the relevant transaction or, at any time, pursuant to or in connection with 'arrangements' entered into within that three-year period; and
(3) there are one or more previous transactions which satisfy all four conditions in paragraph 4A(2) (see below); and
(4) apart from the provisions of paragraph 4A there would be no clawback of the relief given in respect of the relevant transaction.

'Arrangements' includes any scheme, agreement or understanding, whether or not legally enforceable.[477]

There is a 'change of control'[478] of a company if:

- any person who controls the company (alone or with others) ceases to do so;
- a person obtains control of the company (alone or with others); or
- the company is wound up.

---

[476] Economic Secretary to the Treasury Hansard Standing Committee B, 30 June 2005 p.m., Col 288.

[477] Paragraph 4A(5)

[478] Using the test of control in section 416(2)-(6) ICTA 1988.

The four conditions set out in paragraph 4A(2) are:

(1) the previous transaction benefited from group, reconstruction or acquisition relief under Schedule 7;
(2) the effective date of the previous transaction was within three years of the change of control of the purchaser;
(3) the chargeable interest acquired by the purchaser under the relevant transaction is the same as or is derived from the chargeable interest which was the subject of the previous transaction; and
(4) since the previous transaction there has not been a transaction involving the chargeable interest acquired under that previous transaction which was not relieved from charge under Schedule 7.

Where paragraph 4A is in point, the provisions of paragraph 3 and 4 of Schedule 7 (clawback of group relief) apply as if the vendor in relation to the earliest previous transaction were the vendor in relation to the relevant transaction. Sub-paragraph 4A(4) provides that where two or more previous transactions were entered into at the same time all the vendors under those transactions are to be taken into account.

It is not clear whether multiple levels of clawback could arise where there has been a chain of intra-group transactions.

3.4.6. Clawed-back group relief – recovery from third parties

(Paragraphs 5 and 6 Schedule 7)

Once the SDLT due as a result of a withdrawal of group relief in relation to a land transaction has been finally determined, liability to pay that tax is the responsibility of the purchaser. Where such tax (or any part of it) has not been paid within a period of six months of the date on which it became payable, recovery of the unpaid amount is possible from other persons.[479]

The persons from whom the SDLT may be recovered are[480]:

- the vendor;
- any company which at any 'relevant time' was a member of the same group as the purchaser and was above it in the group structure;
- any person who at any 'relevant time' was a controlling director of the purchaser or of a company having control of the purchaser.

To enable recovery, a notice must be served on the person from whom the tax is to be recovered[481]. The notice will require the unpaid amount of tax to be paid within 30 days of the service of the notice and:

---

[479] Paragraph 5 and 6 Schedule 7.

[480] Paragraph 5(3) Schedule 7.

1) must be served before the end of the period of three years beginning with the date on which the tax was finally determined;
2) must state the amount of tax to be paid by the person on whom it is served;
3) has effect for recovery of the tax and any interest on the unpaid tax and also for the purposes of appeals as if it were a notice of assessment and the amount shown on it were an amount of tax due from the person on whom it was served.

Once the person on whom a notice was served has paid the tax (and interest), he is legally entitled to recover the amount he paid from the purchaser.[482]

No deduction is allowed in computing any income, profits or losses for any tax purpose for the amount so paid.

Relevant definitions:[483]

Any 'relevant time' means any time between the effective date of the relevant transaction and the date the purchaser ceased to be a member of the same group as the vendor.

A company (company A) is above another company (company B) in a group structure if company B (or another company that is above company B in the group structure) is a 75% subsidiary of company A.

'Director' (in relation to a company) has the meaning given by section 67(1) ITEPA 2003 and includes any person falling within section 417(5) ICTA 1988.

'Controlling director' (in relation to a company) means a director of the company who has control of the company in accordance with section 416 ICTA 1988.

3.4.7. Assignment of exempt lease[484]

If the grant of a lease is exempt from charge as a result of group relief then the first assignment of that lease that is not itself exempt from charge under any of certain specified provisions[485] is treated for SDLT purposes as a chargeable

---

[481] Paragraph 6 Schedule 7

[482] This potential liability (under paragraph 6(4) Schedule 7) may need to be specifically covered in standard form tax documentation on company purchases.

[483] Paragraph 5(3) and 5(4) Schedule 7.

[484] Paragraph 11 Schedule 17A as re-enacted in amended form by Part 2 Schedule 39 to FA 2004 with effect for transactions with an effective date on or after 22 July 2004.

[485] The specified provisions are:
(a) section 57A (sale and leaseback relief);
(b) Part 1 or 2 Schedule 7 (group relief or reconstruction or acquisition relief);
(c) section 66 (transfers involving public bodies);
(d) Schedule 8 (charities relief);

transaction comprising the notional grant of a new lease by the assignor (unless the assignee acquires the lease as bare trustee of the assignor).

The grant is treated as being for a term equal to the unexpired term of the actual lease, and on the same terms as those on which the assignee holds that lease after the assignment.

This provision does not however apply where the relief in question is group relief and the relief is withdrawn as a result of a disqualifying event occurring before the effective date of the assignment of the original lease, since in that situation the exemption given in relation to the original grant of the lease would be the subject of clawback.

3.5. Reconstruction relief

(Section 62 and paragraph 7 and Part 2 Schedule 7)

The stamp duty relief in section 75 FA 1986 is preserved in amended form in paragraph 7 and Part 2 Schedule 7.

Paragraph 7 provides that where a company ('the acquiring company') acquires the whole or part of the undertaking of another company ('the target company') in pursuance of a scheme for the reconstruction of the target company and three conditions are met, a land transaction entered into for the purposes of or in connection with the transfer of the undertaking or part of the undertaking is exempt.

3.5.1. What is a scheme of reconstruction?

The SDLTM describes the circumstances in which the relief is available as follows:

> "This relief allows land and buildings to be transferred between two companies, as part of a transfer of an undertaking in exchange for shares, where there is no change of ownership, without any charge to SDLT.
>
> An example is where a company decides to split an existing business, which is carried on by one company, into two."[486]

A reconstruction in company law is generally understood to involve the formation of a new company to acquire the undertaking of an existing company.[487] A scheme for the reconstruction of a company under section 55 FA

(e) any such regulations as are mentioned in section 123(3) (regulations reproducing in relation to SDLT the effect of enactments providing for exemption from stamp duty).

[486] At SDLTM23200

[487] See *Hooper v Western Counties and South Wales Telephone Co Ltd* (1892) 68 LT 78; *Re South African Supply and Cold Storage Co* [1904] 2 Ch 268 at 286 to 287.

1927[488] was held to comprise a transfer of the undertaking, or part of the undertaking, of an existing company to a new company with substantially the same persons as members as were members of the existing company, and the scheme had to involve the carrying on by the new company of substantially the same business as the business transferred to it.[489]

The requirements of a 'reconstruction' for the purpose of section 55 FA 1927 were also considered in *Baytrust Holdings Ltd v. IRC* [490] where it was held that the scheme in question was not a scheme of 'reconstruction'. The reconstruction of a company normally involved the transfer of a company's undertaking (or part of it) to a new company which was going to carry on substantially the same business as that transferred to it[491] but the transfer of assets which did not form a part of the business did not qualify for the exemption.

3.5.2. The three conditions for SDLT reconstruction relief[492]

(Paragraph 7 Schedule 7)

The first condition for reconstruction relief is that the consideration for the acquisition consists wholly or partly of the issue of non-redeemable shares in the acquiring company to all the shareholders of the target company. Where the consideration for the acquisition consists partly of the issue of non-redeemable shares, the first condition is met only if the rest of the consideration consists wholly of the assumption or discharge by the acquiring company of liabilities of the target company.

The second condition is that after the acquisition has been made, each shareholder of each of the companies is a shareholder of the other and the proportion of shares of one of the companies held by any shareholder is the same, or as nearly as may be the same, as the proportion of shares of the other company held by that shareholder:

---

488 Section 55 FA 1927 was repealed by section 74 FA 1986 and replaced by the stamp duty exemptions and reliefs set out in sections 75 to 77 FA 1986.

489 See *Brooklands Selangor Holdings Ltd v. IRC* [1970] 2 All ER 76 and *Baytrust Holdings Ltd v. IRC* [1971] 3 All ER 76

490 [1971] 3 All ER 76

491 Dicta of Chitty J. in *Hooper v. Western Counties and South Wales Telephone Co Ltd* (1892) 68 LT 78 at 80, of Buckley J. in *Re South African Supply and Cold Storage Co* [1904] 2 Ch 268 at 286, Lord Hanworth MR in *Oswald Tillotson Ltd v. IRC* [1933] 1 KB 134 at 155, and Pennycuick J. in *Brooklands Selangor Holdings Ltd v. IRC* [1970] 2 All ER 76 at 87 applied.

492 Note: there is no third condition for stamp duty reconstruction relief (under section 75 FA 1986)

> "The only time the proportions do not have to match exactly is when there are insufficient shares of one company to allow the shareholders to match their proportions of shares in the other company. In this case, any reasonable disposition of the shares to allow matching as nearly as possible is acceptable (but so that control of one company is the same as control of the other company)."[493]

This second condition means that the relief is only available where both companies have share capital.

From Royal Assent to FA 2007[494], the rules governing SDLT reconstruction relief have been changed, so that a company that has purchased its own shares is no longer be regarded as a shareholder in determining whether the conditions for relief have been met[495]. In practice this means it will no longer be necessary for such a company to cancel its own shares or accept shares in the acquiring company in order to qualify for the relief. This change arises from the fact that quoted companies can hold their own shares in treasury without the need to cancel them.

The third condition is that the acquisition is effected for bona fide commercial reasons and does not form part of a scheme or arrangement of which the main purpose, or one of the main purposes, is the avoidance of liability to stamp duty, income tax, corporation tax, capital gains tax or SDLT.

A unit trust is not treated as a company for this purpose (section 101(7)).

3.5.3. Claiming reconstruction relief

Relief is claimed by completing the land transaction return (form SDLT1), checking Box 9 to show that a relief is being claimed and inserting code 13.

3.5.4. Clawback of reconstruction and acquisition relief

Paragraph 9 Schedule 7 provides that where a transaction is exempt by virtue of reconstruction relief (or is subject to a reduced rate of tax by virtue of acquisition relief) and:

(1) control of the acquiring company changes before the end of the period of three years beginning with the effective date of the transaction or in pursuance of, or in connection with, arrangements made before the end of that period; and

---

[493] SDLTM23210

[494] 19 July 2007

[495] By section 74(1) and (4) FA 2007 which inserted a new section 75(5A) in FA 1986.

(2) at the time control of the acquiring company changes ('the relevant time'), it or a relevant associated company holds a chargeable interest that was acquired by the acquiring company under the relevant transaction, or that is derived from an interest so acquired and that has not subsequently been acquired at market value under a chargeable transaction in relation to which reconstruction or acquisition relief was available but was not claimed,

then reconstruction or acquisition relief in relation to the relevant transaction, or an appropriate proportion of it, is withdrawn and SDLT is chargeable.

References to control of a company changing are to the company becoming controlled:

(1) by a different person;
(2) by a different number of persons; or
(3) by two or more persons at least one of whom is not the person, or one of the persons, by whom the company was previously controlled.[496]

During the Standing Committee debates on paragraph 9 the Chief Secretary to the Treasury gave the following assurance in answer to a concern that as the circumstances in which a change of control is regarded as occurring are broadly drawn the relief could be clawed back as a result of a small change in shareholdings[497]:

> "I assure the hon. Gentleman that if control of a publicly owned company changes as a result of an ordinary market transfer of its shares, there will be no recovery, because we do not intend to interpret change of control so widely that simple day-to-day transactions by unconnected minority shareholders on the stock exchange could trigger a clawback."

The amount chargeable is the SDLT (or an appropriate proportion of the SDLT that would have been chargeable in respect of the relevant transaction (but for reconstruction or acquisition relief) if the chargeable consideration for that transaction had been an amount equal to the market value of the subject matter of the transaction and, if the acquisition was the grant of a lease at a rent, that rent.[498]

---

[496] Paragraph 9(5)(c) Schedule 7

[497] Hansard Standing Committee B 10 June 2003 a.m. at Cols 424 to 425

[498] Paragraph 9(2) Schedule 7 as substituted by paragraph 9 Schedule 10 F(No.2)A 2005 where the effective date of the transaction benefiting from relief under paragraph 9 of Schedule 7 is on or after 20 May 2005 (subject to the transitional relief in paragraph 16(7) Schedule 10 F(No.2)A 2005). Therefore it does not alter the rules determining clawback where the effective date of the relieved transaction was before 20 May, even if the event giving rise to clawback is on or after that date.

There is no clawback of reconstruction or acquisition relief if control of the acquiring company changes as a result of any of the following five events[499]:

(1) a share transaction effected as mentioned in any of paragraphs (a) to (d) of paragraph 3 Schedule 3 (transactions in connection with divorce etc.);
(2) a share transaction that is effected as mentioned in paragraph 4(1) Schedule 3 and meets the conditions in paragraph 4(2) Schedule 3 (variation of testamentary dispositions etc);
(3) an exempt intra-group transfer, namely a transfer of shares effected by an instrument to which stamp duty group relief applies (the relief is however withdrawn if there is a subsequent non-exempt transfer (see below));
(4) a transfer of shares to another company in relation to which share acquisition relief applies for stamp duty purposes[500](the relief is however withdrawn where there is a subsequent non-exempt transfer (see below));
(5) a loan creditor becoming, or ceasing to be, treated as having control of the company and the other persons who were previously treated as controlling the company continuing to be so treated. 'Loan creditor' has the meaning given by section 417(7) to (9) ICTA 1988.

Where clawback is prevented because the change of control of the acquiring company is a result of an exempt intra-group transfer[501] but:

(1) a company holding shares in the acquiring company to which the exempt intra-group transfer related, or that are derived from shares to which that transfer related, ceases to be a member of the same group as the target company before the end of the period of three years beginning with the effective date of the relevant transaction or in pursuance of or in connection with arrangements made before the end of that period; and
(2) the acquiring company or a relevant associated company, at that time ('the relevant time'), holds a chargeable interest that was transferred to the acquiring company by the relevant transaction or that is derived from an interest that was so transferred and that has not subsequently been transferred at market value by a chargeable transaction in relation to which reconstruction or acquisition relief was available but was not claimed,

reconstruction or acquisition relief in relation to the relevant transaction, or an appropriate proportion of it, is withdrawn and tax is chargeable.

---

[499] Paragraph 10 Schedule 7

[500] Pursuant to section 77 FA 1986

[501] Pursuant to section 42 FA 1930

Where clawback is prevented because the change of control of the acquiring company is as a result of a transfer to which stamp duty share acquisition relief applies[502] but:

(a) control of the other company mentioned in that provision changes before the end of the period of three years beginning with the effective date of the relevant transaction or in pursuance of or in connection with arrangements made before the end of that period, at a time when that company holds any shares transferred to it by the exempt transfer, or any shares derived from shares so transferred; and

(b) the acquiring company or a relevant associated company, at that time ('the relevant time'), holds a chargeable interest that was transferred to the acquiring company by the relevant transaction or one that is derived from an interest that was so transferred, and that has not subsequently been transferred at market value by a chargeable transaction in relation to which reconstruction or acquisition relief was available but was not claimed,

reconstruction or acquisition relief in relation to the relevant transaction, or an appropriate proportion of it, is withdrawn and tax is chargeable.

The amount chargeable is the SDLT(or an appropriate proportion of the SDLT) that would have been chargeable in respect of the relevant transaction but for reconstruction or acquisition relief if the chargeable consideration for that transaction had been an amount equal to the market value of the subject-matter of the transaction.

Where the clawback applies, a further land transaction return must be delivered by the acquiring company as purchaser within 30 days of the disqualifying event.[503] This return is not yet available from HMRC and, in the meantime, full details of the event requiring the return should be forwarded in a letter to Birmingham Stamp Office, attaching a copy of the original land transaction return and the appropriate payment[504].

Relevant definitions[505]:

'An appropriate proportion' means an appropriate proportion having regard to the subject-matter of the relevant transaction and what is held at the relevant time by the acquiring company or, as the case may be, by that company and any relevant associated companies.

---

[502] Pursuant to section 77 FA 1986

[503] Section 81

[504] See 'Where to send your SDLT paper work' available at http://www.hmrc.gov.uk/so/mctu.htm

[505] Paragraph 9(3)-(5) Schedule 7

'Relevant associated company', in relation to the acquiring company, means a company that is controlled by the acquiring company immediately before the control of that company changes and of which control changes in consequence of the change of control of that company.

'Arrangements' includes any scheme, agreement or understanding, whether or not legally enforceable.

'Control' is construed in accordance with section 416 ICTA 1988.

3.5.5. Clawed-back reconstruction relief – recovery from third parties

(Paragraphs 12 and 13 Schedule 7)

Once the SDLT due as a result of a withdrawal of relief has been finally determined, liability to pay the tax is the responsibility of the acquiring company.

Where that SDLT (or any part of it) has not been paid within a period of six months of the date on which it became payable, recovery of the unpaid amount is possible from other persons.

The persons from whom the SDLT may be recovered are:

(1) any company which at any relevant time was a member of the same group as the acquiring company and was above it in the group structure; and
(2) any person who at any relevant time was a controlling director of the acquiring company or of a company having control of the acquiring company.

'Any relevant time' means any time between the effective date of the relevant transaction and the date of change of control by virtue of which tax is chargeable.

'A company ('company A') is above another company ('company B') in a group structure if company B (or another company that is above company B in the group structure) is a 75% subsidiary of company A.

'Director' has the meaning given by section 67(1) ITEPA 2003 and includes any person falling within section 417(5) ICTA 1988.

'Controlling director' means a director of the company who has control of the company in accordance with section 416 ICTA 1988.

To enable such a recovery, a notice must be served on the person from whom the SDLT is to be recovered. The requirements are the same as for group relief (see 3.4 above).

3.5.6. Assignment of exempt lease[506]

If the grant of a lease is exempt from charge as a result of reconstruction relief then the first assignment of that lease that is not itself exempt from charge under any of the specified provisions[507] is treated for SDLT purposes as a chargeable transaction comprising the notional grant of a new lease by the assignor (unless the assignee acquires the lease as bare trustee of the assignor).[508]

The grant is treated as being for a term equal to the unexpired term of the actual lease, and on the same terms as those on which the assignee holds that lease after the assignment.

The provision does not apply where the relief in question is reconstruction relief and the relief is withdrawn as a result of a disqualifying event occurring before the effective date of the assignment of the original lease.

3.6. Acquisition relief

(Section 62 and paragraph 8 and Part 2 Schedule 7)

The stamp duty relief in section 76 FA 1986 is carried over in amended form for SDLT purposes in Part 2 of Schedule 7. Paragraph 8 of Schedule 7 provides that where a company (the 'acquiring company') acquires the whole or part of the undertaking of another company (the 'target company') and four conditions are met, the rate of tax chargeable on a land transaction entered into for the purposes of or in connection with the transfer of the undertaking or part of the undertaking is limited to 0.5%.

3.6.1. The four conditions for SDLT acquisition relief

(Paragraph 8 Schedule 7)

The first condition for acquisition relief is that the consideration for the acquisition consists wholly or partly of the issue of non-redeemable shares in the acquiring company to the target company or to all or any of the target company's shareholders.

---

[506] Paragraph 11 Schedule 17A

[507] The specified provisions are:
(*a*) section 57A (sale and leaseback relief);
(*b*) Part 1 or 2 Schedule 7 (group relief or reconstruction or acquisition relief);
(*c*) section 66 (transfers involving public bodies);
(*d*) Schedule 8 (charities relief)
(*e*) any such regulations as are mentioned in section 123(3) (regulations reproducing in relation to SDLT the effect of enactments providing for exemption from stamp duty).

[508] Paragraph 11 Schedule 17A as re-enacted in amended form by Part 2 Schedule 39 to FA 2004 with effect for transactions with an effective date on or after 22 July 2004.

Where the consideration for the acquisition consists partly of the issue of non-redeemable shares, the first condition is met only if the rest of the consideration consists wholly of cash not exceeding 10% of the nominal value of the non-redeemable shares issued as consideration or the assumption or discharge by the acquiring company of liabilities of the target company or both.

'Cash' means a sum paid at the time of the transaction - deferred payment will give rise to a debt and will prevent relief.

This condition means that the relief is only available where the acquiring company has a share capital but identity of shareholders is not required.

The second condition for acquisition relief is that the acquiring company is not 'associated' with another company that is a party to arrangements with the target company relating to shares of the acquiring company issued in connection with the transfer of the undertaking or part. This is an anti-avoidance provision intended to ensure that the issue of shares is not used as a device to disguise what is, in effect, a sale of land for cash.

A unit trust is not treated as a company for this purpose (section 101(7).

The third condition for acquisition relief (in paragraph 8(5A) Schedule 7)[509] is that the undertaking or part acquired has as its main activity the carrying on of a trade that does not consist wholly or mainly of 'dealing in chargeable interests.' This means that neither a property-dealing trade nor a property investment business will qualify for the relief.

The fourth condition for acquisition relief (in paragraph 8(5B) Schedule 7)[510] is that the acquisition of the undertaking (or part) is:

(1) effected for bona fide commercial reasons; and
(2) does not form part of 'arrangements' of which the main purpose or one of the main purposes is the avoidance of SDLT, stamp duty, corporation tax, income tax or capital gains tax.[511]

Relevant definitions

Companies are 'associated' if one has control of the other or both are controlled by the same person or persons.

---

[509] Inserted by paragraph 8 Schedule 10 F(No. 2)A 2005 for transactions with an effective date on or after 20 May 2005 subject to transitional relief in paragraph 16(7) Schedule 10.

[510] Inserted by paragraph 20 Schedule 10 F(No. 2)A 2005 for transactions with an effective date on or after 20 July 2005 subject to transitional relief in paragraph 22 Schedule 10.

[511] VAT and inheritance tax are not in the list.

'Arrangements' include` any scheme, agreement or understanding, whether or not legally enforceable.

'Control' is construed in accordance with section 416 ICTA 1988.

'Trade' has the same meaning as in ICTA 1988.[512] This is not particularly helpful as there is no definition of 'trade' in ICTA 1988 and the meaning depends to a large extent on case law which has identified the so-called 'badges of trade'.

3.6.2. Claiming acquisition relief

Relief is claimed by completing the land transaction return (form SDLT1), checking Box 9 to show that a relief is being claimed and inserting code 14.

3.6.3. Clawback of acquisition relief

The provisions of paragraph 9 apply in the same way as they do for reconstruction relief. These are summarised at 3.5 above. Where the clawback applies, a further land transaction return must be delivered by the acquiring company as purchaser within 30 days of the disqualifying event.[513] This return is not yet available from HMRC and, in the meantime, full details of the event requiring the return should be forwarded in a letter to Birmingham Stamp Office, attaching a copy of the original land transaction return and the appropriate payment[514].

3.6.4. Clawed-back acquisition relief – recovery from third parties

Once the SDLT due as a result of a withdrawal of relief has been finally determined, liability to pay the tax is the responsibility of the acquiring company.

Where such tax (or any part of it) has not been paid within a period of six months of the date on which it became payable, recovery of the unpaid amount is possible from other persons. The same provisions apply to enable that recovery as apply for reconstruction relief (see section 3.5 above).

3.6.5. Assignment of exempt lease[515]

If the grant of a lease is exempt from charge as a result of acquisition relief then the first assignment of that lease that is not itself exempt from charge under any of the specified provisions[516] is treated for SDLT purposes as a chargeable

---

[512] Paragraph 8(5A) Schedule 7

[513] Section 81

[514] See 'Where to send your SDLT paper work' available at http://www.hmrc.gov.uk/so/mctu.htm

[515] Paragraph 11 Schedule 17A

[516] The specified provisions are:

transaction comprising the notional grant of a new lease by the assignor (unless the assignee acquires the lease as bare trustee of the assignor).[517]

The grant is treated as being for a term equal to the unexpired term of the actual lease, and on the same terms as those on which the assignee holds that lease after the assignment.

The provision does not apply where the relief in question is acquisition relief and the relief is withdrawn as a result of a disqualifying event occurring before the effective date of the assignment of the original lease, since in that situation there would be clawback of the original relief.

3.7. Charities relief

(Section 68 and Schedule 8 as amended)[518]

A land transaction is exempt from charge where the purchaser is a charity and two conditions are met at the effective date of the transaction. The conditions are:

(1) At the effective date the charity must intend to hold the land which is the subject matter of the transaction for 'qualifying charitable purposes' - that is for use in furtherance of the purposes of the charity or of another charity, or as an investment the profits of which will be applied to the charitable purposes of the acquiring charity.[519] Intention is a question of fact.

(2) The transaction must not have been entered into for the purpose of avoiding SDLT (whether by the purchaser or anyone else).

'Charity' is defined as a body or trust established for charitable purposes only.[520] This follows the general law meaning. HMRC regard the relief as restricted to bodies constituted under the laws of the UK.[521]

(*a*) section 57A (sale and leaseback relief);

(*b*) Part 1 or 2 Schedule 7 (group relief or reconstruction or acquisition relief);

(*c*) section 66 (transfers involving public bodies);

(*d*) Schedule 8 (charities relief);

(*e*) any such regulations as are mentioned in section 123(3) (regulations reproducing in relation to SDLT the effect of enactments providing for exemption from stamp duty).

[517] Paragraph 11 Schedule 17A as re-enacted in amended form by Part 2 Schedule 39 to FA 2004 with effect for transactions with an effective date on or after 22 July 2004.

[518] Amendments made by section 302 FA 2004 in relation to any transaction the effective date of which is on or after 22 July 2004.

[519] For stamp duty purposes, a charity did not need to hold the property for charitable purposes to obtain relief.

[520] Paragraph 1(4) Schedule 8

[521] SDLTM26010

Amendments made by FA 2004 dealt with cases where the charity does not hold the whole of the relevant land for qualifying charitable purposes (see below) and extended the relief to charitable trusts (as defined in paragraph 4 Schedule 8).[522] If a charitable trust claims charities relief then the same two tests set out above must be met.

Charities relief also applies to the transfer of an interest in a partnership that is a chargeable transaction by virtue of paragraph 14 or 17 Schedule 15 with the modifications set out in paragraph 28 of Schedule 15.

3.7.1. Partial relief

Paragraph 3 Schedule 8 provides that where a land transaction is not exempt from charge because the first condition for charities relief is not met, but the purchaser intends to hold the 'greater part' of the subject-matter of the transaction for qualifying charitable purposes, the land transaction is exempt from charge. If the intention relates to less than the 'greater part' no relief is available.

'Greater part' is interpreted by HMRC by reference to the value of the interest acquired, rather than area and is equated to 51% or more by value.[523]

A lease is granted 'at a premium' if there is consideration other than rent, and a lease is a 'low-rental' lease if the annual rent (if any) does not exceed £600 a year.

3.7.2. Claiming charities relief

Relief is claimed by completing the land transaction return (form SDLT1), checking Box 9 to show that a relief is being claimed and inserting code 20. The charities registration number which should be entered should be that of the charity which is the purchaser.

Example:

A charity takes a lease with a provision for a rent review within the first five years. Charities relief applies. An SDLT1 must be submitted, in which the charity will claim exemption. An NPV calculation (including a reasonable estimate of the rent after the rent review) is required to be included in the SDLT1, notwithstanding that charities relief applies. Once the rent review has actually taken place, the charity needs to submit a further SDLT1 reflecting the actual rather than the estimated figures for rent, again claiming relief.

[522] For these purposes a charitable trust is a trust of which all the beneficiaries are charities or a unit trust scheme in which all the unit holders are charities.

[523] See SDLTM26030 and Example 3 at SDLTM26030a.

3.7.3. Clawback of charities relief

If within three years of the effective date of the land transaction (or as a result of arrangements made before the end of that period) the charity ceases to be established for charitable purposes only or the land or any interest or right derived from it ceases to be held or used for charitable purposes then the relief or an appropriate proportion of it is withdrawn. These occurrences are referred to in the legislation as 'disqualifying events'.

Where partial relief has been claimed there are two further disqualifying events. These events are:

(1) any transfer of a 'major interest'[524] in the whole or any part of the subject-matter of the transaction, or

(2) any grant of a low-rental lease of the whole or any part of that subject-matter at a premium,

which, in either case, is not made in furtherance of the charitable purposes of the charity. The date of the disqualifying event is the effective date of the transaction.

At the time of the disqualifying event the purchasing charity must hold a chargeable interest that was acquired under the relevant land transaction, or which derives from it. In the case of partial relief, the charity must hold such an interest immediately before the disqualifying event.

Where the clawback applies, SDLT is chargeable on the amount that would have been chargeable in respect of the original transaction but for charities relief or an appropriate proportion of it. A further land transaction return must be delivered within 30 days of the disqualifying event.[525] This return is not yet available from HMRC and, in the meantime, full details of the event requiring the return should be forwarded in a letter to Birmingham Stamp Office, attaching a copy of the original land transaction return and the appropriate payment[526].

Where full relief was given, an 'appropriate proportion' means an appropriate proportion having regard to what the purchaser acquired under the relevant transaction and what the purchaser holds at the time of the disqualifying event, and the extent to which what the purchaser holds at that time is used or held for purposes other than qualifying charitable purposes.

---

[524] Defined in section 117(2) (in relation to England and Wales) as a fee simple absolute or a term of years absolute at law or in equity. The definitions applying to Scotland and Northern Ireland are in section 117(3) and (4) respectively.

[525] Section 81

[526] See 'Where to send your SDLT paper work' available at http://www.hmrc.gov.uk/so/mctu.htm

In the case of partial relief, an 'appropriate proportion' means an appropriate proportion having regard to what the purchaser acquired under the relevant transaction and what the purchaser holds immediately before and immediately after the disqualifying event.

3.7.4. Assignment of exempt lease[527]

If the grant of a lease is exempt from charge as a result of charities relief then the first assignment of that lease that is not exempt from charge under any of the specified provisions[528] is treated for SDLT purposes as if it were the grant of a new lease by the assignor (unless the assignee acquires the lease as bare trustee of the assignor). This rule is not subject to a time limit.

The deemed grant is treated as being for a term equal to the unexpired term of the original lease, and on the same terms as those on which the assignee holds that lease after the assignment.

The provision does not apply where the relief in question is charities relief and the relief is withdrawn as a result of a disqualifying event occurring before the effective date of the assignment of the lease which qualified for relief, since in that situation there would already have been a clawback of the original relief.

3.8. Relief for certain residential property

(Section 58A and Schedule 6A[529])

The relief for acquisitions of residential property applies in six situations:

(1) the acquisition by a house-building company of an individual's old dwelling in consideration (wholly or partly) of the acquisition by that individual of a new dwelling from the house-building company ('new home – part exchange');

---

[527] Paragraph 11 Schedule 17A as re-enacted in amended form by Part 2 Schedule 39 to FA 2004 with effect for transactions with an effective date on or after 22 July 2004.

[528] The specified provisions are:
(*a*) section 57A (sale and leaseback relief);
(*b*) Part 1 or 2 Schedule 7 (group relief or reconstruction or acquisition relief);
(*c*) section 66 (transfers involving public bodies);
(*d*) Schedule 8 (charities relief)
(*e*) any such regulations as are mentioned in section 123(3) (regulations reproducing in relation to SDLT the effect of enactments providing for exemption from stamp duty).

[529] Substituted for sections 58 and 59 as originally enacted by paragraph 3 of the Schedule to the Stamp Duty and Stamp Duty Land Tax (Variation of the Finance Act 2003) (No.2) Regulations 2003 (SI 2003/2816) with effect from 1 December 2003. The Stamp Duty and Stamp Duty Land Tax (Variation of the Finance Act 2003) (No.2) Regulations 2003 were revoked by paragraph 14(2) Schedule 39 FA 2004 and in this respect replaced in amended form by paragraph 17 Schedule 39 with effect for any transaction of which the effective date is on or after 22 July 2004.

(2) the acquisition by a property trader of an individual's old dwelling where that individual acquires a new dwelling from a property trader, where the property trader is in business to make such acquisitions ('new home – part exchange');
(3) the acquisition by a property trader of property from personal representatives, where the property trader is in business to make such acquisitions;
(4) the acquisition by a property trader, in business to make such acquisitions, of an individual's old dwelling where the individual has made arrangements to sell the old dwelling and acquire a new one, where the arrangements to sell the old dwelling fail ('chain breaking');
(5) the acquisition by an individual's employer of the individual's dwelling in connection with a change of residence by the individual resulting from relocation of employment; ('employee relocations')
(6) the acquisition by a property trader of an individual's dwelling in connection with a change of residence by the individual resulting from relocation of employment, where the property trader is in business to make such acquisitions ('employee relocations').

There are two conditions that apply for all six Schedule 6A reliefs:
(1) the individual(s) (or the deceased individual in the case of an acquisition from personal representatives) must have occupied the dwelling which is being disposed of as his only or main residence at some time in the period of two years ending with the date of its acquisition by the house-building company or property trader (or ending with the date of the individual's death in the case of an acquisition from personal representatives); and
(2) the area of land acquired by the house-building company or property trader does not exceed the 'permitted area.'

The first condition may cause problems as the purchaser (who is claiming the relief) will not be in a position to know with certainty whether it has been fulfilled and will have to rely on information provided by the vendor.

Where all the other conditions for relief are fulfilled but the area of land acquired by the house-building company or property trader exceeds the permitted area, the chargeable consideration for the acquisition is the amount calculated by deducting the market value of the permitted area from the market value of the old dwelling.

In addition, there are conditions which are specific to each of the reliefs and these are described below.

Four of the six Schedule 6A reliefs are subject to clawback:

3.8.1. New home part-exchanges

Acquisition by house-builder[530]

Where a 'dwelling' ('the old dwelling') is acquired by a 'house-building company' from an individual (whether alone or with other individuals), that acquisition is exempt from the charge to SDLT provided that the three additional conditions set out below are met.

The additional conditions are that:

(1) the individual (whether alone or with other individuals) acquires a 'new dwelling' from the house-building company;
(2) the individual intends to occupy the new dwelling as his only or main residence; and
(3) each acquisition is entered into in consideration of the other.

Relief is claimed by completing the land transaction return (form SDLT1), checking Box 9 to show that a relief is being claimed and inserting code 08 (part-exchange (house building company)).

The company's CIS (Construction Industry Scheme) reference number should be included in the space provided in Box 9. The CIS gives a registered subcontractor s unique taxpayer reference.

Acquisition by property trader[531]

Where a 'dwelling' ('the old dwelling') is acquired by a 'property trader' from an individual (whether alone or with other individuals), that acquisition is exempt from the charge to SDLT provided that the four additional conditions set out below are met.

The additional conditions are that:

(1) the acquisition is made in the course of a business that consists of or includes acquiring dwellings from individuals who acquire 'new dwellings' from 'house- building companies';
(2) the individual (whether alone or with other individuals) acquires a new dwelling from a house-building company;
(3) the individual intends to occupy the new dwelling as his only or main residence; and
(4) the property trader does not intend:
    a. to spend more than the 'permitted amount' on 'refurbishment' of the old dwelling, or

---

[530] Paragraph 1 Schedule 6A

[531] Paragraph 2 Schedule 6A

b. to grant a lease or licence of the old dwelling (other than the grant of a licence to the individual for a period of no more than six months)[532] or
c. to permit any of its 'principals' or employees (or any person 'connected' with any of its principals or employees) to occupy the old dwelling.

Relief under paragraph 2 is withdrawn[533] if the property trader:
(1) spends more than the permitted amount on refurbishment of the old dwelling, or
(2) grants a lease or licence of the old dwelling (other than the grant of a lease or licence to the individual for a period of no more than six months),[534] or
(3) permits any of its principals or employees (or any person connected with any of its principals or employees) to occupy the old dwelling.

The amount of tax chargeable is the amount that would have been chargeable in respect of the acquisition but for the relief.

Where relief is withdrawn the property trader must deliver a further return before the end of the period of 30 days beginning on the date on which the disqualifying event occurred.[535] This return is not yet available from HMRC and, in the meantime, full details of the event requiring the return should be forwarded in a letter to Birmingham Stamp Office, attaching a copy of the original land transaction return and the appropriate payment[536].

3.8.2. Sale by personal representatives[537]

Where a 'dwelling' is acquired by a property trader from the personal representatives of a deceased individual, that acquisition is exempt from the charge to SDLT provided that the two additional conditions set out below are met.

The additional conditions are that:
(1) the acquisition is made in the course of a business that consists of or includes acquiring dwellings from personal representatives of deceased individuals; and
(2) the property trader does not intend:

---

[532] This provision was amended when Schedule 6A was re-enacted by FA 2004.

[533] Paragraph 11 Schedule 6A

[534] This provision was amended when Schedule 6A was re-enacted by FA 2004.

[535] Section 81

[536] See 'Where to send your SDLT paper work' available at http://www.hmrc.gov.uk/so/mctu.htm

[537] Paragraph 3 Schedule 6A.

a. to spend more than the 'permitted amount on 'refurbishment' of the dwelling; or
b. to grant a lease or licence of the dwelling; or
c. to permit any of its 'principals' or employees (or any person 'connected' with any of its principals or employees) to occupy the dwelling.

Clawback of the relief [538]

Relief under paragraph 3 Schedule 6A is withdrawn if the property trader:
(1) spends more than the permitted amount on refurbishment of the dwelling; or
(2) grants a lease or licence of the dwelling; or
(3) permits any of its principals or employees (or any person connected with any of its principals or employees) to occupy the dwelling.

The amount of tax chargeable is the amount that would have been chargeable in respect of the acquisition but for the relief.

Where relief is withdrawn the property trader must deliver a further return before the end of the period of 30 days after the date on which the disqualifying event occurred.[539]

3.8.3. Chain breaking transactions[540]

Where a 'dwelling' ('the old dwelling') is acquired by a 'property trader' from an individual (whether alone or with other individuals), that acquisition is exempt from the charge to SDLT provided that the six additional conditions set out below are met.

The additional conditions are that:
(1) the individual has made arrangements to sell a dwelling ('the old dwelling') and acquire another dwelling ('the second dwelling');
(2) the arrangements to sell the old dwelling fail; and
(3) the acquisition of the old dwelling is made for the purpose of enabling the individual's acquisition of the second dwelling to proceed;
(4) the acquisition is made in the course of a business that consists of or includes acquiring dwellings from individuals in those circumstances;
(5) the individual intends to occupy the second dwelling as his only or main residence;
(6) the property trader does not intend:

---

[538] Paragraph 11 Schedule 6A

[539] Section 81

[540] Paragraph 4 Schedule 6A

a. to spend more than the 'permitted amount' on 'refurbishment' of the old dwelling, or
b. to grant a lease or licence of the old dwelling (other than the grant of a licence to the individual for a period of no more than six months),[541] or
c. to permit any of its 'principals' or employees (or any person 'connected' with any of its principals or employees) to occupy the old dwelling.

Clawback of the relief[542]

Relief under paragraph 4 Schedule 6A is withdrawn if the property trader:

(1) spends more than the permitted amount on refurbishment of the old dwelling, or
(2) grants a lease or licence of the old dwelling other than the grant of a lease or licence to the individual for a period of no more than six months,[543] or
(3) permits any of its principals or employees (or any person connected with any of its principals or employees) to occupy the old dwelling.

The amount of tax chargeable is the amount that would have been chargeable in respect of the acquisition but for the relief.

Where relief is withdrawn the property trader must deliver a further return before the end of the period of 30 days after the date on which the disqualifying event occurred.[544]

3.8.4. Employee relocations[545]

Acquisition by employer

Where a 'dwelling' is acquired from an individual (whether alone or with other individuals) by his 'employer', that acquisition is exempt from the charge to SDLT provided that the two additional conditions set out below are met.

The additional conditions are that:

(1) the acquisition is made in connection with a change of residence by the individual 'resulting from' 'relocation of employment'; and
(2) the consideration for the acquisition does not exceed the market value of the dwelling.

---

541 This provision was amended when Schedule 6A was re-enacted by FA 2004

542 Paragraph 11 Schedule 6A

543 See footnote 532

544 Section 81

545 Paragraph 5 Schedule 6A

Acquisition by property trader [546]

Where a 'dwelling' is acquired by a 'property trader' from an individual (whether alone or with other individuals), that acquisition is exempt from the charge to SDLT provided that the four additional conditions set out below are met.

The additional conditions are that:

(1) the acquisition is made in the course of a business that consists of or includes acquiring dwellings from individuals in connection with a change of residence 'resulting from' 'relocation of employment';

(2) the acquisition is made in connection with a change of residence by the individual resulting from relocation of employment;

(3) the consideration for the acquisition does not exceed the market value of the dwelling; and

(4) the property trader does not intend:

    a. to spend more than the 'permitted amount' on 'refurbishment' of the dwelling; or

    b. to grant a lease or licence of the dwelling (other than the grant of a lease or licence to the individual for a period of no more than six months);[547] or

    c. to permit any of its 'principals' or employees (or any person 'connected' with any of its principals or employees) to occupy the dwelling.

Clawback of the relief [548]

Relief under paragraph 6 Schedule 6A is withdrawn if the property trader:

(1) spends more than the permitted amount on refurbishment of the dwelling; or

(2) grants a lease or licence of the dwelling (other than the grant of a lease or licence to the individual for a period of no more than six months);[549] or

(3) permits any of its principals or employees (or any person connected with any of its principals or employees) to occupy the dwelling.

The amount of tax chargeable is the amount that would have been chargeable in respect of the acquisition but for the relief.

Where relief is withdrawn the property trader must deliver a further return before the end of the period of 30 days after the date on which the disqualifying event occurred.[550]

---

[546] Paragraph 6 Schedule 6A

[547] This provision was amended when Schedule 6A was re-enacted by FA 2004.

[548] Paragraph 11 Schedule 6A

[549] See footnote 532

[550] Section 81

Relevant definitions

'Connected' has the meaning given by section 839 ICTA 1988.[551]

'Dwelling' includes land occupied and enjoyed with the dwelling as its garden or grounds.

A building or part of a building is a 'new dwelling' if:
(1) it has been constructed for use as a single dwelling and has not previously been occupied, or
(2) it has been adapted for use as a single dwelling and has not been occupied since its adaptation.

A 'house-building company' means a company that carries on the business of constructing or adapting buildings or parts of buildings for use as 'dwellings'. References to such a company include any company connected with it.

'The 'permitted area', in relation to a dwelling, means land occupied and enjoyed with the dwelling as its garden or grounds that does not exceed:
(1) an area (inclusive of the site of the dwelling) of 0.5 of a hectare, or
(2) such larger area as is required for the reasonable enjoyment of the dwelling as a dwelling having regard to its size and character, in which case the permitted area is taken to consist of that part of the land that would be the most suitable for occupation and enjoyment with the dwelling as its garden or grounds if the rest of the land were separately occupied.

A 'property trader' means:
(1) a company,
(2) a limited liability partnership, or
(3) a partnership whose members are all either companies or limited liability partnerships, that carries on the business of buying and selling dwellings.

In relation to a property trader a 'principal' means:
(1) in the case of a company, a director;
(2) in the case of a limited liability partnership, a member;
(3) in the case of a partnership whose members are all either companies or limited liability partnerships, a member or a person who is a principal of a member.

'The permitted amount', in relation to the 'refurbishment' of a dwelling, is:
(1) £10,000, or
(2) 5% of the consideration for the acquisition of the dwelling, whichever is the greater, but subject to a maximum of £20,000.

---

[551] This provision is set out in full in the Glossary in Part Five.

'Refurbishment' of a dwelling means the carrying out of works that enhance or are intended to enhance the value of the dwelling, but does not include:

(1) cleaning the dwelling, or
(2) works required solely for the purpose of ensuring that the dwelling meets minimum safety standards.

'Relocation of employment' means a change of the individual's place of employment due to:

(1) his becoming an employee of the employer, or (in the case of paragraph 6 Schedule 6A) of a new employer;
(2) an alteration of the duties of his employment (with the employer, in the case of paragraph 5 Schedule 6A); or
(3) an alteration of the place where he normally performs those duties.

A change of residence is one 'resulting from' relocation of employment if:

(1) the change is made wholly or mainly to allow the individual to have his residence within a reasonable daily travelling distance of his new place of employment, and
(2) his former residence is not within a reasonable daily travelling distance of that place.

The individual's 'new place of employment' means the place where he normally performs, or is normally to perform, the duties of his employment after the relocation.

For the purposes Schedule 6A anything done by or in relation to a company connected with a property trader is treated as done by or in relation to that property trader, and references to the principals or employees of a property trader include the principals or employees of any such company.

References to the acquisition of the new dwelling are to the acquisition, by way of grant or transfer, of a 'major interest'[552] in the dwelling.

References to the acquisition of the old dwelling are to the acquisition, by way of transfer, of a major interest in the dwelling.

References to the acquisition of the dwelling are to the acquisition, by way of transfer, of a major interest in the dwelling.

References to an individual's employer include a prospective employer.

---

[552] Defined in section 117(2) (in relation to England and Wales) as a fee simple absolute or a term of years absolute at law or in equity. The definitions applying to Scotland and Northern Ireland are in section 117(3) and (4) respectively.

References to the market value of the dwelling, the old dwelling or the new dwelling and to the market value of the permitted area are to the market value of that major interest in that dwelling and of that interest so far as it relates to that area.

Claiming the relief

Relief is claimed by completing the land transaction return (form SDLT1), checking Box 9 to show that a relief is being claimed and inserting code 09 (re-location of employment).

3.9. Relief for compulsory purchases facilitating development

(Section 60)

A compulsory purchase facilitating development is exempt from SDLT. This relief is designed to relieve developers from a potential double charge where they acquire land by way of a compulsory purchase from the original owner via a local authority.

'Compulsory purchase facilitating development' means:

- in relation to England and Wales or Scotland, the acquisition by a person of a chargeable interest in respect of which that person has made a compulsory purchase order for the purpose of facilitating development by another person;
- in relation to Northern Ireland, the acquisition by a person of a chargeable interest by means of a vesting order made for the purpose of facilitating development by a person other than the person who acquires the interest.

As there are two purchases, one from the owner by the local authority and one from the local authority by the developer, there would normally be two SDLT charges. The local authority would usually pass its tax charge on to the developer and, hence, the developer would be subject to a double charge. By claiming the relief under section 60, the local authority relieves itself of the first SDLT charge and does not need to pass it on to the developer.

For the purposes of the relief it does not matter how the acquisition is effected and relief therefore applies where the acquisition is effected by agreement.

The relief is only available where a party other than a local authority develops the land. If the developer is the local authority, there is no need for relief as there is no double charge.

3.9.1. Relevant definitions

'Vesting order' means an order made under any statutory provision to authorise the acquisition of land otherwise than by agreement or by order.[553]

'Development' in England and Wales has the same meaning as section 55 Town and Country Planning Act 1990; in Scotland, it has the same meaning as section 26 of the Town and Country Planning (Scotland) Act 1997; and in Northern Ireland, has the same meaning as in article 11 of the Planning (Northern Ireland) Order 1991.[554]

3.9.2. Claiming the relief

Relief is claimed by completing the land transaction return (form SDLT1), checking Box 9 to show that a relief is being claimed and inserting code 10.

3.10. Relief for land transactions entered into in fulfilment of planning obligations by a public authority or developer

(Section 61)

A land transaction that is entered into in order to comply with a planning obligation or a modification of a planning obligation is exempt provided that:

(1) the planning obligation or modification is enforceable against the vendor, and
(2) the purchaser is a public authority, and
(3) the transaction takes place within the period of five years beginning with the date on which the planning obligation was entered into or modified.

This relieves defined classes of public authorities from having to pay SDLT in these circumstances.

3.10.1. Relevant definitions

In relation to England and Wales 'planning obligation' means either of the following:

(1) a planning obligation within the meaning of section 106 of the Town and Country Planning Act 1990 that is entered into in accordance with subsection (9) of that section; or
(2) a planning obligation within the meaning of section 299A of that Act that is entered into in accordance with subsection (2) of that section,[555]

---

553 Section 60(4)

554 Section 60(5)

555 Section 61(2)(a)

'Modification' of a planning obligation means modification as mentioned in section 106A(1) of the Town and Country Planning Act 1990.[556]

In relation to Scotland, 'planning obligation' means an agreement made under section 75 or section 246 of the Town and Country Planning (Scotland) Act 1997.[557]

In relation to Northern Ireland 'planning obligation' means a planning agreement within the meaning of article 40 of the Planning (Northern Ireland) Order 1991 that is entered into in accordance with paragraph (10) of that article and 'modification' of a planning obligation means modification as mentioned in article 40A(1) of that Order.[558]

The following are 'public authorities' for the purposes of the exemption:[559]

- A Minister of the Crown or government department, the Scottish Ministers, a Northern Ireland department and the National Assembly for Wales.
- A county or district council constituted under section 2 of the Local Government Act 1972, the council of a London borough, the Common Council of the City of London, the Greater London Authority, Transport for London and the Council of the Isles of Scilly.
- A county or county borough council constituted under section 21 of the Local Government Act 1972.
- A council constituted under section 2 of the Local Government etc (Scotland) Act 1994.
- A district council within the meaning of the Local Government Act (Northern Ireland) 1972.
- A Strategic Health Authority or Health Authority established under section 8 of the National Health Service Act 1977, a Special Health Authority established under section 11 of that Act, a Primary Care Trust established under section 16A of that Act, a Local Health Board established under section 16BA of that Act and a National Health Service Trust established under section 5 of the National Health Service and Community Care Act 1990.
- The Common Services Agency established under section 10(1) of the National Health Service (Scotland) Act 1978, a Health Board established under section 2(1)(a) of that Act, a National Health Service Trust established under section 12A(1) of that Act and a Special Health Board established under section 2(1)(b) of that Act.

---

[556] Ibid

[557] Section 61(2)(b)

[558] Section 61(2)(c)

[559] Section 61(3)

- A Health and Social Services Board established under article 16 of the Health and Personal Social Services (Northern Ireland) Order 1972 (SI 1972/1265 (NI 14)) and a Health and Social Services Trust established under article 10 of the Health and Personal Social Services (Northern Ireland) Order 1991 (SI 1991/194 (NI 1)).
- Any other authority that is a local planning authority within the meaning of the Town and Country Planning Act 1990 or is the authority for any of the purposes of the planning Acts within the meaning of the Town and Country Planning (Scotland) Act 1997.
- A person prescribed by Treasury Order.

Where improvements are carried out to a public highway pursuant to section 278 Highways Act 1980, and the resulting section of highway is transferred to the local planning authority, county council or highways authority, the land transfer will not qualify for relief as it is not done to comply with a planning obligation entered into under section 106 Town and Country Planning Act 1990. The cost of the highway construction works would form part of the chargeable consideration for the land transaction, if the relieving conditions in paragraph 10(2) Schedule 4 FA 2003 are not satisfied.

3.10.2. Claiming the relief

Relief is claimed by completing the land transaction return (form SDLT1), checking Box 9 to show that a relief is being claimed and inserting code 11.

3.11. Demutualisation relief for insurance companies

(Section 63)

A land transaction is exempt from charge if it is entered into for the purposes of or in connection with a qualifying transfer of the whole or part of the business of a mutual insurance company ('the mutual') to a company that has share capital ('the acquiring company'). The relief replicates the relief from stamp duty which existed pursuant to section 96 FA 1997.

A transfer of an insurance business is a qualifying transfer if:

(1) it is a transfer of business consisting of the effecting or carrying out of contracts of insurance and takes place under an insurance business transfer scheme,[560] or

(2) it is a transfer of business of a general insurance company carried on through a permanent establishment in the UK and takes place in accordance with authorisation granted outside the UK for the purposes of article 14 of the Council Directive of 5 November 2002 concerning life

---

[560] As defined in Part 7 Financial Services and Markets Act 2000

assurance[561] or article 12 of the Council Directive of 18 June 1992[562] on the co-ordination of laws, regulations and administrative provisions relating to direct insurance other than life insurance and amending Directives 73/239/EEC and 88/357/EEC

and, in either case, the requirements set out below are met in relation to the shares of a company ('the issuing company') which is either the acquiring company or a company of which the acquiring company is a wholly-owned subsidiary.

In addition, certain of the group relief clawbacks are disapplied where the offending arrangements are for the purpose of facilitating a transfer of the whole or part of the business of a company to another company which is intended to fall within section 96 Finance Act 1997 (stamp duty relief: demutualisation of insurance companies).[563]

3.11.1. Requirements in relation to shares in the issuing company:

Shares in the issuing company must be offered to at least 90% of the persons who are members of the mutual immediately before the transfer.

All of the shares in the issuing company that will be in issue immediately after the transfer has been made, other than shares that are to be or have been issued pursuant to an offer to the public, must be offered to the persons who (at the time of the offer) are:

(1) members of the mutual;
(2) persons who are entitled to become members of the mutual; or
(3) employees, former employees or pensioners of the mutual, or of a wholly-owned subsidiary of the mutual.

The Treasury may by regulations substitute a lower percentage or provide that any or all of the references to members shall be construed as references to members of a class specified in the regulations.[564]

3.11.2. Relevant definitions

(Section 63(6) and 63(7))

A company is the wholly-owned subsidiary of another company ('the parent') if the company has no members except the parent and the parent's wholly-

---

[561] 2002/83/EC (the Life Assurance directive)

[562] 92/49/EEC (the Third Non-Life Assurance directive)

[563] Paragraph 2(3A) Schedule 7 inserted by section 167 FA 2006 with effect in relation to any transfer which took place (or was intended to take place) after 22 March 2006.

[564] Section 63(5) – no such regulations have been made to date.

owned subsidiaries or persons acting on behalf of the parent or the parent's wholly-owned subsidiaries.

'Contract of insurance' has the meaning given by article 3(1) of the Financial Services and Markets Act 2000 (Regulated Activities) Order 2001.[565]

'Employee', in relation to a mutual or its wholly-owned subsidiary, includes any officer or director of the company or subsidiary and any other person taking part in the management of the affairs of the company or subsidiary.

'General insurance company' means a company that has permission under Part 4 of the Financial Services and Markets Act 2000, or paragraph 15 Schedule 3 to that Act (as a result of qualifying for authorisation under paragraph 12(1) of that Schedule), to effect or carry out contracts of insurance.

'Insurance company' means a company that carries on the business of effecting or carrying out contracts of insurance.

'Insurance business transfer scheme' has the same meaning as in Part 7 of the Financial Services and Markets Act 2000.

'Mutual insurance company' means an insurance company carrying on business without having any share capital.

'Pensioner', in relation to a mutual insurance company or its wholly-owned subsidiary, means a person entitled (whether presently or prospectively) to a pension, lump sum, gratuity or other like benefit referable to the service of any person as an employee of the company or subsidiary.

3.11.3. Claiming the relief

Relief is claimed by completing the land transaction return (form SDLT1), checking Box 9 to show that a relief is being claimed and inserting code 15.

3.12. Demutualisation relief for building societies

(Section 64)

A land transaction effected by section 97(6) or (7) of the Building Societies Act 1986 (transfer of building society's business to a commercial company) is exempt from charge. Section 64 is based on section 109 of the Building Societies Act 1986 (which relates to stamp duty) and extends that relief to SDLT.

In addition section 109A(1) Building Societies Act 1986[566] provides that a land transaction effected by or in consequence of:

---

[565] SI 2001/544

(a) an amalgamation of two or more building societies under section 93 Building Societies Act 1986; or

(b) a transfer of engagements between building societies under section 94 Building Societies Act 1986

is exempt from charge for the purposes of SDLT.

3.12.1. Claiming the relief

The relief must be claimed in the land transaction return or an amendment to that return by checking Box 9 to show that a relief is being claimed and inserting code 16.

3.13. Relief for incorporation of limited liability partnership ('LLP')

(Section 65)

This provision is intended to prevent a charge to SDLT arising when a partnership converts into an LLP. It re-enacts in slightly amended form the stamp duty relief in section 12 Limited Liability Partnerships Act 2000. This relief is probably no longer necessary as the application of the rules in Part 3 of Schedule 15[567] (see section (1) below) should result in there being no SDLT charge on a conversion of a land-owning partnership into an LLP provided there is no change in the partners' shares.

Section 65 exempts a land transaction by which a chargeable interest is transferred by a person to an LLP in connection with its incorporation where the following three conditions are met:

(1) the effective date of the transaction is not more than one year after the date of incorporation of the LLP; and

(2) at the 'relevant time' the transferor is a partner in a partnership comprising only persons who are or are to be members of the LLP or is a person who holds the interest transferred as nominee or bare trustee for one or more of the partners in such a partnership; and

(3) either:

   a. the proportions of the interest transferred to which the partners/members are entitled immediately after the transfer to the LLP are the same as those to which they were entitled at the 'relevant time', or

---

[566] Inserted by the regulation 2 of and the Schedule to the Stamp Duty Land Tax (Consequential Amendment of Enactments) Regulations 2003 (SI 2003/2867) with effect from 1 December 2003.

[567] See paragraph 14 of Schedule 15 after amendment by FA 2006 and FA 2007.

b. no difference in those proportions has arisen as part of a scheme or arrangement of which the main purpose, or one of the main purposes, is avoidance of liability to any duty or tax.

Condition (2) prevents the relief applying where two or more partnerships merge to form an LLP.

Condition (3) may cause difficulties where a new partner joins the partnership after the incorporation of the LLP but before the transfer of the interest unless at the 'relevant time' it was not contemplated that the new partner would join the LLP. To avoid any problem with condition (2) it should be ensured that all (and only) the persons who are to be members of the LLP are members of the partnership immediately before the incorporation of the LLP.

3.13.1. Relevant definitions

The 'relevant time' means where the transferor acquired the interest after the incorporation of the LLP, immediately after he acquired it and, in any other case, immediately before the incorporation.[568]

'Limited liability partnership' means an LLP formed under the Limited Liability Partnerships Act 2000 or the Limited Liability Partnerships Act (Northern Ireland) 2002.[569]

3.13.2. Claiming the relief

Relief is claimed by completing the land transaction return (form SDLT1), checking Box 9 to show that a relief is being claimed and inserting code 17.

3.14. Relief for land transfers involving public bodies in the case of a re-organisation under statute

(Section 66)

A land transaction entered into on, or in consequence of, or in connection with, a reorganisation effected by or under a statutory provision is exempt from charge if the purchaser and vendor are both 'public bodies'.

The Treasury may by order provide that a land transaction that is not otherwise exempt but that is entered into by way of such a re-organisation is exempt if the transaction is effected by or under a prescribed statutory provision and either the purchaser or the vendor is a public body.

Orders made to date exempt:

---

568 Section 65(5)

569 Section 65(6)

(1) land transactions which are effected under section 38 of the Energy Act 2004 (nuclear transfer schemes);[570]

(2) land transactions effected under paragraph A23(2), 4(2), 5(4B) or 8(2)(b) of Schedule 22 to the School Standards and Framework Act 1998 (transfer of land to local education authority), and transfers required by virtue of regulations made under section 27(2)(b) of the Education and Inspections Act 2006 (transfer of land on removal of foundation or reduction in foundation governors).[571]

3.14.1. Relevant definitions

A 're-organisation' means changes involving the establishment, reform or abolition of one or more public bodies, the creation, alteration or abolition of functions to be discharged or discharged by one or more public bodies or the transfer of functions from one public body to another.[572]

References to a 'public body' include a company in which all the shares are owned by such a body and a wholly-owned subsidiary of such a company.[573] A 'company' for this purpose is as defined by section 735(1) Companies Act 1985.[574] That definition is more restrictive than the general definition of company for SDLT purposes in section 100(1) as it includes only companies formed under the Companies Acts.

The following are 'public bodies' for the purposes of the exemption:[575]

- A Minister of the Crown, the Scottish Ministers, a Northern Ireland department, the National Assembly for Wales, the Corporate Officer of the House of Lords, the Corporate Officer of the House of Commons, the Scottish Parliamentary Corporate Body and the Northern Ireland Assembly Commission.
- A county or district council constituted under section 2 of the Local Government Act 1972, the council of a London borough, the Greater London Authority, the Common Council of the City of London and the Council of the Isles of Scilly.
- A county or county borough council constituted under section 21 of the Local Government Act 1972.

---

[570] The Finance Act 2003, Section 66 (Prescribed Transactions) Order 2005 (SI 2005/645)

[571] The Finance Act 2003, Section 66 (Prescribed Transactions) Order 2007 (SI 2007/1385)

[572] Section 66(3)

[573] Section 66(5)

[574] Or in Northern Ireland, by article 3(1) Companies (Northern Ireland) Order 1986

[575] Section 66(4)

- A council constituted under section 2 of the Local Government etc (Scotland) Act 1994.
- A district council within the meaning of the Local Government Act (Northern Ireland) 1972.
- A Strategic Health Authority or Health Authority established under section 8 of the National Health Service Act 1977, a Special Health Authority established under section 11 of that Act, a Primary Care Trust established under section 16A of that Act, a Local Health Board established under section 16BA of that Act and an NHS Trust established under section 5 of the National Health Service and Community Care Act 1990.
- The Common Services Agency established under section 10(1) of the National Health Service (Scotland) Act 1978, a Health Board established under section 2(1)(a) of that Act, an NHS Trust established under section 12A(1) of that Act and a Special Health Board established under section 2(1)(b) of that Act.
- A Health and Social Services Board established under article 16 of the Health and Personal Social Services (Northern Ireland) Order 1972[576] and a Health and Social Services Trust established under article 10 of the Health and Personal Social Services (Northern Ireland) Order 1991.[577]
- Any other authority that is a local planning authority within the meaning of the Town and Country Planning Act 1990 or is the planning authority for any of the purposes of the planning Acts within the meaning of the Town and Country Planning (Scotland) Act 1997.
- A body (other than a company) that is established by or under a statutory provision for the purpose of carrying out functions conferred on it by or under a statutory provision.
- Any person prescribed for the purposes of section 66 by Treasury Order.[578]

3.14.2. Claiming the relief

Relief is claimed by completing the land transaction return (form SDLT1), checking Box 9 to show that a relief is being claimed and inserting code 18.

---

[576] SI 1972/1265 (NI 14)

[577] SI 1991/194 (NI 1))

[578] NHS foundation trusts constituted in accordance with Schedule 1 to the Health and Social Care (Community Health and Standards) Act 2003 were prescribed by the Finance Act 2003, Section 66 (Prescribed Persons) Order 2005 (SI 2005/83) with effect from 11 February 2005.

3.14.3. Assignment of exempt lease[579]

If the grant of a lease is exempt from charge as a result of section 66 then the first assignment of that lease that is not itself exempt from charge under any of certain specified provisions[580] is treated for SDLT purposes as a chargeable transaction comprising the grant of a new lease by the assignor (unless the assignee acquires the lease as bare trustee of the assignor).

The grant is treated as being for a term equal to the unexpired term of the actual lease, and on the same terms as those on which the assignee holds that lease after the assignment.

3.15. Relief for local political constituency associations on land transfers made as a result of a parliamentary constituency re-organisation

(Section 67)

Relief from SDLT may be claimed by a new local constituency association where a land transaction is entered into as a consequence of an Order in Council under the Parliamentary Constituencies Act 1986 specifying new parliamentary constituencies and an existing local constituency association transfers a chargeable interest to a new association that is a successor to the existing association or to a related body that as soon as practicable transfers the interest or right to a new association that is a successor to the existing association.

This allows for relief where parliamentary constituencies change and, in consequence of that change, the previous local constituency association transfers a chargeable interest to a new local constituency association. This may be needed, for example, where an old constituency is split into two and two new associations are formed, or where two previous constituencies merge and one is formed.

---

[579] Paragraph 11 Schedule 17A as re-enacted in amended form by Part 2 Schedule 39 to FA 2004 with effect for transactions with an effective date on or after 22 July 2004.

[580] The specified provisions are:

(*a*) section 57A (sale and leaseback relief);

(*b*) Part 1 or 2 Schedule 7 (group relief or reconstruction or acquisition relief);

(*c*) section 66 (transfers involving public bodies);

(*d*) Schedule 8 (charities relief);

(*e*) any such regulations as are mentioned in section 123(3) (regulations reproducing in relation to SDLT the effect of enactments providing for exemption from stamp duty).

The relief also covers those occasions where the chargeable interest is temporarily transferred to a related body before eventual transfer to the new association.

Where an Order in Council is made, the transfer, or each of the transfers, is exempt from charge.

3.15.1. Claiming the relief

Relief is claimed by completing the land transaction return (form SDLT1), checking Box 9 to show that a relief is being claimed and inserting code 19.

3.16. Relief for land transactions involving certain museums and cultural organisations

(Section 69)

A land transaction is exempt from charge if the purchaser is:

- the Historic Buildings and Monuments Commission for England;
- the National Endowment for Science, Technology and the Arts;
- the Trustees of the British Museum;
- the Trustees of the National Heritage Memorial Fund;
- the Trustees of the Natural History Museum.

3.16.1. Claiming the relief

Relief is claimed by completing the land transaction return (form SDLT1), checking Box 9 to show that a relief is being claimed and inserting code 21.

3.17. Relief for right to buy transactions, shared ownership leases, share ownership trusts and related transactions

(Section 70 and Schedule 9)

These provisions can be split into three parts:

- relief for right to buy transactions;
- relief for shared ownership leases; and
- relief for rent to mortgage and rent to loan transactions.

The relief for right to buy transactions works by limiting the consideration for the transaction by disapplying some of the provisions relating to chargeable consideration. Thus the consideration does not include any contingent consideration.

Shared ownership leases involve the granting to the tenant of a long lease for a premium equivalent to the share acquired, with rent payable for the remaining portion. Some schemes allow the tenant to acquire the freehold reversion whilst others only allow a maximum proportion on leasehold. The relief works by giving the tenant the choice between paying SDLT on the separate parts as each is purchased or on what would be payable if the whole property was purchased. The legislation also provides that where SDLT is paid at the outset as if the whole house was purchased no further tax is payable when the freehold is eventually purchased. Thus the tenant can fix the SDLT payable at the outset to that which would be payable if the property was purchased outright rather than paying SDLT on each part that they purchase which may mean that more tax is paid if prices rise or the rates increase.

The reliefs for rent to mortgage(in the UK) and rent to loan transactions (the Scottish equivalent of rent to mortgage) apply to certain purchases under the Housing Act 1985 and the Housing (Scotland) Act 1987 by limiting the SDLT payable to that which would be payable if the chargeable consideration was that calculated under (in England) section 126 of the Housing Act 1985 or (in Scotland) section 62 of the Housing (Scotland) Act 1987, rather than the actual purchase price.

3.17.1. Right to buy[581]

(Paragraph 1 Schedule 9)

In the case of a 'right to buy transaction', paragraph 1 Schedule 9 provides that section 51 (1) does not apply and any consideration that would be payable only if a contingency were to occur, or that is payable only because a contingency has occurred, does not count as chargeable consideration.

A grant under section 20 or 21 of the Housing Act 1996 (purchase grants in respect of disposals at a discount by registered social landlords) does not count as part of the chargeable consideration for a right to buy transaction in relation to which the vendor is a registered social landlord.

3.17.2. Relevant definitions

A 'right to buy transaction' means the sale of a dwelling at a discount, or the grant of a lease of a dwelling at a discount, by a 'relevant public sector body' or the sale of a dwelling, or the grant of a lease of a dwelling, 'in pursuance of the preserved right to buy'.

The following are 'relevant public sector bodies' for this purpose:

- A Minister of the Crown, the Scottish Ministers and a Northern Ireland department.
- A local housing authority within the meaning of the Housing Act 1985, a county council in England, a council constituted under section 2 of the Local Government etc (Scotland) Act 1994, the common good of such a

---

[581] See SDLTM27015

council or any trust under its control and a district council within the meaning of the Local Government Act (Northern Ireland) 1972.

- The Housing Corporation, Scottish Homes, the Northern Ireland Housing Executive, a registered social landlord[582] and a housing action trust established under Part 3 of the Housing Act 1988.
- The Commission for the New Towns, a development corporation established by an order made, or having effect as if made, under the New Towns Act 1981, a development corporation established by an order made, or having effect as if made, under the New Towns (Scotland) Act 1968, a new town commission established under section 7 of the New Towns Act (Northern Ireland) 1965, an urban development corporation established by an order made under section 135 of the Local Government, Planning and Land Act 1980 and the Welsh Development Agency.
- A police authority within the meaning of section 101(1) of the Police Act 1996, a police authority within the meaning of section 2(1) or 19(9)(b) of the Police (Scotland) Act 1967 and the Northern Ireland Policing Board.
- An education and libraries board within the meaning of the Education and Libraries (Northern Ireland) Order 1986[583] the United Kingdom Atomic Energy Authority, any person mentioned in paragraphs (g), (k), (l) or (n) of section 61(11) of the Housing (Scotland) Act 1987 and a body prescribed for these purposes by Treasury order.

The transfer of a dwelling, or the grant of a lease of a dwelling, is made 'in pursuance of the preserved right to buy' if:

- the vendor is, in England and Wales, a person against whom the right to buy under Part 5 of the Housing Act 1985 is exercisable by virtue of section 171A of that Act, or, in Scotland, a person against whom the right to buy under section 61 of the Housing (Scotland) Act 1987 is exercisable by virtue of section 81A of that Act, (which provides for the preservation of the right to buy on disposal to a private sector landlord); and
- the purchaser is the qualifying person for the purposes of the preserved right to buy, and
- the dwelling is the qualifying dwelling house in relation to the purchaser.

3.17.3. Claiming the relief

Relief is claimed by completing the land transaction return (form SDLT1), checking Box 9 to show that a relief is being claimed and inserting code 22.

---

[582] A 'registered social landlord' is defined in section 121

[583] SI 1986/594 (NI 3)

In Box 10 for freeholds or assigned leases and Box 22 and/or 23 for new leases the actual consideration paid by the purchaser should be entered.

The tax payable on this consideration should be entered in Box 14. The market value of the property should not be included anywhere on the form.

3.17.4. Shared ownership leases[584]

Shared ownership leases may be granted either by a 'qualifying body' or 'in pursuance of the preserved right to buy'. They work by granting the tenant a long lease for a premium equivalent to the share acquired, with rent payable for the remaining portion. Some schemes allow the tenant to acquire the freehold reversion whilst others only allow a maximum proportion on leasehold.

The SDLT relief works by giving the tenant the choice between paying SDLT on each separate stage of a phased purchase by reference to the prevailing rates of tax in force at the time, or alternatively, making a market value election and paying tax as if the property had been purchased outright from the beginning.

The legislation also provides that where SDLT is paid at the outset as if the whole interest was purchased no further tax is payable when the freehold is eventually purchased.

For the purposes of the shared ownership leases provisions, 'qualifying body' means:[585]

- a local housing authority within the meaning of the Housing Act 1985

a housing association within the meaning of the Housing Associations Act 1985 or Part 2 of the Housing (Northern Ireland) Order 1992[586]

- a housing action trust established under Part 3 of the Housing Act 1988
- the Northern Ireland Housing Executive
- the Commission for the New Towns
- a development corporation established by an order made, or having effect as if made, under the New Towns Act 1981.

A lease is granted 'in pursuance of the preserved right to buy' if:[587]

(1) the vendor is a person against whom the right to buy under Part 5 of the Housing Act 1985 is exercisable by virtue of section 171A of that Act,

(2) the lessee is, or lessees are, the qualifying person for the purposes of the preserved right to buy, and

---

584 See SDLTM27080

585 Paragraph 5 Schedule 9

586 SI 1992/1725 (NI 15)

587 Paragraph 5 Schedule 9

(3) the lease is of a dwelling that is the qualifying dwelling-house in relation to the purchaser.

3.17.5. Shared ownership lease - election for market value treatment

(Paragraphs 2, 3 and 4A Schedule 9)

Where:

(1) a lease is granted by a 'qualifying body' or 'in pursuance of the preserved right to buy',

(2) certain conditions relating to the lease (set out below) are met, and

(3) the purchaser elects for SDLT to be charged in accordance with paragraph 2 Schedule 9,

then the chargeable consideration for the grant of the lease is treated as the amount stated in the lease as the market value of the dwelling (or the sum calculated by reference to that value) by reference to which the premium is calculated.

Section 118 (meaning of 'market value') does not apply in relation to the 'market value of the dwelling' in this calculation.

The transfer of the reversion to the lessee or lessees under the terms of a lease to which the election applies is exempt from charge if any tax chargeable in respect of the grant of the lease has been paid. The position was summarised in the SDLT Practitioner's Newsletter:[588]

> 'Q8 How is SDLT calculated on the final stages of shared ownership leases?
>
> If a market value election was made under FA 1980 s97 (for leases executed under the stamp duty regime), then the acquisition of the reversion is exempt from charge.
>
> If the lessee chose not to make a market value election, then on the reversion, SDLT will be charged (as before) on the premium paid to secure the reversion. The rate at which this premium will be charged to SDLT will be determined (as before) by aggregating the premium for the lease and any other premiums or capital payments made in consideration of a reduction of the rent.
>
> If after having made a market value election the lessee assigns the lease, then the new lessee (the assignee) will also be able to benefit from the exemption of the reversion should he acquire a full share of the property.'

The conditions which have to be met in relation to the lease are set out in paragraph 2(2) Schedule 9 and are that:

---

[588] Issue 2, 21 July 2004 (HMRC publication)

(a) the lease must be of a dwelling;
(b) the lease must give the lessee or lessees exclusive use of the dwelling;
(c) the lease must provide for the lessee or lessees to acquire the reversion;
(d) the lease must be granted partly in consideration of rent and partly in consideration of a premium calculated by reference to:
    i. the market value of the dwelling, or
    ii. a sum calculated by reference to that value;
(e) the lease must contain a statement of:
    i. the market value of the dwelling, or
    ii. the sum calculated by reference to that value

by reference to which the premium is calculated.

Paragraph 4A was inserted into Schedule 9 by section 303 FA 2004 and applies to acquisitions after 17 March 2004. This provision makes clear that where a shared ownership lease is granted and the lessee or lessees make a market value election under paragraph 2 or paragraph 4 Schedule 9, no further liability to SDLT will arise if the lessee or lessees acquire an additional share of the property (commonly called 'staircasing') at a later date. However, if the lessee staircases to 100%, acquiring the freehold reversion or the full leasehold interest, then this final transaction will be notifiable, even though no further tax is payable.

Section 303(3) FA 2004 (deemed to have come into force on 1 December 2003) ensures that those who were granted a shared ownership lease under the old stamp duty provisions and made a market value election do not become liable to SDLT if they acquire an additional share of their property.

If the lessee decides not to pay by reference to the market value method then intermediate transactions are neither notifiable nor chargeable providing the lessee does not staircase above 80%. However, if the lessee staircases above 80%, or staircases to 100% so acquiring the freehold reversion or full leasehold interest, then such transactions are both notifiable and chargeable.

FA 2007[589] has clarified the SDLT treatment of shared ownership leases to ensure that where a market value election is made the rent payable under the lease is disregarded for all SDLT purposes. The new treatment applies to transactions on or after 19 July 2007.

3.17.6. Claiming the relief

An election for tax to be charged in accordance with this provision must be included in the land transaction return made in respect of the grant of the

---

[589] Section 78 FA 2007 inserting a newparagraph2(4A) in Schedule 9

lease, or in an amendment of that return, and is irrevocable so that the return may not be amended in order to withdraw the election.[590] See examples A to C at SDLTM27080 for detailed guidance on how to complete the land transaction return.

3.17.7. Shared ownership lease - election where staircasing allowed

(Paragraphs 4 and 4A Schedule 9)

Where a lease is granted by a 'qualifying body' or 'in pursuance of the preserved right to buy', certain conditions are met in relation to the lease (see below) and the purchaser elects for tax to be charged in accordance with paragraph 4(3), the rent in consideration of which the lease is granted is taken to be the minimum rent stated in the lease and the chargeable consideration for the grant other than rent is taken to be the amount stated in the lease.

The conditions in relation to the lease are that:

(a) the lease must be of a dwelling;

(b) the lease must give the lessee or lessees exclusive use of the dwelling;

(c) the lease must provide that the lessee or lessees may, on the payment of a sum, require the terms of the lease to be altered so that the rent payable under it is reduced;

(d) the lease must be granted partly in consideration of rent and partly in consideration of a premium calculated by reference to:
   (i) the premium obtainable on the open market for the grant of a lease containing the same terms as the lease but with the substitution of the minimum rent for the rent payable under the lease, or
   (ii) a sum calculated by reference to that premium;

(e) the lease must contain a statement of the minimum rent and:
   (i) the premium obtainable on the open market, or
   (ii) the sum calculated by reference to that premium.

'Minimum rent' means the lowest rent which could become payable under the lease if it were altered as mentioned in (c) at the date when the lease is granted.

Paragraph 4A[591] makes clear that that where a shared ownership lease is granted and the lessee or lessees make a market value election under paragraph 2 or paragraph 4 Schedule 9, no further liability to SDLT will arise if the lessee or lessees acquire an additional share of the property at a later date.

Paragraph 4A also provides for relief from SDLT for certain staircasing transactions (known as 'intermediate staircasing') where the lessee or lessees

---

[590] Paragraph 2(3) Schedule 9

[591] Inserted into Schedule 9 by section 303 FA 2004 and applies to acquisitions after 17 March 2004.

have not made a market value election. The relief is conditional on the share of the dwelling held by the lessee or lessees immediately after the transaction not exceeding 80% and is intended to bring the SDLT relief into line with the reliefs which applied for stamp duty.

Section 303(3) FA 2004 (deemed to have come into force on 1 December 2003) ensures that those who were granted a shared ownership lease under the old stamp duty provisions and made a market value election do not become liable to SDLT if they acquire an additional share of their property.

3.17.8. Claiming the relief

An election for tax to be charged in accordance with this provision must be included in the land transaction return made in respect of the grant of the lease, or in an amendment of that return, and is irrevocable so that the return may not be amended in order to withdraw the election.[592]

3.17.9. Shared ownership leases: Guidance for completing SDLT1

HMRC give detailed guidance at SDLTM27080 (in examples E to I) on how to complete the first two pages of the land transaction return when a shared ownership lease is granted and when a tenant acquires a greater share of the property by staircasing.

3.17.10. Rent to mortgage or rent to loan: chargeable consideration

(Paragraph 6 Schedule 9)

Paragraph 6 provides that the chargeable consideration for a 'rent to mortgage transaction' (defined as the transfer or grant of a lease of a dwelling under Part 5 of the Housing Act 1985) is the price that, by virtue of section 126 of the Housing Act 1985, would be payable for a transfer of the dwelling to the person (where the rent to mortgage transaction is a transfer), or the grant of a lease of the dwelling to the person (where the rent to mortgage transaction is the grant of a lease), if the person were exercising the right to buy under Part 5 of that Act.

The chargeable consideration for a 'rent to loan transaction' is the price that, by virtue of section 62 of the Housing (Scotland) Act 1987, would be payable for the house if the person were exercising the right to purchase under section 61 of that Act.

A 'rent to loan transaction' means the execution of a heritable disposition in favour of a person pursuant to the exercise by that person of the right to

---

[592] Paragraph 4(3) Schedule 9

purchase a house by way of the rent to loan scheme in Part 3 of the Housing (Scotland) Act 1987.

3.17.11. Relief for shared ownership trusts[593]

Legislation in FA 2007 extended the same SDLT reliefs to shared ownership trusts as were available for shared ownership leases. The relief applies to all transactions involving shared ownership trusts provided by qualifying bodies the effective date of which is on or after 19 July 2007.

Shared ownership trusts have developed out of an interest in trying to use commonhold as a way of providing affordable housing. Commonhold is an alternative to leaseholds and has come into existence recently following the Commonhold and Leasehold Reform Act 2002.

As shared ownership leases are not feasible for commonholds a new structure (shared ownership trusts) has been developed to make commonholds attractive to those seeking affordable housing. With a shared ownership trust legal ownership is vested in trustees. There is a declaration of trust which gives the purchaser a share in the property, and the exclusive right to occupy the property in return for making regular payments in relation to that share of the property he does not owned. The purchaser can staircase up (make capital payments to increase their share) and so reduce their regular payments or in certain circumstances staircase down to full rent.

'Qualifying body' has the same meaning as for shared ownership leases[594].

3.18. Relief for certain acquisitions by a registered social landlord

(Section 71)

A land transaction under which the purchaser is a 'registered social landlord' is exempt if:

(1) the registered social landlord is 'controlled by its tenants',
(2) the vendor is a 'qualifying body'; or
(3) the transaction is funded with the assistance of a public subsidy.

Many registered social landlords are charities and may also be eligible for charities relief. However, relief under section 71 is preferable as it is not subject to clawback.

---

593 Paragraphs 7 to 11 of Schedule 9 introduced by section 77 FA 2007 with effect from 19 July 2007.

594 Defined in paragraph 5(2) Schedule 9 - see 3.17.4 above.

3.18.1. Relevant definitions

A 'registered social landlord' means:[595]

- in relation to England and Wales, a body registered as a social landlord in a register maintained under section 1(1) Housing Act 1996;
- in relation to Scotland, a body registered in the register maintained under section 57 Housing (Scotland) Act 2001;
- in relation to Northern Ireland, a housing association registered in the register maintained under Article 14 Housing (Northern Ireland) Order 1992.[596]

A registered social landlord is 'controlled by its tenants' if the majority of the 'board members' of the registered social landlord are tenants occupying properties owned or managed by it.[597]

'Board member', in relation to a registered social landlord, means:[598]

- if it is a company, a director of the company,
- if it is a body corporate whose affairs are managed by its members, a member,
- if it is body of trustees, a trustee, or
- otherwise, a member of the committee of management or other body to which is entrusted the direction of the affairs of the registered social landlord.

'Qualifying body' means:[599]

- a registered social landlord
- a housing action trust established under Part 3 of the Housing Act 1988
- a principal council within the meaning of the Local Government Act 1972
- the Common Council of the City of London
- the Scottish Ministers
- a council constituted under section 2 of the Local Government etc (Scotland) Act 1994
- Scottish Homes
- the Department for Social Development in Northern Ireland
- the Northern Ireland Housing Executive.

'Public subsidy' means[600] any grant or other financial assistance:

---

[595] Section 121

[596] SI 1992/1725 (NI 15)

[597] Section 71(2)

[598] Ibid

[599] Section 71(3)

- made or given by way of a distribution pursuant to section 25 of the National Lottery etc Act 1993
- under section 18 of the Housing Act 1996
- under section 126 of the Housing Grants, Construction and Regeneration Act 1996
- under section 2 of the Housing (Scotland) Act 1988
- under article 33 of the Housing (Northern Ireland) Order 1992[601]

3.18.2. Claiming the relief

Relief is claimed by completing the land transaction return (form SDLT1), checking Box 9 to show that a relief is being claimed and inserting code 23.

3.19. Alternative property finance relief – Sharia'a mortgages

(Sections 71A[602] to 73)

Interest-based mortgages do not comply with Sharia'a law and were therefore largely unacceptable to Muslims. Sharia'a-compliant products may be based on several different methods.[603] The purpose of the SDLT provisions is to exempt 'alternative' finance transactions in the same way as a standard mortgage (which is not a 'chargeable interest').[604] However the exemptions are not, in terms, limited in their application to Sharia'a-compliant products or to persons of any particular religion.

3.19.1. Method One

A lender (the 'funder') purchases property, either from the customer or from a seller identified by the funder's customer. The customer lives in the property and makes payments to the funder to repay them the exact purchase price, spread over a period. The customer is also charged rent for the property. Once the purchase price has been repaid the property is sold (or re-sold) to the customer.

This method is sometimes used for a joint purchase by the funder and the customer in which case the ownership is split in the ratio of funding

600 Section 71(4)

601 SI 1992/1725 (NI 15

602 Inserted by section 94 and paragraph 2 Schedule 8 FA 2005 with effect in any case where the effective date of the 'first transaction' (within the meaning of section 71A) falls on or after 7 April 2005 (paragraph 7(1) and (3) Schedule 8 FA 2005). A similar provision, section 72A, is inserted in relation to Scotland.

603 See 'An Introduction to Islamic Banking' Tax Journal Issue 808 at page 24 (10 October 2005).

604 Security interests are excluded by section 48(2).

contributed by the parties and the funder 'rents' its part of the property to the customer.

Using this method the funder makes its profit from the payments for use of the property, rather than a charge for borrowing money.

3.19.2. Method Two

A funder purchases the property (either from the customer or from a seller identified by the funder's customer) and sells it on to the customer at an agreed higher price to be paid over a period. The funder's profit arises from the profit on the sale of the property.

Both methods of lending against the property are structured so that the same property is bought and sold twice (that is, the vendor who may be the customer or a third party sells to the funder which then, in turn, sells (or sells back) to the customer). This ensures that the funder can charge a 'profit element' rather than interest. Such a structure would typically result in SDLT being borne twice - once by the funder and again by the customer – whereas a conventional mortgage funding would involve only one charge to SDLT. Consequently, Sharia'a-compliant mortgages would have resulted in an additional SDLT cost.

Relief from multiple charges to SDLT is available for several types of alternative finance scheme. These reliefs were, until 19 July 2006, relevant to individuals only but were extended to persons other than individuals by section 168 FA 2006.[605] 'Person' includes a body of persons corporate or unincorporated.[606]

Sections 71A and 73 which are summarised below do not apply to land in Scotland.[607]

No alternative property finance relief is available where the 'first transaction' is one to which any of the reliefs under Schedule 7 (group, reconstruction and

[605] With effect in any case where the effective date of the 'first transaction' is on or after Royal Assent, 19 July 2006. Until that date the requirements for relief under sections 71A to 73 could not be not met if an individual entered into the arrangement (or held the lease or sub-lease in question) as trustee, and any beneficiary of the trust was not an individual, or as a partner, and any of the other partners was not an individual.

[606] Schedule 1 Interpretation Act 1978

[607] Sections 72 and 72A apply similar reliefs to Scotland

acquisition reliefs) apply.[608] This is an anti-avoidance provision consequent on the extension of the alternative property finance reliefs to companies.

3.19.3. Section 71A relief – land leased back[609]

This relief applies where a 'financial institution' buys property (or an undivided share in it) and a lease (or sub-lease) is granted (or granted back) to a person who has the right to acquire the reversion. The relief also applies where the property is sold in instalments. This relief covers transactions that, in normal circumstances, would be ordinary mortgages or re-mortgages by the person already owning the property.

In detail, the relief applies where arrangements are entered into between a person and a financial institution under which:

(1) the financial institution purchases a 'major interest' in land or an undivided share in a major interest, ('the first transaction'), and, where the interest is an undivided share, the interest acquired is held on trust for the institution and the person entering into the arrangements as beneficial tenants in common;

(2) the institution (or trustee) grants a lease[610] or a sub-lease[611] out of the interest acquired in the first transaction to the person entering into the arrangements (the 'second transaction'); and

(3) the institution enters into an agreement under which the person who is a party to the second transaction has a right to require the institution or its successor in title to transfer to that person the major interest purchased under the first transaction (in one transaction or a series of transactions).

The first transaction (the acquisition by the financial institution) is exempt from SDLT only if the seller to it is also the person involved in the second transaction or is another financial institution by whom the relevant interest was acquired under alternative property finance arrangements falling within section 71A which were entered into with the person involved in the second transaction.

The second transaction (the grant of the lease or the sub-lease) is exempt from charge if the SDLT provisions relating to the first transaction are complied with in relation to the first transaction (including the payment of any tax chargeable).

Any transfer to the person involved in the second transaction resulting from the exercise of the right referred to in (3) (the 'further transaction') is exempt

---

608 Section 73A inserted by section 168(4) FA 2006 with effect in any case where the effective date of the 'first transaction' is on or after Royal Assent, 19 July 2006

609 See SDLTM28100-SDLTM28340

610 If the interest acquired is a freehold

611 If the interest acquired is leasehold

from charge if the SDLT provisions relating to the first and second transactions are complied with. To secure this relief, the interest purchased under the first transaction must, at all times between the second and further transactions be held by a financial institution (so far as it has not been transferred by a previous further transaction), and the lease or sub-lease granted under the second transaction must be held by the person in question.

The agreement referred to in (3) above is not to be treated as 'substantially performed' (by the relevant person taking possession or paying a substantial amount of the consideration) unless and until the whole interest purchased under the first transaction has been transferred and section 44(5) is disapplied, nor is that agreement treated as a distinct land transaction by virtue of the provisions relating to options and rights of pre-emption in section 46.[612]

Section 71A(7) provides that further transactions which are exempt from charge are not notifiable until the final transaction takes place and the whole interest purchased under the first transaction goes (or has gone) across. This means that where the financial institution sells the property in instalments, only the final transfer triggers the obligation to file a land transaction return.

3.19.4. Section 73 relief – land sold back[613]

This relief operates where a financial institution purchases a property and sells it on (or sells it back) at a higher price secured by an interest-free mortgage over the property. This relief covers transactions that, in normal circumstances, would be ordinary mortgages or re-mortgages by the person already owning the property.

In detail, the relief applies where arrangements are entered into between a person and a financial institution under which:

(1) the institution purchases a major interest in land ('the first transaction'), and
(2) sells that interest ('the second transaction'), and
(3) the buyer grants the institution a 'legal mortgage' over that interest.

The first transaction is exempt from charge only if the seller is also the person involved in the second transaction or is a financial institution which acquired the interest from that person under arrangements falling within section 71A, 72(1) or 72A entered into between it and that person.

The second transaction is exempt from charge provided that the SDLT provisions relating to the first transaction are complied with and SDLT is paid

---

[612] Section 71A(5)

[613] See SDLTM28400-SDLTM28430

on at least the market value of the interest being acquired (including any rent in the case of a lease).[614]

With effect from 20 May 2005[615] where the second transaction is exempt from charge by reason of section 73(3) and arises from a 'secondary contract' within the meaning of section 45(3) (transfer of rights), the substantial performance or completion of the original contract in relation to that exempt transaction will not be disregarded under section 45(3). This is designed to stop avoidance structures that sought to utilise the relieving effect of section 45(3) in conjunction with relief under section 73 and ensures that, in such a case, SDLT is payable on the acquisition of the property from the original vendor. Where the second transaction is not exempt under section 73(3), the subsale relief provided by section 45 is, in principle, available.

Section 73 relief allows the obtaining of finance against a property already owned using a Sharia'a compliant product or the setting-up of a new arrangement with an existing financial institution without an SDLT 'penalty'. It also allows financial institutions to transfer title between themselves where the 'borrower' is not involved.

3.19.5. Alternative property finance relief - exempt interests

(Section 73B[616])

Section 73B provides that where a financial institution has provided an alternative property finance product falling within the scope of sections 71A, 72 or 72A the next dealing in the interest held by the institution or in any interest derived from it, is exempt from SDLT unless the first transaction was exempt by reason of Schedule 7 (Group relief etc.). The provision applies where the effective date of the dealing is on or after 22 March 2007.

3.19.6. Relevant definitions

'Financial institution' means:

- a bank within the meaning of section 840A ICTA 1988,
- a building society within the meaning of the Building Societies Act 1986
- a 'wholly-owned subsidiary' of such a bank or building society

---

[614] Section 73(3) as amended by section 168(3) FA 2006 with effect in any case where the effective date of the 'first transaction' is on or after Royal Assent, 19 July 2006.

[615] Section 45(3) (transfer of rights) was amended by section 49 and paragraph 2 Schedule 10 F(2)A 2005 with effect for any transaction with an effective date after 19 May 2005 to except from its relieving effect any case where the secondary contract gives rise to a transaction that is exempt from SDLT by virtue of section 73(3).

[616] Inserted by section 75(1) and (4) FA 2007.

- a person authorised by a licence under Part 3 of the Consumer Credit Act 1974 to carry on a consumer credit business or consumer hire business within the meaning of that Act, or
- a person authorised in a jurisdiction outside the UK to receive deposits or other repayable funds from the public and to grant credits for its own account.[617]

A company is a 'wholly-owned subsidiary' of a bank or building society ('the parent') if it has no members except the parent and the parent's wholly-owned subsidiaries or persons acting on behalf of the parent or the parent's wholly-owned subsidiaries.

'Major interest' is defined in section 117(2) (in relation to England and Wales) as a fee simple absolute or a term of years absolute at law or in equity. The definitions applying to Scotland and Northern Ireland are in section 117(3) and (4) respectively.

'Legal mortgage' means:[618]

- in relation to land in England or Wales, a legal mortgage as defined in section 205(1)(xvi) Law of Property Act 1925;
- in relation to land in Scotland, a standard security;[619]
- in relation to land in Northern Ireland, a mortgage by conveyance of a legal estate or by demise or sub-demise or a charge by way of legal mortgage.

3.19.7. Claiming the relief

The relief is claimed by completing the land transaction return (form SDLT1), checking Box 9 to show that a relief is being claimed and inserting code 24.

3.20. Relief for certain public bodies - PFI Projects[620]

(Paragraph 17 Schedule 4[621])

Many PFI transactions involve exchanges of interests in land (a sale and leaseback or lease and leaseback and sometimes an additional transfer or lease

---

[617] Section 71A(8) (after amendment by FA 2007 with effect from 22 March 2007) incorporating the definition in section 46 FA 2005.

[618] Section 73(5)

[619] Section 121 provides that 'standard security' has the same meaning as in the Conveyancing and Feudal Reform (Scotland) Act 1970.

[620] See 'Deep Thought: SDLT on PFI Projects' by Mathew Scott, Tax Journal Issue 803 22 August 2005 at page 9.

[621] Inserted by SI 2003/3293 with effect from 19 December 2003 and amended by SI 2004/1069 from 7 April 2004 and further amended from 27 April 2004 by SI 2004/1206. Further amended by section 296 and paragraphs 9(1) and (3) Schedule 39 FA2004 for transactions with an effective date after 17 March 2004.

of what paragraph 17 refers to as 'surplus land') between a public sector body and a private sector service supplier. Without specific provisions, significant SDLT charges could have arisen for both sides (subject to the availability of the Crown Exemption in section 107 for the public sector body).

The rules set out in paragraph 17 Schedule 4 apply (and the exchange provisions in paragraph 5 Schedule 4 do not) where an exchange or a sale and leaseback takes place which involves certain public bodies. The overall result is that in a typical PFI transaction SDLT is only chargeable to the extent that the private sector supplier gives cash for any surplus land. There are four conditions for the application of the relief, all of which must be fulfilled.

The conditions for paragraph 17 relief are that arrangements are entered into under which:

(1) there is a transfer, or the grant or assignment of a lease, of land by a qualifying body ('A') to a non-qualifying body ('B') ('the main transfer');
(2) in consideration (whether in whole or in part) of the main transfer there is a grant by B to A of a lease or under-lease[622] of the whole, or substantially the whole, of that land ('the leaseback');
(3) B undertakes to carry out works or provide services to A; and
(4) some or all of the consideration given by A to B for the carrying out of those works or the provision of those services is consideration in money,

whether or not there is also a transfer, or the grant or assignment of a lease, of any other land by A to B (a 'transfer of surplus land').

There is no need for the main transfer and the transfer, lease or assignment of any surplus land to be separate transactions. For example there may be a lease by A to B which acts both as the main transfer in respect of part of the subject matter and as the transfer of surplus land in respect of the rest.[623]

Where the relief applies:

(1) neither the leaseback nor the carrying out of works by B for A[624] nor the provision of services by B to A[625] is chargeable consideration for the main transfer, or for any transfer of the surplus land (this means that SDLT will generally be charged only on any cash premium or rent paid by the private sector supplier);
(2) there is no chargeable consideration for the leaseback (in other words there is no charge on the qualifying body).

---

622 'Under-lease' includes a sub-lease – paragraph 17(6) Schedule 4.

623 See SDLTM29500

624 Paragraph 10 Schedule 4 is disapplied

625 Paragraph 11 Schedule 4 is disapplied

The relief does not apply to payments in respect of VAT and overage.

The following are 'qualifying bodies' for this purpose:

- public bodies within section 66[626]
- institutions within the further education sector or the higher education sector within the meaning of 91 of the Further and Higher Education Act 1992
- further education corporations within the meaning of section 17 of the Further and Higher Education Act 1992
- higher education corporations within the meaning section 90 of the Further and Higher Education Act 1992
- persons who undertake to establish and maintain, and carry on, or provide for the carrying on, of an Academy within the meaning of section 482 of the Education Act 1996
- in Scotland, institutions funded by the Scottish Further Education Funding Council or the Scottish Higher Education Funding Council.

If, as a result of the application of paragraph 17 there is no chargeable consideration, the land transaction will be exempt under paragraph 1 of Schedule 4. However, the provisions of paragraph 17 are disregarded in determining whether a land transaction is notifiable.[627] This means that both parties will need to file land transaction returns as the transaction will be treated as an exchange for notification purposes. In such a case the consideration on both returns should be shown as nil.

3.21. Relief for new zero-carbon homes

FA 2007 inserted a regulation-making power in FA 2003, section 58B and 58C, allowing HMRC to give relief from the charge to SDLT on sales of new zero-carbon houses.[628]

From 1 October 2007 until 30 September 2012, new zero-carbon homes liable to SDLT on the first sale will be eligible for relief. Qualifying homes costing under £500,000 will bear no SDLT; dwellings with a price in excess of £500,000 will be entitled to £15,000 relief. Where a home qualifies for the relief the rules for linked transactions[629] will be modified so that each home purchased at the same time will be treated as a separate purchase and can therefore qualify for the relief of up to £15,000

---

[626] See 3.14 above

[627] Paragraph17(4A) Schedule 4

[628] As at the date of publication the draft regulations introducing relief for zero-carbon homes had been published for consultation

[629] See 2.1.1 above

New homes are defined as dwellings which are first occupied for residential purposes at the time of the transaction which leads to the SDLT charge. Relief will not be available on second and subsequent sales nor on existing homes.

The zero-carbon standard will be measured using the Government's Standard Assessment ('GSA') procedure for the energy rating of dwellings and will effectively require zero-carbon emissions from all energy use in the home averaged over the course of a year. Existing homes or second and subsequent sales will not be entitled to the relief.

Qualifying criteria for the relief[630] will require zero-carbon emissions from all energy use in the home over a year. To achieve this, the fabric of the home will be required to reach a very high energy efficiency standard and to be able to provide onsite renewable heat and power.

There will be a certification process for all new homes and qualification for the exemption which will be dependant on homebuyers having a certificate. Certification of the exemption will be provided as part of the building control process and will not be provided by HMRC.

The new relief will be claimed on the land transaction return.

3.22. Miscellaneous reliefs

Relief from SDLT is also conferred by specific provisions in the following primary and secondary legislation which carry over a previous stamp duty relief:[631]

Access to Justice Act 1999, section 34A
Airports Act 1986, section 76A
Broadcasting Act 1996, Schedule 7, paragraph 25
Chequers Estate Act 1917, section 3A
Chevening Estate Act 1959, section 2A
Communications Act 2003, Schedule 2, paragraph 5A
Criminal Justice and Court Services Act 2000, section 19(5)
Education Act 1997, section 53A
Finance Act 1960, section 74A (visiting forces and allied headquarters)
Friendly Societies Act 1974, section 105A
Friendly Societies Act 1992, section 105A
Further and Higher Education (Scotland) Act 1992, section 58A

---

[630] To be set out in regulations to be laid before Parliament by the end of the 2007 Summer Recess.

[631] Inserted by Stamp Duty Land Tax (Consequential Amendment of Enactments) Regulations 2003 (SI 2003/2867) with effect from 1 December 2003 and amended by Stamp Duty Land Tax (Consequential Amendment of Enactments) Regulations 2005 (SI 2005/82) with effect from 11 February 2005.

Further and Higher Education Act 1992, section 88A
Health Authorities Act 1995, Schedule 2, paragraph 5
Highways Act 1980, section 281A
Inclosure Act 1845, section 163A
Industry Act 1980, section 2A (exemption where s 66(1) FA 2003 does not apply)
Learning and Skills Act 2000, section 94A
Merchant Shipping Act 1995, section 221(24)
Metropolitan Commons Act 1866, section 33
Museums and Galleries Act 1992, section 8A
National Health Service (Scotland) Act 1978, sections 12DA and 104A
National Health Service and Community Care Act 1990, section 61
National Heritage Act 1980, section 11A
Ports (Northern Ireland) Order 1994
Ports (Northern Ireland) Order 1994 (SI 1994/2809), Article 23A
Ports Act 1991, section 36A
Regional Development Agencies Act 1998, section 39A
School Standards and Framework Act 1998, section 79A[632]
Transport Act 2000, Schedule 2, paragraph 40A
Water Resources Act 1991, Schedule 2, paragraph 8
Welsh Development Agency Act 1975, Schedule 1, paragraph 20A (transfers to the Agency from the Crown or a Crown company)

Relief is claimed by completing the land transaction return (form SDLT1), checking Box 9 to show that a relief is being claimed and inserting code 28 ('Other').

3.23. Property authorised investment funds: proposed relief for conversion of an authorised unit trust to an OEIC

The Treasury discussion paper on Property Authorised Investment Funds ('Property AIFs') issued in July 2007 envisages the introduction of full SDLT relief for funds converting from authorised unit trusts to open-ended investment companies ('OEICs')[633] to take advantage of the Property AIF regime. The new tax regime for Property AIFs is likely to be introduced by April 2008.

---

[632] Repealed by section 79 FA 2007 and relief replaced by a Treasury Order under section 66 – see BN25 'Stamp Duty land Tax – Surplus School Land' (21 March 2007).

[633] For the SDLT treatment of OEICs see 7.16 below

4. Land transactions involving partnerships

(Section 104 and Schedule 15)

4.1. Background

Until after the passing of FA 2004 on 22 July 2004, transfers of UK land by or to partners into and out of a partnership and transfers of partnership interests were exempt from SDLT but remained subject to the old stamp duty rules. Partnerships purchasing UK land in other circumstances, i.e. acquisitions of land by partnerships other than transfers into, within or out of partnerships, were subject to SDLT on the purchase in the same way as other purchasers. This is still the case and such transactions, for example, a firm of solicitors acquiring a lease of new office premises from an unconnected third party, are referred to as 'ordinary partnership transactions' (see 4.4 below).

The SDLT rules for extraordinary transactions have been substantially modified since they came into force by provisions in F(No.2)A 2005[634], FA 2006[635], the Stamp Duty Land Tax (Variation of the Finance Act 2003) Regulations 2006[636] and FA 2007[637] and the rules in their present form are considered in detail in 4.5 below.

When reading Schedule 15, it is important to bear in mind that the three parts of the Schedule have different applications and care must be taken because of this. Part 1 is of general application and regard must be had to these provisions, summarised in 4.3 below, whether a partnership is entering into an ordinary land transaction (acquiring UK land in the market chargeable under the general SDLT provisions) or where there is a contribution, distribution or transfer of a partnership interest within the special charging provisions in Part 3. Part 2 of Schedule 15 (responsibility and liability of partners) is only relevant to ordinary partnership transactions and not to Part 3 transactions.

---

634 Inter alia, F(No.2)A 2005 inserted a new paragraph 17A (Withdrawal of money from a partnership after transfer of a chargeable interest) in Schedule 15 for transactions with an effective date after 19 May 2005, subject to transitional provisions.

635 Schedule 24 FA 2006 modified paragraphs 10, 11, 13, 14, 17A, 18, 19, 23, 24 of Schedule 15 for transactions with an effective date on or after 19 July 2006.

636 SI 2006/3237 paragraph 2 of the Schedule to which amended paragraphs 12, 14 and 20 of Schedule 15, deleted paragraph 13 and inserted a new paragraph 27A with effect from December 2006.

637 FA 2007, to the extent provided in section 72, replaced and amended the changes to Schedule 15 made by the Stamp Duty Land Tax (Variation of the Finance Act 2003) Regulations 2006 (SI 2006/3237) with effect from 19 July 2007, subject to transitional provisions as well as making other amendments to the Schedule.

The sections of the SDLTM dealing with partnerships (SDLTM33150 to SDLTM35500) are still in draft[638] and have not always been updated to cover the changes to the provisions since their enactment nor to reflect changes in HMRC's interpretation of the provisions.

4.2. Overview of the current rules for extraordinary transactions

In outline, the position after the FA 2007 changes is as follows:

(1) Where there is a transfer by one or more (existing or incoming) partners or a person connected with them, of a chargeable interest to a partnership there is a charge to SDLT on that proportion of the market value effectively transferred to the other partners (that is, the proportion of the market value of the contributed property that is attributable to the shares of the other partners immediately after the contribution) regardless of whether any payment was made.

(2) A transfer of an interest in a property-investment partnership is a land transaction chargeable to SDLT.

(3) Transfers of UK land out of a partnership to a partner are taxed at market value with a reduction in certain cases for SDLT or stamp duty previously paid.

The SDLT treatment puts property-investment partnerships, both UK and offshore, at a disadvantage, particularly compared to offshore unit trusts which, at the moment, can offer a vehicle similar to a partnership to pool UK real estate, with more favourable SDLT treatment (even after the withdrawal of seeding relief by FA 2006). The difference is that, unlike a partnership, a unit trust is not a look-though vehicle for SDLT purposes, so a sale of the units will be free of tax and there will be no SDLT charge on the underlying land held by the unit trust.

4.3. Application of SDLT to partnerships – general principles

(Part 1 Schedule 15)

A partnership is defined for SDLT purposes in paragraph 1 Schedule 15 as:

- a partnership within the Partnership Act 1890
- a limited partnership registered under the Limited Partnerships Act 1907
- a limited liability partnership formed under the Limited Liability Partnerships Act 2000 or the Limited Liability Partnerships Act (Northern Ireland) 2002; or
- a firm or entity of a similar character to any of those listed above formed under a law of a country or territory outside the UK.

If the partnership has legal personality, this is disregarded for all SDLT purposes - a chargeable interest held by or on behalf of a partnership is treated

---

[638] As at 20 July 2007

as held by or on behalf of the partners and a land transaction entered into by a partnership is treated as entered into by or on behalf of the partners.

Changes in the membership of the partnership are ignored if any person who was a member before the change remains a member after the change.

A partnership is not to be regarded as a unit trust scheme or as an open-ended investment company (OEIC).

4.4. Application of SDLT to ordinary partnership transactions

(Part 2 Schedule 15)

The rules in Part 2 of Schedule 15 apply only to transactions entered into as purchaser by or on behalf of members of a partnership, which are not transactions dealt with under the special provisions in Part 3 of Schedule 15 (which are, broadly, contributions of chargeable interests to and distributions of chargeable interests from partnerships and transfers of interests in property-investment partnerships – see 4.5 below)[639].

The transactions to which the rules in Part 2 apply are therefore acquisitions of chargeable interests by partnerships from third parties. The partners at that time will, in effect, be treated as joint purchasers. Subject to the rule relating to representative partners (see below), it is the 'responsible partners' who must do whatever is required of a purchaser in such a transaction.

The 'responsible partners' in relation to a transaction are:

1) the persons who are partners at the effective date of the transaction, and
2) any person who becomes a member of the partnership after the effective date of the transaction.

The liability to:

1) make a payment of tax or interest on unpaid tax,
2) make a payment in accordance with an assessment under paragraph 29 Schedule 10 (recovery of excessive repayment), or
3) a penalty or interest on a penalty,

is a joint and several liability of all the responsible partners. No amount may be recovered from a person who did not become a responsible partner for SDLT purposes until after the effective date of the transaction in respect of which the tax is payable or, in the case of a penalty, after the time when the act or omission occurred that caused the penalty to become payable[640].

---

[639] Paragraph 5(1) Schedule 15

[640] Paragraph 7(1A) Schedule 15 as inserted by FA 2004 with effect from 23 July 2004. Before that date an incoming partner could be personally liable for payment of tax or interest on unpaid tax in respect of a land transaction occurring before he became a partner. The only limitation was that a

A representative partner may be nominated by a majority of partners to do anything required to be done by the responsible partners, but such nomination has effect only after notice of the nomination has been given to HMRC.[641] The nomination can be revoked but the revocation is effective only after notice has been given to HMRC[642].

4.5. Partnership transactions to which special provisions apply ('extraordinary transactions')

(Part 3 Schedule 15)[643]

4.5.1. Application of the rules for extraordinary transactions

The special rules in Part 3 of Schedule 15 apply to the partnership transactions listed in paragraph 9 of Part 3. These transactions are:

- the transfer of a chargeable interest to a partnership[644];
- the transfer of an interest in a partnership[645]; and
- the transfer of a chargeable interest from a partnership[646].

Paragraph 9 also provides that references to a 'transfer' of a chargeable interest for the purposes only of Part 3 Schedule 15 include:

- the grant or creation of a chargeable interest
- the variation of a chargeable interest
- the surrender, release or renunciation of a chargeable interest.

This extended meaning applies for Part 3 of Schedule 15 only.

Except as charged under paragraphs 10, 14 or 17 the acquisition of an interest in a partnership is not a chargeable transaction for SDLT purposes, notwithstanding that the partnership property includes land[647].

4.5.2. Transfer of a chargeable interest to a partnership

(Paragraphs 10 to 12 Schedule 15)

Where there is a transfer by one or more (existing or incoming) partners, or a person connected with them, of a chargeable interest to a partnership the aim is

---

penalty or interest on a penalty for such a land transaction could not be recovered from such an incoming partner.

641 Paragraph 8(4) Schedule 15

642 Ibid.

643 Substituted by section 304 and Schedule 41 FA 2004 for partnership transactions with an effective date effect after 22 July 2004

644 Paragraph 10 Schedule 15 – see 4.5.2 below

645 Paragraphs 14, 17, 31 and 32 Schedule 15 – see 4.5.3 below

646 Paragraph 18 Schedule 15 – see 4.5.4 below

647 Paragraph 29 Schedule 15

to charge that proportion of the market value effectively transferred to the other partners (that is, the proportion of the market value of the contributed property that is attributable to the shares of the other partners immediately after the contribution). The detail of the charging provisions is set out below.

Before FA 2006 there was also a charge on any actual consideration paid or given on a transfer in to a partnership (e.g. where debt was assumed by the partnership). However, HMRC acknowledged that the charging formula in its then form was both complicated and prone to producing unintended and excessive charges to SDLT. Accordingly, HMRC simplified the formula and now rely on various anti-avoidance provisions to ensure that the simplification does not result in the use of partnerships for SDLT planning. Further changes to the charging provisions were introduced from 6 December 2006. The main changes are identified below.

There is a transfer of a chargeable interest to a partnership whenever a chargeable interest becomes 'partnership property'.[648]

Partnership interests of 'individuals' connected with the transferor are assumed to belong to the transferor. Somewhat confusingly, an 'individual' includes a corporate trustee in certain circumstances[649].

The charging provisions apply whether the transfer is in connection with the formation of a partnership or is a transfer to an existing partnership.

Partnership property

'Partnership property' is an interest or right held by or on behalf of the partnership or the members of the partnership for the purposes of the partnership business.[650] The test of partnership property is therefore two-fold:

(1) It must be held by or on behalf of the partnership or all of the members of the partnership (not a single member or some of the members); and
(2) It must be held for the purposes of the partnership business (not merely used for the purposes of that business)[651].

Therefore, in practice, a chargeable interest which is partnership property by virtue of section 20 of the Partnership Act 1890 is likely to be partnership property for SDLT purposes. So a chargeable interest acquired, whether by purchase or otherwise, on account of the firm, or for the purposes and in the

---

[648] Paragraph 35 Schedule 15

[649] When calculating the SLP pursuant to paragraph 12 Schedule 15

[650] Paragraph 34(1) Schedule 15

[651] Draft SDLTM35100 and the third paragraph of draft SDLTM33400 no longer represent HMRC's views on paragraph 34(1) – see article in .SDLT Technical News Issue 5 (August 2007)

course of the partnership business, will be partnership property for SDLT purposes. However the mere fact that a business is carried on on property belonging to either one or more partners (but not all partners) does not make the chargeable interest held by that partner or those partners partnership property[652].

The detail of the charge
(Paragraph 10 Schedule 15[653])

Where:
(a) an existing partner transfers a chargeable interest to a partnership;
(b) a person transfers a chargeable interest to a partnership in return for an interest in the partnership; or
(c) a person 'connected with'[654] either a partner or with a person who becomes a partner as a result of, or in connection with, the transfer transfers a chargeable interest to the partnership,

the chargeable consideration for the transfer, subject to the provisions of paragraph 13 of Schedule 15[655], is:

MV x (100-SLP)%

Where:
MV is the market value of the interest transferred.

In determining the market value of a lease for the purposes of paragraph 10, an obligation of the tenant under the lease is to be taken into account only if it is one of those listed in paragraph 10(1) Schedule 17A as not counting as chargeable consideration or it is an obligation to make a payment to a person.[656]

---

652 With acknowledgement to the Stamp Taxes Practitioners' Group for this formulation.

653 As amended by FA 2006 for transactions with an effective date on or after 19 July 2006.

654 The provisions of section 839 ICTA (connected persons) apply with the omission of sub-section (4) (partners connected with each other) (paragraph 39 Schedule 15).

655 The legislation still refers to paragraph 13 (Transfer of chargeable interest to a partnership consisting wholly of bodies corporate) even though this provision was removed from Schedule 15 by the Schedule to the Stamp Duty Land Tax (Variation of the Finance Act 2003) Regulations 2006 (SI 2006/3237) with effect from 6 December 2006. Paragraph 13 was again repealed by FA 2007 in respect of transfers occurring on or after 19 July 2007. The repeal by FA 2007 was in relation to paragraph 13 as it stood before amendment by the Stamp Duty Land Tax (Variation of the Finance Act 2003) Regulations 2006 (SI 2006/3237). Section 72(17) FA 2007 provides that the transitional provisions of sub-paragraphs (8) to (10) of paragraph 2 of the Schedule to the Stamp Duty Land Tax (Variation of the Finance Act 2003) Regulations 2006 continue to have effect.

656 Paragraph 38 Schedule 15

SLP is the sum of the lower proportions determined in accordance with paragraph 12 (see *Determining the SLP* below). In the simple case where a partner is the 100% owner of a land asset before the transfer to a partnership and he is not connected with any of the other partners the SLP will be the transferor's partnership share after the transfer.

Paragraph 10 as originally enacted by FA 2004 gave rise to a charge which was partly based on a proportion of the market value of the land and partly based on 'actual consideration' given by the transferee[657]. In practice it was not always clear what constituted 'actual consideration'. For all transactions with an effective date on or after 19 July 2006, FA 2006 removed the references to 'actual consideration' in paragraph 10 (and paragraph 18) so that the charge is now based solely on a proportion of market value. In a case where rent forms all or part of the consideration for the transfer of a chargeable interest to a partnership, there is a substituted computation for the chargeable consideration[658].

Example: Transfer of land into a partnership

A transfers land worth £1,000,000 to a partnership consisting of himself and B (an unconnected person for the purposes of Schedule 15). B has (and retains) a 60% share in the partnership and the partnership pays nothing to A. The SDLT charge will be calculated as:

Chargeable consideration = MV x (100-SLP)%

= £1 m x(100-40)% = £1 million x 60% = £600,000.

If A had received consideration the SDLT charge would still have been on 60% of market value.

If, in the case where the land was transferred to the partnership by A, A had taken a proportionately increased partnership share (from 40% to 52%), the SDLT charge would have been based on 48% of market value = £480,000. This reflects the fact that A remained the owner of 52% of the property transferred, but had disposed of a 48% share in it.

Responsible partners
(Paragraph 10(7) Schedule 15)

The responsible partners on a transfer to a partnership are those who were partners immediately before and after the transaction and any person

[657] As did paragraph 18 on transfers out of a partnership

[658] See *'Chargeable consideration includes rent'* below

becoming a partner as a result of or in connection with the transfer. The former relates to a contribution to an existing partnership whilst the latter includes a contribution on formation.

Determining the SLP
(Paragraph 12 Schedule 15[659])

There are five steps to determining the SLP. In a simple case, the SLP is broadly the proportion of the interest in land retained by the transferor and certain of those connected with him after the transfer.

Step One: Identify the 'relevant owner' or owners.

A 'relevant owner' is a person who immediately before the transaction was entitled to a proportion of the chargeable interest and immediately after the transaction is a partner or is 'connected with' a partner.

Step Two: For each relevant owner, identify the 'corresponding partner' or partners.

A person is a 'corresponding partner' in relation to a relevant owner if immediately after the transaction he is a partner and he is either the relevant owner or is an 'individual' 'connected with'[660] the relevant owner.

In applying the rules in paragraph 12 to determine the SLP the provisions of section 839 ICTA 1988 (connected persons) apply with the omission of sub-section (3)(c) (trustee connected with a body corporate which is connected with a settlement) and sub-section (4) (partners connected with each other). The disapplication of the connected persons test in section 839(3)(c) by FA 2007 is intended to block a disclosed[661] SDLT scheme which relied on a purchaser engineering a connection between a vendor and the partners in a property partnership created by trustees for the purchaser and into which the vendor sold the property.

For the purposes of *Step Two* a company is to be treated as an 'individual' connected with the relevant owner in so far as it owns property as trustee and is connected with the relevant owner only because of section 839(3) ICTA 1988

---

[659] As amended by FA 2007 which replaced the amendments to paragraph 12 Schedule 15 made with effect from 6 December 2006 by the Stamp Duty Land Tax (Variation of the Finance Act 2003) Regulations 2006 (SI 2006/3237) with effect from 19 July 2007, subject to transitional provisions.

[660] Paragraph 39 Schedule 15 as amended by FA 2007 with effect for transfers occurring on or after 19 July 2007. This definition of 'connected' also applies for the purposes of determining the SLP on a transfer out of a partnership under paragraph 20 Schedule 15.

[661] For the rules on disclosure of SDLT avoidance schemes see Section 5.1 below

(trustee of settlement connected with settlor etc.)[662]. This allows a relevant owner to contribute land to a property partnership in which a corporate trustee of land (under a trust created by him) is the other partner without generating an SDLT charge. Other than a corporate trustee, only partners connected with a relevant owner who are individuals can be corresponding partners. This means that even where a corporate partner is wholly owned by a partner an SDLT charge may arise in respect of part of the interest transferred to that corporate partner although a form of group relief may be available[663].

Where the contributing partner is a company it will be a corresponding partner for the purposes of calculating the SLP.

If there are no corresponding partners the SLP is nil (and the whole of the market value of the interest transferred will be chargeable).

Step Three: For each relevant owner, find the proportion of the chargeable interest to which he was entitled immediately before the transaction.

Apportion that proportion between any one or more of the relevant owner's corresponding partners. There is no set method of performing this apportionment and it should be carried out to give the best result (as it is the lower of this apportioned amount and the partner's share immediately after the transaction that is to be taken into account – see *Step Four* below).

Step Four: Find the 'lower proportion' for each person who is a corresponding partner in relation to one or more relevant owners. This will include the proportion attributable to the relevant owner if he is also a corresponding partner.

The 'lower proportion' is the lower of:
(a) the proportion of the chargeable interest attributable to that partner (at *Step Three*); and
(b) the partner's partnership share immediately after the transaction.

It is income entitlement (and not capital share) which is used to measure partnership share[664]. This is surprising given that the SDLT charge relates to what would normally be a capital asset of the partnership.

If the partner in question is a corresponding partner in relation to only one relevant owner, the proportion attributable to him for the purposes of (a) is the

---

[662] See footnote 659 above

[663] Pursuant to paragraph 27A Schedule 15 – see *Transfer of chargeable interest to a partnership that consists of or includes companies* below

[664] Paragraph 34(2) Schedule 15)

proportion (if any) of the chargeable interest apportioned to him at *Step 3* in respect of that owner.

If the partner in question is a corresponding partner in relation to more than one relevant owner, the proportion attributable to him for the purposes of (a) is the sum of the proportions (if any) of the chargeable interest apportioned to him at *Step 3* in respect of each of those owners.

Step Five: Add together the lower proportions of each person who is a corresponding partner in relation to one or more relevant owners.

The result is the SLP.

Example of SLP calculation:

A, B, C and D are in equal partnership. B and C but not D are connected to A for the purposes of paragraph 10 of Schedule 15. A transfers land to the partnership worth £1,000,000, for which B and C each pay £100,000 and D pays £400,000.

Step One: A is the 'relevant owner'.

Step Two: The 'corresponding partners' are A, B and C.

Step Three: The proportion of the chargeable interest to which A was entitled immediately before the transaction was 100% apportioned equally between A, B and C.

Step Four: The lower proportion is 25% for each of A, B and C as their partnership share of 25% is lower than their proportion of the chargeable interest immediately before the transfer (which was 33.3%).

Step Five: The SLP is therefore 25% + 25% + 25% = 75%.

The chargeable consideration is:
MV x (100-SLP)%
£1,000,000 x (100-75)% = £250,000
Note: D could be a company wholly-owned by A and 25% of the value transferred would still be chargeable whereas if D was an individual connected with A the SLP would be 100% and there would be no chargeable consideration.

Chargeable consideration includes rent
(Paragraph 11 Schedule 15[665])

In a case where rent forms all or part of the consideration for the transfer of a chargeable interest to a partnership (as it may be on the grant of a lease or agreement for lease, but not on an assignment of an existing lease (unless it is deemed to be a grant)), there is a substituted computation for determining the chargeable consideration. In effect, it becomes the Relevant Chargeable

[665] As amended by FA 2006 for transactions with an effective date on or after 19 July 2006.

Proportion (RCP) of the NPV of the rent (calculated in accordance with Schedule 5 subject to modifications set out in paragraphs (2A) to (2C) of paragraph 11).

The RCP is (100-SLP)% so that where a lease is contributed only the proportion of the NPV of rent attributable to the other unconnected parties is charged to SDLT. SLP is determined in accordance with paragraph 12.

Paragraph 10 Schedule 5 charges to SDLT the proportion of any market value (after allowing for the obligation to pay rent taxed under paragraph 10) that is attributable to unconnected parties and this amount is treated as consideration other than rent for the purpose of the rule in paragraph 9 Schedule 5 so that the 0% band is not available for other chargeable consideration where the average annual rent exceeds £600.

Transfer from a partnership to a partnership

Where there is a transfer of a chargeable interest from a partnership to a partnership and the transfer is within both the provision for a transfer to a partnership (in paragraph 10) and from a partnership (in paragraph 18), and none of the chargeable consideration is rent, the chargeable consideration is taken to be whichever is the greater under the two provisions. If the whole or part of the chargeable consideration is rent, the chargeable consideration is taken to be whichever is the greater under paragraphs 11 and 19[666].

Transfer of chargeable interest to a partnership that consists of or includes companies

(Paragraph 13[667] and paragraph 27A[668] Schedule 15)

Paragraph 13 was removed from Schedule 15 by the Schedule to the Stamp Duty Land Tax (Variation of the Finance Act 2003) Regulations 2006 with effect from 6 December 2006[669].

---

[666] Paragraph 23 Schedule 15

[667] Paragraph 13 was repealed by FA 2007 for transfers occurring on or after 19 July 2007. The repeal is in relation to this paragraph as it stood before the Stamp Duty Land Tax (Variation of the Finance Act 2003) Regulations 2006 (SI 2006/3237) which repealed paragraph 13 with effect from 6 December 2006. The repeal by FA 2007 replaces the change made by the 2006 regulations, subject to transitional provisions in section 72(17) FA 2007.

[668] Paragraph 27A was inserted by FA 2007 for transfers occurring on or after 19 July 2007. The amendment is in relation to Schedule 15 as it stood before the Stamp Duty Land Tax (Variation of the Finance Act 2003) Regulations 2006 (SI 2006/3237) which inserted an identical paragraph 27A with effect from 6 December 2006. The repeal by FA 2007 replaces the amendment made by the 2006 regulations, subject to transitional provisions in section 72(17) FA 2007.

Before repeal, the provisions of paragraph 13 had the result that, in a case where the transferee partnership consisted entirely of corporate partners and the SLP was 75 or more (either because the contributing partner retained that interest through its partnership share or did so when its interest after the contribution is aggregated with other group company partners), there was no reduction for prior ownership or participation by connected companies and, on a transfer to such a partnership, the chargeable consideration in paragraph 10 was taken to be equal to the full market value of the interest transferred. There was a corresponding adjustment to paragraph 11 where the chargeable consideration included rent.

From 6 December 2006, where the corresponding partners are part of the same corporate group as the transferor, the transferee partners may be able to claim a type of group relief group relief pursuant to new paragraph 27A in order to benefit from relief from the charge, with the possibility of a clawback of that relief should they leave the group within three years. This relief is not available on a transfer of land out of a partnership that consists of or includes companies.

Paragraph 27A provides that, in a case where:

(1) in calculating the SLP under paragraph 12 , a company would have been a corresponding partner of a relevant owner but for the fact that for the purposes of *Step Two* connected persons are included only if they are individuals[670], and
(2) the connected company and the original owner are members of the same group

the charge in respect of the transaction (chargeable under paragraph 10) is reduced to the amount that would have been payable had the connected company been a corresponding partner of the original owner for the purposes of calculating the SLP.

The SDLT group relief provisions are then applied to treat the SLP reduction as a form of group relief[671] which is subject to clawback under paragraph 3 of Schedule 7 if:

---

669 Paragraph 13 was repealed by FA 2007 (see footnote 667 above). Section 72(17) FA 2007 provides that the transitional provisions of sub-paragraphs (8) to (10) of paragraph 2 of the Schedule to the Stamp Duty Land Tax (Variation of the Finance Act 2003) Regulations 2006 continue to have effect.

670 For the purposes of *Step Two* a company is to be treated as an individual connected with the relevant owner in so far as it owns property as trustee and is connected with the relevant owner only because of section 839(3) ICTA 1988 (trustee of settlement connected with settlor etc.)

671 Paragraph 27A(3) Schedule 15.

(1) the corporate partner ceases to be a member of the same group as the transferor before the end of three years beginning with the date of the transfer (or at any time in pursuance of or in connection with arrangements made before the end of the period); and
(2) at that time the land is held by the partnership.

The amount of tax chargeable if relief is clawed back is the SDLT that would have been paid but for the group relief under paragraph 27A if the chargeable consideration had been the market value of the land or an 'appropriate proportion' of the SDLT that would have been payable. An 'appropriate proportion' means the proportion to which the corporate partner is entitled at the time of de-grouping to share in the income profits of the partnership[672].

Relief under paragraph 27A is claimed by completing the land transaction return (form SDLT1), checking Box 9 to show that a relief is being claimed and inserting code 28 ('Other relief'). *Not* code 12 ('Group relief').

Anti-avoidance: withdrawal of money or money's worth from partnership after transfer of chargeable interest
(Paragraph 17A Schedule 15)[673]

F(No.2)A 2005[674] introduced an anti-avoidance provision, new paragraph 17A, into Schedule 15 to impose an SDLT charge where there has been an transfer of a chargeable interest to a partnership chargeable under paragraph 10 (i.e. a transfer of a chargeable interest by a new or existing partner or a person 'connected with[675]' him) and within three years of that transfer a 'qualifying event' occurs.

A 'qualifying event' occurs where:
(1) a 'relevant person' withdraws money or money's worth from the partnership (which does not represent income profit) by:
  a. withdrawing capital;
  b. reducing his partnership interest; or
  c. ceasing to be a partner.
(2) in the case where the 'relevant person' has made a loan to the partnership:
  a. there is a repayment (to any extent) by the partnership of the loan; or

---

672 Paragraph 27(3) and (4) Schedule 15.

673 Inserted by paragraph 10 Schedule 10 F(No.2)A 2005 where the effective date of the transaction transferring the chargeable interest to the partnership is on or after 20 May 2005 subject to transitional provisions in paragraph 16(7) Schedule 10.

674 Section 49 and Schedule 10 paragraphs 1 and 10.

675 As defined in paragraph 39 Schedule 15.

b. there is a withdrawal by that person of money or money's worth which does not represent income profit.

A 'relevant person' is broadly the transferor or a connected person[676].

The qualifying event is deemed to be a land transaction chargeable to SDLT. The partners are deemed to be the purchasers under this land transaction and paragraphs 6 to 8 of Schedule 15 are applied so that they are jointly and severally liable for the SDLT and to make returns.

The chargeable consideration for the transaction is taken to be, depending on the qualifying event, the value of the money or money's worth withdrawn from the partnership or the amount of the loan repaid. Paragraph 17A(7) limits the charge to the market value of the land or interest in land contributed at the outset, further reduced by the amount, if any, in respect of which the initial transfer to the partnership was liable to SDLT.

Paragraph 17A applies to transactions transferring an interest to a partnership with an effective date on or after 20 May 2005 subject to transitional provisions[677]. Whereas the charge under paragraph 14 (see 4.5.3 below) has since 19 July 2006 been restricted to property-investment partnerships, the restriction has not been mirrored in paragraph 17A. To deal with the possibility of a double charge arising (under paragraph 14 (transfer of an interest in a property-investment partnership) and paragraph 17A), FA 2006 introduced a credit mechanism into paragraph 17A. Where a qualifying event under paragraph 17A gives rise to a charge, and the same event gives rise to a charge under paragraph 14, the amount of the charge under paragraph 17A is reduced, but not below nil, by the amount of charge under paragraph 14[678].

Paragraph 17(8) would not apply to prevent a double-charge to SDLT where one partner contributes land and the other partner contributes a cash equalisation payment which is then paid out to the partner contributing the land. The contribution of the land will be taxed on the market value of the proportionate share of the land attributable to the other partner under paragraph 10, and a further tax charge would then arise under section 17A by reference to the money paid out to equalise their respective contributions.

---

[676] Paragraph 17A(3)

[677] In paragraphs 16(3) and 16(6) to (8) of Schedule 10 to F(No.2)A 2005.

[678] Paragraph 17A(8) inserted by paragraph 10 Schedule 24 FA 2006 with effect in relation to any qualifying event with an effective date of on or after 19 July 2006.

4.5.3. The charge on certain transfers of a partnership interest

(Paragraphs 14 to 17 Schedule 15)

Transfers of interests in property-investment partnerships

(Paragraph 14 as amended[679])

A transfer of an interest in a partnership is a land transaction chargeable to SDLT where:

- it is a transfer of an interest in a 'property-investment partnership'; and
- the 'relevant partnership property' includes a chargeable interest.

A 'property-investment partnership' ('PIP') is defined in paragraph 14(8) as a partnership whose sole or main activity is investing in or dealing in chargeable interests (whether or not that involves carrying out construction operations on land[680]). This means that from 19 July 2006 a partnership need not be concerned about SDLT when partnership interests change unless its business is dealing or investing in land (or it is caught by the anti-avoidance provisions in paragraph 17 or paragraph 17A Schedule 15).

There is no definition of an 'interest in a partnership' - SDLTM refers to it as 'that bundle of rights and obligations assumed by partners in a partnership'[681].

There is no exhaustive definition of what constitutes a 'transfer' for the purposes of paragraph 14. However, it is specifically provided that there is a transfer of an interest in a partnership (to the acquiring partner from the other partners) for the purposes of Part 3 of Schedule 15 (i.e. other than for ordinary partnership transactions) whenever a person acquires or increases a partnership share.[682] Accordingly, the charge may arise where partners join or leave a PIP, or transfer interests in the assets of a PIP between themselves.

---

[679] By FA 2006 with effect in relation to any transfer that had an effective date on or after 19 July 2006, by the Stamp Duty Land Tax (Variation of the Finance Act 2003) Regulations 2006 (SI 2006/3237) with effect from 6 December 2006 and by FA 2007 in relation to paragraph 14 as it stood before amendment by the Stamp Duty Land Tax (Variation of the Finance Act 2003) Regulations 2006 (SI 2006/3237). Section 72(17) FA 2007 provides that the transitional provisions of sub-paragraphs (8) to (10) of paragraph 2 of the Schedule to the Stamp Duty Land Tax (Variation of the Finance Act 2003) Regulations 2006 continue to have effect.

[680] 'Construction operations' has the same meaning as in Chapter 3 of Part 3 FA 2004

[681] See SDLTM34500 (draft)

[682] Paragraph 36 Schedule 15 as substituted by FA 2007 with effect from 19 July 2007 subject to transitional provisions in section 72(14) FA 2007. Before the substitution of the new paragraph 36 a mere change in the income profit-sharing ratio would not have been be treated as a transfer of an interest in the partnership because either an actual transfer of an interest to another person or a

It is understood that HMRC will interpret the 'wholly or mainly' test in the definition of a PIP in the same way as they interpret the test in section 105(3) IHTA 1984 (the test of business property relief for inheritance tax purposes)[683].

Paragraph 14(6) provides that 'relevant partnership property' means every chargeable interest that was held as partnership property[684] immediately after the transfer, other than:

(a) an interest that was transferred to the partnership in connection with the transfer; and
(b) certain leases to which paragraph 15 Schedule 15 applies (see 'market rent leases' below).

The 'purchaser' for SDLT purposes is the person who acquires an increased partnership share or who becomes a partner as a result of the transfer[685]. There is no longer any requirement that consideration be given for the transfer to be chargeable to SDLT[686].

The chargeable consideration is deemed to be a proportion of the market value of the relevant partnership property. That proportion is:

(a) if the purchaser was not a partner before the transfer, his partnership share immediately after it; and
(b) if he was a partner before the transfer, the difference between his partnership share before and after the transfer[687].

It is income entitlement and not capital which is used to measure partnership share.[688]

---

deemed transfer (where a person became a partner and another partner withdrew or reduced his interest under the same arrangement) was required.

683 The test in section 105(3) IHTA 1984 was considered in *Farmer and another (executors of Farmer, deceased) v. Inland Revenue Commissioners* [1999] STC (SCD) 321 where the Special Commissioner held that section 105(3) was concerned with what the business consisted of, and it was necessary to look at the business and its activities in the round and to consider all the relevant factors

684 Partnership property is an interest or right held by or on behalf of the partnership or the members of the partnership for the purposes of the partnership business (paragraph 34(1) Schedule 15)

685 Paragraph 14(3) Schedule 15

686 Paragraphs 14(1)(b) and 14(4) Schedule 15 were removed by FA 2007 with effect from 19 July 2007. From 6 December 2006 to 18 July 2007 transfers of an interest in a PIP were chargeable if consideration was given or, if no consideration was given, where the transferee was a person connected with the transferor.

687 Paragraphs 14(6) and 14(7) Schedule 15

688 Paragraph 34(2) Schedule 15

An interest the transfer of which would be within paragraph 14 of Schedule 15 is treated as a chargeable interest for group relief purposes to the extent that the relevant partnership property consists of a chargeable interest[689]. This is to enable the group relief clawback provisions to apply to it.

Following the introduction of section 75A[690] (Anti-avoidance – see Section 5 below) an interest in a partnership has been treated as a chargeable interest for the purposes of that section. Taxpayers will need to be careful that a charge under section 75A does not arise on the transfer of an interest in a partnership even where paragraph 14 may not apply.

Example: Transfer of interest in a PIP

A and B are in partnership. The partnership property includes chargeable interests valued at £2,000,000 and the partnership is a PIP. C joins the partnership by buying a 10% interest from B for £250,000.

The transaction between B and C is a land transaction in which B is the purchaser and the chargeable consideration for SDLT purposes is 10% of £2,000,000 = £200,000

Note: FA 2007 amendments – transitional provisions

Section 72(14) FA 2007 provides that certain amendments to Schedule 15 made by section 72(6) and 72(10)) of that Act do not affect anything done in respect of a PIP established before 19 July 2007 (the date of Royal Assent to FA 2007) if:

(1) the partnership does not acquire a chargeable interest on or after that day, and
(2) SDLT was paid in respect of each chargeable interest acquired before that day, by reference to chargeable consideration of not less than the market value.

The relevant amendments are:

(1) the omission of sub-paragraphs (1)(b) and (4) of paragraph 14 (removing the requirement for consideration),
(2) the insertion of a new sub-paragraph 9 in paragraph 14 (treating a partnership interest as itself a chargeable interest for group relief purposes as described above); and

---

689 Paragraph 14(9) Schedule 15 inserted by FA 2007 with effect for transfers occurring on or after 19 July 2007 subject to transitional provisions in section 72(14).

690 From 2 pm on 6 December 2006 by the Stamp Duty Land Tax (Variation of the Finance Act 2003) Regulations 2006 SI 2006/3237. Sections 75A to 75C were substituted for section 75A by FA 2007 with effect from 6 December 2006 subject to transitional provisions.

(3) the substitution of a new paragraph 36 (Interpretation: transfer of interest in a partnership).

Market rent leases
(Paragraph 15 Schedule 15)

'Market rent leases' are excluded from the definition of 'relevant partnership property' and are therefore outside the ambit of the charge in paragraph 14. There are four conditions for 'market rent leases' and, where all the conditions are fulfilled a lease held as partnership property[691] immediately after a transfer of an interest in the partnership is not relevant partnership property for the purposes of paragraph 14(5). The conditions are that:

(1) no chargeable consideration other than rent has been given in respect of the grant of the lease and no arrangements are in place at the time of the transfer for any such consideration to be given in respect of that grant;
(2) the rent payable under the lease was a market rent at the time of the grant;
(3) the term of the lease is five years or less or, if more than five years, there is a rent review to market rent at the review date at least once every five years. The market rent for this purpose is the rent that the lease might reasonably be expected to fetch at that time in the open market. It is important to note that a provision for 'upwards-only' reviews would not be a rent review to market rent for these purposes;
(4) there has been no change to the lease since it was granted the result of which is that, immediately after the change takes effect, the rent payable under the lease is less than a market rent.

The exclusion of market rent leases from being relevant partnership property is intended to exclude from the paragraph 14 charge leases which have no inherent capital value. However, the fact that leases with upward-only rent reviews fall outside the definition of 'market rent leases' may seriously reduce the number of leases that come with this exclusion.

Exchanges involving partnership interests
(Paragraph 16 Schedule 15)

A special rule applies where there is an acquisition of an interest in a land-owning partnership in consideration of transferring land to an existing partner. The partnership interest acquired is regarded as a major interest in land where

---

[691] Partnership property is an interest or right held by or on behalf of the partnership or the members of the partnership for the purposes of the partnership business (paragraph 34(1) Schedule 15).

the 'relevant partnership property' (as defined in paragraph 14(5)[692]) includes a 'major interest[693]' in land so that the provisions on exchanges in paragraph 5 Schedule 4 will apply. This has the result that the exchange will be treated as two separate land transactions and the amount of the consideration for each transaction is taken to be the market value of the subject matter acquired. There will, in effect, be a double market value charge.

The relief allowed in calculating the chargeable consideration of the existing share of an interest in land which is the subject of a partition in paragraph 6 Schedule 4 is disapplied.

Anti-avoidance: transfer of partnership interest pursuant to earlier arrangements
(Paragraph 17 Schedule 15)

Avoidance provisions are in place to deal with cases where transfers are separated or staggered in order to reduce SDLT. A partnership share that is acquired in exchange for the transfer of land into a partnership may have been artificially increased and that would lower the proportion of the other partners' partnership interests and reduce the SDLT charge. Where paragraph 17 applies there is a deemed chargeable transaction (to counteract the SDLT advantage) when there is a later transfer of a partnership interest.

Paragraph 17 provides that where there is a transfer of a chargeable interest to a partnership within the meaning of paragraph 10(1) ('the land transfer') followed by a transfer of a partnership interest by the relevant partner ('the partnership transfer') pursuant to arrangements that were in place at the time of the land transfer, and the transfer of the partnership interest would not otherwise be chargeable, the partnership transfer is deemed to be a chargeable land transaction. The partners are taken to be the purchasers and the consideration is taken to be the proportion of the market value, as at the date of the transaction, of the interest transferred on the land transfer that corresponds to the partnership interest disposed of by the partner.

---

[692] Every chargeable interest that was held as partnership property immediately after the transfer, other than an interest that was transferred to the partnership in connection with the transfer; and certain leases to which paragraph 15 Schedule 15 applies.

[693] A 'major interest' is defined in section 117(2) (in relation to England and Wales) as a fee simple absolute or a term of years absolute at law or in equity. The definitions applying to Scotland and Northern Ireland are in section 117(3) and (4) respectively.

'Arrangements' include any scheme, agreement or understanding, whether or not legally enforceable[694].

Where paragraph 17 applies, the responsible partners in relation to the transfer of the partnership interest are those who were partners immediately before the transfer and who remain partners after the transfer and any person becoming a partner as a result of or in connection with the transfer.[695]

Transfer of a partnership interest: notification
(Paragraph 30 Schedule 15)

The acquisition of a partnership interest in respect of which a charge arises under paragraph 14 or paragraph 17 is a notifiable transaction only if SDLT is chargeable in relation to it at a rate of 1% or more. The thresholds apply for individual partners unless they are 'connected' (otherwise than by reason of partnership).[696]

4.5.4. Transfer of a chargeable interest from a partnership

(Paragraphs 18 to 24 Schedule 15[697])

Where a chargeable interest is transferred:

- from a partnership to a person who is or has been one of the partners for his personal benefit (i.e. not as partnership property); or
- from a partnership to a person 'connected with'[698] a person who is or has been one of the partners

there is a chargeable transaction for SDLT purposes. The intention of the legislation is to charge SDLT on the proportion of the market value of the land to which the recipient partner was not previously beneficially entitled by virtue of the partnership's interest in the land.

There is a transfer of a chargeable interest from a partnership where a chargeable interest that was partnership property ceases to be partnership property or where a chargeable interest is granted or created out of partnership

---

[694] Paragraph 40 Schedule 15

[695] Paragraph 17(7) Schedule 15

[696] The provisions of section 839 ICTA 1988(connected persons) apply with the omission of sub-section (4) (partners connected with each other) (paragraph 39 Schedule 15).

[697] Paragraph 20 was amended by the Stamp Duty Land Tax (Variation of the Finance Act 2003) Regulations 2006 (SI 2006/3237) with effect from 6 December 2006 and by FA 2007 in relation to paragraph 20 as it stood before amendment by the Stamp Duty Land Tax (Variation of the Finance Act 2003) Regulations 2006 (SI 2006/3237).

[698] The provisions of section 839 ICTA 1988(connected persons) apply with the omission of sub-section (4) (partners connected with each other) (paragraph 39 Schedule 15).

property and that interest is not partnership property.[699] 'Partnership property' is an interest or right held by or on behalf of the partnership or the members of the partnership for the purposes of the partnership business[700].

It is expressly provided in paragraph 18(7) that property which was partnership property before dissolution or other cessation of a partnership is treated as remaining as partnership property until it is distributed.

The chargeable consideration is found in the same way as for a transfer of a chargeable interest to a partnership under paragraph 10 (MV x (100-SLP)%), with the qualification that for a group transaction paragraph 27A does not apply. Paragraph 19 applies in the same way as paragraph 11 when the chargeable consideration includes rent.

Transfer from a partnership: determining the SLP
(Paragraphs 20 to 22 Schedule 15)

The SLP is determined under paragraph 20 in the same way as it is in relation to the transfer of a chargeable interest to a partnership,[701] with the exception of *Step Four*, where the 'partnership share attributable to the partner' needs to be found by applying paragraphs 21 and 22.

Where the chargeable interest was transferred to the partnership before 20 October 2003[702], or, where it was transferred on or after that date but the transfer was stamped, either ad valorem or with fixed duty, or SDLT was paid, a charge to tax under paragraph 20 will arise only on the proportion of the market value of the property interest transferred on which tax has not previously been paid. This proportion is calculated by a statutory formula (set out in paragraphs 21 and 22) which takes account of increases or decreases in partnership shares since the property was transferred to partnership. These rules are set out in detail below.

The 'partnership share attributable to the partner' is zero where the effective date of the transfer of the 'relevant chargeable interest' to the partnership was on or after 20 October 2003 and neither ad valorem stamp duty nor SDLT was paid on the transfer. The 'relevant chargeable interest' is the interest that ceases to be partnership property as a result of the transfer or, where the transaction is

---

[699] Paragraph 37 Schedule 15

[700] Paragraph 34(1) Schedule 15

[701] Under paragraph 12 Schedule 15 – see 4.5.2 above

[702] The date of publication by HMRC of the draft legislation amending Schedule 15 which was enacted in FA 2004

the grant or creation of a chargeable interest, is the chargeable interest out of which that interest is granted or created.

Where:

(1) the effective date of the transfer of the 'relevant chargeable interest' to the partnership was before 20 October 2003; or
(2) the effective date of the transfer of the relevant chargeable interest to the partnership was on or after 20 October 2003 and either ad valorem stamp duty or SDLT was paid on the transfer

the partnership share attributable to the partner is determined as follows:

Step One: Find the partner's actual partnership share on the 'relevant date'. The 'relevant date' is:

- in a case falling within (1) above, the later of 19 October 2003 and the date on which he became a partner
- in a case falling within (2) above, the later of the effective date of the transfer of the relevant chargeable interest to the partnership and the date on which he became a partner.

Step Two: To that partnership share add any increases in the partner's partnership share which occurred in the period beginning on the day after the relevant date and ending immediately before the transfer of the chargeable interest from the partnership and which 'count' for this purpose. The result is the 'increased partnership share'. An increase 'counts' for this purpose only where (in the case where the transfer which resulted in the increase took place on or before 22 July 2004) the instrument of transfer has been duly stamped with ad valorem stamp duty or (in the case where the transfer which resulted in the increase took place after 22 July 2004) SDLT which was payable has been paid on the transfer.

Step Three: Deduct from the increased partnership share any decreases in the partner's partnership share which occurred in the period beginning on the day after the relevant date and ending immediately before the transfer of the chargeable interest from the partnership.

The result is the partnership share attributable to the partner. If the effect of applying *Step Three* would be to reduce the partnership share attributable to a partner below zero, the partnership share attributable to that partner is zero. The partnership share will also be zero if:

- in a case falling within (1) above, the partner ceased to belong to the partnership before 19 October 2003; or
- in a case falling within (2) above, the partner left the partnership before the effective date of the transfer of the relevant chargeable interest to the partnership.

Example: Transfer of land out of a partnership

A initially has a 75% interest in a land-owning partnership. When the value of the property held by the partnership is £2 million A purchases an additional 10% interest in the partnership from the other partners who are unconnected with him and pays SDLT on a chargeable consideration of £200,000. Some time later, when the property is worth £3 million it is transferred to A on his retirement from the partnership.

The chargeable consideration on the transfer to A will be calculated as follows:

A's interest in the partnership when the property was contributed = 75%

Subsequent interest acquired = 10%

SLP = 75% + 10% = 85%

Chargeable consideration = MV x (100-SLP)%
=(15% x £3,000,000)
= £450,000

Transfer from a partnership to a partnership
(Paragraph 23 Schedule 15[703])

This provision deals with the case where there could be two possible SDLT charges, one on land going in, and the other on land coming out, of a partnership.

Where there is a transfer of a chargeable interest from a partnership to a partnership and the transfer is within both the provision for a transfer to a partnership (in paragraph 10) and from a partnership (in paragraph 18), and none of the chargeable consideration is rent, the chargeable consideration is taken to be whichever is the greater under the two provisions. If the whole or part of the chargeable consideration is rent, the chargeable consideration is taken to be whichever is the greater under paragraphs 11 and 19.

A change in the identity of the partners will not amount to a transfer to another partnership as long as any person who was a member before the change remains a member after the change[704].

Transfer out of a wholly corporate partnership
(Paragraph 24 Schedule 15[705])

Where immediately before the transfer out of a partnership the partners are all bodies corporate and the SLP is 75 or more, there is no reduction under

---

[703] As modified by FA 2006 with effect from 19 July 2006

[704] Paragraph 3 Schedule 15

[705] As amended by FA 2006 from 19 July 2006

paragraph 18 of Schedule 15. The charge in such a case bites on market value and the full NPV of any rent. This is an anti-avoidance measure and the transferee will have to be in a position to claim group relief to escape the charge, with the possibility of a clawback of that relief should it leave the group within three years.

There is no equivalent provision on transfers of land out of a partnership to paragraph 27A Schedule 15 (which applies a modified form of group relief on the transfer of land into a partnership which includes corporate partners who are members of the same group of companies as the transferor[706]).

4.5.5. Application of exemptions and reliefs

(Paragraphs 25 to 28 Schedule 15)

The exemption from SDLT in paragraph 1 Schedule 3 (transfers for no chargeable consideration) does not apply to partnership transactions to which the special provisions in Schedule 15 apply. This allows the market value rules to operate on contributions and distributions of capital for which no consideration is given.

All the other SDLT exemptions do apply, subject to modification in the case of disadvantaged areas relief[707], group relief[708] and charities relief.[709] The modifications are intended to ensure that these reliefs apply in the same way as for non-partnership transactions.

4.5.6. Continued application of stamp duty to transfers of partnership interests

(Paragraphs 31 to 33 Schedule 15)

Paragraph 31 Schedule 15 provides for the continued application of stamp duty to instruments transferring a partnership interest,[710] but paragraph 32 modifies the consideration in the case of a land-owning partnership.

Where stamp duty is charged on an instrument transferring an interest in a partnership and the relevant partnership property includes an interest in land, the consideration for the transaction for stamp duty purposes is reduced by the

---

[706] See *Transfer of chargeable interest to a partnership that consists of or includes companies* in 4.5.2 above.

[707] Paragraph 26 Schedule 15

[708] Paragraph 27 Schedule 15

[709] Paragraph 28 Schedule 15

[710] Paragraph 31 has the effect of preserving the stamp duty which would have been chargeable under FA 1999 Schedule 13, where a transfer is not on sale. For example, a transfer otherwise than on sale of a partnership interest would still be chargeable with a fixed duty of £5.

'excluded amount'. The intention is to avoid a double charge to both stamp duty and SDLT. Arguably paragraph 32 is not necessary in view of paragraph 33 which limits the stamp duty charge to the net value of any stock or marketable securities held as partnership property (see below).

The 'excluded amount' is a proportion of the 'net market value' of the 'relevant partnership property' immediately after the transfer. Where the person acquiring the interest was not a partner before the transfer, the proportion is equal to his partnership share immediately after the transfer. Where the person acquiring the interest in the partnership was previously a partner, the proportion is the difference in his partnership share, before and after the transfer.

'Relevant partnership property' in relation to a transfer of a partnership interest is every chargeable interest held as partnership property[711] immediately after the transfer other than any interest that was transferred to the partnership in connection with the transfer.

The 'net market value' of the relevant partnership property is the market value of the interest in land at the transfer date less the amount of any loan secured solely on the interest in land at that date. Where this produces a negative result the net market value is taken as nil. Where the excluded amount is greater than the actual consideration paid, the reduced amount is taken as nil.

The relevant instrument will need to be adjudicated [712]

Paragraph 33 was amended by F(No.2)A 2005[713] because, as originally drafted, it did not reflect what was intended, namely only to charge stamp duty on that proportion of the value of a partnership interest being transferred as was attributable to interests in stock and marketable securities, net of debt secured on the stock etc immediately after the transaction (ignoring any such stock etc transferred into the partnership in connection with the transfer of the partnership interest)[714]. Paragraph 33(1A) now states that if the partnership property does not include any stock or marketable securities, no stamp duty shall be chargeable on the instrument.

---

[711] Partnership property is an interest or right held by or on behalf of the partnership or the members of the partnership for the purposes of the partnership business (paragraph 34(1) Schedule 15)

[712] Paragraph 32(9) Schedule 15

[713] The amendments were effective for transactions on or after 20July 2006 although HMRC practice was already to operate paragraph 33 as if it were correctly worded before that date.

[714] See new paragraph 33(3A)

If the partnership property does not include any stock or marketable securities, paragraph 33 will not apply and therefore the instrument will not require to be adjudicated.

5. SDLT – General anti-avoidance measures

When SDLT was introduced in 2003 one of the main drivers was to counter stamp duty avoidance in relation to real property. In spite of this aim in designing the new tax HMRC have felt the need to introduce further anti-avoidance measures every year since then, beginning in 2004 (when the tax was barely six months old). There are some specifically targeted anti-avoidance provisions and these are dealt with elsewhere in this book[715]. This chapter deals only with those of more general application – the disclosure rules and the general anti-avoidance rule in new sections 75A to 75C.

5.1. Disclosure of SDLT schemes

(Part 7 FA 2004[716])

In FA 2004, HMRC introduced a regime under which details of schemes or arrangements, the main purpose of which was the avoidance of tax, had to be disclosed to them. From 1 August 2005, the regime was extended to SDLT schemes involving commercial property of a value of £5 million or more. The reason given for the extension was that:

> "HMRC has been hampered in countering avoidance schemes by a particular form of the information gap .... SDLT avoidance schemes usually involve a series of transactions. One transaction (usually the first) may be a land transaction on which a claim to relief is made, or indeed for which no return at all is required. Any HMRC enquiry into that return is restricted to verifying that the right amount of SDLT has been paid on that particular transaction. However, the other transactions in the series are not land transactions at all (e.g. because the land is wrapped up in the sale of a company) and it is all the transactions taken together that effectively transfer ownership of the property to a third party without a charge to SDLT arising. Consequently, the normal return and enquiry system will often not provide HMRC with sufficient information to identify when a land transaction is part of an avoidance scheme, or the details of how that

---

[715] The following specific anti-avoidance provisions are discussed: subsale relief 1.4.2, linked transactions 2.1.1, lease loans and deposits 2.6.6, group relief 3.4.1, reconstruction relief 3.5.2, acquisition relief 3.6.1, alternative property finance 3.19 and partnerships 4.5.2.

[716] Extended to SDLT by the Stamp Duty Land Tax Schemes (Prescribed Descriptions of Arrangements) Regulations 2005 (SI 2005/1868) and the Tax Avoidance Schemes (Information) (Amendment) Regulations 2005 (SI 2005/1869) which were amended by the Tax Avoidance Schemes (Information) Regulations 2006 (SI 2006/1544).

scheme works. This information gap inhibits HMRC from taking quick and effective action against such schemes[717]."

HMRC statistics to March 2007[718] show that 670 disclosures had been made since 1 August 2005 in relation to SDLT schemes and the figures indicate an upward trend.

5.1.1. What has to be disclosed?

Disclosure is required of SDLT arrangements and proposals for arrangements which are prescribed by regulations:

(1) where an SDLT advantage might be expected to be obtained ('Test One'); and

(2) the obtaining of that SDLT advantage might be expected to be a main benefit or one of the main benefits of the arrangements ('Test Two'),[719] where:
   a. the scheme does not relate solely to 'residential property';
   b. the 'market value' of all the chargeable interests[720] in non-residential property subject to the arrangements is at least £5 million (or this is not known); and
   c. none of the exceptions from disclosure[721] applies.

HMRC has given a public assurance that the provision of 'every day tax advice does not trigger a disclosure obligation'[722].

Test One

The following points emerge from the HMRC Guidance in relation to the application of Test One[723]:

(1) As the definition of 'tax advantage' for these purposes is drawn from the definition in section 709 ICTA 1988 (anti-avoidance legislation targeted at certain transactions involving securities) HMRC expect the existing body of case law on section 709 to apply equally for disclosure purposes.

---

[717] Explanatory memorandum to SI 2005/1869 (the Tax Avoidance Schemes (Information) (Amendment) Regulations 2005) at paragraph 7.10.

[718] http://www.hmrc.gov.uk/avoidance/stats_2007.xls

[719] Section 306(1)(b) and (c) FA 2004

[720] 'Chargeable interest' is defined in section 48

[721] See 5.1.3 below

[722] See CIOT Technical Note of 23 August 2004 available at: http://www.tax.org.uk/showarticle.pl?id=270b

[723] 'Disclosure of Tax Avoidance Schemes (Income Tax, Corporation Tax, Capital Gains Tax and Stamp Duty Land Tax) The Main Guidance' (August 2006) at paragraph 5.1.2.

(2) The definition of tax advantage in section 709 is very widely drawn. It includes the avoidance or reduction of a charge to tax, a relief from tax, repayment of tax and the deferral of tax or the avoidance of an obligation to deduct tax. HMRC expect that section 318 FA 2004 (which sets out the definition of advantage for disclosure purposes) will also be construed widely.

(3) Where the scheme is expected to result in tax being avoided or reduced then the test formulated by Lord Wilberforce in *IRC v. Parker*[724] applies and the existence of a tax advantage is tested on a comparative basis. Lord Wilberforce's test was that:

> "there must be a contrast as regards the 'receipts' between the actual case where these accrue in a non-taxable way with a possible accruer in a taxable way, and unless this contrast exists the existence of the [tax] advantage is not established"

In other words, if a transaction is structured in such a way that no tax liability arises, but it could have been structured differently so that a tax liability did arise, a tax advantage exists.

In the *Sema Case*[725] Lord Justice Parker summarised what the draftsman was trying to do when defining 'tax advantage' in section 709(1) as intending to cover every situation in which the position of the taxpayer vis-à-vis HMRC was improved in consequence of the particular transaction or transactions. A 'tax advantage' presupposed that a better position had been achieved vis-à-vis HMRC.

A relief or exemption from tax can give rise to a tax advantage as defined.

Test Two

The main benefit test is objective. The expected tax advantage must be weighed against any other benefits likely to result from the arrangements.

Relevant definitions

'Advantage' in relation to a tax is defined in section 318(1) FA 2004 and includes relief or increased relief from tax, deferral of payment and the avoidance of any obligation to account for tax.

'Arrangements' include any scheme, transaction or series of transactions[726].

The definitions of 'residential property' and 'non-residential property' in section 116 apply[727] so a single transaction involving six or more dwellings is

---

[724] [1966] AC 141

[725] *IRC v. Trustees of the Sema Group Pension Scheme* [2003] STC 95

[726] Section 318 FA 2004

treated as involving non-residential property and may therefore be disclosable. If a promoter does not know whether a proposal will be used for non-residential property, he is required to assume that it will be.

'Market value' is to be determined in accordance with the capital gains tax rules in sections 272 to 274 TCGA 1992[728] and is, broadly, the price that might be expected to be obtained on a sale on the open market. There is no indication in the legislation of whether or how encumbrances (which would reduce the value of the interest transferred) should be taken into account. All chargeable interests held by all 'connected persons[729]' in the same property are to be aggregated[730]. The market value is to be determined at the time the requirement to disclose arises.

If a promoter does not know the market value of the property at the date the obligation to disclose arises or makes a proposal available 'generally', it is assumed that the market value is £5 million or more.

If a user dealing with a non-UK promoter does not know the market value at the time the obligation to disclose arises, it is assumed to be at least £5 million.

5.1.2. Who has to disclose and when?

The primary obligation to disclose falls on the 'promoter' of the scheme. 'Promoters' are defined in section 307 FA 2004. In summary, a person is a promoter if, in the course of providing services in relation to tax, he designs or makes available for implementation, proposals or arrangements of a prescribed type. Where there are co-promoters, only one of them needs to disclose. The rules apply to UK and non-UK based promoters.

There are three exceptions from the definition of 'promoters' for persons who, although involved in the design of the arrangements, do not make a proposal available for implementation. Those exceptions are:

(1) tax advisers who are instructed to advise only on the technical merits of the scheme but who do not advise on its design. This is referred to in the HMRC guidance[731] as the 'benign test[732]' and could apply, for example, to tax counsel who advises on the merits of a tax adviser's scheme..

---

[727] See 2.4.1 above

[728] Section 118 applies to determine market value for this purpose.

[729] The definition of 'connected' in section 839 ICTA applies.

[730] Regulation 2(2) SDLT Arrangements Regulations

[731] 'Disclosure of Tax Avoidance Schemes (Income Tax, Corporation Tax, Capital Gains Tax and Stamp Duty Land Tax) The Main Guidance' (August 2006).

[732] See regulation 4(1) and 4(2) Tax Avoidance Schemes (Promoters and Prescribed Circumstances) Regulations 2004 (SI 2004/1865).

(2) advisers who do provide tax advice from time to time and who are to some extent responsible for the design of the scheme, such as the property law aspects, but who do not actually provide tax advice in relation to the particular arrangements. This is referred to in the HMRC guidance as the 'non-adviser test[733]'.

(3) advisers who are responsible for some elements of the scheme, but who are insufficiently involved to know whether disclosure is required or lack the detailed information required to be disclosed. This is referred to in the HMRC guidance as the 'ignorance test'

Barristers and solicitors (unless covered by legal professional privilege[734]), accountants, chartered tax advisers, estate agents, chartered surveyors and other advisers whose work includes an element of tax advice can all, potentially, be promoters (as can banks and securities houses regardless of whether they supply tax services or not).

For marketed schemes, disclosure is required within five days of the earlier of:

(1) the date on which a promoter first makes the scheme available for implementation by another person; and

(2) the date on which a promoter becomes aware that the scheme has been implemented by a transaction taking place that forms part of it.

HMRC guidance indicates that they regard a scheme as being made available for implementation by another person when it:

(1) has been developed to such a stage that the promoter has a high degree of confidence in the tax analysis applying to it; and

(2) is communicated to a potential user in sufficient detail that he could be expected to: understand the way in which the scheme works, including its key elements; realise the expected tax advantages; and decide whether or not to enter into it.

For individual or 'bespoke' SDLT schemes there is an obligation to disclose within five days of the date when the promoter becomes aware that a transaction forming part of the arrangements has occurred[735].

---

[733] See regulation 4(1) and 4(3) Tax Avoidance Schemes (Promoters and Prescribed Circumstances) Regulations 2004 (SI 2004/1865).

[734] Section 314 FA 2004

[735] 'Disclosure of Tax Avoidance Schemes (Income Tax, Corporation Tax, Capital Gains Tax and Stamp Duty Land Tax) The Main Guidance' (August 2006) at paragraph 10.3.1.

Persons dealing with non-UK promoters

Where a non-UK promoter fails to comply with a disclosure obligation, the disclosure obligation falls on the user and disclosure is required within five days of entering into the first transaction forming part of the scheme. HMRC have indicated that they will not seek to penalise users who have relied upon written assurances given to them by non-UK based promoters that either the disclosure obligation has been complied with or does not arise, providing it was reasonable in the circumstances to rely upon the assurance given[736].

No promoter[737]

When there is no promoter, any person who enters into a transaction forming part of the arrangements must disclose within 30 days of entering into the first transaction forming part of the scheme. In other words, only schemes that have been implemented need to be disclosed.

The promoter is covered by legal professional privilege[738]

The disclosure obligation in principle falls on the user unless he chooses to waive his right to privilege (but subject to the same exemption in the user's hands for information that is the subject of a claim to legal professional privilege). Disclosure of any information that is not subject to legal professional privilege is required within 30 days of entering into the transaction. If the user waives his right to privilege the disclosure obligation reverts to the promoter, who must disclose within five days.

The SDLT disclosure rules have been built onto and incorporate most of the direct tax scheme disclosure rules that were already in existence (the 'basic rules'). The basic rules contain many of the definitions and other matters relating to disclosure generally which also apply to SDLT.

The key differences between the basic rules and the SDLT disclosure rules are:

(1) In order to trigger a disclosure obligation under the basic rules, certain 'hallmarks' of avoidance must be present. The direct tax 'hallmarks'[739] do not apply to oblige SDLT disclosure.[740]

(2) For SDLT schemes only, there is a list of six excluded steps (A to F[741]) and disclosure may not be required for a single step or certain combinations of

---

[736] 'Disclosure of Tax Avoidance Schemes (Income Tax, Corporation Tax, Capital Gains Tax and Stamp Duty Land Tax) The Main Guidance' (August 2006) at paragraph 10.4.1

[737] Section 310 FA 2004

[738] Section 310 FA 2004 and regulation 6 Tax Avoidance Schemes (Promoters and Prescribed Circumstances) Regulations 2004 (SI 2004/1865)

[739] Also sometimes referred to as 'filters'

[740] SI 2005/1868

steps on this list. The list is set out in the Schedule to the Stamp Duty Land Tax Schemes (Prescribed Descriptions of Arrangements) Regulations 2005 (the 'SDLT Arrangements Regulations')[742].

(3) Users of 'in-house' SDLT schemes where there is no "promoter", and users of schemes whose promoter is covered by legal professional privilege must make the disclosure themselves within 30 days of entering into arrangements.

(4) Promoters of disclosed SDLT schemes are not required to provide a user with a reference number and there is no requirement for users of SDLT schemes to include a reference number for the scheme when filing an SDLT return.

For SDLT schemes, the Anti-Avoidance Group in HMRC will issue a reference number to promoters solely to help the promoter identify the scheme to internal and external stakeholders (i.e. employees and clients). This will help to ensure that the same scheme is not disclosed more than once, either by the same promoter or by other co-promoters[743].

There is no statutory obligation on the promoter to provide a user with the reference number. If a promoter does provide the user with the number, they should make clear that it is for reference purposes only and that the user is not required to notify the number to HMRC.

5.1.3. Exclusions from disclosure

A scheme need only be disclosed once provided that it is 'substantially the same'[744].

The SDLT Arrangements Regulations[745] provide that arrangements need not be disclosed if:

(1) they comprise one or more of six steps (A to F), subject to two rules (Rules 1 and 2) which specify arrangements involving combinations of steps which are not excluded from disclosure; and

(2) they do not include any step, which is necessary for the purpose of securing a tax advantage, other than one of steps A to F.

Steps A to F are as set out below.

---

[741] See 5.1.3 below

[742] SI 2005/1868

[743] Disclosure of Tax Avoidance Schemes (Income Tax, Corporation Tax, Capital Gains Tax and Stamp Duty Land Tax) The Main Guidance' (August 2006) at paragraph 31.1.

[744] Section 308(5) FA 2004

[745] Regulation 2(3)(c) and Schedule

The purpose of the exclusions is to avoid the need to disclose certain basic SDLT avoidance techniques which are common and known to HMRC. In summary, disclosure is not required of SDLT schemes which consist of either a single step from the list or a combination of steps, unless the combination of steps is prevented from being excluded by Rules 1 and 2. However the inclusion of an unlisted step necessary to obtain the SDLT advantage will make the scheme disclosable where all the other requirements for disclosure are met.

Step A: Acquisition of a chargeable interest by special purpose vehicle
The acquisition of a chargeable interest in land by a company created for that purpose (a special purpose vehicle).

It would appear that the use of an 'off-the-shelf' company created for general purposes, but which is then used to acquire land, may not be an excluded step. It is not clear whether 'company' includes a unit trust scheme, which generally is treated as a company for SDLT purposes[746].

Step B: Claims to relief
(a) Making a 'single claim' to relief under any of the following provisions:
- (i) section 57A (sale and leaseback arrangements);
- (ii) section 60 (compulsory purchase facilitating development);
- (iii) section 61 (compliance with planning obligation);
- (iv) section 64 (demutualisation of building society);
- (v) section 64A (initial transfer of assets to trustees of unit trust scheme)[747];
- (vi) section 65 (incorporation of limited liability partnership);
- (vii) section 66 (transfers involving public bodies);
- (viii) section 67 (transfer in consequence of reorganisation of parliamentary constituencies);
- (ix) section 69 (acquisition by bodies established for national purposes);
- (x) section 71 (certain acquisitions by registered social landlords);
- (xi) section 74 (collective enfranchisement by leaseholders);
- (xii) section 75 (crofting community right to buy);
- (xiii) Schedule 6 (disadvantaged areas relief);
- (xiv) Schedule 6A (relief for certain acquisitions of residential property);
- (xv) Schedule 7 (group relief, reconstruction and acquisition reliefs);

---

[746] The better view is that it does not as the section 101 definition is not applied by the SDLT Arrangements Regulations.

[747] Section 64A was repealed by FA 2006 subject to transitional provisions – see 3.1.1 above.

(xvi) Schedule 8 (charities relief);
(xvii) Schedule 9 (right to buy, shared ownership leases etc);

(b) Making one or more claims to relief under any one of the following provisions:
(i) section 71A (alternative property finance: land sold to financial institution and leased to individual);
(ii) section 72 (alternative property finance in Scotland: land sold to financial institution and leased to individual);
(iii) section 72A (alternative property finance in Scotland: land sold to financial institution and leased to individual in common); or
(iv) section 73 (alternative property finance: land sold to financial institution and resold to individual).

A 'single claim' will include one of a number of identical claims being made in respect of separate properties[748].

HMRC accept that steps taken to avoid a clawback of group, reconstruction or acquisition relief by ensuring that the purchaser ceases to be a member of the vendor's group or that control of the purchaser changes only at the end of the three-year clawback period, can be included within Step B[749].

Step C: Sale of shares in special purpose vehicle
The sale of shares in a special purpose vehicle, which holds a chargeable interest in land, to a person with whom neither the special purpose vehicle, nor the vendor, is connected.

It is unclear whether an issue of shares, as distinct from a transfer of existing shares to a purchaser, is included within step C.

Step D: Not exercising election to waive exemption from VAT
No election is made to waive exemption from VAT contained in paragraph 2 of Schedule 10 to VATA 1994 (treatment of buildings and land for VAT purposes).

Step E: Transfer of a business as a going concern
Arranging the transfer of a business, connected with the land which is the subject of the arrangements, in such a way that it is treated for the purposes of VAT as the transfer of a going concern.

---

[748] See 'Disclosure of Tax Avoidance Schemes (Income Tax, Corporation Tax, Capital Gains Tax and Stamp Duty Land Tax) The Main Guidance' (HMRC August 2006) at paragraph 9.8.
[749] Ibid

Step F: Undertaking a joint venture
The creation of a partnership (within the meaning of paragraph 1 of Schedule 15) to which the property which is subject to a land transaction is to be transferred.

Certain combinations of steps A to F are not excluded. Those non-excluded combinations are identified by Rules 1 and 2.

Rule 1: Arrangements which involve Steps B (Claims to relief), D (Not waiving exemption from VAT), E (Transfer of going concern for VAT purposes) or F (Creation of a partnership) are excluded from disclosure unless Rule 2 applies.

Rule 2: Arrangements are not excluded from disclosure if they:
(a) include all, or at least two of, Steps A (Acquisition by special purpose vehicle), C (Sale of shares in special purpose vehicle) and D (Not waiving exemption from VAT); or
(b) involve more than one instance of Step A (Acquisition by special purpose vehicle), C (Sale of shares in special purpose vehicle), or D (Not exercising election to waive exemption from VAT).'

5.1.4. Making the disclosure

The information required to be disclosed (subject to legal professional privilege) when a scheme is disclosable is[750]:
(1) the name and address of the promoter or other person required to make the disclosure;
(2) details of the provisions of the SDLT Arrangements Regulations by virtue of which the proposal or arrangement is notifiable;
(3) a summary of the proposal or arrangement and the name (if any) by which it is known;
(4) information explaining each element of the proposal or arrangement from which the expected SDLT advantage arises; and
(5) the statutory provisions on which that SDLT advantage is based.

Copies of the relevant forms on which to make disclosure are available on the Anti Avoidance Group section of HMRC's website[751]. The forms can be completed and submitted online.

---

[750] Regulation 3 Tax Avoidance Schemes (Information) Regulations 2004(SI 2004/1864) as amended by SI 2004/2613, SI 2005/1869 and SI 2006/1544.

[751] At http://www.hmrc.gov.uk/aiu/forms-tax-schemes.htm. Paper copies of the forms can be obtained from the Order Line on 08459 000404.

5.1.5. Penalties[752]

A failure to make the required disclosure of an SDLT scheme renders the offender liable to an initial penalty of up to £5,000 and is determined by the Special Commissioners. If the failure to make disclosure continues after the initial penalty is imposed by the Special Commissioners, HMRC can impose a further penalty of up to £600 per day while the failure continues.

Reasonable excuse

No penalty will be charged where the promoter or user (as applicable) has a reasonable excuse and the failure to comply is remedied within a reasonable time after the excuse ceased.

5.2. SDLT general anti-avoidance rule

(Sections 75A, 75B and 75C)

A general anti-avoidance rule ('GAAR') for SDLT was announced in the 2006 pre-Budget report and was introduced with effect from 2 pm on 6 December by the Stamp Duty Land Tax (Variation of the Finance Act 2003) Regulations 2006[753]. The provision, new section 75A, was, from Royal Assent to FA 2007, replaced by sections 75A, 75B and 75C, which all have effect from 6 December 2006, although the basic structure of the original section 75A has been retained.

The SDLT GAAR was intended to counter certain known SDLT schemes which had been disclosed to HMRC and is wide-ranging. Proposals to issue a non-statutory 'white list' of transactions which are not caught have been dropped although HMRC issued 'interim guidance' in relation to the application of section 75A as introduced by the 2006 regulations[754] and this was replaced by guidance on sections 75A to 75C in August 2007[755]. It may be that the 'white list' will resurface in a legislative guise as section 75C(11)) allows HMRC to provide, by order, for section 75A not to apply in certain circumstances[756].

The GAAR targets the case where a person disposes of a chargeable interest and another person acquires that interest or an interest derived from it and a number of transactions are inserted with the result that the SDLT payable is less than it otherwise would have been. The inserted steps are ignored and

---

[752] Section 315 FA 2004

[753] SI 2006/3237

[754] In February 2007 (see http://www.hmrc.gov.uk/so/sdlt_regs06_intguidance.htm) – this guidance supplemented the Technical Note which was issued tin December 2006.

[755] See SDLT Technical News Issue 5 (August 2007)

[756] The non-statutory white list concept was criticised as unsatisfactory primarily because it had no legal status and was not subject to Parliamentary scrutiny.

SDLT is chargeable on a notional land transaction, the consideration being the total consideration given or received.

There is no clearance mechanism although it may be possible to use the COP 10 procedure nor is there a tax avoidance motive test.

5.2.1. The detail of the SDLT GAAR

The SDLT GAAR in section 75A applies where the following three requirements are met:

(1) one person (V) disposes of a 'chargeable interest'[757] and another person (P) acquires either it or a chargeable interest deriving from it,

(2) a number of transactions (including the disposal and acquisition referred to in (1)) are involved in connection with the disposal and acquisition (the 'scheme transactions'), and

(3) the sum of the amounts of SDLT payable in respect of the scheme transactions is less than the amount that would be payable on a notional land transaction effecting the acquisition of V's chargeable interest by P on its disposal by V (the 'tax-saving test').

There is no requirement that, in order for section 75A to apply, the acquisition by P referred to in (1) be from V directly.

An interest in a property investment partnership is treated as a chargeable interest for the purposes of section 75A. Where V or P is a partnership the provisions in Part 3 of Schedule 15 apply as they would to the transfer of a chargeable interest into or out of a partnership[758].

The result of the SDLT GAAR applying is that the individual scheme transactions are disregarded for SDLT purposes and there is instead a notional transaction by which P acquires V's chargeable interest (which was the subject matter of the disposal by V) by P and the chargeable consideration for that notional transaction is the 'notional consideration'. Any SDLT paid in respect of a land transaction which is to be disregarded is taken to have been paid in respect of the notional transaction[759].

'Transaction' is defined to include[760]:

- a non-land transaction;
- an agreement, offer or undertaking not to take specified action;

---

[757] As defined in section 46

[758] Section 75C(8)

[759] Section 75C(10)

[760] Section 75A(2)

- any kind of arrangement whether or not it could otherwise be described as a transaction;
- a transaction which takes place after the acquisition by P of the chargeable interest;
- the exercise of a right to terminate a lease or to take some other action;
- an agreement not to exercise a right to terminate a lease or to take some other action; and
- the variation of a right to terminate a lease or to take some other action

Scheme transactions

The second requirement for section 75A to apply is that there are 'scheme transactions' which are a number of transactions (including the disposal and acquisition) involved in connection with the disposal by V and acquisition by P.

Section 75A(3), unusually, gives examples of 'scheme transactions':

- the acquisition by P of a lease deriving from a freehold owned or formerly owned by V;
- a sub-sale to a third person;
- the grant of a lease to a third person subject to a right to terminate.

The HMRC guidance[761] in relation to when a number of transactions will be 'involved in connection with' a disposal and acquisition and result in there being scheme transactions is as follows:

> "The phrase 'involved in connection with' implies that there must be some connection between the disposal and acquisition on the one hand and the transactions on the other which goes beyond the fact that a number of transactions happen in chronological order, and that they affect the same property. In particular it is unlikely that (except on a transfer of rights) section 75A can apply to a disposal by V and an acquisition by P where neither P nor his associates nor his advisers have had any involvement in or any connection with transactions other than the one by which P acquired the property, and neither P nor his associates obtains any SDLT benefit from the way in which the acquisition is effected. However section 75A will apply where the acquisition by P is effected by a 'transfer of rights' within the meaning of section 45, for example a sub-sale. So if V agrees to sell to X and X agrees to sell on to P section 75A applies to the disposal by V and the acquisition by P whether or not P or his associates or his advisers had any involvement in or connection with the V–X contract. Section 75A(1)(b) refers to the scheme transactions as being 'involved in connection with' the disposal and acquisition. Thus scheme transactions need not necessarily be

[761] See SDLT Technical News Issue 5 (August 2007)

connected with each other. For example, if V agrees to sell to X and X agrees to sell to P the two transactions are 'involved in connection with' the disposal by V and the acquisition by P even if V is unaware of the sale on by X."

The HMRC guidance[762] gives the following examples of where section 75A would not apply because there are no scheme transactions:

1) V sells two properties at arm's length to third party purchasers N1 and N2. At some later stage, and in transactions which are not connected in any way with the purchases by N1 and N2, P buys both properties at arm's length.

   Section 75A does not apply as regards the disposal by V and the acquisition by P.

2) V grants a long lease to X. At a later stage, and in a transaction which is not connected in any way with the grant of the lease, X assigns the lease to an unconnected third party P. P exercises a statutory right of enfranchisement.

   Section 75A does not apply as regards the disposal by V and the acquisition by P.

3) V grants an option to purchase land to X. At a later stage, and in a transaction which is not connected in any way with the grant of the option, X assigns the benefit of the option to an unconnected third party P. P exercises the option.

   Section 75A does not apply as regards the disposal by V and the acquisition by P.

4) V agrees to sell land to H. H agrees to sell on to his spouse W. These transactions are completed at the same time. At a later stage W sells on to an unconnected third party P.

   Section 75A does not apply as regards the disposal by V and the acquisition by P (although section 75A will apply as regards the disposal by V and the acquisition by W).

5) V agrees to sell land to P. P agrees to sell on to C. The transactions are completed at the same time.

   Section 75A does not apply as regards the disposal by V and the acquisition by P (although section 75A will apply as regards the disposal by V and the acquisition by C). The sale on to C is not 'involved in

[762] See SDLT Technical News Issue 5 (August 2007)

connection with' the disposal by V and the acquisition by P because it does not in any way affect the nature of the interest acquired by P.

The HMRC guidance[763] gives the following examples of where section 75A would apply because there are scheme transactions:

(1) V grants a 999-year lease to N for no premium and a peppercorn rent. V assigns the freehold reversion to P for a nominal sum. P pays N £X in consideration of N's agreement to vary the lease by the insertion of a provision giving the landlord the right to terminate the lease for no payment. P exercises the right to terminate.
(2) V grants a 999-year lease to N for no premium and a peppercorn rent. The lease includes a right for the landlord to terminate the lease on payment of £X to the tenant. V assigns the freehold reversion to P for a nominal sum. P exercises the right to terminate and pays N £X.
(3) V grants a 999-year lease to P for no premium and a peppercorn rent. The lease gives the landlord a right to terminate it within 14 days of the date of grant. P offers to pay V £X if V allows the 14 days to elapse without exercising the right to terminate. V does so (an example of a scheme transaction which occurs after the acquisition of the chargeable interest by P).
(4) V agrees to sell property to N for £10 million. N agrees to sub-sell the property to P. Both transactions are completed at the same time. (See the note above on the application of section 75A where an acquisition is effected by means of a 'transfer of rights').
(5) V agrees to sell property to N Ltd for £10 million. N Ltd declares a dividend in favour of P, its sole shareholder, the dividend to consist of the property and to be paid at the same time as completion of the V–N Ltd contract. The contract is completed and the property transferred to P.

A transfer of shares or securities (or units in a unit trust) is ignored for the purposes of section 75A if it would otherwise be the first of a series of scheme transactions (and several such transfers are likewise ignored if they all precede any other scheme transaction)[764].

The notional transaction

The chargeable consideration for the notional transaction for the purposes of applying the tax-saving test and for taxing a notional transaction to which section 75A applies (the 'notional consideration') is the largest amount (or aggregate amount):

---

763 Ibid

764 Section 75C(1)

(1) given by or on behalf of any one person by way of consideration for the scheme transactions, or
(2) received by or on behalf of V (or a person 'connected with' V[765]) by way of consideration for the scheme transactions[766].

An amount given or received partly in respect of the chargeable interest acquired by P and partly in respect of another chargeable interest is to be determined on a just and reasonable apportionment. Consideration includes monies worth.

In calculating the notional consideration the consideration properly attributable to 'incidental' transactions is disregarded[767]. Incidental transactions are those that are merely incidental to the disposal by V and the acquisition by P.

A transaction is not incidental to the transfer of the chargeable interest from V to P:
(1) if or in so far as it forms part of a process, or series of transactions, by which the transfer is effected,
(2) if the transfer of the chargeable interest is conditional on the completion of the transaction, or
(3) if it is one of the examples listed in section 75A(3).

A transaction may, subject to (1) to (3) above, be incidental if or in so far as it is undertaken only for a purpose relating to:
(1) the construction of a building on property to which the chargeable interest relates,
(2) the sale or supply of anything other than land, or
(3) a loan to P secured by a mortgage, or any other provision of finance to enable P, or another person, to pay for part of a process, or series of transactions, by which the chargeable interest transfers from V to P.

Reference to the transfer of a chargeable interest from V to P includes a reference to a disposal by V of an interest acquired by P.

The effective date of the notional transaction is the last date of completion for the scheme transactions, or if earlier, the last date on which a contract in respect of the scheme transactions is substantially performed[768].

---

[765] Applying the test in section 839 ICTA 1988

[766] Section 75A(5) – there are examples of how the notional consideration is calculated in the guidance in SDLT Technical News Issue 5 (August 2007).

[767] Section 75B

[768] Section 75A(6)

The notional transaction attracts any relief which it would attract if it were an actual land transaction[769]. In addition the consideration attributable to any scheme transaction which would qualify for relief under section 60, 61, 63, 64, 65, 66, 67, 69, 71, 74 or 75, or Schedules 6A or 8, is disregarded in calculating the notional consideration[770]. Some reliefs involve a number of transactions where the tax-saving test will almost certainly be satisfied. Accordingly, section 75A is disapplied where the tax-saving test is satisfied by reason only of sections 71A to 73 (alternative property finance) or a provision in Schedule 9 (right to buy, shared ownership leases, etc).

If any of the scheme transactions is entered into for the purposes of or in connection with the transfer of an undertaking or part of an undertaking for the purposes of paragraphs 7 or 8 of Schedule 7 (reconstruction and acquisition relief) then the notional transaction is also deemed to be entered into for such purposes or in such connection[771]. This enables the notional transaction to qualify for reconstruction or acquisition relief if the other conditions for availability of relief are satisfied.

The notional transaction will be subject to the market value rule in section 53 if P is a company connected with V[772].

If part of the consideration for the notional transaction is a land transaction entered into by V as purchaser, or by P as vendor, then the market value rules in paragraph 5 of Schedule 4 will apply[773].

5.2.2. The transitional provisions[774]

As explained above, section 75A exists in two versions. The first was introduced by The Stamp Duty Land Tax (Variation of the Finance Act 2003) Regulations 2006[775] from 2 p.m. on 6 December 2006 (the 'relevant time'). The second was introduced by section 71 FA 2007 (which also introduced supplementary provision in sections 75B and 75C).

The FA 2007 provisions have effect in respect of disposals and acquisitions if the disposal takes place on or after 6 December 2006, and all the scheme

---

[769] Section 75C(2)

[770] Section 75C(4)

[771] Section 75C(3)

[772] Section 75C(6)

[773] Section 75C(7)

[774] Section 75C (3) FA 2007 which retains the transitional provisions in paragraph 1 of the Schedule to SI 2006/3237

[775]SI 2006/3237.

transactions take place after that time. However section 75C does not have effect where a disposal takes place before 19 July 2007[776] and the effect of section 75C would be to impose a higher tax charge than that provided for in the Regulations.

Section 75A, and the Regulations, do not have effect in relation to:

(1) any land transaction which is effected in pursuance of a contract entered into and substantially performed before the relevant time;
(2) any other land transaction which is effected in pursuance of a contract entered into before the relevant time and which is not an 'excluded transaction'.

A scheme transaction effected in pursuance of a contract is an excluded transaction if:

(1) at or after the relevant time the contract is varied in a way that significantly affects the scheme transaction,
(2) the subject-matter of the scheme transaction is not identified in the contract in a way that would have enabled its acquisition before the relevant time,
(3) rights under the contract are assigned at or after the relevant time,
(4) the scheme transaction is effected in consequence of the exercise, at or after the relevant time, of any option, right of pre-emption or similar right, or at or after the relevant time there is an assignment, sub-sale or other transaction (relating to the whole or part of the contract's subject-matter) as a result of which a person other than the purchaser under the contract becomes entitled to call for a conveyance to him.

A contract is varied in a way that significantly affects the scheme transaction if:

(1) it is varied so as to substitute a different purchaser in relation to the scheme transaction,
(2) it is varied so as to alter the subject-matter of the scheme transaction, or
(3) it is varied so as to alter the consideration for the scheme transaction.

---

[776] The date of Royal Assent to FA 2007

6. The SDLT regime - Commencement and transitional provisions

(Sections 124 and 125 and Schedules 19 and 20[777])

6.1. Commencement of SDLT Regime

Paragraph 2 Schedule 19 states the general rule which is that a land transaction is within the scope of SDLT (an 'SDLT transaction') if the effective date of the transaction was on or after the 'implementation date'. The 'implementation date' was 1 December 2003.[778] Section 125(5)(a) provides that an instrument effecting a land transaction is not subject to stamp duty if the transaction is an 'SDLT transaction' or would be such a transaction but for an exemption or relief.

6.2. The SDLT transitional regime

(Schedule 19)

Only 'SDLT transactions' are capable of being chargeable transactions or notifiable transactions or are transactions to which the prohibitions on registration without production of a certificate set out in section 79 apply.[779]

A contract both made and completed before 1 December 2003 will not be an SDLT transaction. A contract both made and completed on or after 1 December 2003 will be an SDLT transaction. In relation to other transactions the rules set out below apply to determine whether the transaction falls into the stamp duty or SDLT regime.

6.2.1. SDLT transactions – the detailed rules

Rule One: Effective date on or after 1 December 2003

(Paragraph 2 Schedule 19)

A transaction is not an SDLT transaction unless the 'effective date' is on or after 1 December 2003.

---

[777] There are examples of the operation of the transitional provisions at SDLTM49000 to SDLTM49700.

[778] The 'implementation date' appointed by the Stamp Duty Land Tax (Appointment of the Implementation Date) Order 2003 (SI 2003/2899).

[779] Paragraph 1(2) Schedule 19

Rule Two: Contracts entered into before 11 July 2003 (the date on which FA 2003 received Royal Assent)
(Paragraph 3 Schedule 19)

A transaction is not an SDLT transaction if it is effected in pursuance of a contract[780] entered into[781] before 11 July 2003 unless:

- there is a variation[782] of the contract or assignment of rights under the contract on or after 11 July 2003; or
- the transaction is effected in consequence of the exercise after 11 July 2003 of an option, right of pre-emption or similar right; or
- on or after 11 July 2003 there is an assignment, subsale or other transaction (relating to the whole or part of the subject-matter of the contract) as a result of which a person other than the purchaser under that contract becomes entitled to call for a conveyance to him.[783]

Rule Three: Contracts entered into and substantially performed before 11 July 2003 but completed on or after 1 December 2003
(Paragraph 4 Schedule 19)
A transaction is not an SDLT transaction if:

- it is completed on or after 1 December 2003;
- it is effected in pursuance of a contract[784] entered into[785] and substantially performed before 11 July 2003; and
- it is not within exceptions (1), (2) or (3) to Rule Two.

Where the contract is substantially performed on or after 11 July 2003, but before 1 December 2003, the effective date of the transaction is the date of

---

[780] Contract' includes any agreement (paragraph 10 Schedule 19)

[781] In a case where section 44 has effect in accordance with section 45 (effect of transfer of rights) and there is a deemed secondary contract with the transferee this date is taken to be the date of the assignment, subsale or other transaction in question – paragraph 4B Schedule 19.

[782] SDLTM49300 gives as an example of what would constitute a variation for these purposes a change to the subject matter of the contract, to the parties, to the contractual consideration, or, in an agreement for a lease, to the term length. The same paragraph in the SDLTM continues "on the other hand some changes, for example, to prescribed colour schemes or to contractual completion date, may be too insignificant to amount to a variation".

[783] Paragraph 3(3) Schedule 19 as substituted by section 296 and paragraph 12 Schedule 39 FA 2004 with effect for any transaction of which the effective date is after 17 March 2004. The amendment does not apply in relation to a contract that was substantially performed before 17 March 2004 (paragraphs 13(3) and 13(4) Schedule 39 FA 2004). Paragraph 3(c) previously read:
'where the purchaser under the transaction is a person other than the purchaser under the contract because of a further contract made on or after that date.'

[784] 'Contract' includes any agreement (paragraph 10 Schedule 19)

[785] See footnote 781.

completion (regardless of the fact that substantial performance occurred before 1 December 2003), so if completion is 1 December 2003 or later this would make it an SDLT transaction. This means that where the effective date would have occurred by reason of the substantial performance before 1 December, that date is, in effect, displaced by the date of completion.

Rule Four: Contracts entered into before 11 July 2003 and substantially performed after 1 December 2003
(Paragraph 4A Schedule 19)
Where a transaction is effected in pursuance of a contract[786] entered into[787] before 11 July 2003, and:

- the contract is substantially performed (without having been completed) after 1 December 2003; and
- there is subsequently:
- a variation[788] of the contract or assignment of rights under the contract; or
- the exercise of an option, right of pre-emption or similar right in consequence of which the transaction is effected; or
- an assignment, subsale or other transaction (relating to the whole or part of the subject-matter of the contract) as a result of which a person other than the purchaser under that contract becomes entitled to call for a conveyance to him,
- by virtue of which the transaction becomes an SDLT transaction, then the effective date of the transaction is the date of the event falling within (2) above and not the date of substantial performance.[789]

Table - Summary of transitional rules:

Contract 'made' before 11 July 2003 In a case where section 44 has effect in accordance with section 45 (effect of transfer of rights) and there is a deemed secondary contract with the transferee, any reference to the date a contract is made in paragraph 3, 4 and 4A Schedule 19 is taken to be a reference to the date of the	Completed before 1 December 2003	Not an SDLT transaction – stamp duty payable on completion

786 'Contract' includes any agreement (paragraph 10 Schedule 19)

787 See footnote 781

788 See footnote 782

789 Paragraph 4A Schedule 19

assignment, subsale or other transaction in question – paragraph 4B Schedule 19		
Contract made before 11 July 2003	Substantially performed before 11 July 2003	Not an SDLT transaction – stamp duty payable when completed
Contract made before 11 July 2003	Substantially performed on or after 11 July 2003 but before 1 December 2003 and not completed before 1 December 2003	Not an SDLT transaction – stamp duty payable when completed unless: a) the contract was varied or assigned on or after 11 July 2003; or b) the transaction is in consequence of the exercise after 11 July 2003 of an option, right of pre-emption or similar right; or c) where the purchaser is a person other than the purchaser under that contract because of a further contract made on or after 11 July 2003 in which case SDLT transaction
Contract made before 11 July 2003	Neither substantially performed nor completed before 1 December 2003	Not an SDLT transaction – stamp duty payable when completed unless: a) the contract was varied or assigned on or after 11 July 2003; or b) the transaction is in consequence of the exercise after 11 July 2003 of an option, right of pre-emption or similar right; or c) (in a case where the effective date is before 17 March 2004) d) the purchaser is a person other than the purchaser under that contract because of a further contract made on or after 11 July 2003 e) (in a case where the effective date is on or after 17 March 2004 and the contract was not substantially performed before 17 March 2004) f) there is an assignment, subsale or other transaction (relating to the whole or part of the subject-matter of the contract) as a result of which a person other than the purchaser under that contract becomes entitled to call for a conveyance to him in which case SDLT transaction
Contract made on or after 11	Completed before	Not an SDLT transaction

July 2003 but before 1 December 2003	1 December 2003	Stamp duty payable on completion
Contract made on or after 11 July 2003 but before 1 December 2003	Substantially performed (but not completed) before 1 December 2003	SDLT transaction
Contract made on or after 11 July 2003 but before 1 December 2003	Neither substantially performed nor completed before 1 December 2003	SDLT transaction
Contract made after 1 December 2003	In all cases	SDLT transaction

Credit for ad valorem stamp duty paid:
(Paragraph 5 Schedule 19)
Where a transaction chargeable to SDLT is completed pursuant to a contract entered into before 1 December 2003, any ad valorem stamp duty paid on the contract is available as a credit against the SDLT payable (but no refund is available should the stamp duty exceed the SDLT). An example of this would be where a contract for the sale of land was chargeable to stamp duty under section 115 FA 2002 and that contract was completed on or after 1 December 2003. A credit would be available for the stamp duty paid against the charge to SDLT.

Stamping of contract where transaction on completion subject to SDLT
(Paragraph 7A Schedule 19)
Where a contract is entered into before 1 December 2003 which would not be stampable apart from the provisions of paragraph 7 Schedule 13 FA 1999 and a conveyance is effected 'in conformity with' the contract on or after 1 December 2003, so on completion an SDLT liability potentially arises or would but for a relief or exemption, then presentation of the contract for stamping together with HMRC certificate for SDLT purposes will result in the contract being deemed to be duly stamped.

Transitional provisions – agreements for lease
(Paragraph 8 Schedule 19)
Where an agreement for lease has been entered into before 1 December 2003 and stamped, and the lease is executed on or after that date and the transaction is an SDLT transaction, the protection against interest and penalties on the presentation of the agreement for stamping is continued.

Accordingly, if the lease is produced when the agreement is presented for stamping and the stamp duty (if any) chargeable on the agreement is paid, the interest and penalty provisions for stamp duty apply in relation to the agreement as if it had been executed on the date the lease was executed. The lease must be either in conformity with the agreement or relate to substantially the same property and term as the agreement. The stamp duty will be available as a credit against any SDLT chargeable on the transaction.

Transitional provisions – options and rights of pre-emption
(Paragraph 9 Schedule 19

Where an option to enter into a land transaction or a right of pre-emption relating to a land transaction was acquired before 1 December 2003 and was exercised on or after 1 December 2003:

- if the option or right was acquired on or after 17 April 2003[790] any consideration given for the grant of the option or right is treated as part of the chargeable consideration for the land transaction resulting from the exercise of the option or right.
- if the option or right was varied on or after 17 April 2003 but before 1 December 2003 any consideration for the variation is treated as part of the chargeable consideration for the land transaction resulting from the exercise of the option or right.
- whether or not the option or right was entered into or varied on or after 17 April 2003 the acquisition or variation of the option is treated as linked with the land transaction resulting from the exercise of the option or right.
- any ad valorem stamp duty paid on the acquisition or variation of the option or right goes to reduce the SDLT payable on the transaction resulting from its exercise.

6.2.2. Miscellaneous transitional provisions

Paragraph 6(2) and 6(3) Schedule 19 deal with transitional provisions for stamp duty group relief and acquisition relief.

Paragraph 7(1) Schedule 19 makes provision for transactions which are not themselves SDLT transactions but are linked to SDLT transactions. The linked transactions rules for SDLT purposes have, in effect, replaced the certificate of value provisions under stamp duty. A non-SDLT transaction linked to an SDLT transaction may have the effect of increasing the rate of SDLT payable. Paragraph 7(4) provides that in applying the linked lease provisions no account is to be taken of any transaction that is not an SDLT transaction.

Paragraph 7(2) Schedule 19 makes provision for transitional relief in relation to shared-ownership leases which were granted before 1 December 2003.

---

[790] One week after the 2003 Budget (9 April 2003)

Paragraph 7(3) Schedule 19 makes provision for the disapplication of the market value rule for transactions with a connected company in section 53 where stamp duty group relief has been claimed by the vendor within the three year period immediately preceding the effective date of the transaction.

6.3. Counterparts and duplicates

From 1 December 2003 counterparts and duplicates no longer need to be denoted against the original and stamped with £5 fixed duty. These instruments are not subject to SDLT.

7. The administration and collection of SDLT

(Sections 76 to 99 and Schedules 10 to 14)

Whereas stamp duty was essentially a voluntary tax, SDLT is backed by full assessment machinery. Liability for and payment of SDLT are governed by sections 85-92. Detailed provisions about the making of land transaction returns, assessments and related matters are contained in sections 76-82 and Schedule 10. These provisions are similar to those governing the direct tax self assessment regime in TMA 1970 and Schedule 18 FA 1998.

7.1. Notifiable transactions

(Section 77)

Notifiable transactions are not only those transactions for which SDLT is payable. They include those where tax is chargeable at the 0% rate and cases where a relief is claimed which reduces or extinguishes the liability.[791] However, transactions are not notifiable if they are exempt from charge under Schedule 3.[792]

Where a 'notifiable' land transaction is entered into, the purchaser must deliver a land transaction return to HMRC within 30 days of the effective date of the transaction (section 76(1)).

A land transaction is notifiable if it is:

(1) the grant or deemed grant[793] of a lease:

  a. for a term of seven years or more[794] for chargeable consideration;[795] or

  b. for a term of less than seven years where either:

    i. the chargeable consideration consists of or includes a premium in respect of which SDLT is chargeable at a rate of 1% or more (or would be but for a relief) or

---

[791] Paragraph 13 Schedule 6 inserted by section 298 FA 2004 with effect from 22 July 2004

[792] Section 77(5) as inserted by section 98(2) FA 2004 with effect from 22 July 2004

[793] For example, where there are successive linked leases (see 2.6.4 above), where an assignment of a lease is treated as a grant (see 1.5 above), where an agreement for lease is substantially performed without being completed (see 1.3 above), where a lease is varied in the first five years to increase the rent (see 2.6.21 above) or where there is an 'abnormal' rent increase after the fifth year of a lease (see 2.6.15 above).

[794] For the purposes of section 77 a lease for an indefinite term is treated as a lease for a term of less than seven years – paragraph 4(1) Schedule 17A.

[795] A peppercorn is not regarded as chargeable consideration – it is seen by HMRC as neither rent nor premium – SDLTM11010 (April 2007 draft).

ii. the chargeable consideration consists of or includes rent in respect of which SDLT is chargeable at a rate of 1% or more (or would be but for a relief);

(2) the assignment of a lease for chargeable consideration where:[796]

a. the lease is for seven years or more; or

b. the consideration for the assignment is chargeable at a rate of 1% or higher (or would be but for a relief);

(3) any other acquisition of a 'major interest'[797] in land unless the transaction is exempt under Schedule 3[798] or the land consists of residential property and the chargeable consideration for the acquisition, together with that for any linked transaction, is less than £1,000;[799]

(4) any other acquisition of a chargeable interest if SDLT is chargeable at the rate of 1% or more, (or would be but for a relief).

(5) a land transaction which a person is treated as entering into by virtue of section 44A(3) (contract and conveyance to third party);.[800]

(6) a lease to which paragraph 3 Schedule 17A applies (leases that continue after a fixed term) whatever the length of its fixed term.[801]

For the purposes of section 77 a lease for an indefinite term is treated as a lease for a term of less than seven years.[802]

---

796 Section 77(2A) inserted by section 164(1) FA 2006 with effect in relation to any assignment of which the effective date is on or after 19 July 2006. As originally enacted, section 77(2A) required notification of an assignment if the grant of the lease being assigned, if occurring on the same terms but at the time of the assignment, would be notifiable.

797 Defined in section 117(2) (in relation to England and Wales) as a fee simple absolute or a term of years absolute at law or in equity. The definitions applying to Scotland and Northern Ireland are in section 117(3) and (4) respectively.

798 For exempt transactions see 1.1.1 above. There is no need to file a land transaction return but self-certification is required

799 Section 77(3) as amended by section 98(2) FA 2004 with effect from 22 July 2004 – the transaction can then be self-certified.

800 See 1.1.1 above. Section 77(5) inserted by paragraph 4 Schedule 39 FA 2004 in relation to any contract entered into after 17 March 2004.

801 Paragraph 3(5) Schedule 17A inserted by paragraph 22 Schedule 39 FA 2004 with effect from 22 July 2004

802 Paragraph 4(4A) Schedule 17A inserted by paragraph 22 Schedule 39 FA 2004 with effect from 22 July 2004

7.1.1. Later linked transactions

(Section 81A)

A later transaction may make an earlier transaction to which it is linked a notifiable transaction. If the earlier transaction becomes notifiable in such circumstances or tax or additional tax becomes payable in respect of the earlier transaction, the purchaser under the earlier transaction must deliver a land transaction return within 30 days of the effective date of the later transaction.[803]

Before FA 2007 the return had to be accompanied by any tax payable calculated by reference to the rates in force at the effective date of the earlier transaction. Legislation was introduced in FA 2007 (taking effect from Royal Assent, 19 July 2007) amending section 81A so that payment of any SDLT due no longer has to accompany the land transaction return[804]. The tax is still payable by the filing date for the return.

7.2. The land transaction return

(Sections 76[805] and 78 and Schedule 10)

Section 76 effectively imposes the liability to SDLT. In the case of every 'notifiable transaction', the purchaser must within 30 days[806] after the effective date of the transaction (the 'filing date')[807] deliver a land transaction return to HMRC (section 76(1).

Legislation was introduced in FA 2007 (taking effect from Royal Assent[808]) amending section 76(3) so that payment of SDLT no longer has to accompany the land transaction return. This measure is intended to facilitate electronic conveyancing. The tax will still be payable within 30 days of the effective date of the transaction.

Where no land transaction return is delivered HMRC have power to determine the SDLT chargeable to the best of their information and belief. Such a

---

[803] Section 81A – Where a return has been submitted in respect of the earlier transaction an additional return will be required. This return is not yet available from HMRC and, in the meantime full details of the event requiring the return should be forwarded in a letter to Birmingham Stamp Office, attaching a copy of the original land transaction return and the appropriate payment - see 'Where to send your SDLT paper work' available at http://www.hmrc.gov.uk/so/mctu.htm.

[804] Section 81A(1)(d) as substituted by section 80 with effect from 19 July 2007.

[805] As amended by FA 2007 with effect from 19 July 2007

[806] The 30 day period can be shortened by regulations.

[807] Section 76(1) and paragraph 2 Schedule 10

[808] 19 July 2007

determination must be made within six years of the effective date of the transaction. Notice of the determination must be given to the purchaser and the notice must state the date on which it is issued.[809]

Where there are linked transactions with the same effective date the purchaser, or all the purchasers if more than one, may make a single land transaction return as if all those linked transactions that are 'notifiable' were a single notifiable transaction (section 108(2)). Where a single return is made in these circumstances, the provisions relating to joint purchasers in section 103 (see 7.17 below) apply as if the transactions were a single transaction and the purchasers were acting jointly.

Where SDLT relief is later withdrawn, for example, if charities relief is withdrawn because the property is no longer being used for charitable purposes, a further land transaction return must be made within 30 days of the date of the disqualifying event.[810] This return is not yet available from HMRC and, in the meantime, full details of the event requiring the return should be forwarded in a letter to Birmingham Stamp Office, attaching a copy of the original land transaction return and the appropriate payment[811].

In addition to the basic return in form SDLT1, the following supplemental returns have to be delivered:
SDLT2 – where there are more than two vendors and/or purchasers.
SDLT3 – where additional information is required to identify the property or the transaction involves more than one property
SDLT4 – where additional information is required about the transaction.

These forms are described in detail at 8.2 below.

The land transaction return must:

- be in the 'prescribed' form;
- contain the 'prescribed' information; and
- include a declaration by the purchaser (or each of them) that the return is to the best of his knowledge correct and complete.

(paragraph 1 Schedule 10)

'Prescribed' means prescribed by regulations made by HMRC which may require the provision of information corresponding to any of the particulars formerly required under Schedule 2 to FA 1931.[812] Section 28 FA 1931 required

---

[809] Paragraph 25 Schedule 10

[810] Section 81

[811] See 'Where to send your SDLT paper work' available at http://www.hmrc.gov.uk/so/mctu.htm.

[812] Paragraph 1(2) and 1(4) Schedule 10

a return to HMRC of details listed in Schedule 2 in the following circumstances:

- any transfer on sale of the fee simple of land.
- the grant of a lease for more than seven years.
- any transfer on sale of a lease with a term of more than seven years

The information was provided in the so-called Particulars Delivered ('PD') form (technically, form Stamps L(A)451) for stamp duty purposes and gave particulars of:

(a) the description of the instrument;
(b) the date of the instrument;
(c) the names and addresses of the transferor and transferee or lessor and lessee;
(d) the situation of the land to which the transaction relates, including any dimensions stated in the instrument and, if necessary for the identification of the land, a description of the boundaries of the land, or a plan;
(e) the estate or interest transferred, including, where the transaction is the assignment or grant of a lease or the transfer of a fee simple subject to a lease, the term of the lease, the date of the commencement of the term and the rent reserved;
(f) the consideration, if any, other than the rent shown under sub-paragraph (e), showing separately any capital payment, any debt released, any debt covenanted to be paid or to which the transaction is made subject, any periodical payment (including any charge) covenanted to be paid, any terms surrendered, any land exchanged and any other thing representing money or money's worth comprised in the consideration for the transaction;
(g) any minerals, mineral rights, sporting rights, timber or easements reserved, and of any restrictions, covenants or conditions affecting the value of the estate or interest transferred or granted; and
(h) the information given to the transferee or lessee by any relevant authority when requested, in connection with the transaction, to state what entries (if any) relating to the land to which the transaction relates were shown in any relevant register.

The form and content of the land transaction return (SDLT1) and the other supplementary returns (SDLT2, SDLT3 and SDLT4) is prescribed by regulation 9 Stamp Duty Land Tax (Administration) Regulations 2003.[813] The regulation provides as follows:

(1) A land transaction return must be in writing and completed in black ink.
(2) A land transaction return must be -

---

[813] SI 2003/2837

(a) on the form prescribed by Part 1 Schedule 2 of the Regulations together with any of the forms prescribed by Parts 2 to 4 of that Schedule which are relevant;[814] or

(b) in a form that has been approved by the Board.

(3) A land transaction return must contain the information required by the forms prescribed by Schedule 2 of the Regulations.

Online filing[815]

Since July 2005 online filing has been possible. Case management software can be used to generate the necessary forms. In order to use the online facility it is necessary to register and then activate the Stamp Taxes Online service[816]. See 1.1 below.

7.2.1. Amendment of land transaction return

(Paragraph 6 Schedule 10)

The purchaser can amend his land transaction return by notice to HMRC within 12 months of the filing date[817]. If the purchaser amends his return in this way then this alters the time periods for the enquiry window. The basic rule is that HMRC have nine months from the date of amendment to raise an enquiry[818]. However if the return has already been the subject of an enquiry, a second enquiry can only relate to the consequences of the amendment[819].

7.2.2. Relief in case of mistake in return

(Paragraph 34 Schedule 10)[820]

A person who believes he has paid tax under an assessment that was excessive by reason of some mistake in a land transaction return may make a claim to HMRC for relief against any excessive charge. The claim must be made not more than six years after the effective date of the transaction. The claim should be made to:

---

[814] The forms prescribed by Parts 2 to 4 are SDLT2, SDLT3 and SDLT4. The land transaction return (SDLT1) is prescribed by Part 1 of the Schedule.

[815] See Stamp Duty Land Tax (Electronic Communications) Regulations 2005 (SI 2005/844) as amended by SI 2006/3427 with effect from 31 January 2007

[816] To register for Stamp Taxes Online go to the HMRC homepage and under 'do it online' select 'Stamp Duty Land Tax'

[817] See SDLTM80585 for details of how to do this

[818] Paragraph 12(2)(c) Schedule 10

[819] Paragraph 13(2) Schedule 10

[820] As amended by section 299(8) FA 2004 with effect from 22 July 2004

Birmingham Stamp Office
9th Floor
City Centre House
30 Union Street,
Birmingham B2 4AR
Tel: 0845 603 0135
Fax: 0121 643 8381

The envelope and the letter should be marked 'SDLT'.

No relief is given in respect of a mistake as to the basis on which the liability ought to have been computed when the return was in fact made on the basis or in accordance with the practice generally prevailing at the time when it was made, nor is relief given in respect of a mistake in a claim or election included in the return.

In determining a claim, HMRC are required to have regard to all the relevant circumstances of the case and, in particular, consider whether the granting of relief would result in amounts being excluded from charge to tax.

An appeal can be made to the Special Commissioners against HMRC's decision on the claim.

7.2.3. Correction of land transaction return by HMRC

(Paragraph 7 Schedule 10[821])

HMRC can, by notice to the purchaser, amend a land transaction return to correct obvious errors or omissions. Such a correction can only be made within nine months after the delivery of the return or, if the purchaser has amended the return, within nine months after the amendment. The purchaser can amend the return to reject the correction or, if the period for amending the return has expired, he has three months from the date of issue of the notice of correction to give notice that he rejects the correction.

7.2.4. Lost or damaged returns

(Section 82)

Section 82 applies to returns lost or damaged before details can be recorded at HMRC's Central Processing Unit in Netherton (also known as the Rapid Capture Data Centre). If details have been recorded, credit will be given for tax paid and accounted for at the time the original return was submitted. No penalty will be charged if the return and payment were originally received on time.

---

821 As amended by F(No.2)A 2005 to allow HMRC by regulation to specify that this power can be exercised by the Chief Land Registrar – presumably to facilitate e-conveyancing.

Where a land transaction return delivered to HMRC or any other document relating to tax made by or provided to HMRC has been lost or destroyed, or been so defaced or damaged as to be illegible or otherwise useless, HMRC may treat the land transaction return as not having been delivered or the document as not having been received.

If, as a result of the loss, a person is charged with tax and they prove to the satisfaction of the General or Special Commissioners that they have already paid tax in respect of the transaction in question, relief shall be given by reducing the charge or by repayment as the case may require.

7.2.5. Formal notice to deliver a land transaction return

(Paragraph 5 Schedule 10)

HMRC have power to issue a notice where the filing date for a land transaction return has passed and the purchaser has failed to deliver a return.

7.2.6. Disclosure of information contained in land transaction returns

(Section 78A[822])

'Relevant information' contained in land transaction returns (whether before or after the commencement of this section) is to be available for use:

(1) by listing officers appointed under section 20 of the Local Government Finance Act 1992, for the purpose of facilitating the compilation and maintenance by them of valuation lists in accordance with Chapter 2 of Part 1 of that Act,

(2) as evidence in an appeal by virtue of section 24(6) of that Act to a valuation tribunal established under Schedule 11 to the Local Government Finance Act 1988,

(3) by the Commissioner of Valuation for Northern Ireland, for the purpose of maintaining a valuation list prepared, and from time to time altered, by him in accordance with Part 3 of the Rates (Northern Ireland) Order 1977, and

(4) by such other persons or for such other purposes as the Treasury may by regulations prescribe.

'Relevant information' means any information of the kind mentioned in paragraph 1(4) of Schedule 10 (information corresponding to particulars required under previous legislation).

The Treasury may by regulations amend the definition of 'relevant information'.

---

[822] Inserted by section 48 F(No.2)A 2005 from a day to be appointed by Treasury order.

7.3. Registration of land transactions

(Section 79[823])

The Land Registry is prohibited from registering, recording or otherwise reflecting in an entry on the Register any land transaction or any document effecting or recording it (other than where the entry is required to be made without any application or so far as the entry relates to an interest or right other than the chargeable interest acquired by the purchaser under the land transaction that gives rise to the application) unless a Revenue certificate or self-certificate is produced[824].

The requirement for a certificate applies to every land transaction, other than a transaction treated as taking place:

- under section 44(4) (contract and conveyance) or under that section as it applies by virtue of:
- section 45 (contract and conveyance: effect of transfer of rights); or
- paragraph 12B Schedule 17A (assignment of agreement for lease)
- under section 44A(3) (contract providing for conveyance to a third party) or under that section as it applies by virtue of section 45A (contract providing for conveyance to a third party: effect of transfer of rights); or
- under paragraph 12A(2) or 19(3) Schedule 17A ((agreement for lease substantially performed without being completed) or
- under paragraph 13 (increase of rent in first five years) or 15A (reduction of rent or term or variation of a lease for consideration) Schedule 17A.

So far as relating to the entry of a notice under section 34 of the Land Registration Act 2002 or section 38 of the Land Registration Act (Northern Ireland) 1970 (notice in respect of interest affecting registered land) the restriction on registration does not apply where the land transaction in question is the variation of a lease.

The certificate must be included with the documents submitted to the Land Registry when applying for registration of title. There are two types of certificate:

- a Revenue certificate that a land transaction return has been filed in respect of the land transaction (form SDLT5 – see 7.3.1 below);
- a self-certificate (form SDLT 60 – see 7.3.2 below) by the purchaser confirming that no land transaction return is required in respect of the transaction.

---

[823] As amended by F(No.2)A 2005 with effect from 20 July 2005

[824] Or such information about compliance as HMRC specify in regulations – presumably to facilitate e-conveyancing.

7.3.1. The Revenue certificate[825]

Three conditions must be met before a Revenue certificate is issued:[826]

(1) A land transaction return in respect of the transaction must have been received by HMRC.

(2) The land transaction return (together with any other returns that are required) must have been completed and must include a declaration that the return is correct and complete.

(3) A self-assessment must be included in the return; and on the basis of the information contained in the return, the self-assessment must appear to be correct.

Until 19 July 2007 there was a fourth condition, that payment of the amount of tax chargeable in respect of the transaction accompanied the return, but this was removed by FA 2007. The tax is still be payable by the filing date for the return.

A Revenue certificate must be in writing and must contain the following information:[827]

- the address of the land to which the transaction relates
- any number recorded as the title number of the land, for England and Wales, at the Land Registry
- any NLPG UPRN[828]
- a description of the transaction
- the effective date in relation to the transaction
- the name of the purchaser
- the name of the vendor

If HMRC are satisfied that a Revenue certificate has been lost or destroyed a duplicate Revenue certificate may be issued.[829] The duplicate Revenue certificate may be either, a Revenue certificate equivalent to, and replacing, the original certificate or, a new Revenue certificate superseding the original certificate.

Where a land transaction return is made relating to more than one transaction, then if the purchaser requests on the return that separate Revenue certificates

---

[825] This appears still to be the correct terminology even after the passage of the Commissioners for Revenue and Customs Act 2005

[826] Regulation 4 Stamp Duty Land Tax (Administration) Regulations 2003 (SI 2003/2837)

[827] Regulation 5 Stamp Duty Land Tax (Administration) Regulations 2003 (SI 2003/2837)

[828] The NLPG UPRN is the National Land and Property Gazette Unique Property Reference Number which is entered in Box 30 of the land transaction return– see 8.4.6 below

[829] Regulation 6 Stamp Duty Land Tax (Administration) Regulations 2003 (SI 2003/2837)

be issued in respect of each of the transactions to which the return relates, HMRC may provide separate certificates in respect of any of those transactions.[830]

7.3.2. The self-certificate

(Schedule 11)

The self-certificate must be on form SDLT60 which is the 'prescribed form' for the purposes of paragraph 2 Schedule 11.[831] FA 2007 amended these provisions to allow HMRC to provide that the self-certificate may include a declaration by an agent authorised by the purchaser to complete the self-certificate, or by the relevant Official Solicitor[832]. The form of the agents' and Official Receiver's declaration and electronic submission of the self-certificate will be provided for in regulations to be made by HMRC pursuant to this power.

SDLTM60050 gives a useful list of the circumstances in which an SDLT60 should be used and (after updating to take into account the changes to section 77(2A) made by section 164(1) FA 2006 in relation to assignments)[833] that list would read as follows:

1) The transfer or conveyance of a freehold interest in land for no chargeable consideration.[834]
2) The grant of a lease for a term of seven years or more for no chargeable consideration.[835]
3) The grant of a lease where:
    a) the term of the lease is less than seven years; and
    b) the amount of any premium is not such as to attract a charge to SDLT at a rate of 1% or higher (ignoring the availability of any relief); and
    c) the amount of any rent is not such as to attract a charge to SDLT at a rate of 1% or higher (ignoring the availability of any relief).[836]
4) The assignment of a lease for chargeable consideration where:
    a) the term of the lease is for seven years or more; or
    b) the consideration for the assignment would attract a charge to tax at a rate of 1% or higher (ignoring the availability of any relief).[837]

---

[830] Regulation 7 Stamp Duty Land Tax (Administration) Regulations 2003 (SI 2003/2837)

[831] Prescribed by regulation 8 Stamp Duty Land Tax (Administration) Regulations 2003 (SI 2003/2837) - form SDLT 60 is reproduced in the Appendix.

[832] In relation to transactions with an effective date on or after 19 July 2007

[833] Where the effective date is on or after 19 July 2006

[834] Section 77(3) and paragraph 1 Schedule 3

[835] Section 77(2)(a)

[836] Section 77(2)(b)

5) Land transactions, other than the acquisition of a 'major interest[838]' where the amount of the consideration is such as to attract SDLT at a rate of 1% or higher (ignoring the availability of any relief).[839]
6) Land transactions exempt from SDLT as transactions in connection with divorce or the dissolution of a civil partnership.[840]
7) Land transactions exempt from SDLT as variations of testamentary dispositions.[841]
8) The transfer or conveyance of a freehold interest in land consisting entirely of residential property, where the chargeable consideration, together with that of any linked transactions, is less than £1,000.[842]
9) The transfer to a beneficiary entitled under a will or on intestacy, where the only consideration given is the assumption of a 'secured debt'.[843]
10) The transfer of interest in a partnership for chargeable consideration not exceeding the nil-rate threshold.[844]

A purchaser who is required to give a self-certificate has similar record-keeping obligations to a purchaser who is required to deliver a land transaction return (paragraph 2 Schedule 11). HMRC have power to open an enquiry into a self-certificate.[845] A purchaser who fraudulently or negligently gives a self-certificate is liable to a tax-related penalty not exceeding the amount of tax chargeable in respect of the transaction[846].

7.3.3. Land Registry practice

The Land Registry regards transactions in relation to property as falling into three categories:[847]

---

[837] Section 77(2A) as inserted by section 164 FA 2006 in relation to any assignment of which the effective date is on or after 19 July 2006.

[838] A 'major interest' is defined in section 117(2) (in relation to England and Wales) as a fee simple absolute or a term of years absolute at law or in equity. The definitions applying to Scotland and Northern Ireland are in section 117(3) and (4) respectively.

[839] Section 77(4)

[840] Paragraph 3 Schedule 3

[841] Paragraph 4 Schedule 3

[842] Section 77(3)(b)

[843] As defined in paragraph 3A Schedule 3

[844] Not notifiable by virtue of paragraph 30 of Schedule 15

[845] Part 3 Schedule 11

[846] Paragraph 3 Schedule 11

[847] See Land Registry Practice Guide 49 (December 2006) at paragraph 5.3

1) Transactions requiring notification to HMRC and requiring the completion of a land transaction return. An original Revenue certificate must be submitted to the Land Registry when registering such a transaction.
2) Transactions not requiring notification to HMRC, but requiring a self-certificate form signed by the purchaser. The Land Registry will accept a photocopy of form SDLT60.[848]The certificate must be in the prescribed form.
3) Transactions that are exempt from SDLT or outside the scope of SDLT and do not require either notification to HMRC or self-certification.

The Land Registry requires the third category to be accompanied by a letter explaining why no certificate is necessary, except in the case of the following[849]:

- Discharge of charge
- Charge (including floating and fixed equitable charges)
- Transfer of charge
- Mortgage of a contract for sale or agreement for lease
- Postponement of registered charge
- Deed of variation of charge

Deed of variation of lease dated on or after 17 March 2004 which does not take effect as a surrender and re-grant of the existing lease (i.e. adds land to the demise or lengthens the term of the lease), or increase the rent payable

- Equitable charge
- Statutory charge
- Charging order
- Contract for sale
- Relocation grant scheme charge under s.138 of the Housing Grants, Construction and Regeneration Act 1996
- Property balancing agreement
- Land charge under statutes relating to the improvement of lands (i.e. the Improvement of Lands Acts 1864 and 1899 or the Land Improvement Company's Act 1853 to 1969)
- Deed of substituted security
- Vendor's unpaid lien
- Licence
- Franchise
- Other security interest

---

[848] See Land Registry Practice Guide 50 (November 2006) at paragraph 7.2

[849] See Land Registry Practice Guide 49 (December 2006) at paragraph 5.3

HMRC have the power to inspect any Revenue certificates or self-certificates produced to the Land Registry and are given the power to enter into arrangements with the Land Registry to obtain information.[850]

7.4. Claims not included in the land transaction return

(Section 82A and Schedule 11A)[851]

The usual mechanism for claiming repayment of tax within the time limit for amending the return is by way of an amended land transaction return.[852] The rules in Schedule 11A deal with claims to relief from SDLT which cannot be made in a land transaction return or amended return because they are outside the twelve month time limit.

Claims must include a declaration that they are correct to the best of the claimant's information and belief. The claim should be in a form required by HMRC and should include statements and documents to support it.

There is a duty to keep and preserve records. Records to support the claim for amendment must be kept for one year from the time of the claim or until the closure of any enquiry whichever is the later. This provision does not affect the requirement in paragraph 9 Schedule 10 to keep records relating to the preparation and delivery of the return for six years from the effective date of the transaction (see below).

The claimant can amend the claim within 12 months of the date of the claim or during an enquiry. HMRC can correct a claim to remove obvious errors within nine months of the date of claim.

HMRC have the power to enquire into a claim or an amendment of a claim. The enquiry must be commenced within nine months of the date of the claim or amendment. HMRC can issue a notice to produce documents and information for the purposes of an enquiry. The same rules apply to an enquiry under Schedule 11A as apply to an enquiry into a return under paragraph 14 Schedule 10.

7.5. Preservation of records

(Section 78 and Schedule 10 Part 2)

A purchaser who is required to deliver a land transaction return must keep such records as may be needed to deliver a correct and complete return and

---

[850] Section 79(6)

[851] Inserted by FA 2004 with effect from 22 July 2004

[852] Pursuant to paragraph 6 Schedule 10.

preserve those records for at least six years from the date of the transaction and until any later date on which an enquiry into the return is completed or HMRC no longer have power to enquire into the return. Failure to do so carries a penalty of up to £3,000. HMRC have indicated their view that there can only be one failure in respect of each return.[853]

The records required to be kept and preserved under this paragraph include:

- relevant instruments relating to the transaction, in particular, any contract or conveyance, and any supporting maps, plans or similar documents
- records of relevant payments, receipts and financial arrangements.

Paragraph 10 Schedule 10 allows for the preservation of information instead of the original records. Records may be kept in an alternative form, such as microfiche or an electronic facsimile, as long as the information they contain is preserved.[854]

> "It is not [HMRC]'s intention to seek penalties under this legislation in every case where there is evidence that the purchaser had failed to maintain and retain the required records.
>
> In the majority of cases where the purchaser has failed to keep adequate records and where, as a result, offences under paragraph 11 Schedule 10 FA 2003 have been brought to light, it will be sufficient simply to continue to reflect those failures in calculating the abatements considered appropriate.
>
> Assurances should be given that paragraph 11 Schedule 10 FA 2003 penalties will only be sought in more serious cases where, for example, records have been deliberately destroyed to obstruct an enquiry or where there has been a history of serious record-keeping failures."[855]

7.6. Enquiries into returns[856]

(Section 78 and Part 3 Schedule 10)

HMRC can make an enquiry into a land transaction return within nine months of submission of the return or of the date on which an amendment was made to a return[857]. The scope of an enquiry covers the question of whether tax is chargeable and the amount of tax so chargeable. HMRC can amend the return

---

[853] See SDLTM86230

[854] Ibid

[855] See SDLTM86230

[856] See Code of Practice 24 'Stamp Duty Land Tax Enquiries', Code of Practice 25 'Stamp Duty Land Tax Enquiries into companies and partnerships' and 'Enquiries into land transaction returns' dated April 2005 – all available on the HMRC website.

[857] Amendments to a return can be made within 12 months of the filing date.

during the course of an enquiry to prevent loss of tax and the purchaser also has the opportunity to amend a return while an enquiry is in progress[858].

HMRC can require the production of documents for the purposes of the enquiry. An enquiry is completed when HMRC issue a closure notice informing the purchaser that they have completed their enquiries and stating their conclusions.

7.7. Payment of tax

(Section 86[859])

In accordance with the legislation in force at the date of publication any SDLT due must be paid at the same time as the land transaction return is made (which must be by the filing date).

Section 86 was amended by FA 2007 with effect from 19 July 2007 so that payment of any SDLT due no longer has to accompany the land transaction return. The tax is still payable by the filing date for the return.

If a land transaction return is amended before the filing date payment of tax remains due at the filing date. If a land transaction return is amended after the filing date payment of tax is due immediately.

If tax is not paid because group relief, reconstruction or acquisition relief or charities relief has been claimed and such relief is withdrawn because a disqualifying event occurs, SDLT is payable and a land transaction return must be made within 30 days of such disqualifying event[860].

In cases where HMRC issues a determination or assessment in respect of an amount of SDLT, the tax is due within 30 days of the date of issue of the determination or assessment.

7.7.1. Liability for tax

(Section 85)

The 'purchaser' is liable for the SDLT due in respect of a chargeable transaction. Joint purchasers are jointly and severally liable for the tax (section 103(2)(c)). There are special rules for trustees (see 7.18 below).

---

[858] Subject to the time limit in paragraph 6 Schedule 10.

[859] As amended by FA 2007

[860] Section 86(2) which was also amended by FA 2007 (with effect from 19 July 2007) to require the tax to be paid not later than the filing date for the land transaction return relating to the withdrawal.

Any SDLT due can be recovered, subject to certain procedures, by HMRC pursuant to the provisions Schedule 12.

7.8. Deferring payment of SDLT in the case of uncertain or contingent consideration[861]

(Section 90 and Part 4 Stamp Duty Land Tax (Administration) Regulations 2003)[862]

An application to defer the SDLT payable on a transaction may be made by the purchaser where the whole or part of the chargeable consideration:

1) is contingent or uncertain as defined in section 51 and
2) becomes payable or may become payable more than six months after the effective date of the transaction.

Deferral is not available to the extent that the consideration consists of rent.[863] Where the application is successful, interest will run only from 30 days after the deferred SDLT becomes payable.

An application under section 90 does not affect the purchaser's obligation to pay SDLT on any consideration that:

- has already been paid when the application is made
- will become payable within six months of the effective date of the transaction
- is not contingent
- is ascertained or ascertainable at the time the application is made.

Deferral can apply to consideration which is payable within six months if there is any part of the uncertain or contingent consideration payable after six months.

Deferral is not available where the amount of the consideration is ascertainable at the effective date but has not yet been ascertained. This is because in order to be within section 51 the amount has to depend on uncertain future events by virtue of section 51(3). Where consideration is ascertainable but not ascertained, the land transaction return (Box 10) should be completed on the basis of a best estimate of the purchase price which will be payable (which may be nil). When the final consideration is known an amendment to the land transaction return should be made.[864]

---

[861] See SDLTM50900 and SDLTM50910

[862] SI 2003/2837

[863] Section 90(7)

[864] Under paragraph 6 Schedule 10

A payment on account may be made where a purchaser considers interest may accrue on any SDLT outstanding.

The application for deferral must be made before the filing date for the land transaction return.[865] There is no express power for HMRC to grant an extension for late applications.

The application must be made in writing and should be sent the Birmingham Stamp Office (and *not* to the Complex Transaction Unit, see 8.3.20).

The application must set out:[866]

1) the identity of the purchaser;
2) the location of the land;
3) the nature of the contingency/uncertain payment;
4) the amount of consideration for which deferment is sought;
5) as full details of the times of expected payments as possible to give;
6) a reasoned opinion as to when this part of the consideration will cease to be contingent or can be ascertained;
7) a calculation of the SDLT payable on the total of the actual and the contingent/uncertain consideration;
8) a calculation of the SDLT in respect of which the application to defer payment refers.

Where the consideration to which an application relates, or any element of that consideration, consists of the carrying out of works of construction, improvement or repair of a building or other works to enhance the value of land or the provision of services (other than the carrying out of such works) the application must contain a scheme for payment of tax.[867] Such a scheme must include:

- a proposal for the payment of tax in respect of the consideration, or element of the consideration, consisting of the carrying out of such works or the provision of such services within 30 days after the carrying out or from when the provision is substantially completed; and
- if the carrying out of such works or the provision of such services is expected to last for more than six months, proposals for a scheme of payment of tax at intervals of not more than six months.

HMRC may make a request for further information in order to determine if an application may be accepted.

---

[865] Regulation 10 Stamp Duty Land Tax (Administration) Regulations 2003 (SI 2003/2837). This will normally be 30 days from the effective date of the land transaction

[866] Regulation 12 Stamp Duty Land Tax (Administration) Regulations 2003 (SI 2003/2837). See also SDLTM50910

[867] Regulation 13 Stamp Duty Land Tax (Administration) Regulations 2003 (SI 2003/2837)

Payment of any SDLT which would not be due and payable if the deferral application were accepted is postponed pending the reaching of a decision on the application. If an application is refused and there is no appeal against the refusal of the application, the date on which any tax, the payment of which had been postponed pending a decision, is due and payable, is determined as if it were charged by an assessment of which notice was issued on the date on which HMRC issues to the applicant a notice of the total amount payable in consequence of the refusal of the application.

HMRC must give notice in writing to the person by whom the application was made of their decision whether to accept or refuse an application. Where HMRC accept an application, the notice must set out the terms on which the application has been accepted and, in particular, the 'relevant events' which will trigger an obligation to pay the SDLT which has been deferred.[868] SDLT may still be payable before the additional consideration is paid.

Where HMRC refuse an application, the notice must set out the grounds for the refusal and the total amount of tax payable in consequence of the refusal.[869] An application for deferral may be refused, inter alia, if there are 'tax avoidance arrangements' in relation to the transaction in question.[870]

Arrangements are 'tax avoidance arrangements' in relation to a transaction if their main object or one of their main objects is to enable payment of the tax payable in respect of the transaction to be deferred; or to avoid the amount or value of the whole or part of the chargeable consideration for the transaction being determined in accordance with section 51(1). Broadly, therefore, the avoidance targeted is the exploitation of the rules on deferred consideration.

'Arrangements' include any scheme, agreement or understanding, whether or not legally enforceable.

There is a right of appeal against a refusal by HMRC to accept an application for deferral. Notice of an appeal must be given in writing within 30 days after the date on which the notice of the decision to refuse the application was issued.

Where HMRC accept a deferral application which relates to SDLT that has already been paid, the amount already paid is repaid together with interest as

[868] Regulation 16(2)(a) Stamp Duty Land Tax (Administration) Regulations 2003 (SI 2003/2837)

[869] Regulation 16(3)(a) Stamp Duty Land Tax (Administration) Regulations 2003 (SI 2003/2837)

[870] Regulation 17 Stamp Duty Land Tax (Administration) Regulations 2003 (SI 2003/2837)

from the date of payment. An application which has been accepted ceases to have effect if 'the facts and circumstances relevant to it materially change'[871].

Where an application for deferral has been accepted, the purchaser must make a return or further return by the date determined in accordance with regulation 24(3).[872] The return must be accompanied by payment of any tax or additional tax payable. As at the date of publication the specific form of return had not been produced by HMRC so notification should be by letter to the Birmingham Stamp Office, attaching a copy of the original land transaction return and payment.

If the effect of the return is that less tax is payable in respect of a transaction than has already been paid, the amount overpaid will be repaid on a claim by the purchaser, together with interest as from the date of payment.

7.9. Assessments

(Paragraphs 28 to 32 Schedule 10)

HMRC have power to make assessments if they discover that:
a) an amount of tax that ought to be assessed has not been assessed; or
b) an assessment to tax is or has become insufficient; or
c) relief has been given that is or has become excessive
and may also make assessments to recover excessive repayments of tax.

Where the purchaser has delivered a land transaction return in respect of the transaction HMRC may make a discovery assessment only if there has been fraud or negligence by the purchaser or a partner of his or a person acting on his behalf, or in certain circumstances where HMRC could not previously have been expected to be aware of the situation.[873] Notice of an assessment must be served on the purchaser in the appropriate form.

7.9.1. Discovery assessments – effect of Langham v. Veltema

The question of when HMRC can be expected to be aware of a situation was considered in the direct tax case of *Langham v. Veltema*[874] the facts of which were as follows:

A company director was liable to income tax on the value of a house. In his 1997/98 tax return, which he submitted in July 1998, he submitted a valuation of £100,000. In September 1998 HMRC advised him that his return had been

---

[871] Regulation 28 Stamp Duty Land Tax (Administration) Regulations 2003 (SI 2003/2837)

[872] Even if the purchaser no longer owns the land.

[873] Paragraph 30 Schedule 10

[874] [2004] EWCA Civ. 193, [2004] STC 544 applied in *McQueen v. HMRC* [2007] SSCD 457 (Sp C 601).

processed 'without any need for correction'. In October 1999 the company submitted a corporation tax return, and HMRC subsequently formed the opinion, on the basis of information in that return, that the value of the house had been more than the £100,000 included on the director's personal tax return. In June 2000 they issued a further assessment on the basis that the true value had been £145,000. The director appealed, contending that the issue of a further assessment was not authorised by section 29 TMA 1970 as HMRC could have been reasonably expected, on the basis of information made available to them in the self-assessment return, to be aware that his assessment to tax was insufficient so as to cause a loss of tax for the purpose of section 29 TMA 1970.

The Court of Appeal unanimously upheld the assessment on the taxpayer, holding that section 29(5) [875] did not prohibit the issue of the assessment. The underlying purpose of the self-assessment scheme was to simplify and bring about early finality of assessment to tax, based on an assumption of an honest and accurate return and accompanying documentation by the taxpayer. Where a taxpayer made an inaccurate self-assessment, but without any fraud or negligence on his part, it would frustrate the scheme's aim to interpret section 29(5) TMA 1970 so as to introduce an obligation on HMRC to conduct an intermediate scrutiny of self-assessment returns when they did not disclose insufficiency but only circumstances whose further investigation might show insufficiency. It was plain from the wording of the statutory test in section 29(5) that it was concerned with what a tax inspector could have been reasonably expected to be aware of, not what he could reasonably have been expected to do. Section 29(5) spoke of an inspector's objective awareness, from the information made available to him by the taxpayer, of an actual insufficiency in the assessment. HMRC was shut out from making a discovery assessment under section 29 only when a taxpayer, in making an honest and accurate return, or in responding to an inquiry, had clearly alerted them to the insufficiency of the assessment, not where HMRC might have some other information that could put the sufficiency of the assessment in question. Accordingly, applying the proper statutory test, there had been no basis upon which it could have been found that the inspector ought reasonably to have been aware of the insufficiency of the assessment on the basis of the information provided in the taxpayer's self-assessment return.

HMRC have published guidance on the application of *Langham v. Veltema* to SDLT transactions[876]. The guidance is as follows:

---

[875] Section 29(5) is identical, in all material respect, to paragraph 30 Schedule 10.

[876] In SDLT Technical Newsletter 4 (6 March 2007)

Stamp Duty Land Tax: Finality and 'Discovery'

1. After a land transaction return has been filed or amended HM Revenue & Customs (HMRC) may decide to open an enquiry into the return so that we can be satisfied that the correct amount of SDLT has been paid. Such an enquiry must be opened within a certain time period. For example, where a return is filed on time and no later amendment is made HMRC must open an enquiry within nine months of the filing date (the filing date is the date by which the return must be filed to avoid a penalty and in normal circumstances is 30 days after the effective date of the transaction). At the conclusion of the enquiry HMRC will decide whether the right amount of SDLT has (in our opinion) been paid. If we think the right amount of SDLT has not been paid we can amend the return in order to assess the right amount of tax. There is the right of appeal to an independent tax tribunal

2. However in some circumstances HMRC can make an assessment even where an enquiry has not been opened during the nine-month period.

Such as assessment is referred to as a 'discovery' assessment (because we 'discover' that not enough SDLT has been paid). In most cases a discovery assessment is made because we consider that tax has been underpaid because of the fraudulent or negligent conduct of the purchaser, a person acting on behalf of the purchaser or a business partner of the purchaser. This article is not concerned with fraudulent or negligent conduct and nothing in this article affects our approach where we consider there has been fraudulent or negligent conduct.

3. But a discovery assessment can also be made where, at the time the nine-month enquiry period came to an end or (if later) the time HMRC completed their enquiries, we could not reasonably have been expected, on the basis of the information available to us before that time, to have been aware that insufficient tax had been paid.

4. This provision is similar to an income tax provision, which was considered by the Court of Appeal in the case of *Langham v Veltema* [2004] STC 544. This case gave rise to some uncertainty among taxpayers, first, as regards the lack of finality for the taxpayer at the close of the enquiry window and second, as regards the inherent difficulty of complying with the law as expounded in the Court of Appeal.

5. For this reason we issued a Statement of Practice, SP1/06, in 2006 (Statements of Practice explain how we intend to apply the law in cases of uncertainty). This explained what taxpayers had to do to guard against the possibility of a

subsequent discovery assessment. You can find the text of the Statement of Practice at http://www.hmrc.gov.uk/practitioners/sp01-06.pdf.

6. We intend to apply the Statement of Practice to SDLT. However it would be very unusual for purchasers to have to make a disclosure in ordinary residential or small commercial transactions. For example it is very common in such transactions to apportion part of the purchase price to chattels. There is no need to disclose to us that you have done so. Similarly, on the sale of a business, there is no need to provide us with any information additional to that in box 1 of form SDLT4.

7. If purchasers or their advisers do feel that they need to protect themselves from discovery by making a disclosure in relation to a land transaction they should do so by writing to the Complex Transactions Unit in Manchester, quoting the UTRN, at or before the time they submit the land transaction return for that land transaction. Information disclosed in this way will be treated, for the purposes of paragraph 30(4)(a) of Schedule 15 Finance Act 2003, as if it had been contained in the land transaction return for that land transaction. Please do not send disclosures to the Rapid Data Capture Centre at Netherton, or put them in the same envelope as land transaction returns, as this causes difficulty for the automated processing system.

The general guidance given by SP1/06 is that a taxpayer should provide enough information for HMRC to realise within the enquiry period that the self-assessment is insufficient. Taxpayers are encouraged to submit the minimum information necessary to make disclosure of an insufficiency. Where the taxpayer has alerted HMRC to the full circumstances of an entry on the return, then HMRC are in a position to determine whether or not there is an insufficiency and the conditions set by the Court of Appeal in *Langham v Veltema* be met and the assessment will not be open to discovery on that point.

For SDLT purposes, protection from a discovery assessment by making a disclosure of the insufficiency only seems to be available when a land transaction return has been submitted. Where the transaction concerned has also given rise to a requirement to disclose under the Tax Avoidance Schemes (Information) (Amendment) Regulations 2005[877] a disclosure under these regulations will not provide protection against a discovery assessment, especially where the disclosure is by the promoter, because such disclosures are not client or transaction specific.

[877] SI 2005/1869 – see Chapter 5 above

Where no land transaction return is required it seems that the safest method of making a disclosure is to file a nil return (on form SDLT1) and disclose by covering letter.

7.9.2. Time limit for assessments

(Paragraph 31)

The general time limit for an assessment is six years after the effective date, although this time limit is extended in cases of fraud or negligence to 21 years. If a purchaser has died, assessments on his or her personal representatives must be made within three years of the date of death and only in relation to transactions within the six years prior to the death.

7.10. Interest and penalties

The general rules in relation to penalties are set out in section 99 and Schedule 14. Penalties can be mitigated and an appeal lies to the General or Special Commissioners against the imposition of a penalty.

Section 99(2A) provides that where there are two tax related penalties under SDLT, penalties after the first are reduced so that the total does not exceed the amount of the greatest penalty. This is similar to the rule for Income Tax in section 97A of TMA 1970. The maximum total penalty that is chargeable is the amount of the tax.

7.10.1. Penalties in relation to the land transaction return

Schedule 10 makes provision for penalties in the following cases in relation to the land transaction return:

- a flat-rate penalty of £100 if the land transaction return is 'delivered' within three months of the filing date and £200 in any other case;[878]
- a tax related penalty equal to the amount of the unpaid SDLT where the return is not delivered within twelve months of the filing date. This is in addition to any flat-rate penalty;
- a daily penalty of up to £60 a day for failure to comply with an HMRC notice to deliver a land transaction return;
- a tax-related penalty of an amount not exceeding the tax understated where a return is incorrect through fraud or negligence;[879]
- a tax-related penalty of an amount not exceeding the tax understated where an incorrect return is not remedied without unreasonable delay.[880]

---

[878] 'Delivered' for the purposes of Schedule 10 means that the return has been made in the prescribed form (paragraph 2(2) Schedule 10) – see 7.2 above.

[879] The same penalty applies by reason of paragraph 3 Schedule 11 in relation to self-certificates.

[880] See footnote 879

7.10.2. Other penalties

The following penalties are also chargeable:

- a penalty not exceeding £3,000 for failure to keep and preserve the records required by paragraph 9 Schedule 10 or paragraph 4 Schedule 11 (in relation to a self-certificate). HMRC have indicated their view that there can only be one failure in respect of each return.[881]
- a penalty of £50 for failing to comply with a notice to produce documents for the purposes of an enquiry together with a penalty of £30 or £150 where the failure continues after the first penalty has been imposed.
- a penalty not exceeding £300 for failure to comply with a notice under Part 1, 2 or 3 Schedule 13 to deliver a document or to provide information, or to make a document available for inspection.[882] If the failure continues after a penalty has been imposed, there is a further penalty or penalties not exceeding £60 for each day on which the failure continues after the day on which the penalty was imposed (but excluding any day for which a penalty has already been imposed).[883]
- a penalty not exceeding £3,000 where a person who is required by a notice under Part 1, 2 or 3 Schedule 13 to deliver a document or to provide information, or to make a document available for inspection, fraudulently or negligently delivers, provides or makes available any incorrect document or information.
- a maximum penalty of £3,000 for assisting in the preparation of an incorrect return, information or other document. The penalty applies to a person who assists in such preparation or delivery which he knows will be or is likely to be used for the purposes of the tax and which will be incorrect.[884]

7.10.3. Interest

(Sections 87 to 89)

Sections 87, 88 and 89 provide for the charging of interest on SDLT, the charging of interest on SDLT penalties and the payment of interest on repayments of SDLT. In each case the rate of interest is the rate applicable under section 178 FA 1989.

Interest runs on unpaid SDLT from the end of the period of 30 days after the 'relevant date' until payment.

---

[881] See SDLTM86230

[882] Section 93(3)

[883] Section 93(4)

[884] Section 96

The 'relevant date' is:

1. in the case of an amount payable because relief is withdrawn under:
   Schedule 6A (relief for certain acquisitions of residential property)
   Part 1 Schedule 7 (group relief)
   Part 2 Schedule 7 (reconstruction or acquisition relief)
   Schedule 8 (charities relief)
   the date of the 'disqualifying event';
2. in the case of an amount payable under section 81A in respect of an earlier transaction because of the effect of a later linked transaction, the effective date of the later transaction;
3. in the case of an amount payable under paragraph 3(3) or 4(3) Schedule 17A (leases that continue after a fixed term and treatment of leases for an indefinite term), the day on which the lease becomes treated as being for a longer fixed term;
4. in the case of a deferred payment under section 90, the date when the deferred payment is due;
5. in any other case, the effective date of the transaction.

Disqualifying event is defined in section 87(4).

In a case falling within section 51 (contingent, uncertain or unascertained consideration) where payment is not deferred, interest on any tax payable under section 80 (adjustment where contingency ceases or consideration is ascertained) runs from the effective date of the transaction.

If an amount is lodged with HMRC in respect of the tax, the amount on which interest is payable is reduced by that amount.

HMRC had to admit that regulations laid in 2003 were defective, and that during the period between 1 December 2003, when SDLT was introduced, and 26 September 2005 (when the regulations referred to below came into force), they had not been statutorily empowered to charge interest on unpaid SDLT nor to pay interest on overpaid SDLT. Any interest paid by taxpayers during that period will be refunded and interest paid by HMRC will not be recovered.[885]

The Taxes (Interest Rate) (Amendment) Regulations 2005[886] amended the Taxes (Interest Rate) Regulations[887] to add provisions about interest rates in connection with SDLT and to make provision for the setting of the rate of

---

[885] See 'Incorrect charging of SDLT Interest: Briefing' at: www.hmrc.gov.uk/so/sdlt_interest_qa.htm

[886] SI 2005/2462

[887] SI 1989/1297

interest on SDLT which is not paid on time, the rate of interest on SDLT penalties and the rate of interest on repayments of SDLT. The regulations are not retrospective and interest will run from the date the Taxes (Interest Rate) (Amendment) Regulations 2005 came into force, 26 September 2005.

7.10.4. Fraudulent evasion of SDLT

(Section 95)

The offence of fraudulent evasion of SDLT is committed by a person who is knowingly concerned in the fraudulent evasion either of his own tax liability or that of another person. The penalty, on summary conviction, is imprisonment not exceeding six months or a fine not exceeding the statutory maximum or both. On conviction on indictment, the penalty is imprisonment for a term not exceeding seven years or a fine or both.

7.11. Information powers

(Section 93 and Schedule 13)

Schedule 13 provides HMRC with extensive information powers:
Part 1 confers power on an authorised officer to call for documents or information from the taxpayer;
Part 2 confers power on an authorised officer to call for documents from a third party;
Part 3 confers power on an authorised officer to call for the papers of a tax accountant;
Part 4 imposes restrictions on the powers under Parts 1 to 3;
Part 5 confers powers on the Board to call for documents or information;
Part 6 provides for an order of a judicial authority for the delivery of documents;
Part 7 provides for entry with a warrant to obtain evidence of an offence;
Part 8 relates to falsification etc of documents

Schedule 13 is based on sections 20 to 20D TMA 1970 and gives general information powers, in addition to the power to issue a notice for documents etc. for the purposes of an enquiry. The powers apply to third parties. Penalty provisions are included.

7.12. Appeals

(Part 7 Schedule 10 and Stamp Duty Land Tax (Appeals) Regulations 2004)[888]

There are four grounds of appeal to the General or Special Commissioners:

---

[888] SI 2004/1363

1. against an amendment of a self-assessment by HMRC during an enquiry in order to prevent loss of tax (pursuant to paragraph 17 Schedule 10)
2. against a conclusion stated or amendment made by a closure notice (after an enquiry)
3. against a discovery assessment
4. against an assessment to recover an excessive repayment (pursuant to paragraph 29 Schedule 10).

An appeal must be lodged within 30 days of the specified date (determined in accordance with paragraph 36 Schedule 10).

7.13. Collection of unpaid SDLT

Schedule 12 deals with HMRC's powers to recover unpaid SDLT.

7.14. Application of SDLT to companies

(Section 100)

Except where a specific definition applies,[889] 'company' for SDLT purposes means any body corporate or unincorporated association. A company's proper officer or another person authorised to act for the company, except in liquidation, is responsible for notifying and paying the SDLT.

The proper officer of a body corporate is the secretary or person acting as secretary and the proper officer of an unincorporated association or body corporate that does not have a secretary is the treasurer or person acting as treasurer.

SDLTM30200 gives the following guidance on company signatories:

> "In practice, a return or amended return should be accepted provided that it contains a signature and there is no reason to doubt the authority of the person signing.
>
> On this basis, the signature of any company official, employee or agent can be accepted. This includes a tax advisor, accountant, solicitor or licensed conveyancer.
>
> In addition, a land transaction return that is signed in the name of a firm of accountants, solicitors or licensed conveyancers on behalf of a company may also be accepted."

If a company is in liquidation or administration the proper officer is the liquidator or administrator. If two or more persons are appointed to act jointly or concurrently, the proper officer is the person who is specified in a notice

[889] For example, section 66(6)

given to HMRC by those persons for the purpose of this section. If no notification has been made, HMRC may designate a proper officer.

Service of any document is given effect by serving on the proper officer and tax due from a company that is not a body corporate or is incorporated outside the UK may be recovered from such officer. The proper officer may retain company monies in order to pay SDLT and where he is not reimbursed he may be indemnified by the company in respect of that liability.[890]

7.15. Application of SDLT to unit trusts

(Section 101)

Section 101 provides that the trustees of a unit trust scheme are treated as if they were a company for SDLT purposes, except that group relief, reconstruction and acquisition reliefs do not apply to them.[891] The rights of unit holders are treated for SDLT purposes as if they were shares in that company. This means that there is no 'look-through' a property-owning unit trust to the underlying land and a unit can be transferred without SDLT because it is not a chargeable interest[892].

Unit trusts are carved out of the trust rules in Schedule 16. The effect of this is that the units are not chargeable interests under section 48 and SDLT does not apply to the acquisition of those units, but an acquisition of a chargeable interest by the trust in exchange for the issue of units will, for SDLT purposes, be treated as a complete alienation of the property by the contributor.

The deemed market value rule for transactions between connected companies in section 53 applies to unit trusts as it does to companies.[893]

A unit trust scheme has the same meaning as in the Financial Services and Markets Act 2000 and a unit holder means a person entitled to a share of the investments subject to the trusts of a unit trust scheme.

An umbrella scheme is a unit trust which has arrangements for separate pooling of the contributions of participants and the profits or income out of

---

890 Section 100(5)

891 For capital gains tax purposes it is the scheme (not the trustees) which is deemed to be a company (section 99(1) TCGA 1992) but this difference has no significance.

892 Contrast the treatment of a partnership owning UK land even if the at partnership has legal personality – paragraph 2 Schedule 15 and see Section 1 above.

893 Section 101(7) was amended by section 166(3) FA 2006 to apply the market value rule to unit trusts in relation to any land transaction of which the effective date was on or after 22 March 2006, subject to transitional provisions – see 3.1.1 above.

which payments are to be made and under which the participants are entitled to exchange rights in one pool for rights in another. A part of an umbrella scheme means such of the arrangements as relate to a separate pool.

Where there is an umbrella scheme each part is regarded as a separate unit trust and the scheme as a whole is not treated as a unit trust scheme for SDLT purposes. Therefore, where part of an umbrella scheme acquires land, that part is treated as a unit trust in its own right and the trustees of that part will be treated as a company by virtue of section 101(1)(a).

Unit trust seeding relief was withdrawn with effect from 22 March 2006[894].

7.16. Application of SDLT to open-ended investment companies ('OEICs')

(Section 102)

OEICs are companies for SDLT purposes and the SDLT provisions can apply to them in the same way as they apply to unit trust schemes. The Treasury has power to make regulations to secure this result. No regulations have been made to date so for the time being the normal SDLT rules apply.

7.17. Application of SDLT to joint purchasers

(Section 103)

Section 103 applies to a land transaction where there are two or more purchasers who are or will be jointly entitled to the interest acquired. It does not, however, apply to partnerships or trustees for whom there are separate provisions (set out in Chapter 1 above and section 7.18 below).

Section 103(2) sets out the general rules for joint purchasers which are:

- Any obligation imposed on a purchaser is imposed on the purchasers jointly but may be discharged by any one of them.
- Anything required or authorised to be done in relation to the purchaser must be done in relation to all joint purchasers.
- Any liability of a purchaser is joint and several, so a failure to submit a land transaction return and pay the tax due will attract interest and penalties which can be recovered from all or any of the joint purchasers.

If the joint transaction is a notifiable transaction, only a single land transaction return is required, although the declaration that the land transaction return or

---

[894] See 3.1.1 above

self-certificate is complete and correct must be made by all the joint purchasers.[895]

Any formal notice issued by HMRC must be issued to all purchasers and will not be effective against any of them unless notice of it is given to each of them (provided their identity is known).

7.18. Application of SDLT to trusts and trustees

(Section 105 and Schedule 16)

The general SDLT rules apply to trusts in conjunction with the special rules set out in Schedule 16. Trustees may be chargeable in the normal way when they acquire land and the beneficial interest[896] under a trust is a chargeable interest where the underlying property includes land. Trustees are treated as a continuing body of persons for SDLT purposes and so changes in the trustees are ignored where the trust continues[897].

The SDLT legislation distinguishes between bare trusts and settlements (which are defined as trusts which are not bare trusts).

7.18.1. Bare trusts/nominee arrangements

A 'bare trust' for SDLT purposes means 'a trust under which property is held by a person as trustee:

(a) for a person who is absolutely entitled as against the trustee, or who would be so entitled but for being a minor or other person under a disability, or
(b) for two or more persons who are or would be jointly so entitled,

and expressly includes a case in which a person holds property as nominee for another'.[898]

The references to a person being absolutely entitled to property as against the trustee are references to a case where the person has 'the exclusive right, subject only to satisfying any outstanding charge, lien or other right of the trustee, to resort to the property for payment of duty, taxes, costs or other outgoings or to direct how the property is to be dealt with.'[899]

---

[895] Section 103(3) and (4)

[896] Other than an interest as the object of a discretionary power

[897] See SDLTM31745

[898] Paragraph 1(2) Schedule 16 This wording should be compared to the definition of 'absolutely entitled as against a trustee 'in section 60(1) TCGA 1992:
"the exclusive right, subject only to satisfying any outstanding charge, lien or other right of the trustees to resort to the property for payment of duty, taxes, costs or other outgoings, to direct how that property shall be dealt with."

[899] Paragraph 1(3) Schedule 16

The general rule[900] is that where a person acquires a chargeable interest or an interest in a partnership as bare trustee, the SDLT legislation applies as if the interest were acquired by the beneficial owner - the acts of the trustee in relation to the chargeable interest are treated as if they were the acts of the person or persons for whom he is trustee.[901] In such a case, the beneficiaries are responsible for paying the SDLT.

The general rule does not apply in a case where the transaction is the grant of a lease to or by a nominee (not necessarily by or to the beneficial owner). Paragraphs 3(3) and 3(4) of Schedule 16[902] make such a transaction chargeable to SDLT as if the nominee was the purchaser or vendor of the whole interest (legal and beneficial) in the lease. This should not have any adverse consequences in the case of a grant to a nominee unless the nominee gives consideration for the grant. A group relief claim may be necessary where a lease is granted by one group company to a connected company as its nominee (so as to avoid a market value charge arising under section 53). Where a nominee takes a grant of a lease as bare trustee for a purchaser the nominee (and not the beneficial owner) will be responsible for filing the land transaction return and paying any SDLT due.

This rule applies to leases granted after 19 May 2005 (subject to transitional provisions) and is an anti-avoidance provision. It may cause problems in relation to the application of sale and leaseback relief under section 57A where the leaseback is to a nominee. Similar concerns may apply on a surrender and re-grant involving a nominee.[903]

Transfers of the mere legal title (other than the grant of a lease to a bare trustee) are not land transactions where the beneficial ownership remains with same person. Therefore, for example, where legal title to a partnership's real property is acquired by trustees this is not a land transaction and does not need to be self-certified.

7.18.2. Settlements

Where persons acquire a chargeable interest or an interest in a partnership as trustees of a settlement, they are treated for SDLT purposes as purchasers of the whole of the interest acquired (including the beneficial interest).[904] In such a

---

[900] In paragraph 3(1) Schedule 16

[901] Paragraph 3 Schedule 16 as amended by FA 2007 with effect from 19 July 2007

[902] Inserted by paragraph 11 Schedule 10 F(No. 2)A 2005 and applies to leases granted after 19 May 2005 – there are transitional provisions in paragraph 16(7) Schedule 10.

[903] Paragraphs 9 and 16 Schedule 17A

[904] Paragraph 4 Schedule 16 as amended by FA 2007 with effect from 19 July 2007

case, there is no second charge on a beneficiary with an interest in possession – the only charge is on the trustees.

For SDLT purposes the trustees of a settlement are treated as a single and continuing body of persons. It follows that for a continuing settlement a change in the composition of trustees is not a land transaction and a land transaction return should not be completed in respect of the change. Where such a change results in an application to the Land Registry, an explanatory letter should accompany the application unless it is obvious from the documents that they relate to such a change.[905]

7.18.3. Consideration for exercise of power of appointment or discretion

(Paragraph 7 Schedule 16)

Where a chargeable interest is acquired by virtue of the exercise of a power of appointment or the exercise of a discretion vested in the trustees of a settlement, any consideration given by the person in whose favour the appointment was made is treated as consideration for the acquisition of the chargeable interest.

HMRC have indicated that this provision will have no application to normal trust transactions. It is intended to deal with the unusual case where a person pays trustees, or someone else, in order that the power or discretion may be exercised in their favour.[906]

7.18.4. Reallocation of trust property between beneficiaries

(Paragraph 8 Schedule 16907)

For a long time it was HMRC's view that where trustees reallocated land between sub-funds (swapping land within sub-fund A for investments in sub-fund B), such transactions were to be treated as land transactions in respect of which SDLT was chargeable. This view was eventually abandoned in the case where the trustees were not required to have the consent of the relevant beneficiaries.

Paragraph 8, which applies from 20 July 2006, deals with the more difficult case of where a beneficiary's consent is required to the changes in investments within sub-funds of a single settlement. Paragraph 8 provides that, where a

---

[905] See SDLTM31745

[906] See SDLTM31760

[907] Inserted by section 165 FA 2006 in relation to any acquisition the effective date of which is on or after 19 July 2006.

beneficiary consents to no longer having an interest in one type of trust property and acquires an interest in other trust property which includes a chargeable interest in land, that consent does not of itself trigger a charge to SDLT; as the giving of consent does not constitute chargeable consideration for SDLT purposes. The limitation in paragraph 8 is without prejudice to other provisions such as paragraph 7 Schedule 16 (consideration for exercise of power or discretion).[908]

7.18.5. Removal of anti-avoidance rule – leases assigned by a nominee

The anti-avoidance rule at paragraph 11 Schedule 17A charges the first assignments of certain leases that are not exempt from charge under any of the specified provisions[909] as if they are grants and prevents leases on which relief had been claimed being assigned to a third-party (instead of granted directly to the third-party) in order to avoid the SDLT charge. However, it was possible to sidestep these rules by granting a market rent lease to a nominee who would then assign the lease on to the third party. As the grant of a lease by a person to his nominee was not a land transaction for SDLT purposes (since the newly created leasehold interest was deemed to be held by the person for whom the nominee was a bare trustee), the result was that, although a lease had been created, no land transaction had taken place for SDLT purposes. On the assignment by the nominee to a third party the charge to SDLT on the rent payable under the lease would be avoided.

This route was closed with effect from 22 July 2004 by providing that where a lease was granted to a person as bare trustee of the grantor (with the result that the lease was treated as vested in the grantor by virtue of paragraph 3 Schedule 16 in its then form), then the first assignment of that lease that was not exempt under any of the specified provisions is treated for SDLT purposes as if it were the grant of a lease by the assignor (except where the assignee acquired the lease as bare trustee of the assignor).[910]

The amendments made by FA 2004 referred to above making the grant of a lease to or by a nominee chargeable to SDLT as if the nominee was the

---

[908] See 7.18.3 above

[909] The specified provisions are:

(*a*) section 57A (sale and leaseback relief);

(*b*) Part 1 or 2 Schedule 7 (group relief or reconstruction or acquisition relief);

(*c*) section 66 (transfers involving public bodies);

(*d*) Schedule 8 (charities relief)

(*e*) any such regulations as are mentioned in section 123(3) (regulations reproducing in relation to SDLT the effect of enactments providing for exemption from stamp duty)

[910] Paragraph 11(2) Schedule 17A as re-enacted in amended form by Part 2 Schedule 39 FA 2004 - see also 7.18.1 above

purchaser or vendor of the beneficial interest meant that paragraph 11(1)(b) of Schedule 17A was no longer necessary and it was removed.[911]

7.18.6. Trusts: SDLT compliance

In the case of a bare trust SDLT compliance is for the beneficiaries and the normal rules apply to them.

In the case of settlements, SDLT and penalties can be recovered from any one or more of the 'responsible trustees'. Under paragraph 5 of Schedule 16 an incoming trustee can be personally liable (SDLT liabilities being joint and several) for payment of tax or interest on unpaid tax in respect of a land transaction occurring before he became a trustee. However, a penalty or interest on a penalty cannot be recovered from a person who did not become a trustee until after the penalty became payable or after the time when the act or omission occurred which caused the penalty to be payable.

The land transaction return or self-certificate may be completed by one or more of the trustees who are responsible trustees in relation to the transaction. All the trustees who make the return or certificate must complete the declaration at the end.[912]

7.19. Application of SDLT to persons acting in a representative capacity

(Section 106)

7.19.1. Trustees, guardians etc of incapacitated persons

The person having the direction, management or control of the property of an incapacitated person is responsible for discharging any obligations in relation to a transaction affecting that property, to which the incapacitated person would be subject if they were not so incapacitated. The person having control of the property of an incapacitated person may retain, out of money they hold on behalf of the incapacitated person, sums to meet any payment they are liable to make and so far as they are not reimbursed, is entitled to be indemnified in respect of any such payment.

7.19.2. Parent or guardian of a minor

The parent or guardian is responsible for discharging any obligations of the minor that are not discharged by the minor themselves.

---

[911] By paragraph 11(2) Schedule 10 F(No. 2)A 2005 which applies to leases granted after 19 May 2005 – there are transitional provisions in paragraph 16(7) Schedule 10.

[912] Paragraph 6 Schedule 16

7.19.3. Personal representatives

The personal representatives of a person who was the purchaser under a land transaction are responsible for discharging the obligations of the purchaser in relation to the transaction. They are not the nominees or bare trustees for those named in the will as beneficiaries or entitled on intestacy. It follows that where personal representatives acquire a chargeable interest for SDLT purposes they must notify in their own names as joint purchasers.

They may deduct any payment made by them in respect of SDLT out of the assets and effects of the deceased person.

7.19.4. Receiver appointed by a UK court

A receiver appointed by a UK court and having direction and control of any property is responsible for discharging any obligations in relation to a transaction affecting that property, as if the property were not under the direction and control of the court.

7.20. Application of SDLT to the Crown

(Section 107)

In principle SDLT applies in relation to public offices and departments of the Crown, but section 107 provides that nothing in FA 2003 requires the payment by any such office or department of SDLT that would ultimately be borne by the Crown and nothing renders the Crown liable to prosecution. The powers of entry with warrant to obtain information conferred by Part 7 Schedule 3 are not exercisable in relation to premises occupied for the purposes of the Crown.[913]

A land transaction is exempt if the purchaser is listed in section 107(2):

- A Minister of the Crown, the Scottish Ministers and a Northern Ireland department.
- The Corporate Officer of the House of Lords, the Corporate Officer of the House of Commons, the Scottish Parliamentary Corporate Body, the Northern Ireland Assembly Commission and the National Assembly for Wales.

7.21. SDLT and pension funds[914]

There are no special SDLT rules for pension funds. Where there is a transfer of assets and obligations from one pension fund[915] to another (for example, on the payment of a statutory cash equivalent transfer value for an individual or on a

---

[913] Section 107(3)

[914] See SDLTM31750

[915] Including FURBS

merger of funds) and those assets include a chargeable interest in land, the transfer is, in principle, within the scope of SDLT.

SDLT will only be due where there is chargeable consideration for the transaction. It follows that in the normal circumstance where a new trustee is appointed in addition to or in place of a former trustee and property is conveyed into the name of the new trustee, there will be no chargeable consideration and therefore no SDLT due. On that basis the transfer would be exempt and could be self-certified under paragraph 1 Schedule 3 (see 3.6 above).

Equally it is HMRC's view that where land is conveyed from the trustees of one pension fund to another in return for the assumption by the transferee fund, or the trustees of that fund, of obligations to provide benefits there is no chargeable consideration.

If, in either of the above cases, separate consideration is given by the transferee fund, or the trustees of that fund, in the form of money or money's worth then that will be chargeable consideration for SDLT purposes. This would also be the case if the transfer of obligations was in consideration of a defined monetary sum to be satisfied by the release of obligations by the former trustees.

A pension fund may borrow money and may grant a mortgage or other charge over land as security. If a transferee fund, or the trustees of that fund:

- assumes an existing liability of the transferor fund or trustees of the transferor fund to repay borrowings or
- otherwise brings about the release of the transferor fund or trustees of the transferor fund from the debt
- and they do so as part of an in-specie transfer between funds then HMRC have indicated[916] that they would not treat paragraph 8 Schedule 4 (debt as consideration) as meaning that there is chargeable consideration given for the land transaction.

7.22. Assignment of lease - responsibility of assignee for returns

(Paragraph 12 Schedule 17A)

This paragraph shifts to the assignee of a lease certain continuing responsibilities, which would otherwise have fallen on the original grantee, for

[916] At SDLTM31750

adjustments to the original land transaction return. These responsibilities arise by reason of the following provisions:

- section 80 (adjustment where contingency ceases or consideration is ascertained[917]),
- section 81A (return or further return in consequence of later linked transaction[918]),
- paragraph 3 or paragraph 4 Schedule 17A (return or further return required where lease for indefinite period continues[919]), or
- paragraph 8 Schedule 17A (adjustment where rent ceases to be uncertain[920]).

Anything previously done by or in relation to the assignor is treated as if it had been done by or in relation to the assignee. Accordingly, an assignee needs to make sure that he has (or is given the contractual right to obtain) the information from the assignor which is necessary to enable him to fulfil his statutory obligations and avoid incurring penalties. This provision results in a possible trap for the unwary.

The provision does not apply if the assignment falls to be treated as the grant of a lease by the assignor[921], since the assignee in such a case will be treated as the grantee of the lease.

---

[917] See 1.7.10 above

[918] See 7.1.1 above

[919] Dealt with at 2.6.17 and 2.6.1 above respectively

[920] See 2.6.12 above

[921] Pursuant to paragraph 11 Schedule 17A – see 1.5 above

PART THREE

THE SDLT PROCESS

8. THE SDLT PROCESS[922]

8.1. Forms and letters in the SDLT process

SDLT1	Land transaction return – Notification form required for all transactions
SDLT2	Land transaction return – Additional vendor/purchaser details
SDLT3	Land transaction return – Additional details about the land
SDLT4	Land transaction return – Additional transaction or lease details
SDLT5	Certificate – Confirming that the transaction has been notified and that the Land Registry may proceed with registration
SDLT6	Land Transaction Return Guidance Notes (for completing forms SDLT1, 2, 3 and 4)
SDLT7	Standard letter – Response to purchaser enquiry
SDLT8 and 8A	Standard letter – Further information required and reminder
SDLT9 and 9A	Standard letter – Potential overpayment of tax and reminder
SDLT10	Standard letter – Confirmation that repayment will follow
SDLT11 and 11A	Standard letter – Reminder that Disadvantaged Area relief is available for residential property
SDLT12 and 12A	Standard letter – Further tax/penalty/interest due and reminder
SDLT14	Standard letter – Inform purchaser that no further reminders and no certificate will be issued
SDLT15 and 15A	Standard letter – Potential overpayment of tax due to availability of relief and reminder
SDLT38	Form - SDLT refund authorisation form
SDLT60	Certificate that no land transaction return is required for a land transaction
SDLT68	Self certification guidance notes

These "informal" forms might be acceptable to HMRC instead of a letter:

(a) Notification under s80 FA2003 (Adjustment where contingency ceases or consideration is ascertained);

(b) Notification under s81A FA2003 (Return or further return in consequence of later linked transaction);

(c) Notification under Sch.17A paragraph 3 or 4 FA2003 (Return where the lease term is affected by those provisions, i.e. "growing lease");

(d) Notification under Sch.17A paragraph 8 FA2003 (Adjustment where rent ceases to be uncertain).

---

922 This part draws heavily on the latest version of Land Transaction Return Guidance Notes (SDLT6) available before going to press (August 2007) and other HMRC materials. The reader is advised to refer to the HMRC website before undertaking any transaction, as SDLT6 is updated regularly and can be found at:
http://www.hmrc.gov.uk/so/sdlt6.pdf or http://www.hmrc.gov.uk/sdlt6/index.htm.

8.2. The forms

8.2.1. The land transaction return

The SDLT legislation requires completion of a land transaction return for notifiable transactions.[923] The land transaction return (SDLT1) replaces the old PD form, which needed to be completed for instruments liable to stamp duty.

Even transactions where tax is not chargeable may need to be notified to HMRC on the land transaction return e.g. where there is consideration of £125,000 or less for residential property or £150,000 for non-residential and mixed use property.

8.2.2. Supplementary land transaction returns

In the vast majority of cases it will only be necessary to submit an SDLT1. However, forms SDLT2, SDLT3 and SDLT4 need to be completed in the following circumstances:

An SDLT2 is required for each additional vendor above two, where there are more than two vendors and/or purchasers. The online return (see 1.1 below) allows extra vendors or purchasers to be included.

SDLT3 is required where there is more than one property in code F or O (not leases) and/or where the land involved requires detailed description in the absence of a postal address e.g. 'land lying south of....'

SDLT4 is required where any of the following applies:

- any purchaser is a company;
- the property transferred, leased etc is non-residential or is mixed residential and non-residential;
- the property is included in the sale of a business or part of a business;
- any of the consideration (apart from rent) is contingent or uncertain (whether or not tax is being paid by instalments);
- the transaction reserves minerals or mineral rights;
- HMRC have been asked for a post transaction ruling under COP10 or for advice on the application of the law to the transaction;
- there is a single acquisition of multiple leasehold properties by grant or transfer;
- there are grants of linked leases being notified together (using a form SDLT4 for the second and each subsequent lease with the same effective date and between the same parties).[924]

---

[923] See 2.6.1 above

[924] Use a schedule where a transaction is subject to existing leases.

8.2.3. Obtaining land transaction returns

Supplies of the forms can be obtained by ringing HMRC Orderline on 0845 302 1472.[925] The Orderline can also be contacted by fax: 01726 201015, or by email: saorderline.ir@gtnet.gov.uk

The postal address is:
IRCC
PO Box 37
St Austell
PL35 5YN

Obtaining and maintaining a supply of forms will be particularly important because each land transaction return obtained from the Orderline will contain a unique pre-printed transaction reference number ('TRN') which means that it cannot be photocopied.

On-line services

We discuss the online service in detail at section 8.6 below.

It should be noted that the questions in the online service are not in the same sequence as for the hard-copy form filing.

8.3. Submission and processing of the return

Sections 8.3 and 8.4 deal with all submissions of paper forms. The online lease calculator is discussed in section 8.5, and E-filing, and the key differences between e-filing and paper filing are dealt with in section 8.6.

By 30th March 2008 50% of returns are expected to be filed online. By the end of 2008 the 2D barcode will no longer be used. Beyond that there will be e-conveyancing incorporating SDLT data (already available in Scotland).

8.3.1. Postal submission

The land transaction return (the original, not a photocopy) should be sent to the Rapid Data Capture Centre which is the SDLT processing centre in Netherton, near Liverpool to be received by the filing date:

HMRC SDLT
Comben House
Farriers Way
NETHERTON
Merseyside
L30 4RN

Or using the Document Exchange facility to:

[925] The Orderline is open 7 days a week from 8am to 10pm (except Bank Holidays). Calls are charged at local rates.

Rapid Data Capture Centre
DX 725593
Bootle 9
marking the sender's DX number onto the envelope for charging purposes.

Returns cannot be submitted by fax or email.

Proof of sending and a copy of the SDLT1 and any supplementary forms should be retained.

8.3.2. Role of Stamp Offices

Stamp Offices will not have the ability to process land transaction returns or to issue a certificate.

All SDLT work (other than data capture) is now dealt with by the Birmingham Stamp Office. This includes correspondence on complex transactions. The address is:

Birmingham Stamp Office
9th Floor, City Centre House
30 Union Street
Birmingham
B2 4AR
Tel: 0845 603 0135
Fax: 0121 643 8381

HMRC has issued the following guidance to help ensure that the post is sorted more quickly and referred to the relevant team:

Correspondence should be marked with:

- The topic (examples given below); and
- Any reference number

Topic	**Please mark**
Stamp Duty	Stamp Duty
Stamp duty reserve tax (SDRT)	SDRT
Stamp duty land tax (SDLT)	
Financial enquiries	SDLT finance
Multiple property transactions, where a schedule is included	Multiple Properties
Completion following substantial performance	Substantial performance
Ending of Disadvantaged Area Relief – Transitional Provisions	DAR
Returns under Section 80, 81 and 81A FA2003	Section 80, 81 and 81A FA2003

Section 80, 81 and 81A Returns under Sch 17A FA2003	Sch 17A FA2003
Returns relating to cases of contingent or uncertain consideration where tax has been deferred under s.90 FA2003	SDLT Deferment Application
Request for information and advice – Code of Practice 10	COP10

HMRC will issue certificates only where SDLT1s have been correctly completed. Land transaction returns that do not meet the requirements will be returned. Only when any missing information has been supplied will HMRC issue a certificate.

As those land transaction returns submitted in hard copy are to be scanned electronically, it is important that they are not folded or stapled and that they are returned in the envelopes provided. These will be automatically provided with the printed land transaction returns and are also available from HMRC Orderline. Additionally, HMRC has requested that only one application, with payment, be sent in each envelope. No other information or documents (such as a covering letter or compliment slip) should be submitted with the land transaction return. In particular plans should only be submitted when for Valuation Office Agency purposes it is needed to identify development land, agricultural land and small 'garden' plots. In these circumstances HMRC have arrangements with the Rapid Data Capture Centre to pass the plans to the Valuation Office Agency.

The land transaction return must be accompanied by a cheque for the relevant amount of SDLT made payable to 'Inland Revenue Only' and with the TRN inserted after the payee. Payment can be made by the following methods:

1) BACS or CHAPS, Internet or telephone banking. The following information must be given:

- the payment account
- the TRN from the payslip
- the sort code (10-50-41)
- HMRC account number (23456000)
- the amount of duty.

Separate payment should be made through BACS for each transaction otherwise HMRC accounting function has problems allocating payments to specific transactions:

2) At the bank, via the payment slip, cheque made payable to Inland Revenue Only.

3) At the Post Office, by cheque made payable to Post Office Ltd.
Alliance & Leicester/GIRO account, completed payslip sent direct to Girobank.

There is an HM Revenue & Customs Payments Office enquiry line on 01274 530750.[926]

8.3.3. Amended land transaction returns[927]

An amendment may not be made more than 12 months after the filing date (which is 30 days after the effective date).

If a land transaction return has been submitted containing errors, the purchaser or their agent, should submit:

- a letter explaining fully how and where the land transaction return should be amended;
- a copy of the original land transaction return;
- a copy of the certificate issued by the Stamp Office; and
- payment of any outstanding tax and interest payable, if applicable.

If:

- Box 59 of the original land transaction return was left blank or 'No' was entered; or
- a different agent other than that entered at Box 60 of the original SDLT1 is required to act on behalf of the purchaser in respect of the amendment.

HMRC Agent Authorisation form 64-8 must be completed by the purchaser and submitted with the amendment.

It was previously the case that if the effect of the amendment was that more tax was due, the letter and enclosures had to be sent to the Complex Transactions Unit in Manchester. This is no longer so, and these should now be sent to:

Birmingham Stamp Office
9th Floor City Centre House
30 Union Street
Birmingham B2 4AR
DX: 15001 Birmingham 1

If the effect of the amendment is that less tax is due, a claim for repayment should be made by amending the return under paragraph 6 Schedule 10 if within the twelve-month time limit and under Schedule 11A if outside that time limit.

---

[926] Open from 8am to 5pm Monday to Friday (except Bank Holidays)

[927] SDLTM80585

8.3.4. The certificate of notification

A certificate of notification will be issued by HMRC provided that:

- All information expected is provided
- The system check verifies the calculation of SDLT due
- A payment is enclosed for the amount declared (or the amount is paid using one of the other payment options).

The certificate will be sent to the client unless the solicitor completes the authority box on the land transaction return (Box 58 on page 5 of SDLT1).

This certificate should be presented with documents submitted to HM Land Registry when applying for registration of title. The certificate also acts as a receipt.

8.3.5. Multiple transactions[928]

Special arrangements are offered to customers making multiple acquisitions of property, i.e. situations where a six or more land transactions take place on the same day between the same purchaser and vendor. The purchaser or their agent is encouraged to contact the Stamp Office Help Line on 0845 603 0135 before the land transaction return is prepared.

The Help Line will provide initial advice. Where the caller was previously referred to the Complex Transaction Unit in Manchester, all new matters will be handled by the Birmingham office[929]. They may suggest that the information is sent in Schedular format rather than multiple SDLT3s or SDLT4s. The Schedule can be obtained via e-mail from the Birmingham Stamp Office. The precise form of the Schedule will depend on the nature of the interests being acquired and how they should be coded. Copies of the Schedular information will be required both on paper accompanying the SDLT1 and in electronic format. This will to help reduce the time taken to produce the certificate for the transaction.

It may also be suggested that callers liaise with the Land Registry to establish their minimum requirements for any transaction in advance of submitting their return.

When 'No' is checked Box 27 on the land transaction return, the Stamp Office will issue a single certificate, supported by a list detailing the properties included in the customers schedule. When 'Yes' is checked at Box 27 the Stamp Office will produce separate certificates for each property.

---

[928] See SDLTM60215

[929] From July 2007, the Complex Transactions Unit has only been dealing with ongoing issues which started prior to the announced transfer of responsibility to the Birmingham Stamp Office.

8.3.6. Self-certificates (certificate that no SDLT1 is required) – SDLT60

Some transactions need not be notified to HMRC.[930] In these cases the purchaser will sign a 'self-certificate' stating why no notification to is needed and that self-certificate (form SDLT60) is included with any application to the Land Registry for registration[931].

A paper SDLT 60 cannot be signed as agent (unless by power of attorney).

HMRC has announced that, with effect from 17 April 2007, only the current version of SDLT 60 (version dated "03/06") is acceptable. It has also issued a statement pointed out that SDLT60s are being sent to the Stamp Office in error – the completed SDLT60 should be sent to the nearest Land Registry office for the property.

8.3.7. The enquiry regime

HMRC will enquire into some land transaction returns, including those where a Revenue certificate has been issued. A small selection of land transaction returns will be selected for review. Some enquiries will be selected at random and others will be selected on a risk basis. The overwhelming majority of transactions will be accepted and certificates issued without an enquiry.

HMRC will have a fixed time within which they can start an enquiry – this is known as the enquiry window - and is a period of 9 months beginning:

- after the filing date, if the land transaction return was delivered on or before that date;
- after the date on which the land transaction return was delivered, if the land transaction return was delivered after the filing date;
- after the date on which any amendment was made to the land transaction return.

Enquiries can also be conducted into self-certificates provided to the land registries.

Any enquiry will start with a letter to the purchaser with a copy sent to the solicitor, if the solicitor has completed the correspondence Box on the land transaction return (Box 58 on page 5). At the end of the enquiry a letter closing the enquiry will be issued to the client and copied to the solicitors, again where the correspondence Box has been completed.

---

[930] See 7.1 above

[931] The Land Registry will now accept a photocopy of form SDLT 60 – see Land Registry Practice Guide 50 (November 2006) at paragraph 7.2

8.3.8. Retention of records

In line with other taxes, records supporting transactions must be retained for six years (this is also the case where a self-certificate is given). The obligation to retain the records remains with the purchaser as the liable person.

An example of the types of records which may need to be kept includes the following:

- a contract/agreement for sale and any related side papers
- professional valuations of both the land and apportionments of fixtures and loose fittings
- relevant instruments relating to the transaction, in particular any contract of conveyance, and any supporting maps, plans or similar documents
- partnership agreements
- completion documents
- records of relevant payments, receipts and financial arrangements.
- deed of attorney

8.3.9. Late filing - fixed penalties

If the return is filed late and/or the SDLT is not paid the purchaser will be charged a flat-rate penalty of £100 if the return is delivered within three months of the filing date, and £200 in any other case. Interest may also be chargeable on tax paid late (see 7.10 above). If you have not completed Box 59 (see 8.4.8 below) the penalty notice will be sent to the purchaser and not his solicitor. Interest runs on penalties from their date of determination (s.88).

If a late filing penalty is not paid within 30 days of the penalty notification interest will be charged on the penalty.

If the SDLT1 is more than a year late a tax-based penalty may be levied which can be up to the amount of the SDLT due.

Appeals against late filing penalties should be made in writing within 30 days of receiving the notification of a penalty being imposed. There is a form for this purpose which is available from any Stamp Office.

An appeal against a penalty can be made if there is a 'reasonable excuse' for not sending their land transaction return on time. The following are accepted by HMRC as constituting a reasonable excuse:

- an unforeseen event, which disrupted the normal postal service and led to an SDLT return posted in good time being lost or delayed
- serious acute illness (or death) that prevented an adviser from controlling their business and private affairs.

8.4. Completing the forms[932]

The land transaction return (SDLT1) has been devised to meet the needs of the majority of 'straightforward' land transactions. By 'straightforward' HMRC means a sale by one or two vendors of a single property for a cash price, equal to the market value of the property, to one or two purchasers.

The land transaction return SDLT1 is in six main parts with 70 boxes (or sets of boxes) and is completed by a making a signed declaration.

The agent cannot sign on the purchaser's behalf (see below in relation to powers of attorney) so ensure that the purchaser's signature is obtained well before the filing date which is 30 days after the effective date of the transaction.

8.4.1. Who can sign

It was previously the case that the land transaction return could not be signed by an agent (other than an attorney). This requirement has now been relaxed and 2D bar-coded land transaction returns (SDLT1) can be signed by an agent (e.g. solicitor).

An attorney acting under a deed of attorney can sign the land transaction return on behalf of the purchaser. The deed does not need to be submitted with the land transaction return. An attorney must indicate that he is signing in that capacity in the space provided in Box 71 on the return. 'Power of attorney' should be written underneath the signature.

8.4.2. Completing the return - practical points

- The boxes must be completed in black ink in capital letters, using one box for each letter or number and leaving a space between words
- The return must also be signed in black ink
- If a box doesn't apply it should be left blank - do not strike through or put N/A
- Do not write outside the boxes – there is no 'white space'
- A separate land transaction return must be completed in respect of each transaction
- Do not use correcting fluid. Strike through any error and write the correct information immediately to the right of the relevant box
- Fields that have a 'Yes/No' question require further details to be completed where the answer is 'Yes' or the form will be rejected. If the answer 'No' is selected and further information is entered the form will also be rejected.

---

[932] For significant differences in e-filing, please see section 1.1

8.4.3. Form SDLT1 Section 1: About the transaction (Boxes 1-8)

HMRC has issued detailed guidance completion of form SDLT1 in the case of shared ownership leases.[933] These are summarised at 3.17 above.

Box 1 – Type of property

The correct code for the type of property should be inserted:

Residential 01

Mixed 02

Non residential 03

Box 2 - Description of transaction

The appropriate code should be inserted:

Code A:[934]

Acquisition or transfer of

- an existing lease
- an interest, including a freehold interest, which is subject to a lease or lease

Surrender of a lease

Acquisition of a freehold or leasehold reversion by a tenant

Code F:

Other conveyance or transfer

Code L:

The grant of a lease

Code O:

Other (such as grant of an easement)

Box 3 – Interest transferred or created

Enter most appropriate code from the following:

Freehold with vacant possession - FP

Freehold subject to long lease or leases at ground rent or nominal rent - FG

Freehold subject to a lease or tenancy to an occupier - FT

Long leasehold at a ground rent or nominal rent with vacant possession – LG

Long leasehold subject to lease or tenancy to an occupier – LT

Lease to an occupier - LP

All other (such as acquisition of an easement) - OT

---

[933] See SDLTM27080 and, in particular, the examples

[934] See SDLT Practitioner's Newsletter Issue 2, 21st July 2004

In Scotland only:

Owner's interest with vacant possession - FP

Superior's interest, including minutes of waiver - FG

Owner's interest subject to tenancy - FT

Leasehold/tenant's interest - LP

Box 4 – Effective Date
In the majority of cases this will be the date of completion, or the settlement date in Scotland.

Box 5 – Any restrictions, covenants or conditions affecting the value of the interest transferred or granted?
There are only 42 spaces in which to provide the information (which is for the benefit of the Valuation Office Agency). One of the questions asked by practitioners at the SDLT seminars organised by the Law Society in conjunction with HMRC was as follows:[935]
'There was not enough characters available in Box 5 to complete full details of restrictions. What should practitioners do to complete this properly?'

HMRC's answer was:

The important thing is that unusual or unexpected restrictions are entered. Abbreviations are fine.'

It is understood that stating 'ordinary covenants and conditions' will be acceptable.

Box 6 – Date of contract or conclusion of missives
Box 7 – Is any land exchanged or part exchanged?
Box 8 - Is the transaction pursuant to a previous option agreement?

8.4.4. Form SDLT1 Section 2: About the calculation (Boxes 9-15)

Box 9 – Are you claiming relief?
The various reliefs must be claimed by completion of this Box on the SDLT1. If more than one relief applies the code for a combination of reliefs should be selected.[936] No letter of claim is required.

---

[935] See questions from practitioners and the answers provided by the Revenue dated 16th January 2004 available on the Law Society's website: www.lawsociety.org.uk

[936] From October 2007 there will be a zero-carbon relief code, which is not shown in the current table, set out above.

Where partial relief is claimed the amount remaining chargeable must be shown here.

Designated disadvantaged areas (residential)	05
Designated disadvantaged areas (non-residential)	06
Designated disadvantaged areas (mixed)	07
Part-exchange (house building company)[937]	08
Re-location of employment	09
Compulsory purchase facilitating development	10
Compliance with planning obligations	11
Group relief	12
Reconstruction relief	13
Acquisition relief	14
Demutualisation of insurance company	15
Demutualisation of building society	16
Incorporation of limited liability partnership	17
Transfers involving public bodies	18
Transfer in consequence of reorganisation of parliamentary constituencies	19
Charities[938]	20
Acquisition by bodies established for national purposes	21
Right to buy transactions	22
Registered social landlords	23
Alternative property finance	24
Collective enfranchisement by leaseholders (does not apply in Scotland)	25
Crofting community right to buy (applies in Scotland only)	26
Diplomatic Privileges	27
Other	28
Combination of reliefs	29

[937] The CIS (Construction Industry Scheme) gives a registered subcontractor a unique taxpayer reference. Where this relief is claimed the CIS reference number should be included. The CIS (Construction Industry Scheme) gives a registered subcontractor a unique taxpayer reference.

[938] The charity's registration number must be shown.

Box 10 – What is the total consideration?

The amount shown here is the total consideration in money or money's worth, in whatever form, given for the subject matter of the transaction including any VAT payable. For a residential purchase, VAT is not an issue.

Do not use commas between the figures.

The NPV of any rent should NOT be included here. If the transaction is the grant of a new lease (and L has been entered in Box 2) this Box should be left blank (i.e., a value of 0 should not be entered) and Boxes 16 to 25 completed instead.

Any amount properly apportionable to other matters (such as chattels) should be excluded:

'The apportionment agreed between vendor and purchaser, for whatever purposes, may not represent a just and reasonable apportionment. We expect purchasers (who are solely responsible for the accuracy of the information contained in the land transaction return) to consider this question afresh before entering the consideration for the land transaction on the return'[939]

A payment for goodwill that that is part of the land is part of the chargeable consideration for SDLT purposes. The price paid for this goodwill should be included in the figure shown at Box 10 where code A, F or O has been entered at Box 2[940]:

Box 11 – If the total consideration for the transaction includes VAT, please state the amount of VAT

If the vendor has to charge or has elected to charge VAT the amount of VAT should be shown.

If the transaction is the grant of a new lease this Box should be left blank and Boxes 16 to 25 ('About new leases') completed.

Box 12 – What form does the consideration take?

The appropriate code(s) should be inserted from the following list:

Cash	30
Debt (which includes assumption by the purchaser of outstanding mortgage)	31
Building works	32

[939] See SDLTM04010

[940] See 1.7.2 subsection *"Goodwill"* above

Employment	33
Other (such as an annuity)	34
Shares in a quoted company	35
Shares in an unquoted company	36
Other land	37
Services	38
Contingent	39

Box 13 – Is this transaction linked to any other(s)?

Transactions are linked if they form part of a single scheme, arrangement or series of transactions between the same vendor and purchaser or, in either case, persons connected with them.

The total amount paid for all linked transactions including any VAT should be entered. For linked leases the total premium should be shown.

All linked transactions may be notified on the same SDLT1, if they have the same effective date, or a separate SDLT1 can be completed for each property. If only one SDLT1 is completed separate SDLT3s need to be completed in respect of each property. Linked leases must be notified on separate SDLT1s.

Box 14 – Total amount of tax due for this transaction

The calculation should be rounded down to the nearest pound.

This Box should not be left blank. If no tax is due because the rate is 0% or a relief is claimed, enter £0.00.

If the transaction is a new lease this Box should reflect the total of Boxes 24 and 25.

Guidance on using the online lease calculator is set out in section 1.1.

Box 15 – Total amount paid or enclosed with this notification

Show here the total amount due after taking into account any agreed arrangements with HMRC to defer payment of SDLT (for such arrangement see 7.8 above).

If the land transaction return is late (received more than 30 days after the effective date of the transaction shown in Box 3), this Box should reflect the appropriate penalty and any interest in respect of the late payment of the tax.

8.4.5. Form SDLT1 Section 3: About leases (Boxes 16-25)

This section of the form needs to be completed where the property sold is subject to existing leases. There is room for details of one such lease on form SDLT1 and details of any others are to be inserted on separate SDLT4s. The questions asked on SDLT4 (see 8.4.11 below) are different from those on SDLT1. Neither form requires any details which would identify which lease is being referred to in any particular section which can be confusing.

Box 16 - Type of lease
Box 16 on is headed 'Type of lease' but in fact the codes describe the type of premises. A code should be selected:
Residential - R
Non Residential - N
Mixed – M

If the acquisition is of a freehold interest subject to one or more leases give details of the 'first lease' here and of any other leases on a schedule. If the acquisition is of a leasehold interest subject to sub-leases give details of the leasehold interest here and of any other leases on a schedule. You can use form SDLT4 where you notify linked leases together. If the transaction involves a surrender of a lease or the acquisition of a reversionary interest by a tenant, details of the lease which has been brought to an end should be entered here. Where a large number of leases are involved the Stamp Office suggests contacting the Enquiry line. [941]

Box 17 – Start date as specified in lease
This is the date from which the term of the lease runs and may be before the date of execution of the lease. Substantial performance may trigger the start of a term for this purpose.

Box 18 – End date as specified in lease
Any break clause should be ignored.

Box 19 – Rent-free period
The total number of rent-free months, rounded up to a whole number of months should be shown here.

Box 20 – Annual starting rent inclusive of VAT actually payable
If the landlord has elected to charge VAT as at the effective date this amount should include the VAT payable.

If the rent varies throughout the term, the initial rent should be shown here together with the date that this rent will end.

If rents for the remainder of the term are known, this should be indicated by checking the appropriate box.

---

[941] See SDLT6 section *"Additional details for cases involving leases"*.

Box 21 – What is the amount of VAT, if any?
Box 22 – Total premium payable
This amount should include any VAT.

If the lease is linked to another, the total premium for all the linked leases should be entered.

Box 23 – NPV on which tax is calculated
If the transaction is linked to any other, the total NPV of all the linked leases should be shown.

Box 24 – Total amount of tax due - Premium
Box 25 – Total amount of tax due – NPV
If the transaction is linked to any other the total tax due on all the linked leases should be entered.

8.4.6. Form SDLT1 Section 4: About the land including buildings (Boxes 26-33)

SDLT1 assumes that the transaction is a sale of interests in land. In the case of transactions consisting of rights over land, such as easements, rights of pre-emption etc. it must be presumed that a description is required of the land over which the right subsists and the rest of this section completed on the basis that the right over land is a 'property'.

Box 26 – Number of properties included.
The number of properties included in this transaction should be shown, using figures, not words. Where more than one property is being purchased (or there is not enough space in Box 28 on the SDLT1 to describe the property) a supplementary sheet, SDLT3, should be completed for each additional property.

HMRC considers that having a separate address makes a property separate for SDLT purposes.[942] Accordingly if several flats in the same block are acquired a separate form SDLT3 is required to be completed in respect of each one after the first.
Box 27 – Where more than one property is involved do you want a certificate for each?
Generally one certificate will be issued in respect of one land transaction return.

---

942 See Land Transaction Return Guidance Notes (SDLT6) in relation to Box 26.

The certificate issued by HMRC is evidence to the Land Registry of delivery of a land transaction return. If there is more than one property and only one certificate is issued with a schedule of all properties concerned, the properties will have to be registered at the same time.

If this land transaction return includes more than one property and a certificate is required for each of them, this should be shown here otherwise all the properties will be included in one certificate and will have to be registered at the same time.

Box 28 – Address or situation of land

The full postal address including the postcode if there is one and, in Northern Ireland, the county, should be given. A plan must be provided for all transactions where boundaries need defining and provision of a plan should be indicated in Box 33.

If more than one property is part of this transaction that should be shown here and separate forms SDLT 3 completed for each. The SDLT3s should accompany the SDLT1. If there is not enough space in Box 28 on the SDLT1 to describe the property a supplementary sheet, SDLT3, should be completed.

Box 29 – Local authority number

The local authority code for the area in which the 'lead' property is situated should be given. These codes are listed in an Appendix of the Land Transaction Return Guidance Notes (SDLT6).[943]

Box 30 – Title number (if any)

If the property is registered give the title number if any is available. If no title number is available give the parent title number, if it is available.

Box 31 – NLPG UPRN

The NLPG UPRN is the National Land and Property Gazette Unique Property Reference Number.

HMRC have modified their guidance. Previously they have said "it will be vital to include the NLPG UPRN in Box 31 on the SDLT1 return. This is because it's increasingly used as a common property address reference by many Government departments and public authorities."

The current advice is to leave blank if not available, but if you know or are readily able to find the number then enter it here.

[943] The HTML version of SDLT6 has an alphabetical section for local authority codes.

You may be able to obtain the NLPG UPRN from the local authority's planning department. There are also three licensed bodies able to provide the UPRN. These are:

Searchflow, 0870 787 7625 www.searchflow.co.uk

TM Property Services, 0870 740 7833 www.tmproperty.co.uk

Transaction Online, 0800 085 4951 www.transaction-online.co.uk

In Northern Ireland the equivalent is 'Pointer'. For Northern Ireland properties in all cases enter prefix NI followed without any space by the 12 digit 'Pointer' UPRN. Note that 'Pointer' UPRN's do not cover undeveloped land and are not available from the NPLG sources. You can get them directly from their website www.pointer-ni.gov.uk or the Valuation and Lands Agency website at www.vla.nics.gov.uk

In Scotland it is not yet widely used or available.

The full reference should be of 14 characters or less. Do not leave any spaces.

Box 32 – If agricultural or development land, what is the area, if known?

This Box is for the benefit of the Valuation Office Agency and HMRC has indicated that, in spite of the heading, it should be completed in respect of any land acquired without buildings. The area of land can be shown in hectares or square metres, not acres.

Box 33 – Is a plan attached?

A plan will not be required for the majority of straightforward transactions where there is a full address for the property. However, a plan is needed in all instances where a boundary needs defining. The scale should be shown on the map supplied or the map endorsed 'Not to Scale' if this is the case. The TRN of the land transaction return, the address or description of the land as shown in Box 28 and the local authority code as shown in Box 29 must be shown on the plan.

8.4.7. Form SDLT1 Section 5: About the vendor including transferor, lessor (Boxes 34-48)

Box 34 – Number of vendors

The number of vendors should be entered here using figures, not words. If there is more than one vendor, Boxes 45 to 48 should be completed in respect of the second vendor. If there are more than two vendors, an SDLT2 should also be completed in respect of each additional vendor.

Box 35 – Title of vendor

Box 36 – Vendor (1) surname or company name

If this transaction has more than one vendor the surname of the first named vendor should be entered. If the vendor is a company or (in England, Wales or Northern Ireland) a partnership, the company or partnership name should be entered.

Box 37 –Vendor (1) first name

Only to be completed if the vendor is an individual.

Box 38 – Vendor (1) address

The address of the person named in Box 36 should be entered. If this is a limited company the address of the registered office should be inserted. If the Vendor's address cannot be obtained the address of the property being acquired can be entered as this is a mandatory field.

Box 39 – Agent's name

If the vendor has an agent, (for example, a solicitor, licensed conveyancer or accountant) the agent's name should be entered here and Boxes 40 to 44 completed otherwise this Box should be left blank.

Boxes 40 to 44 – Agent details

Boxes 45 to 48 – Vendor (2) details (Additional vendor(s))

These Boxes should be completed in respect of the second vendor only. Any additional vendors, after the second, should be entered on separate SDLT2s.

8.4.8. Form SDLT1 Section 6: About the purchaser including transferee/lessee (Boxes 49-69)

Box 49 – Number of purchasers

The number of purchasers should be shown using figures, not words. If there is more than one, Boxes 65 to 69 should be completed in respect of the second purchaser. If more than two, supplementary sheet SDLT 2 should also be completed for each additional purchaser after the second.

Purchaser (1) can be any one of the joint purchasers involved in the transaction.

In England and Wales and Northern Ireland a partnership counts as a single purchaser.

Box 50 – National Insurance Number for Purchaser (1)

This box should only be completed if the National Insurance Number (NINO) of the lead purchaser is known. Temporary NINOs with the prefix TN should not be used. In practice, this box is often not completed.

Box 51 – Title of purchaser

Box 52 – Purchaser (1) surname or company name

If the purchaser is a company or other body corporate an SDLT 4 should also be completed.

Box 53 – Purchaser (1) first name

Box 54 – Purchaser (1) address

If this is not the same as the address of the property shown in Box 28, full details should be given.

Box 55 – Is the purchaser acting as a trustee?

Failure to answer this mandatory question is the most common error. Normally the answer is no (co-ownership does not count and of course a bare trustee should not complete the form at all).

Box 56 – Please give a daytime telephone number

Box 57 – Are the purchaser and vendor connected?

The definition of 'connected' is in section 839 ICTA 1988.

Box 58 – To which address shall we send the certificate?

On receipt of a properly completed land transaction return and payment of the correct tax a certificate will be issued for registration purposes. The certificate will be sent to one of the following, according to the preference indicated:
The address of the property shown in Box 28
The purchaser's address shown in Box 54; or
The address of the purchaser's agent shown in Box 61.

There is no provision for sending it to the mortgagee's solicitors so an undertaking may be required from the solicitors acting for a purchaser/mortgagor.

Box 59 – I authorise my agent to handle correspondence on my behalf

The land transaction return has to be signed by the purchaser.

Usually the solicitor acting on their behalf will complete many land transaction returns and the purchasers will want and expect their solicitor to deal with issues arising from the land transaction return.

Without the agent authority box completed HMRC cannot send copies of correspondence to the agent.

Box 60 – Agent's name

Boxes 61 to 64 – Agent's details

If the DX is being used the full DX address including the number and location should be entered in Box 62.

Boxes 65 to 69 - Additional purchaser details

Box 70 – How many supplementary sheets have you enclosed with this land transaction return?

If supplementary sheets have been used for additional vendors and/or purchasers (SDLT2), or land (SDLT3), or for complex commercial transactions, company as purchaser(s) and leases (SDLT4), the total for each should be shown using figures, not words.

Box 71 – Declaration

A declaration is required that the information given on the return is, to the best of the purchaser's knowledge and belief, correct and complete

Who should sign the SDLT1?

Box 71 has space only for signatures by up to two purchasers. The Guidance Notes indicate that 'every purchaser' should sign the declaration. It is understood that the Stamp Office have advised that where there are more than two purchasers two should sign Box 71 and each of the others should complete and sign an SDLT2.

The land transaction return (or self-certificate) may be made by one or more of the trustees who are responsible trustees in relation to the transaction.[944] All the trustees who make the return or certificate must complete the declaration.[945] Trustees must all be named, but any of them can sign on behalf of them all (Sch 16 para 6(1)).[946]

In the case of a partnership, the return may be signed either by all the partners or by a nominated representative of the partnership. Where a nominated representative signs, proof of the signatory's authority should be kept on file.

2D bar-coded returns can be signed by agents. All co-owners must all sign the declaration (s.103(2)&(3)) at the place relevant.

Companies

The proper officer of the company, usually the company secretary or any other person authorised by the company, should sign the declaration in a land transaction return or amended return.

In practice, a return or amended return will be accepted by HMRC provided that it contains a signature and there is no reason to doubt the authority of the

---

[944] These are the trustees at the effective date of the land transaction in question and any person who subsequently becomes a trustee (paragraph 5 Schedule 16).

[945] Paragraph 6 Schedule 16

[946] See SDLT6 *"Signing the land transaction return"*.

person signing. On this basis, the signature of any company official, employee or agent can be accepted. This includes a tax advisor, accountant, solicitor or licensed conveyancer.[947] In addition, a land transaction return that is signed in the name of a firm of accountants, solicitors or licensed conveyancers on behalf of a company may also be accepted.

The exception is when a company is in liquidation when the liquidator must sign the return or amended return.

Payslip

The land transaction return must be accompanied by a self-assessed payment of the SDLT due. The payslip also needs to be signed.

If any mineral rights are reserved an SDLT4 should be completed and sent with the SDLT1.

8.4.9. Form SDLT2: Additional vendor/purchaser details

The TRN from the SDLT1 payslip should be inserted in the 'Reference' Box.

If the form is being completed in respect of a vendor, the declaration does not need to be completed. Any additional purchaser completing SDLT2 needs to sign the declaration that the information given on the SDLT2 is, to the best of his knowledge and belief, correct and complete.

8.4.10. Form SDLT3: Additional details about the land

The TRN from the SDLT1 payslip should be inserted in the 'Reference' Box.

If mineral or mineral rights are reserved the appropriate code (listed in the Land Transaction Return Guidance Notes (SDLT6)) should be inserted (see page 323 below).

8.4.11. Form SDLT4: About the transaction (Boxes 1-9)

Even if it is only one property, you must still answer any of Boxes 1-9 that is relevant – purchaser a company, property that is non-residential or mixed etc.

Box 1 – If this is part of a purchase of a business?

If this land transaction is part of a sale of a business, the assets being purchased are to be identified here, indicating the non-chargeable assets by type (the options are: stock, goodwill, chattels and moveables, and other). The amount of consideration that is apportioned to these assets (i.e. other than to land and buildings) should be shown. These will not attract SDLT. An apportionment must be made on a just and reasonable basis.[948]

---

[947] See SDLT30200

[948] See SDLTM04010

Box 2 – If the property is for commercial use, what is it?
The options given are office, shop, factory, hotel, warehouse, other industrial unit and 'other'.

HMRC guidance has indicated that "for" is misleading. The purpose is to tie this question in with SDLT1 Box 1 even if conversion into wholly residential use is intended.

Box 3 – Have you applied for and received a post transaction ruling in accordance with Code of Practice 10?
A post-transaction ruling is a ruling by HMRC on the application of tax law to a specific transaction which has already has taken place. Code of Practice 10 sets out when HMRC will give a post-transaction ruling, and how to apply, and also advice on law applicable to the transaction..

Box 4 – Is any part of the consideration contingent or dependent on uncertain future events?
Box 5 – Have you agreed with HMRC that you will pay on a deferred basis?
Box 6 – Are there any minerals or mineral rights reserved?
The Land Transaction Return guidance notes[949] state that 'any mineral rights (historic or new) which are expressly excluded from the sale' should be indicated by entering the appropriate code (listed below).

In practice, the most common code is likely to be 01.

---

[949] Reproduced in the Appendix

More than one type shown below	1
Anhydrite	2
Barytes	3
Brickearth	4
Calcite	5
Chalk	6
Chert	7
Clay – Ball	8
Clay – Brick	9
Clay – Cement	10
Clay – China	11
Clay – Silica	12
Coal	13
Fieldspar	14
Fireclay	15
Flint	16
Fluorspar	17
Fullers Earth	18

Granite	19
Gypsum	20
Ironstone	21
Lead	22
Limestone	23
Marl	24
Oil	25
Peat	26
Potash	27
Salt	28
Sand	29
Sand & Gravel	30
Sandstone	31
Shale	32
Slate	33
Tin	34
Vein Minerals	35
Other	36

Box 7 – If the purchaser is VAT registered, give its VAT registration number

If the lead purchaser ('Purchaser (1)') is VAT registered show his VAT registration number.

Box 8 – If the purchaser is a company, please give the following details:

The tax reference number, company registered number and, if registered abroad, place of registration are to be entered here.

Box9 - Description of the purchaser

Describe the first purchaser by entering all appropriate codes from the list below:

Unincorporated builder	01
Unincorporated sole trader other than a builder	02
Individual other than sole trader	03
Partnership	04
Local authority	05
Central government	06
Public corporation	07

Property company	08
Bank	09
Building society	10
Insurance/Assurance Company	11
Superannuation or pension fund	12
Other financial institution	13
Other company	14
Other, including charity	15

8.4.12. Form SDLT4: About the leases (Boxes 10-39)

HMRC has issued the following guidance:

"Use the About Leases section of SDLT4 for:

(1) the grant of a lease, which is shown as either 'mixed' code 02 or 'non residential' code 03 at SDLT1 Question 1

(2) a single transaction to acquire multiple leasehold properties by grant or assignment or in Scotland assignation - separate chargeable interests or separate plots of land, the number having been entered on form SDLT1 at question 26 and the first property identified at question 28. Enter each property on a separate form SDLT4

(3) linked leasehold transactions. If a lease is linked to the lease shown in the 'About Leases' section of the SDLT1 and it:

(4) shares the same effective date and
   a. has identical purchasers and identical vendors and
   b. comes within the same code, either A or L for question 2 of SDLT1 and
   c. in common with all the other linked leases either is claiming no relief at all, or is claiming exactly the same kind of relief

you may use an SDLT1 for the first lease and multiple forms SDLT4, one each for the other leases giving details of the linked lease in this part. See notes for question 13 of the SDLT1.

Note: if there are six or more properties involved in any one transaction refer to Part 1 paragraph 3.4 [of SDLT6].

DO NOT use the 'About leases' section of an SDLT4 for

- the grant of a lease of a single property used wholly and exclusively as a private residence, shown as 'residential' code 01 at question 1 of the SDLT1
- the assignment or in Scotland assignation, of a lease of a single property
- the surrender or renunciation of a lease of a single property
- notifying one or more leases to which the property is subject. If the chargeable transaction entered on the SDLT1 was the acquisition of a freehold or grant of a head-lease subject to underleases (subleases) make a return by using a schedule. You can download the schedule from the Stamp

Taxes website at www.hmrc.gov.uk/so/sdlt-sublease-guide or call the Helpline on 0845 603 0135.

Note: these schedules are for completion and submission direct to Stamp Taxes, Netherton. They are not part of the special arrangements for six or more properties referred to at paragraph 3.4."

Box 10 – Type of property

The code shown should be the same as for question 1 of SDLT1.

Box 11 – Address or situation of land

If the transaction is of a single property or title, put an X in the box here, and go to question 28.

Boxes 10- 27 (Boxes 24-27 for linked leases)

These boxes collect information on properties in addition to the information on the first property, which is collected on SDLT1.

Box 28 – Any terms surrendered

This applies to any surrender of lease or leases of the same property.

Box 29 – Break clause type

The types of break clause listed are:

- Landlord only
- Tenant
- Mutual

Box 30 – What is the date of the break clause?

Box 31 – Which of the following relate to the lease?

The list is:

- Option to renew
- Market rent
- Turnover rent
- Unascertainable rent
- Contingent reserved rent

Box 32 – Rent review frequency

This heading is misleading as HMRC requires the number of reviews during the term to be inserted.

Box 33 – Date of first review

Box 34 – Rent review clause (type))

The list is:

- Open market
- RPI
- Other

Box 35 – Date of rent change

If the lease provides for specific rent changes, such as "stepped rents" or a mechanism for rent review, then you need to enter the date that the first rent change may occur during the term of the lease.

Box 36 – Service charge/rent (amount)

If the lease provides for payments by the tenant for services, as distinguished from occupational rent, the amount of that payment should be entered here. If the service charge cannot be distinguished from the rent, the total amount of rent should be entered in Box 20 on the SDLT1 and this Box should be left blank.

Box 37 – Service charge frequency

The list is:

- Monthly
- Quarterly
- Annually
- Other

Box 38 – Other considerations - tenant to landlord

If there is any form of consideration given by a tenant other than in money [950] the appropriate code should be selected from the following:

Debt (which includes assumption by the purchaser of an outstanding mortgage)	1
Building works	2
Employment	3
Other (such as an annuity)	4
Shares in a quoted company	5
Share in an unquoted company	6
Other land	7
Services	8
Contingent	9

Box 39 – Other considerations landlord to tenant

If there is consideration moving from the landlord in a non-monetary form this Box needs to be completed. A reverse premium would be shown here (but would not be subject to SDLT).

A description should be selected from the codes below:

[950] The Land Transaction Return Guidance Notes in relation to Box 18 of SDLT4 indicate that this question relates only to premiums. The Guidance Notes are reproduced in the Appendix.

Debt (which includes assumption by the purchaser of an outstanding mortgage)	1
Building works	2
Employment	3
Other (such as an annuity)	4
Shares in a quoted company	5
Share in an unquoted company	6
Other land	7
Services	8
Contingent	9

8.4.13. SDLT8 and SDLT8A: Further information required to allow certificate to be issued[951]

An SDLT8 is automatically issued when there is insufficient data captured from the land transaction return for the issue of a certificate. This may be because information has been omitted, is illegible or is invalid, for example, a letter has been entered where a number should be. The SDLT8 will indicate which items of information are not satisfactory so that the practitioners or clients can provide the information by returning the form.

Before being sent to an agent/purchaser, the SDLT8 is reviewed internally by HMRC. In many cases HMRC can resolve a problem internally, for example a figure written outside the space in the form. In other cases HMRC will attempt to telephone the agent (or, if none, the purchaser) so as to resolve the problem. Most of these problems are avoided if online filing is used.

A certificate will not be provided unless the correct or missing information is provided. The issue of an SDLT8 means that the SDLT1 will remain on HMRC's system to be completed when the SDLT8 is returned. Unlike the SDLT1, the returned SDLT8 does not need to be signed by the purchaser.

In response to representations made by conveyancers, HMRC will now accept SDLT8s from agents/solicitors who are authorised by their clients to act on their behalf[952] without the need for the clients' signature(s) on the SDLT8. SDLT8 responses should be sent by fax or by sending completed SDLT8s to the specific office printed at the top of the letter. If faxing your response to an SDLT8, a further postal copy will not be required. Practitioners or clients may

[951] See SDLTM60220

[952] On the land transaction return – Box 59 - See Practitioners' Newsletter Issue 9 (September 2005) at page 4.

also make amendments via the telephone by ringing the Stamp Taxes Helpline.[953]

Provided that the land transaction return to which the SDLT8 relates has been received within 30 days of the effective date of the transaction the need to issue and SDLT 8 will not result in a late filing penalty.[954]

If the completed SDLT8 is not received after 15 working days a reminder, SDLT8A, is issued automatically. The SDLT8A states that a certificate will not be issued until the outstanding information is received.

8.4.14. SDLT9/9A and SDLT15/15A: Potential overpayment of tax[955]

An SDLT9 is issued where HMRC system has calculated an SDLT overpayment of more than £10.

SDLT15 is issued where tax may have been overpaid due to the availability of a relief, i.e. because relief has been claimed on the return but the purchaser has made a payment.

Where the overpayment is in excess of £150,000 form SDLT9 or SDLT15 will not be issued until the information has been reviewed and the purchaser has been offered the opportunity to receive the repayment via CHAPS.

The purpose of SDLT9 and SDLT15 is to check with the purchaser whether the information captured is correct and confirm that too much tax has been paid.

Responses to an SDLT9 should be sent to:
Customer Service Office
Birmingham Stamp Office
9th Floor City Centre House
30 Union Street
Birmingham B2 4AR
DX: 15001 Birmingham 1

If the purchaser confirms that an overpayment has been made HMRC's finance team accesses the computer record and will locally print a form SDLT38. This is checked and if correct is signed and sent to the Accounts Office. The signed form SDLT38 is their authorisation to issue the refund together with any interest due.

---

[953] 0845 603 0135

[954] See Practitioners' Newsletter Issue 9 (September 2005) at page 6.

[955] SDLTM60230

An SDLT10 is then issued to the purchaser and agent, if applicable, confirming the amount of the repayment.

If the purchaser does not agree that an overpayment has been made they should give their reasons why the original tax paid is in fact correct. As the details on the record will need to be amended and the tax liability is affected, the reasons given must be in writing and signed by the purchaser.

If a response to the SDLT9 or SDLT15 is not received after ten working days a reminder (SDLT9A or SDLT15A) is issued. The SDLT9A or SDLT15A states that the refund will not be made until a response is received.

8.4.15. SDLT12/12A: Request for payment of underpaid tax

If the system calculates that there is an underpayment of tax an SDLT12 is issued to the purchaser automatically, requesting payment of the amount owing within 10 working days. The SDLT12 contains a payslip.

If the payment is not made within 10 days a reminder (SDLT12A) is issued automatically.

8.5. The lease calculator

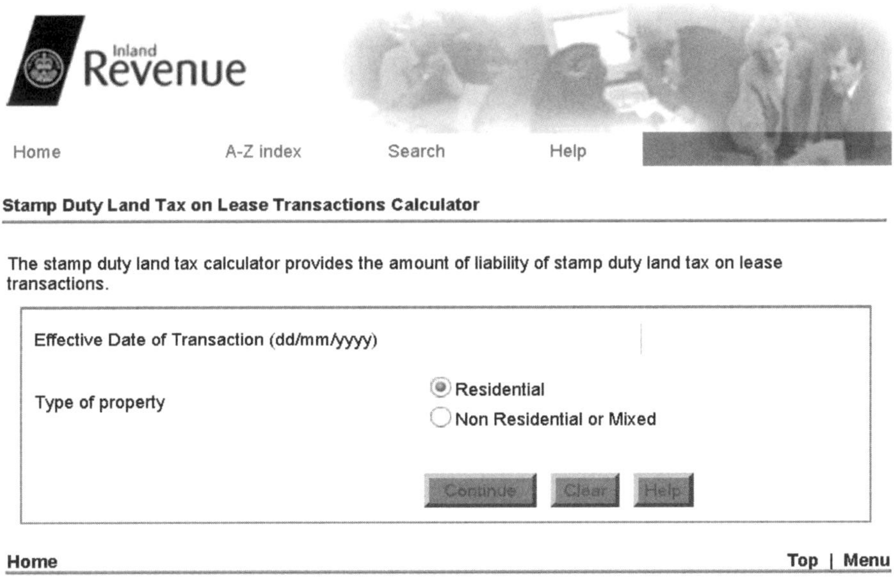

The lease calculator can be found at:
http://ldcalculator.inlandrevenue.gov.uk/

You can also gain access the stamp duty land tax Lease Transactions Calculator by selecting the question mark icon alongside question 1.23 in the online tax return 'Net present value upon which tax is calculated'. This will open a new browser window, giving guidance and a link to the Stamp Taxes website from where the online SDLT lease calculator can be accessed.

HMRC have issued the following advice on using the lease calculator. It can be found by going into the lease calculator (at the URL above) and clicking the help box underneath the data input fields (*not* the help box at the top of the screen).

Advice on using the lease calculator

The First Input Screen

- **Step. 1 Effective Date and Term of Lease:** This section allows you to input details of the term of the lease. Enter the effective date of transaction (the date of grant or substantial performance of the lease) and the start and end dates of the lease in "dd/mm/yyyy" format.
- **Step. 2 Property Type:** You will be able to indicate the type of property concerned in the lease by selecting either the 'Residential' or 'Non residential or Mixed Use' options.

This can be done by left-clicking on the empty circle beside the relevant definition.

The Second Input Screen

- **Step. 1 Disadvantaged Area Relief:** This part of the calculator allows you to take into account if the property is in a 'Disadvantaged Area'. This would then be applied to the tax calculation. ***This does not apply to non residential transactions with an effective date on or after 17th March 2005.*** If the property is in a Disadvantaged Area, left-click on the empty square.

  If the property is not in a Disadvantaged Area, move to the next field.

  If you are unsure as to whether the property is in a Disadvantaged area left-click on the 'here' link. This will open up a second Internet window, enabling you to use the postcode search engine.

- **Step. 2 Start Date as specified in lease:** Enter the start date as specified in the lease. **Please note** that for a '**notional lease**' based on '**substantial performance**', you must enter the '**effective date**' here also.
- **Step. 3 End Date as specified in lease:** Enter the end date of the term of the lease, as specified in the lease.
  Please note: If VAT is payable, you must enter the VAT inclusive figure for any premium and/or rents payable.
- **Step. 4 Premium:** This field allows you to input any premium that may have been paid for the lease.
  Left-click on the vacant field and key-in the amount. If there is no premium on the lease, simply leave the field blank.

- **Step. 5 Annual Rent(s):** Enter the annual rent(s) for the term of the lease. If the annual rent is zero enter a "0" in the field.
  The term of the lease is the period from the later of the start date or effective date until the end date; e.g. a lease 'starts' on 01/01/2001 but is granted on 01/01/04 and runs until 31/12/2010. The term is 7 years exactly (from 01/01/2004 until 31/12/2010).
  If the term of the lease is less than or equal to five years, enter the actual rent payable for each full or part year of the term of the lease in the appropriate boxes. If, for example, the term is for 3 years, you must leave years 4 & 5 blank. Do not complete the 'highest 12 monthly rent' box.

  If the term of the lease is greater than five years, enter the actual rent payable for each of the first five years of the term of the lease.

- **Step. 6 Highest 12 Monthly Rent:** This field should only be answered if the term of the lease is more than 5 years.
  Enter the highest 12 monthly rent in the first five-year period.

- **Step. 7 Average Annual Rent:** This field asks you for the 'average annual rent' for the lease.

  If the consideration includes consideration (Premium) other than rent then:

  a) If the annual rent does not exceed £600 and the relevant consideration (Premium) does not exceed the nil rate threshold, the consideration (premium) other than rent does not count as chargeable consideration.

  b) If the annual rent exceeds £600, the consideration other than rent is counted as chargeable consideration.

  The "annual rent" is the average annual rent over the term of the lease.

Date	Residential Premium	Non Residential Premium	Average Annual Rent	Rate Applied to Premium
Pre 1/12/03	£60,000	£60,000	£600	0%
Pre 1/12/03	£60,000	£60,000	£601	1%
1/12/03 - 16/03/05	£60,000	£150,000	£600	0%
1/12/03 - 16/03/05	£60,000	£150,000	£601	1%
From 17/03/05	£120,000	£150,000	£600	0%
From 17/03/05	£120,000	£150,000	£601	1%
From 23/03/06	£125,000	£150,000	£600	0%
From 23/03/06	£125,000	£150,000	£601	1%

- **Step. 8 Calculate:** Click on the 'calculate' button to submit your data to the calculator. A pop-up box will appear asking 'Are you sure you want to submit the form?'
  Click 'Yes' to go through to the calculation screen.

  Click on 'Cancel' if you want to check your figures before submitting the form.

- **Miscellaneous:** The other buttons on the screen are:-
  'Clear', which will allow you to clear the information you have input and start the lease calculation again.

  'Help', which is how you got here!

The Calculation Screen
The first box on this screen provides a brief synopsis of the various elements of the lease that were input into the lease calculator. These include information about:

- The type of property.
- Whether Disadvantaged Area Relief has been applied.
- The Effective, Start and End dates of the lease.
- What is being paid for the lease in the form of a premium (if any).
- The annual rent for the first 5 years of the lease.
- The highest yearly rent.
- The average annual rent.
- The term of the lease, in years and days, calculated from the later of the Effective or Start Dates up to the End Date.
- The figure of rent used for the final part year if the term is longer than 5 years and is not a whole number of years.

The second box displays the lease calculation result. This includes:

- The effective date of the rates and thresholds used in the calculation.
- The total tax due for the transaction.
- The Net Present Value of the lease upon which tax is calculated (NPV).
- The amount of Stamp Duty Land Tax on Rent.
- The amount of Stamp Duty Land Tax on Premium.

There is also an option at the bottom of the screen to perform another calculation if you so wish.

If you have any difficulty in using the online 'Lease Calculator', please contact the Stamp Taxes Enquiry Line on 0845 6030135.

Legislative Reference: Section 56 & Schedule 5 FA 2003.

8.6. E-filing

HMRC have developed a Stamp Taxes Online service, which has the following features:

- on-line completion of forms SDLT1, 2, 3 and 4, with the ability to save partially completed returns
- an electronic SDLT 5 certificate (submission receipt) which can be printed off to send to the appropriate land register, with the necessary documents, for registration.
- built in guidance to help with the completion of forms
- validation of data
- provision of a unique transaction reference number (UTRN) and an online submission receipt for each return successfully filed
- automatic calculation of any tax due based on the information provided
- the purchaser is able to approve the contents of the return before the effective date is known, and the agent insert the effective date when filing.

The service allows the user to file a land transaction return over the Internet and view the return for up to 30 days following submission, using either HMRC's on-line Service, or third party forms and case management software. Information about this can be found at:
http://www.hmrc.gov.uk/so/online/menu.htm.

The service can also be selected from the 'do it online' link on HMRC homepage.

The on-line service cannot be used in the following circumstances:

- Where the transaction relates to more than two properties
- Where there are more than three vendors
- Where there are more than three purchasers
- Where the transaction is linked to another

In order to use the service it is necessary to register and create a 'Stamp Taxes ID'. HMRC Online Services Helpdesk can be contacted[956] with any technical issues on registering for access to the on-line service:
Email: helpdesk@ir-efile.gov.uk

Telephone: 0845 60 55 999
Fax: 0845 366 7805

---

[956] Open Monday to Friday 8am to 10 pm. Weekends and Bank Holidays 10am to 6pm. Closed Christmas Day, Boxing Day and New Year's Day.

8.6.1. Using the online service

- After you log in there is a page of preliminary questions - basic date for referencing the online return - name of purchaser, address of the property and the nature.
- Next are pages about each purchaser - overview and identity - also the agent of the purchaser.
- Next are pages about each vendor.
- Next are pages about the land.
- Next are pages about the transaction.
- Then there is the SDLT calculation.
- The Return status checks for errors.

The following guidance is reproduced from the HMRC website[957]:

Locate a specific question within our SDLT online return

The HMRC land transaction return software has built in guidance to help you complete only the necessary forms and questions, based on the information you enter. We provide the main return SDLT1 and the supplementary returns SDLT2, 3 and 4 as some transactions may require one or a combination of these. You will be able to identify when you are completing a supplementary return as the question numbers are pre-fixed with the corresponding number e.g. SDLT2 questions are shown as 2.1, 2.2 etc.

SDLT1 – this is the main land transaction return and has to be completed for the majority of transactions involving the purchase or assignment of a lease on property such as houses, flats, other buildings or land.

Question	Section of the return
1.1 Type of property	About the land
1.2 Description of transaction	About the transaction
1.3 Interest transferred or created	About the land
1.4 Effective date of transaction	About the transaction
1.5 Any restrictions, covenants or conditions affecting the value of the interest transferred or granted?	About the transaction
1.6 Date of contract or conclusion of missives	About the transaction

957 http://www.hmrc.gov.uk/so/online/sdlt-faq-guide.htm

1.7 Is any land exchanged or part-exchanged?	About the transaction
1.8 Is the transaction pursuant to a previous option agreement?	About the transaction
1.9 Are you claiming relief?	About the transaction
1.10 What is the total consideration in money or money's worth, including any VAT actually payable for the transaction notified?	About the transaction
1.11 If the total consideration for the transaction includes VAT, please state the amount	About the transaction
1.12 What form does the consideration take?	About the transaction
1.13 Is this transaction linked to any other(s)?	About the transaction
1.14 * Total amount of tax due for this transaction	Tax calculation
1.15 Total amount paid or enclosed with this notification	Tax calculation
1.16 Type of lease	About the lease **
1.17 Start date as specified in lease	About the lease
1.18 End date as specified in lease	About the lease
1.19 Rent-free period	About the lease
1.20 Annual starting rent inclusive of VAT (actually) payable	About the lease
1.21 What is the amount of VAT, if any?	About the lease
1.22 Total premium payable	About the lease
1.23 Net present value upon which tax is calculated	About the lease
1.24 * Total amount of tax due – premium	Tax calculation
1.25 * Total amount of tax due – premium	Tax calculation
1.26 * Number of properties included	About the land
1.27 Where more than one property is involved, do you want a certificate for each property?	Final details **
1.28 Address or situation of land	About the land
1.29 Local authority number	About the land
1.30 Title number, if any	About the land
1.31 NLPG UPRN	About the land

1.32 If agricultural or development land, what is the area (if known)?	About the land
1.33 Is a plan attached?	About the land
1.34 * Number of vendors included	About the vendor
1.35 Title	About the vendor
1.36 Vendor (1) surname or company name	About the vendor
1.37 Vendor (1) first name(s)	About the vendor
1.38 Vendor (1) address	About the vendor
1.39 Agent's name	About the vendor
1.40 Agent's address	About the vendor
1.41 Agent's DX number	About the vendor
1.42 Agent's e-mail address	About the vendor
1.43 Agent's reference	About the vendor
1.44 Agent's telephone number	About the vendor
1.45 Title	About the vendor
1.46 Vendor (2) surname or company name	About the vendor
1.47 Vendor (2) first name(s)	About the vendor
1.48 Vendor (2) address	About the vendor
1.49 * Number of purchasers included	About the purchaser(s)
1.50 National Insurance number (purchaser 1), if you have one.	About the purchaser(s)
1.51 Title	About the purchaser(s)
1.52 Purchaser (1) surname or company name	About the purchaser(s)
1.53 Purchaser (1) first name(s)	About the purchaser(s)
1.54 Purchaser (1) address	About the purchaser(s)
1.55 Is the purchaser acting as a trustee?	About the purchaser(s)
1.56 Please give a daytime telephone number	About the purchaser(s)
1.57 Are the purchaser and vendor connected?	About the

	purchaser(s)
1.58 To which address shall we send the certificate?	Final details
1.59 I authorise my agent to handle correspondence on my behalf.	About the purchaser(s)
1.60 Agent's name	About the purchaser(s)
1.61 Agent's address	About the purchaser(s)
1.62 Agent's DX number	About the purchaser(s)
1.63 Agent's reference	About the purchaser(s)
1.64 Agent's telephone number	About the purchaser(s)
1.65 Title	About the purchaser(s)
1.66 Purchaser (2) surname or company name	About the purchaser(s)
1.67 Purchaser (2) first name(s)	About the purchaser(s)
1.68 Purchaser (2) address	About the purchaser(s)
1.69 Is the purchaser acting as a trustee?	About the purchaser(s)
1.70 * How many supplementary returns have you enclosed with this return?	N/A

* Question will be completed by the software, based on the information you have entered in the return

** About the lease - Questions 1.16 to 1.20 will be asked if question 1.2 'Description of transaction' has been answered Code A – Conveyance/transfer with lease involvement. If Code L – Grant of lease is entered Questions 1.16 to 1.23 will be asked.

*** This question will be asked if the transaction involves more than one property.

SDLT2 – this should be completed if the transaction involves more than 2 purchasers and/or vendors. If you add a third purchaser and/or vendor the software will automatically open the SDLT2.

SDLT3 – this should be completed if the transaction involves more than one property and question 1.2 'Description of transaction' has been answered code 'F – Conveyance/transfer' or 'O – Other'. The software will automatically open the SDLT3.

Note: If you have entered code 'A - Conveyance/transfer with lease involvement' or 'L – Grant of lease' at question 1.2 'Description of transaction', the software will automatically open an SDLT4 for any additional address details or properties.

SDLT4 – this should be completed where additional information about the transaction and/or lease can be provided. As this return can apply to a number of different transactions the following gives guidance on where to find all the questions:

Questions	Location	Section of the return
4.1 to 4.5	Main return	About the transaction – these questions are shown for all transactions. Questions 4.1 'Is this transaction part of the sale of a business?' & 4.2 'Is the property described anything other than residential?' aren't numbered.
4.6	Main return	About the land – this question is shown for all transactions
4.7 to 4.9	Main return	About the purchaser – the purchaser must have been entered as a company. On the overview page above the purchaser name there is a link ' Provide company details' You need to select this to open questions 4.7 to 4.9
4.10 to 4.17	Main return	About the land - these questions will be shown when you add more than one property and have entered code 'A - Conveyance/transfer with lease involvement' or 'L – Grant of lease' at question 1.2 'Description of transaction'
4.18 to 4.27	N/A	Not available as these questions relate to transactions involving multiple leases which currently cannot be notified online
4.28 to 4.39	Main return	About the lease – these questions will be shown when the user has entered code 'L – Grant of lease' at question 1.2 'Description of transaction'

8.6.2. Multiple linked grants of lease

In one sense you cannot file online linked transactions as a single return, but you can do them by going through the sequence for each transaction (indicating linking - for example a transfer plus linked grant of a lease).

You can't do more than 100 properties or more than 103 purchasers/vendors (any combination) in one go but it's rare to have such a deal.

The pages below are from HMRC's guidance, which can be found at: http://www.hmrc.gov.uk/so/multiple-linked-grants.pdf

Multiple Linked Grants of Lease [Code 'L']
Residential/Non Residential/Mixed

Note 1: All mandatory questions will be marked with a 'red asterisk [*]' on screen.

Note 2: The 'Online Return' will not calculate the tax due for this transaction. You must enter your own self-assessed tax due figure.

Note 3: This step-by-step guide contains online links to further guidance.

Multiple Linked Grants of Lease

What is a linked transaction?

- See SDLT 6 [3.3 Linked transaction]
- Guidance on Linked Lease Transactions – See Stamp Duty Land Tax Manual SDLTM13100

1) Complete 'Preliminary questions'

About the purchaser(s) – Purchaser (1) [Q1.52]
About the land – Property (1) [Q1.28]
About the transaction [Q1.2/Q1.63]
<u>**Next**</u>

2) 'About the purchaser - Overview' [new page]

To complete purchaser details click on 'complete details'

3) 'About the purchaser – Identity' [new page]

Complete purchaser details as appropriate [Q1.51/Q1.52/Q1.53/Q1.50/1.54/1.56 /Q1.55/Q1.57]
<u>**Next**</u>

4) 'About the Agent for the purchaser(s) [new page]

Complete Agent details for the purchaser(s) [Q1.60/Q1.61/Q1.62/Q1.64/ Q1.63/Q1.59]
<u>**Next**</u>

5) 'About the purchaser(s) - Overview [new page]

For every subsequent purchaser, please select:
Add another purchaser – Individual [Q1.65/Q1.66/Q1.67/Q1.68/1.69]

- Please note that when adding a 3rd and any subsequent purchasers, it will be SDLT 2 form questions that appear: [Q2.2/Q2.3/Q2.4/Q2.5/Q2.7/Q2.6] **or**

Add another purchaser – Company [Q1.66/Q1.68/Q1.69]

- Please note that when adding a 3rd and any subsequent company purchasers, it will be SDLT 2 form questions that appear: [Q2.3/Q2.5/Q2.7/Q2.6]
- Please note that if you select 'Provide company details', please provide 'Company details' of any 1 company, only. [Q4.7/Q4.8/Q4.9]
- Please note that our online return will not support transactions where there are any more than a combination of ninety nine purchasers & vendors. Go to 'Vendor Details'

6) 'About the vendor – Identity' [new page]
Complete vendor details as appropriate. [Q1.35/Q1.36/Q1.37/Q1.38]

Next

7) 'About the Agent for the Vendor(s)' [new page] Complete agent details for the vendor(s). [Q.1.39/Q1.40/Q1.41/Q1.44/Q1.42/Q1.43]
Next

8) 'About the vendor(s) – Overview' [new page] For every subsequent vendor, please select:
Add another Vendor [Q1.45/Q1.46/Q1.47/Q1.48]

- Please note that when adding a 3rd and any subsequent vendors, it will be SDLT 2 form questions that appear [Q2.2/Q2.3/Q2.4/Q2.5]
- Please note our online return will not support transactions where there are any more than a combination of ninety nine purchasers & vendors.

Go to Land Details

9) 'About the land – Overview' [new page]
To complete subject property details click on **'complete details'**

10) 'About the Land' [new page]
Complete subject property details as appropriate.

[Q.1.1/Q1.3/Q1.28/Q1.29/Q1.30/Q1.31/Q1.32/Q1.33/Q4.6]

Next

11) 'About the Land - Overview [new page]

This section allows you to check the land details and make any amendments if necessary. It also enables you to **'add another property'** for any multi-property transactions.

Add another property [Q4.10/Q4.17/4.11/4.12/Q4.13/Q4.14/Q4.15/Q4.6]

- Please note our online return will not support transactions where there are any more than ninety nine properties.

Go to transaction details

12) 'About the Transaction' [new page]
Complete details. [Q1.4/Q1.6]

Next

13) 'About the Transaction – Consideration' [new page]
Complete further details. [Q1.13/Q1.9/Q4.4/Q4.5]
Please note, you must answer 'Yes' to 'Is this transaction linked to any other?' [Q1.13] & complete the total linked consideration in Q1.13 part 2 – if, there are no premiums payable, please enter '0' here.
Next

14) 'About the Transaction – Additional Details 1' [new page]
Complete additional details as appropriate. [Q4.1 / 4.2 / 4.3]

- Please note: Q4.1: 'Is this transaction part of the sale of a business?' & Q4.2 'Is the property described, anything other than residential?' are not numbered within the online return.

Next

15) 'About the transaction – Additional Details 2' [new page]
Complete additional details as appropriate. [Q1.5 / 1.7 / 1.8]
Go to Lease Details

16) 'About the Lease' [new page]
Complete lease details for subject property.
[Q1.16/Q1.17/Q1.18/Q1.19/Q1.20/Q1.21/Q1.22/Q1.23]

- Please note questions 1.22 - 1.23 must be completed for this 1st lease only, apportioning the correct tax due.
- Please note that the linked rate applies to any 'Premium' payable & complete guidance on the apportionment of tax due on the 'NPV', is within the footnote below.

Next

17) 'About the Lease – Additional Information' [new page]
Complete as appropriate.
[Q4.28/Q4.29/Q4.30/Q4.31/Q4.32/Q4.33/Q4.34/Q4.35/Q4.36/Q4.37/Q4.38/4.39]

View Return Status

18) 'Return Status' [new page]
This is an overview of the information entered so far.

Click on **'Check this Return'**

19) Error Overview [new page]
Any errors on completion of your 'Return' will be listed here. If there are any errors listed: Click on **Correct these errors** & then

Return to the error overview

20) 'There are no errors so far' [new page]
- Tax Calculation
- Final Details

Click on 'Tax Calculation'

21) Tax Due [new page]
Complete Questions Q4.24/Q4.25/Q1.15-with your self-assessed tax calculation.

For this transaction, a linked grant of lease, the 'Online Return' will not calculate the tax due. You must enter your own self-assessed tax due figure for:
- Total amount of tax due – Premium [Q1.24]
- Total amount of tax due - NPV [Q1.25]
- Amount you intend to pay [Q1.15]
    - o Please note we suggest you keep a copy of the 'Tax Calculation' for your records.
    - o Please note that in many cases the 'Online Return' will calculate any tax due based on the information you provide. There are however some circumstances where it won't. SDLT will not be calculated where:
      a) Field 3 on the 'SDLT 1' is 'OT' (all others)
      b) It is a linked lease transaction
      c) Relief code '07' is claimed [designated areas (mixed)]
      d) It is a shared ownership lease (Code 'OT' must be used)
      e) There is stair-casing (Code 'OT' must be used)
      f) Claiming 'Disadvantaged Area Relief' [DAR] for a lease where the 'Average Annual Rent' is over £600, use code 'OT' in field 3

Go to final details

22) Final Details [new page]
Complete further details:
- Check the 'effective date' [Q1.4]
- Do you want a certificate for each property [Q1.27]
- To which address shall we send the certificate [Q1.58]

<u>View, print & store</u>

23) Complete return [new page]

- Please note, we suggest you keep a copy of the return & the tax calculation for your own records.

<u>**Then go to 'Submit this return'**</u>

2nd Grant of Lease [Linked to 1st Lease]

1) Go to <u>'Start new return'</u> for 2nd Lease

Please complete another 'Return' to notify this transaction. The same flow of questions & guidance, as above, will apply.

Footnote:

<u>**1. Example of calculating the SDLT payable on rent for linked grants of new leases**</u>

We have 3 linked leases (not successive linked leases) with no premium.

We need to calculate the total SDLT payable on the rent.

We also need to know how much of this **'total tax' is apportioned to each of these leases. How do we do this?**

- Calculate the **NPV of the first lease** = £180,000 [Q1.23 SDLT 1]
- Calculate the **NPV of the second lease** = £45,000 [Q1.23 SDLT 1]
- Calculate the **NPV of the third lease** = £215,000 [Q1.23 SDLT 1]
- Add these **NPV's** together = £440,000
- **Deduct** the **shared slice** = £150,000 [Non-residential] / £125,000 [Residential]
- **Balance** = £290,000
- **SDLT @ 1%** = £2,900
- **SDLT on the first lease** = £2,900 divided by £440,0000 multiplied by £180,000 = £1,186 [Q1.25 SDLT1]
- **SDLT on the second lease** = £2,900 divided by £440,000 multiplied by £45,000 = £296 [Q1.25 SDLT1]
- **SDLT on the third lease** = £2,900 divided by £440,000 multiplied by £215,000 = £1,417 [Q1.25 SDLT1]

The total SDLT payable will therefore be £2,899

<u>**2. Example of calculating the SDLT payable on the premium for linked grants of new leases**</u>

We have 3 linked leases (not successive linked leases) each with a premium

We need to calculate the total SDLT payable on each of the Premiums.

How do we do this?

- Premium on Lease 1 = £200,000 [Q1.22 SDLT 1]
- Premium on Lease 2 = £250,000 [Q1.22 SDLT 1]
- Premium on Lease 3 = £215,000 [Q1.23 SDLT 1]
- To determine the rate applicable to each of these premiums you must: **Add** all of the Premiums together = £675,000 **[Rate 4/%]**
- To calculate the **'Total amount of tax due – premium' [Q1.24] - Apply** this combined premium **rate of 4 % to each individual premium** when entering the tax due for each linked lease at **Q1.24**
- **SDLT due on Premium [Lease 1]** = £200,000 x 4% = £8,000 [Q1.24 SDLT 1]
- **SDLT due on Premium [Lease 2]** = £250,000 x 4% = £10,000 [Q1.24 SDLT 1]
- **SDLT due on Premium [Lease 3]** = £215,000 x 4% = £8,600 [Q1.24 SDLT 1]

8.6.3. Electronic completion, print and post

Printing out in HTML gives you the running order of answers. Printing out in PDF gives you a replica SDLT1 etc (so that you and the client can see the questions and answers in the order on the paper forms).

With the HMRC software the submission receipt gives you a generated UTRN (top right corner. Ignore the lengthy and prominent reference for the receipt). The UTRN is needed for the payment reference e.g. if payment is by cheque then it should be endorsed with the UTRN for posting to Netherton.

If you use the HMRC software do not send in a payslip (even if amended – as sometimes the cheque is credited to the deleted printed number when read by machine).

Endorse plans with the UTRN and the local authority code, also for sending to Netherton. Likewise schedules of existing leases affecting the property.

If you realise later that there was an error (such as not linking transactions, hence the tax is wrong) then you write to Birmingham to amend the return within 12 months.

Problems arise and are being addressed all the time – at the moment most of the "system busy" signals are false (log out and log in again to the HMRC software). Avoid peak times, but the system has "pooling" so that remaining ones in the system at midnight are picked up.

Some go through quickly (you have to keep the "window" open for several seconds so that the processing goes through). You do not always get the certificate right away, but you can come back later and check the status, and there is a second e-mail on the HMRC software system.

Do not send a printed version of the online filed return to HMRC (it will not scan without a barcode etc).

HMRC has also approved certain software houses for production of the SDLT forms. These suppliers are able to make copies of substitute SDLT forms available to solicitors and conveyancers and their computer systems. A list of suppliers whose products have been approved for release to customers may be inspected at http://www.hmrc.gov.uk/efiling/sdltsoft-dev.htm.

If any of these on-line or electronic form-producing services are used the form is produced un-numbered and without a payslip. The TRN must be inserted from the payslip that is intended to accompany the submission of the form (a stock of paying-in slips can be obtained from the Orderline).

PART FOUR

SDLT BY TRANSACTION

9. SDLT BY TRANSACTION

The purpose of this chapter is to illustrate the main principles of SDLT by reference to typical scenarios which may arise in practice so as to give a working knowledge of the tax. The scenarios build on each other to a certain extent and for each scenario attention is drawn to any particular features of the SDLT forms which would apply in relation to it. In appropriate cases the SDLT calculation is shown.

No consideration is given to those areas of the form SDLT1 which fall within Section 4 (About the land), Section 5 (About the vendor) or Section 6 (About the purchaser).

Reference should, of course, be made to Part Two of this book for a detailed explanation of the tax.

9.1. Purchase of freehold

9.1.1. Freehold residential property: contract with completion by conveyance

S enters into contract to sell a freehold dwelling house to B with vacant possession for £520,000 together with carpets, curtains and fitted wardrobes (which would cost £15,000 new but are a few years old), and completes the sale by a conveyance four weeks later. S's estate agent suggested that £10,000 should be apportioned to fixtures and fittings and that B should agree to pay the agent's fees of £10,000, in order that the price should not exceed the threshold of £500,000.

Commentary:

This is the type of simple transaction for which the land transaction return was designed. B will have an obligation to complete and submit an SDLT1 and pay the tax within 30 days of completion.

The amount paid for the carpet and curtains can be disregarded in calculating the tax due as these are chattels. SDLT must be paid on the amount apportioned to the fitted wardrobes as these are fixtures. A 'just and reasonable' apportionment must be made and evidence of how the apportionment was reached should be retained.

HMRC have indicated that the apportionment of the purchase price may well be one of the aspects of form SDLT1 into which they will make enquiries. They may also undertake enquiries into cases where a deduction has been made for chattels to confirm that those items properly fall within the definition of chattels.

B's payment of the agent's fees incurred by S will be consideration for SDLT purposes (as it is money's worth) and it should be included in the total consideration inserted in Box 10.

Calculation of the SDLT:

Assuming that £3,000 can reasonably be apportioned to the carpets and curtains the SDLT payable will be:

£517,000 x 4% = £20,680

Completion of SDLT1 in relation to the transaction:

Box 1 – Type of property

Code 01 (residential)

Box 2 - Description of transaction

Code F (conveyance or transfer)

Box 3 – Interest transferred or created

Code FP (freehold with vacant possession)

Box 4 – Effective Date

The date of completion

Box 10 –Total consideration

517000

Box 12 – What form does the consideration take?

Code 30 (cash) and Code 31 (debt)

Box 14 – Total amount of tax due for this transaction

20680

Box 15 – Total amount paid or enclosed with this notification

20680 (or 0 if payment does not accompany the SDLT1[958])

Notes:

1) If there were more than two sellers and/or more than two purchasers, additional forms SDLT2 would need to be completed for each additional seller or buyer after the second.
2) If the suggestions of S's estate agent are taken up the SDLT would be £500,000 x 3% = £15,000 but the SDLT1 would be inaccurate and B could be liable to interest and penalties, assuming his conduct did not amount to fraud.

9.1.2. Freehold residential property: sale off-plan

S, a house-builder, contracts to sell to B a freehold house in the course of construction for £525,000 Completion of the sale takes place five months later when the house is ready.

Commentary:

It makes no difference to the SDLT analysis that completion does not take place for five months provided that there is no 'substantial performance' of the contract by the buyer in the intervening period.

Calculation of the SDLT:

The SDLT payable will be £525,000 x 4% = £21,000

Completion of SDLT1 in relation to the transaction:

Box 1 – Type of property

Code 01 (residential)

[958] Since 19 July 2007 payment does not have to accompany the SDLT1 although the tax remains payable within 30 days of the effective date of the transaction.

Box 2 - Description of transaction

Code F (other conveyance or transfer)

Box 3 – Interest transferred or created

Code FP (freehold with vacant possession)

Box 4 – Effective Date

The date of completion

Box 10 –Total consideration

525000

Box 12 – What form does the consideration take?

Code 30 (cash)

Box 14 – Total amount of tax due for this transaction

21000

Box 15 – Total amount paid or enclosed with this notification

21000 (or 0 if payment does not accompany the SDLT1[959])

9.1.3. Freehold residential property: sale off-plan with stage payments

S, a house-builder, contracts to sell to B for £400,000 a freehold house in the course of construction. A 10% deposit is payable on exchange, a further 20% deposit is payable when the brickwork is up to first floor level, a further 20% is payable when the roof structure is installed, and the balance is payable on completion of the sale, once the new house is finished.

Commentary:

The acquisition by B from S is a standard transaction (for which see scenario 9.1.1). The effective date will be completion and SDLT is payable on £400,000 within 30 days of that date.

Note: If the instalments payable more than six months after completion an application to defer payment of the SDLT could be made.

9.1.4. Freehold residential property: house-building company acquires buyer's old house

B buys the freehold of a new house from S, a house-building company. The new house is being sold by S for £300,000. S takes B's existing house in part exchange; it is worth £220,000 so B also pays S £80,000 in cash.

Commentary:

The acquisition by B from S is a standard transaction (for which see scenario 9.1.1).

[959] See footnote 958

Assuming that the detailed conditions are fulfilled the relief for an acquisition of a dwelling by a house-building company from an individual acquiring a new dwelling would apply to the acquisition by S from B. This transaction would therefore be exempt.

Calculation of the SDLT:

The SDLT on B's acquisition would be:

£300,000 x 3% = £9,000

Completion of SDLT1s in relation to the transaction:

There will be two SDLT1s:

In relation to B's acquisition Box 12 of the SDLT1 (Form of consideration) should show Code 30 (cash) and Code 37 (other land).

In relation to S's acquisition the relevant entries on the SDLT1 in relation to the claiming of the relief will be:

Box – 9 – Are you claiming relief?

Code 08 ((part-exchange (house-building company)) The company's CIS (Construction Industry Scheme) reference number should be included in the space provided.

Box 14 – Total amount of tax due for this transaction

0

Box 15 – Total amount paid or enclosed with this notification

0

Note: As there is a corporate purchaser an SDLT4 will need to be completed in respect of the acquisition by the house-building company. The company's tax reference number, registered number and, if registered abroad, place of registration are to be entered in Box 8.

9.1.5. Freehold commercial investment property: contract and completion by conveyance

S enters into contract to sell an office building for £5 million to B subject to and with the benefit of three leases, and completes the sale two weeks later. £1.2 million of the purchase price is allocated, by a capital allowances election, to lifts and air-conditioning plant and equipment. The contract provides that on completion the reserve fund held by S will be handed over to B. The property is elected for VAT but the sale is dealt with as a transfer of a going concern.[960]

[960] Pursuant to article 5 VAT (Special Provisions) Order 1995 (SI 1995/1268)

Commentary:
The capital allowances election apportions £1.2 million to lifts and air-conditioning plant and equipment. These items are likely to be fixtures (rather than chattels) and the amounts paid for them will form part of the chargeable consideration.

The transfer of the reserve fund will not be chargeable consideration given for the land transaction.

As no VAT is charged (although an election has been made) the chargeable consideration will be £5 million.

Calculation of the SDLT:
The SDLT payable will be £5,000,000 x 4% = £200,000

Completion of SDLT1 in relation to the transaction:
Box 1 – Type of property

Code 03 (non-residential)

Box 2 - Description of transaction

Code F (conveyance)

Box 3 – Interest transferred or created

Code FT (freehold subject to lease to an occupier)

Box 4 – Effective Date

The date of completion

Box 10 –Total consideration

5000000

Box 12 – What form does the consideration take?

Code 30 (cash)

Box 14 – Total amount of tax due for this transaction

200000

Box 15 – Total amount paid or enclosed with this notification

200000 (or 0 if payment does not accompany the SDLT1[961])

Box 16 – Type of lease

Code N (non-residential)

Completion of SDLT4s in relation to the transaction:
As the freehold is acquired subject to three leases, details of one should be included on form SDLT1 as indicated above and two SDLT4s (one for each

[961] See footnote 958

additional lease to which the freehold is subject) should be completed. The acquisition of part of a business will be indicated in Box 1 of from SDLT4.

9.1.6. Freehold commercial property: completion by conveyance - no contract

The same scenario as 9.1.5 but the parties go straight to completion without having a contract.

Commentary:

The SDLT analysis would be as for scenario 9.1.5. The same amount of tax would be payable and the SDLT1 entries and SDLT4 entries would not change. There would obviously be no date of contract to insert in Box 6 of the SDLT1.

9.1.7. Freehold commercial property: contract and completion by conveyance – buyer allowed access in period before completion

S enters into contract to sell a warehouse building for £2 million to B with vacant possession. The warehouse was used by S for its own business, and has not been let, but it was elected for VAT six months earlier and so B has to pay VAT on the price. B is allowed to install its warehousing racking system in the property as from exchange of contracts and completion takes place six weeks after exchange.

Commentary:

As VAT is chargeable in addition to the price this need to be included as part of the chargeable consideration.

The entry onto the premises by B in advance of completion could constitute substantial performance of the contract if the terms on which the access was granted amounted to giving possession of the interest in the warehouse to B[962]. On the assumption that this is the case (as there is no indication that B carries out the installation pursuant to a licence), an SDLT1 must be delivered and the SDLT paid within 30 days of possession of the premises being taken by B.

Calculation of the SDLT:

Chargeable consideration = £2,000,000 plus VAT = £2,350,000.

SDLT payable = £2,350,000 x 4% = £94,000

Completion of SDLT1 in relation to the transaction:

The SDLT1 will be completed in the normal way except for the following Boxes:

Box 4 – Effective Date

[Date possession taken by B]

---

[962] See section 1.3.1 above for what amounts to 'giving possession' for this purpose

Box 11 – Amount of VAT

350000

9.1.8. Freehold commercial investment property: with void rent allowances

S enters into a contract to sell a five-storey office building for £13 million to B, subject to and with the benefit of four leases, and with one floor unlet. The four leases were granted recently and still have rent free periods running. The sale contract requires S to allow B, on completion, an amount (which is subsequently calculated as £224,500) equal to rent under the four leases for the period from completion until their rent free periods expire. It also requires S to pay to B, quarterly in advance, notional rent for the vacant floor at £365,000 per annum from completion until that floor is let or until nine months expires, whichever is earlier. That floor remains un-let for seven months, for which S pays B notional rent totalling £210,000.

Commentary

This is a land transaction where part of the consideration is unascertainable at completion. The SDLT payable will be calculated on the basis that the consideration is £13 million less £224,000 (void rent allowance) less a reasonable estimate of the reduction in the consideration in respect of the notional rent for the vacant floor. An SDLT1 will be furnished on this basis and that return amended once the unascertainable element is determined (on the earlier of the expiration of nine months or the letting of the vacant floor). A refund of SDLT may then be due.

Completion of SDLT1 and SDLT4 in relation to the transaction:

The following entry on the SDLT1 would be necessary:

Box 12 – What form does the consideration take?

Codes 30 (cash) and 39 (contingent)

In addition, Box 4 (contingent or uncertain consideration) will need to be completed on SDLT4.

9.1.9. Freehold commercial property: linked transactions

S has a freehold investment portfolio of six small office buildings, each let to separate tenants. B agrees to buy them all for £2.5 million but then suggests that they should be bought by six separate companies in its group at separate prices, the price of each on a fair and reasonable basis falls below £500,000 except in the case of the most valuable building.

Commentary:

These transactions will be linked transactions so in calculating the rate of SDLT the consideration must be aggregated.

Calculation of the SDLT:

Assuming a total price for the two exempt transactions of £800,000 the SDLT payable will be:

£2,500,000 x 4% = £100,000

Completion of SDLT1and SDLT4s in relation to the transaction:

The SDLT1 will be completed in the normal way except for that Box 13 (Linked transactions) will need to be completed.

As there are corporate purchasers an SDLT4 will need to be completed in respect of each of them. Each company's tax reference number, registered number and, if registered abroad, place of registration should be entered in Box 8.

9.1.10. Chargeable consideration: overage payment

P sells B of the freehold of a derelict site, not VAT elected, for £5 million with overage payable if B obtains and implements a planning permission for residential development of more than a specified density.

Commentary:

The overage payment would constitute contingent consideration for SDLT purposes.

If the amount of the overage can be established at the effective date of the transaction, for example, if it is expressed as a fixed sum payable in the event that planning permission in the stated terms is obtained, that sum will form part of the chargeable consideration as it has to be assumed that the contingency will be satisfied. An adjustment would be made later if the required planning permission was not obtained.

If the amount of the overage cannot be determined at the effective date, because, for example, it is based on a formula which takes into account the density for which planning consent is obtained a reasonable estimate of the amount must be made to enable the SDLT liability to be calculated. Again an adjustment is made when the overage becomes ascertainable.

A deferment application can be made where unascertainable or contingent consideration is payable more than six months after the effective date of the transaction. The application must be made within 30 days of completion.

Completion of SDLT1 and SDLT4 in relation to the transaction:

The following entry on the SDLT1 would be necessary to deal with the overage payment:

Box 12 – What form does the consideration take?

Codes 30 (cash) and 39 (contingent)

In addition, Box 4 (contingent or uncertain consideration) will need to be completed on SDLT4.

Note: If a deferment application had been made and accepted this would need to be indicated in Box 5 on SDLT4.

9.2. Purchase of existing lease

9.2.1. Leasehold residential property

S contracts to sell for £320,000 a leasehold flat to B, together with S's share in the company that owns the freehold.

Commentary:

Only the leasehold acquisition is subject to SDLT so a 'fair and reasonable' apportionment of the consideration must be made between the property and the share in the company owning the freehold. As it is the assignment of a single lease no SDLT4 is required.

Calculation of the SDLT:

Assuming that £1 can be apportioned to the share the SDLT payable will be:

£319,999 x 3% = £9,599 (rounded down to nearest pound)

Completion of SDLT1 in relation to the transaction:

Box 1 – Type of property

Code 01 (residential)

Box 2 - Description of transaction

Code F (conveyance or transfer)

Box 3 – Interest transferred or created

Code LG (long lease at ground or nominal rent)

Box 4 – Effective Date

The date of completion

Box 10 –Total consideration

319999

Box 12 – What form does the consideration take?

Code 30 (cash)

Box 14 – Total amount of tax due for this transaction

9599

Box 15 – Total amount paid or enclosed with this notification

9599 (or 0 if payment does not accompany the SDLT1[963])

Box 16 – Type of lease

Code R (residential)

---

[963] See footnote 958

9.2.2. Leasehold residential property with share of freehold

S contracts to sell for £425,000 a leasehold maisonette to B, together with S's one-half share in the freehold which is owned jointly by S and L, the lessee of the other maisonette in the building. S transfers his lease to B, and at the same time S and L transfer the freehold to L and B.

Commentary:

The sale of the leasehold interest is a standard transaction. An amount of the consideration should be apportioned to the share of the freehold and as this is a linked transaction all the consideration will be taxed at the 3% rate. Two SDLT1s need to be submitted as the codes in Box 2 are different[964] and Box 13 (linked transactions) completed on both. As it is the assignment of a single lease no SDLT4 is filed.

9.2.3. Leasehold commercial property – acquisition subject to occupational leases

S enters into a contract to sell a long leasehold parade of five shops, subject to and with the benefit of five separate under-leases of the shops to occupational tenants for £2.5 million. S has not elected to charge VAT. Completion takes place on the same day as exchange of contracts.

Commentary:

This is a standard transaction and completion of the SDLT1 is straightforward.

Calculation of the SDLT:

The SDLT payable will be:

£2,500,000 x 4% = £62,500

Completion of SDLT1 in relation to the transaction:

Box 1 – Type of property

Code 03 (non-residential)

Box 2 - Description of transaction

Code F (conveyance or transfer)

Box 3 – Interest transferred or created

Code LT (long lease subject to lease to an occupier)

Box 4 – Effective Date

The date of completion

Box 10 –Total consideration

2500000

[964] See page 23 of SDLT6 (September 2007)

Box 12 – What form does the consideration take?

Code 30 (cash)

Box 14 – Total amount of tax due for this transaction

62500

Box 15 – Total amount paid or enclosed with this notification

62500 (or 0 if payment does not accompany the SDLT1[965])

Box 16 – Type of lease

Code N (non-residential)

Completion of SDLT4s in relation to the transaction:

As the freehold is acquired subject to five under-leases, details of one should be included on form SDLT1 as indicated above and four SDLT4s (one for each additional lease to which the freehold is subject) should be completed. SDLT1 and SDLT4 require different information.

9.2.4. Commercial property – assignment of leaseback with reverse premium

S Limited, which was formerly the owner-occupier of a property, sold the freehold on 31 March 2004 and took back a 25 year lease at an initial annual rent of £250,000. By the end of September 2007 the market rent has plummeted and S Limited's business is failing. S Limited assigns the leaseback to B, paying B a reverse premium of £150,000.

Commentary:

If sale and leaseback relief was claimed by S Limited in respect of the leaseback element of the transaction which took place in March 2004 there would be a claw-back of that relief. The assignment of that leaseback by S to B would be treated as the grant of a new lease by S to B for a term equal to the unexpired term of the original leaseback, and on the same terms as those on which B holds that lease after the assignment.

The reverse premium is not chargeable to SDLT.

Calculation of the SDLT:

The SDLT would be calculated on the basis of a lease for 21.5 years at an annual rent of £250,000 giving an RRV of £4,067,485. The tax payable on the assignment to B is therefore:

(£3,732,976 - £150,000) x 1% = £35,829 (rounded down to the nearest pound)

---

[965] See footnote 958

Completion of SDLT1 in relation to the transaction:
The original SDLT1 delivered in relation to the March 2004 transaction would need to be amended to reflect the grant of the notional lease to B. The amended return should be accompanied by the tax payable.

Completion of SDLT4 in relation to the transaction:
As the notional lease is a new commercial lease an SDLT4 must also be completed. The reverse premium would be shown in Box 39 by inserting Code 04 (other).

9.3. Grant of new lease

9.3.1. New long lease: residential

S, a house-building company, contracts to sell a flat off-plan to B on a long lease at a premium of £130,000. Completion is nine months after exchange of contracts.

Commentary:

This is a standard transaction and completion of the SDLT1 is relatively straightforward. The fact that completion is not for nine months will not affect matters provided that the contract is not substantially performed by the buyer in the intervening period. As it is the grant of a residential lease no SDLT4 is filed.

Calculation of the SDLT:

The SDLT payable will be:

£130,000 x 1% = £1,300[966]

Completion of SDLT1 in relation to the transaction:

Box 1 – Type of property

Code 01 (residential)

Box 2 - Description of transaction

Code L (grant of a lease)

Box 3 – Interest transferred or created

Code LG (long leasehold at a ground or nominal rent)

Box 4 – Effective Date

The date of completion

Box 10 –Total consideration

130000

Box 12 – What form does the consideration take?

Code 30 (cash)

Box 14 – Total amount of tax due for this transaction

1300

[966] The threshold for residential property was increased from £60,000 to £120,000 for transactions with an effective date after 16 March 2005 by section 95 FA 2005 and was further increased to £125,000 for transactions with an effective date after 22 March 2005 by section 162 FA 2006. Once the threshold is exceeded the whole of the consideration is chargeable except in relation to the charge on rent when only the excess of the RRV over the threshold is taxed.

Box 15 – Total amount paid or enclosed with this notification

1300 (or 0 if payment does not accompany the SDLT1[967])

Box 16 – Type of lease

Code R (residential)

9.3.2. New long lease: residential, with stage payments

S, a house-building company, contracts to sell a flat off plan to B on a long lease at a premium of £350,000. Completion is nine months after exchange of contracts. A 10% deposit is payable on exchange, a further 30% is payable after three months, a further 30% is payable after six months, and the balance is payable on completion of the sale, once the flat is ready.

Commentary:

This is a standard SDLT transaction. The total consideration of £350,000 will be chargeable and the tax is due within 30 days of completion. As it is the grant of a residential lease no SDLT4 is filed.

The SDLT analysis is not affected by the fact that there are stage payments.

9.3.3. New lease: commercial with reverse premium

L grants a five year lease of a shop to T at an annual rent of £40,000 and pays T a reverse premium of £30,000. It is not preceded by a contract.

Commentary:

The reverse premium is not subject to SDLT. The fact that there is no contract makes no difference to the SDLT analysis.

Calculation of the SDLT:

The RRV of the lease is £180,602. The SDLT payable will be:

£180,602 - £150,000 = £30,602 x 1% = £306 (rounded down to nearest pound)

Completion of SDLT1 in relation to the transaction:

Box 1 – Type of property

Code 03 (non-residential)

Box 2 - Description of transaction

Code L (grant of a lease)

Box 3 – Interest transferred or created

Code LP (lease to an occupier)

Box 4 – Effective Date

The date of completion

---

967 See footnote 958

Box 10 –Total consideration

Leave blank

Box 12 – What form does the consideration take?

Code 30 (cash)

Box 14 – Total amount of tax due for this transaction

306

Box 15 – Total amount paid or enclosed with this notification

307

Box 16 – Type of lease

Code N (non-residential)

Box 20- - annual starting rent

40000

Box 23 - NPV

180602

Box 25 – Total amount of tax due - NPV

306

Completion of SDLT4 in relation to the transaction:

As the lease is a new non-residential lease an SDLT4 must also be completed. The reverse premium would be shown in Box 39 by inserting Code 04 (other).

9.3.4. Agreement for lease: commercial with access for fitting-out

S enters into an agreement for a ten year lease of commercial premises with T who is given access three months before the grant of the lease to carry out a fit-out.

Commentary:

If the terms on which T is allowed access to carry out a fit-out are such that T takes possession of the interest in the premises[968], that will amount to substantial performance of the agreement for lease before it has been completed. If this is the case, the substantially performed agreement for lease will be treated as if it were the grant of a lease for a term of ten years and three months, beginning on the date on which the agreement for lease was substantially performed and ending on the date when the actual lease will end.

When the actual lease is granted in pursuance of the agreement which has earlier been substantially performed, this is treated for the purposes of overlap relief as a surrender and re-grant and overlap relief is available.

[968] See section 1.3.1 above for what amounts to 'giving possession' for this purpose

Calculation of the SDLT:

The SDLT will be based on the NPV for a lease of ten years and three months (if the consideration for the grant consists of or includes rent).

Completion of SDLT1 and SDLT4 in relation to the transaction:

An SDLT1 and an SDLT4 will be completed on the basis of the grant of a lease of ten years and three months. The effective date (to be inserted in Box 4 of SDLT1) would be the date possession was taken by B.

On the grant of an actual lease pursuant to a substantially performed agreement for lease, Box 17 on the SDLT1 ('start date as specified in lease') should show the start date of the actual lease. Box 20 ('annual starting rent') should show the full rent payable under the actual lease and not simply the amount left after deducting the rent declared on the SDLT1 for the notional lease. As neither Box 17 nor Box 20 is used to compute the NPV this will not affect the charge to SDLT which will take into account overlap relief.

9.4. Rent reviews and rent variations

9.4.1. New lease – commercial with open market rent review (1)

L grants a 15 year lease of an office to T at an annual rent of £120,000. There are upwards only rent reviews after every five years of the term, which commences on the date of the lease. The building is elected for VAT which is chargeable in addition to the rent.

Commentary:

Before calculating the SDLT the rent must be increased by the amount of the VAT which gives an annual VAT-inclusive rent of £141,000. As the first rent review will take place after the end of year five of the lease it will be ignored unless the rent increase is 'abnormal'.

Calculation of the SDLT:

The RRV of the lease is £1,623,954. The SDLT payable will be:

£1,623,954 - £150,000 = £1,473,954 x 1% = £14,739 (rounded down to nearest pound)

Completion of SDLT1 in relation to the transaction:

Box 1 – Type of property

Code 03 (non-residential)

Box 2 - Description of transaction

Code L (grant of a lease)

Box 3 – Interest transferred or created

Code LP (lease to an occupier)

Box 4 – Effective Date

The date of completion

Box 10 –Total consideration

Leave blank

Box 12 – What form does the consideration take?

Code 30 (cash)

Box 14 – Total amount of tax due for this transaction

14739

Box 15 – Total amount paid or enclosed with this notification

14739 (or 0 if payment does not accompany the SDLT1[969])

[969] See footnote 958

Box 16 – Type of lease

Code N (non-residential)

Box 20 - annual starting rent (inclusive of VAT)

141000

Box 21 - amount of VAT

21000

Box 23 - NPV

1473954

Box 25 – Total amount of tax due - NPV

14739

Completion of SDLT4 in relation to the transaction:

As the lease is a new lease an SDLT4 must also be completed – in particular Boxes 10 to 39.

In relation to the rent review the following Boxes should be completed:

Box 32 – Rent review frequency

05

Box 33 – Date of first review

DD MM YYYY

Box 34 – Rent review clause (type)

Select 'Open market'

9.4.2. New lease – commercial with open market rent review (2)

The same scenario as 9.4.1 but the term is expressed to run from the quarter day before the grant of the lease, so the first rent review is slightly less than five years after the date of the lease.

Commentary:

As the rent review is the first one, is uncertain in its effect and the review date is expressed as falling five years after a specified date which is within three months before the beginning of the term of the lease that review can be ignored[970]. The SDLT analysis would therefore be as for scenario 9.4.1. The same tax would be payable as in respect of scenario 9.4.1 and the SDLT1 entries would not change. The same Boxes on form SDLT4 would need to be completed in respect of the new lease as in scenario 9.4.1.

[970] As paragraph 7A Schedule 17A will apply

9.4.3. New lease – commercial with turnover rent review (3)

T takes a ten year lease of a shop in a new shopping centre at a basic rent of £200,000 per annum subject to upwards only review every five years to 80% of open market value, and at a supplemental turnover rent equal to 3% of the tenant's annual turnover at the premises, with a maximum of £40,000, payable within three months of the end of each year of the term.

At the outset the first year's turnover rent was expected to be around £20,000 but it is in fact found to be only £13,000 due to poor trading. The total rent actually payable is therefore £200,000 in the first year and £213,000 in the second year. After that the turnover is high enough to trigger the maximum total yearly rent of £240,000 until the five year review date is reached when the basic rent increases to £230,000 per annum.

Commentary:

The SDLT payable when the SDLT1 is filed in respect of the grant will be calculated by adding to the basic rent a reasonable estimate of the turnover rent. The review after the end of Year Five will be ignored unless it gives rise to an 'abnormal' increase in rent. Assume that the following figures are estimated:

Year One:
£200,000
Year Two:
£220,000
Year Three:
£220,000
Year Four:
£220,000
Year Five:
£220,000
Years Six to Ten:
£220,000 (highest rent estimated for Years One to Five)

At the end of Year Five a second SDLT1 will be filed based on the following actual rents:

Year One:
£200,000
Year Two:
£213,000
Year Three:
£240,000
Year Four:
£240,000
Year Five:

£240,000
Years Six to Ten:
£240,000 (highest rent in Years One to Five)

Calculation of the SDLT:

The SDLT to be paid in relation to the grant will be based on an RRV of £1,810,329 giving an initial SDLT charge of:
(£1,810,329 - £150,000) x 1% = £16,603 (rounded down to the nearest pound)

The SDLT to be paid when an SDLT1 is filed at the end of Year Five will be based on an RRV of £1,932,133. The additional SDLT payable will be:
(£1,932,133 - £150,000) x 1% = £17,821 - £16,623 = £1,198

9.4.4. New lease – commercial with staged rents and minimum at review

T takes a fifteen year lease of a shop at a rent of £50,000 in the first year, £60,000 in the second year, and £70,000 in each of the third to fifth years, rising to the higher of open market rent and £80,000 pa at the end of the fifth year, and with a review to open market rent at the end of the tenth year.

Commentary:

The review at the end of Year Five will be ignored (as it cannot give rise to an 'abnormal' increase in rent) as will the review at the end of Year Ten (unless it gives rise to an 'abnormal' increase in rent).

The same Boxes on form SDLT4 would need to be completed in respect of the new lease as in scenario 9.4.1.

The SDLT payable when the SDLT1 is filed in respect of the grant will be calculated as follows:

Year One:
£50,000
Year Two:
£60,000
Year Three:
£70,000
Year Four:
£70,000
Year Five:
£70,000
Years Six to Fifteen:
£70,000 (highest rent in Years One to Five)

Calculation of the SDLT:

The SDLT to be paid in relation to the grant will be based on an RRV of £777,559 giving an initial SDLT charge of:

(£777,559 - £150,000) x 1% = £6275 (rounded down to the nearest pound)

9.4.5. New lease – commercial with fixed rent increases

T takes a twenty year lease of a new distribution centre at an initial rent of £1,000,000 per annum subject to fixed rent increases of 1.5% every year, compounded annually.

Commentary:

Any variations in rent after the end of the fifth year of the term will be ignored unless they give rise to an 'abnormal' rent increase. In calculating the SDLT the rent for Years Six to Twenty will be taken to be the same as the Year Five rent.

The same Boxes on form SDLT4 would need to be completed in respect of the new lease as in scenario 9.4.1.

9.4.6. Agreement for lease: variation to increase the rent

L and T enter into an agreement for a 15 year lease at a rent of £20 per square foot, completion to be following construction of the building by L (the landlord) at which time the building will be measured to fix the rent, but the minimum area must be 100,000 square feet. Before the building is completed L and T then enter into a deed of variation which provides for the specification to be improved, the rent to increase to £25 per square foot, and the lease term to increase to 20 years. The lease is later granted to T on the terms as varied.

Commentary:

Provided neither the original agreement for lease nor the agreement as varied are substantially performed before completion, the only land transaction will be the grant of the lease at a rent of £25 a square foot for a term of 20 years. The rent will be ascertainable at that time.

Note: If the lease term had been extended after the grant this would have taken effect as a surrender and re-grant (see scenario 9.7.3). A variation of the lease within the first five years of the term to increase the rent is treated for SDLT purposes as if it were the grant of a lease in consideration of the additional rent made payable by it[971].

---

[971] See 2.6.21 above

9.5. Sub-sales/assignments of rights

9.5.1. Residential property: sub-sale and conveyance direct to third party

S contracts to sell a house to B for £700,000 with completion to take place two months later. The contract precludes assignment but allows B to direct that S will transfer the property to a third party. B contracts to sell the house to B2 for £800,000 with the same completion date, on which S transfers the house directly to B2. B joins in the transfer to direct the transferring to B2 and to acknowledge receipt of the profit of £100,000.

Commentary:

This is a transfer of rights. The only land transaction will be the transfer from S to B2. SDLT will be payable by B2 by reference to chargeable consideration of £800,000.

B is not regarded as entering into a land transaction and therefore does not have to submit an SDLT1.

9.5.2. Residential property: sub-sale and double conveyance

The same scenario as 1.6.1 but the first contract precludes B from requiring S to transfer the property to a third party, so on completion S transfers the house to B and B transfers it to B2.

Commentary:

This is also a transfer of rights. HMRC have confirmed that a double conveyance structure can qualify for relief as a transfer of rights and generate only one charge to SDLT, where the S to B contract is completed by the transfer to B at the same time as (in other words, immediately before) the completion of the B to B2 contract by the transfer to B2[972].

Completion of SDLT1 in relation to the transaction:

B will complete an SDLT in the normal way in respect of his acquisition. The subsale can be ignored and either S or B1 can be shown as the vendor[973].

9.5.3. Residential property: assignment of benefit of contract

S contracts to sell a house to B for £700,000 with completion to take place two months later. The contract does not preclude assignment. A week later, B contracts to sell the house to B2 for £800,000 with the same completion date, but this contract allows B to give B2 seven days notice requiring B2 to take an assignment of the first contract, for a premium of £100,000. B immediately exercises this right and assigns the first contract to B2 for £100,000. B2 thereby

[972] See SDLTM1080

[973] See Land Registry internal guidance NP6

becomes the buyer under the first contract, which he completes (at the price of £700,000) six weeks after the assignment.

Commentary:

This is a transfer of rights. The only land transaction will be the transfer from S to B2. SDLT will be payable by B2 by reference to chargeable consideration of £800,000.

B is not regarded as entering into a land transaction and therefore does not have to submit an SDLT1.

9.5.4. Residential property: use of nominee (bare trustee) to buy

S is selling his house for £500,000. His arch enemy B wants to buy it, and persuades his friend F to agree to buy the house as his secret agent. F purchases the house using B's money. S transfers the house to F for £500,000. F immediately transfers the house to B for no monetary consideration, pursuant to the bare trust

Commentary:

The purchase by B will be a standard SDLT transaction. As this is a bare trust, the SDLT1 will show B as the purchaser (not the nominee) and B will sign the SDLT1.

The Revenue certificate will be issued in the name of the beneficial owner, B. If registration of the legal owner (F) is required this should be explained in a letter to the Land Registry accompanying the certificate.[974] A subsequent transfer from F to B will be exempt. There will be no requirement for an SDLT1 but a self-certificate (SDLT 60) will need to be completed.

---

[974] See SDLT6 (September 2007) at page 30 (SDLT1 Q55)

9.6. Sale and leaseback

9.6.1. Commercial: sale of freehold and leaseback with option to renew

S is the owner-occupier of a factory. S sells the freehold to B and takes back a lease for 20 years at a rent of £2 million per year, increasing annually by 1% compound, with a tenant's option for renewal for a further five years at an open market rent, exercisable by giving notice nine months before the end of the term.

Commentary:

The sale of the freehold to B is a standard transaction. The chargeable consideration will be the market value of the freehold subject to the leaseback (including the value of the rent available from the leaseback) as the transaction is treated as an exchange for SDLT purposes[975].

Sale and leaseback relief will be available to S in relation to the leaseback. On the first assignment of that lease which is not either an assignment to S's nominee or exempt, the relief will be clawed back. Where a clawback occurs, the assignment of the lease would be treated as the grant of a new lease by S for a term equal to the unexpired portion of the 20 year term, and on the same terms as those on which B holds that lease after the assignment. The option to renew will be ignored.

Completion of SDLT1 in relation to the leaseback transaction:

Relief should be claimed by S by entering Code 28 (other) in Box 9.

9.6.2. Commercial: sale of leasehold and sub-leaseback

S has a long lease of a supermarket. S sells the long lease to B and takes back a sub-lease for 15 years at a rent of £50,000 per year with reviews every five years to open market rent.

Commentary:

The sale of the long lease to B is a standard transaction. The chargeable consideration will be the market value of the long lease subject to the leaseback (including the value of the rent available from the leaseback) as the transaction is treated as an exchange for SDLT purposes[976].

Sale and leaseback relief will be available to S in relation to the leaseback. On the first assignment of that lease which is not either an assignment to S's nominee or exempt, the relief will be clawed back. Where a clawback occurs, the assignment of the lease would be treated as the grant of a new lease by S for a term equal to the unexpired portion of the 20 year term, and on the same

---

[975] See 3.3 above

[976] See footnote 975

terms as those on which B holds that lease after the assignment. The option to renew will be ignored.

Completion of SDLT1 in relation to the leaseback transaction:
Relief should be claimed by S by entering Code 28 (other) in Box 9.

9.6.3. Commercial: sale of freehold and leaseback to group companies

S Group Plc operates ten retail shops. The freeholds of four of them are owned by S (Retail) Limited and the other six by S (Properties) Limited, being companies in the same group as S Group Plc. S (Retail) Limited and S (Properties) Limited exchange, simultaneously, ten separate contracts to sell each of the freeholds to B Limited (an unconnected company) and for B Limited to grant a separate leaseback of each shop to S Group Plc for 15 years at certain specified rents. Each individual sale is for under £250,000.

Commentary:
This will be a standard transaction as sale and leaseback relief is not available where the leaseback is not to the seller. The ten sales will be linked transactions as S (Retail) Limited and S (Properties) Limited are connected persons and the sales are part of a series.

Note: Sale and leaseback relief is not available between companies in the same group, although normally group relief would be available where a sale and leaseback takes place between group members

9.7. Surrender and merger of leases

9.7.1. Surrender by deed

T surrenders his lease by deed to L with vacant possession, T pays L £150,000 for accepting the surrender and for releasing T from dilapidations liability. The remedying of the dilapidations would have cost £50,000, although this sum is not mentioned in the deed.

Commentary:

The surrender of the lease is a land transaction however as the purchaser (L) gives no consideration the transaction is not chargeable (on the assumption that L is not a company connected with T when the deemed market value rule would apply[977]).

Note: A self-certificate (SDLT 60) will need to be completed.

9.7.2. Surrender by operation of law

As in scenario 1.1.1 but T surrenders his lease by operation of law.

Commentary:

The SDLT analysis is as in scenario 9.1.1 The absence of a document is irrelevant for SDLT purposes.

9.7.3. Surrender and re-grant

T holds a lease of a shop which now has just under five years unexpired. There is an outstanding rent review almost agreed at £20,000 per annum. The landlord grants T a new 15 year lease of the shop at an initial rent of £22,500 per annum paying T a reverse premium of £12,000.

Commentary:

The grant of the new lease will be a land transaction for SDLT purposes. The surrender of the old lease will not be treated as chargeable consideration for the grant of that new lease.

If SDLT was paid in respect of the old lease relief will be available in respect of the rent payable during the period of the new lease which overlaps with the old.

The reverse premium is not chargeable to SDLT.

Calculation of the SDLT:

Assuming that SDLT had been paid on the grant of the old lease and that the rent taken into account in determining the SDLT chargeable in respect of the acquisition of the old lease was £15,000 per annum then the RRV of the new

---

[977] Which substitutes a consideration of not less than the market value of the property transferred in certain cases where the purchaser is a company – see 9.7.2 above

lease will be calculated on the basis of an annual rent of £7,500 (£22,500 less £15,000) for the period of the new lease which overlaps with the old (just under five years) and £22,500 for the balance of the term.

9.8. Exchanges

9.8.1. Exchange of land: equality money

A transfers the freehold of a field to his neighbour B in exchange for B transferring to him a long lease of a smaller paddock and paying him £40,000. The field is worth £160,000 and the paddock £120,000.

Commentary:

There are two land transactions here – A to B and B to A. The consideration for the A to B transaction is £160,000 (the market value of the field which is acquired by B) and the consideration for the B to A transaction is £120,000 (the market value of the paddock which is acquired by A).

Calculation of the SDLT:

The transactions are not linked transactions. It is assumed that both pieces of land are non-residential property. The SDLT payable on the acquisition by A will be nil as the threshold of £150,000 for non-residential property is not exceeded.

The SDLT payable on the acquisition by B will be:
£160,000 x 1% = £1,600

Completion of SDLT1s in relation to the transaction:

Two SDLT1s will need to be filed (even though no SDLT is payable by A). In relation to each acquisition Box 12 of the SDLT1 (form of consideration) should show Code 37 (Other land).

9.8.2. Exchange of land: no equality money

The boundary between A's land and B's land is irregular. A and B exchange various areas in order to straighten the boundary. No payment is made by either of them since A and B are friends and consider that the values are probably roughly equal, although neither has measured the areas or obtained a valuation.

Commentary:

The analysis will be the same as for scenario 9.1.1. There are two land transactions and the chargeable consideration for each acquisition will be the market value of what is acquired. For this purpose each area of land will have to be valued separately.

9.8.3. Exchange of land: land exchanged for rights over land

A transfers the freehold of a small parcel of his land to his neighbour B, and pays B the sum of £2000 towards B's surveyor's and solicitor's fees. In return B grants A a right of way, for access to A's new barn, across B's adjacent land

Commentary:

As this is an exchange involving a 'major interest'[978] the analysis will be the same as for scenario 9.1.1 There are two land transactions and the chargeable consideration for each acquisition will be the market value of what is acquired.

If the exchange had not involved a major interest the consideration for each leg would exclude the disposal given in exchange for the acquisition and only the equality money would be chargeable[979].

---

[978] A 'major interest' is defined in section 117(2) (in relation to England and Wales) as a fee simple absolute or a term of years absolute at law or in equity. The definitions applying to Scotland and Northern Ireland are in section 117(3) and (4) respectively.

[979] See 1.9.3 above

9.9. Carrying out of works

9.9.1. Commercial: sale of newly constructed building

S contracts to sell the freehold interest in a sports centre for £3 million with vacant possession. The centre includes a new grandstand that has just been completed at a cost to S of £1 million. The property is not elected for VAT.

Commentary:

This is a standard transaction – the value of the building works can be ignored as they were not part of the consideration given by the purchaser for the land transaction as they have been done at S's cost.

As part of the price relates to the sale of the freehold in a new building which is not a 'qualifying building[980]' for VAT purposes (the grandstand) part of the price will be subject to VAT. If the price is VAT exclusive VAT will need to be added to the amount of the total consideration apportioned to the grandstand before the SDLT charge is calculated.

Calculation of the SDLT:

Assuming the price is VAT inclusive, the SDLT will be:
£3 million x 4% = £120,000

9.9.2. Commercial: sale of plot with building works to be executed after completion

S contracts to sell a plot of land to B for £500,000. S's group company, S2, contracts with B to build a factory on the site for £750,000 plus VAT. The sale of the site is to be completed four weeks after exchange of contracts and building work starts immediately after completion.

Commentary:

Provided that it is not a condition of the S-B land transaction that S2 (which is connected with S) carries out the works the value of the building works can be ignored as they are carried out after the effective date on land acquired under the land transaction. If S were the contractor it would make a difference to the SDLT analysis only if it was a condition of the S-B land transaction that S carried out the works as the value of the works may then be chargeable[981].

[980] See Item 1(a) Group 1 Schedule 9 VATA 1994

[981] See 1.7.6 above and Scenario 9.9.3 below

9.9.3. Commercial: sale of plot, to be completed when new building has been built under separate contract

S contracts to sell a plot of land to B for £500,000. S's group company, S2, contracts with B to build a factory on the site for £750,000 plus VAT. The sale of the site is to be completed once the building is completed (six months later), but the building contract price is payable by monthly instalments and building work is to start one week after exchange of these contracts.

Commentary:

The value of the works to be carried out will constitute chargeable consideration for SDLT purposes if, as a matter of construction, the carrying out of the works is part of the consideration given for the land transaction and, in effect, there is a sale of a completed building to B. As the works are carried out on the relevant land before the effective date of the land transaction (completion) the relief in paragraph 10 of Schedule 4 will not apply here[982]. The use of S2 will not avoid the SDLT charge as S1 and S2 are 'connected'.

The stage payments will not affect the position and the SDLT will be payable within 30 days of completion (unless the terms of the building contract are such as to amount to 'substantial performance' by B which is unlikely).

Completion of SDLT1 in relation to the transaction:

Assuming the building works are consideration, total consideration of £1,250,000 would be entered in Box 10 (total consideration). Code 32 (building works) would be entered in Box 12 (form of consideration).

9.9.4. Commercial: sale of plot, to be completed when new building is built

S contracts to sell a plot of land to B for £450,000 and agrees to build a factory on it for £750,000 plus VAT. The sale of the site is to be completed once the building is completed (six months later), but the building contract price is payable by monthly instalments and building work is to start one week after exchange of these contracts.

Commentary:

The same analysis applies as for scenario 9.9.3

9.9.5. Commercial: agreement to build and then grant lease

D contracts with T that D will construct a light industrial building to an agreed specification and that D will procure that a 15 year lease will then be granted to T by the fund which owns the estate and with whom D has a joint venture

---

[982] See 1.7.6 above

agreement. The lease is granted 15 months later, when the construction has been completed.

Commentary:

This is a standard transaction – the value of the building works can be ignored as they were not part of the consideration given by T for the land transaction as they have not been done at T's cost. This would also be the case if D were the landlord, provided that it is not T who pays for the works.

9.9.6. Commercial: agreement to grant a lease once the tenant has constructed a building

L and T enter into an agreement for a 150 year lease, the lease to be granted to T in consideration of the payment of a premium of £1 million and also in consideration of T constructing the building. T enters onto the land as licensee immediately after exchange of the agreement in order to construct the building, the lease to be granted five working days after practical completion of the works.

Commentary:

The value of the works to be carried out will constitute chargeable consideration as the carrying out of the works is part of the consideration given for the land transaction and the works are carried out on the relevant land before the effective date of the land transaction (completion).

Note: If the entering onto the land by T as licensee is in terms that amount to T taking possession of the leasehold interest which is to be granted to him, the works will not form part of the chargeable consideration as they will be carried out after the effective date (the date T takes possession).

Completion of SDLT1 in relation to the transaction:

The total consideration of £1,000,000 plus the value of the works would be entered in Box 10 (total consideration). Code 32 (building works) would be entered in Box 12 (form of consideration)

9.10. Holding over

9.10.1. Holding over: tenant vacates

The lease of a shop which was granted after 1 December 2003 expires on 24 March 2010. The landlord, having previously overlooked the need to serve a six month termination notice under section 25 Landlord and Tenant Act 1954, serves the notice in December 2009 to terminate the tenancy on 23 June 2010. The tenant (T) decides to comply with the notice so he remains in occupation until that date and then vacates. Since the 1954 Act continues his existing tenancy until that date, the tenant continues paying the existing level of rent, which is £120,000 per annum.

Commentary:

The holding over by T will be treated for SDLT purposes as the grant to him of a lease for a fixed term of one year longer than the original fixed term on 25 March 2010. This means that SDLT will be charged on the additional rent payable for a full year, notwithstanding that the tenancy continues only for one quarter.

Overlap relief will be available as the original lease was an SDLT transaction (see scenario 9.7.3)

9.10.2. Holding over: new lease granted

The lease of an office which was granted after 1 December 2003 at an annual rent of £50,000 expires on 23 June 2010. The landlord (L) served a notice on the tenant (T) under section 25 of the Landlord and Tenant Act 1954 to terminate the tenancy on that date. T continues in occupation beyond that date while renewal terms are being negotiated under the Act.

T carries on paying rent at the annual rate of £50,000. On 1 October 2010 it is agreed that L will grant T a new lease expiring on 23 June 2017 at a rent of £65,000 per annum. By the new provisions of the 1954 Act, that yearly amount will also be payable as interim rent backdated to 24 June 2010. L's solicitor submits a draft new lease expressed to grant a term from 24 June 2010 to 23 June 2017.

Commentary:

The analysis in respect of the holding over will be as for scenario 9.1.1 In other words, the holding over by T will be treated for SDLT purposes as the grant to him on 24 June 2010 of a lease for a fixed term of one year longer than the original fixed term. This will enable SDLT to be charged on the rent payable during the holding over period and an SDLT1 based on the rent of £50,000 per annum must be filed within 30 days of the first day of the hold over period. Overlap relief will be available as the grant of the original lease was an SDLT transaction.

Once the interim rent in respect of the hold over period is fixed (on 1 October 2010) the SDLT1 filed in respect of the holding over must be amended (by 31 October 2010) to reflect the increase in the rent to £60,000 per annum.

The grant of the new lease will be a standard transaction. If the new lease covers the hold over period (and the rent is backdated), credit will be given for the SDLT paid in respect of that period from the start of the hold over to the date of grant of the new lease when calculating the SDLT due on the grant of the new lease.

9.11. Options and pre-emption rights

9.11.1. New lease: commercial with option to buy freehold

S wants to sell an industrial building which it built ten years ago and which is let. An investor, B, is to buy it for £10 million. However, S wants to keep the industrial building allowances so, instead of selling the freehold, S grants B a 999 year lease at a premium of £10 million and an annual rent of £1 and gives B an option to buy the freehold for £1, exercisable in 12 years time.

Commentary:
The grant of the 999 year lease to B will be a standard transaction.

The grant of the option to buy is a separate land transaction, linked to the grant of the lease. SDLT on the underlying land transaction to which the option may give rise is chargeable, if and when the option is exercised. The grant of the option is notifiable as SDLT will be chargeable at the rate of 1% or more by virtue of its being linked to the grant of the lease.

Completion of SDLT1 in relation to the transaction:
Code O will be entered in Box 2, Code OT in Box 3 and the fact that the grant of the option is a linked transaction indicated in Box 13.

9.11.2. New lease: commercial with option to buy freehold

S grants B an option over the freehold of a VAT elected retail building for £3 million, the option allowing the grantee to buy the site for £9 million plus an overage if B obtains and implements a planning permission for residential development of more than a specified density.

Commentary:
See scenario 9.1.1

Calculation of the SDLT:
Assuming the price is VAT inclusive, the SDLT payable on the grant of the option will be:
£3,000,000 x 4% = £120,000

On the exercise of the option the SDLT will be calculated on the basis of £9 million plus the overage payment (if it is ascertainable at the effective date of the transaction). If the overage is not ascertainable at that time, a reasonable estimate of the amount of the overage should be included on from SDLT1 and an amended or additional land transaction return submitted when the amount of the overage is ascertained.

9.11.3. Grant of pre-emption right

S grants B, in consideration of £250,000, a right to buy S's land if S decides to sell it within the next four years. The land price is to be the market value of the land at the date when S gives notice of his decision to sell.

Commentary:

The SDLT analysis is the same as for an option to buy – see scenarios 9.1.1 and 9.11.2.

9.12. Grant of Easements and Rights

9.12.1. Grant of parking rights

S grants B, who owns the adjacent building, a permanent right to park six cars in the parking area of S's building, for £400,000.

Commentary:

This is a standard land transaction. The grant is notifiable as tax is chargeable. The grant will be subject to VAT[983] so SDLT will be calculated on the VAT-inclusive consideration at 3%.

9.12.2. Grant of easement

S grants B the right to create a fire escape door in the party wall between their buildings and a right of emergency escape across S's yard to the back lane, in consideration of B paying him £175,000 and allowing S to lay a fibre optic communications cable across B's parking area.

Commentary:

There are two land transactions, S to B and B to S. As the exchange does not involve 'major interests'[984] only the equality money is chargeable (and the exchange element is ignored). This means that B's acquisition is subject to SDLT (and therefore notifiable) and S's is not.

---

[983] Item 1(h) Group 1 Schedule 9 VATA 1994

[984] Defined in section 117(2) (in relation to England and Wales) as a fee simple absolute or a term of years absolute at law or in equity. The definitions applying to Scotland and Northern Ireland are in section 117(3) and (4) respectively.

9.13. Statutory planning etc agreements

9.13.1. Section 106 agreement (1)

The local council resolves to grant planning permission for a commercial development, subject to the developer entering into an agreement under section 106 of the Town and Country Planning Act 1990. The developer enters into the section 106 agreement pursuant to which he agrees to pay £100,000 for nearby road improvements.

Commentary:

There is no land transaction so no SDLT charge arises.

9.13.2. Section 106 agreement (2)

The local council resolves to grant planning permission for a residential development, subject to the developer entering into an agreement under section 106 of the Town and Country Planning Act 1990. The developer enters into the section 106 agreement pursuant to which agrees to grant long leases of a specified number of the flats in the development to a housing association and to construct a playground and transfer it to the council.

Commentary:

The transfer to the local authority of the playground will be exempt as it is in pursuance of a planning obligation within the meaning of section 106 of the Town and Country Planning Act 1990.

The transfer to the housing association will be a standard transaction as in order for the relief for transfers in pursuance of planning obligations to apply the local authority must be the purchaser.

Completion of SDLT1 in relation to the transaction:

Relief will be claimed in respect of the acquisition of the playground by inserting Code 11 in Box 9. Code 34 (other) should be entered in Box 12 (form of consideration).

9.14. Gifts and transfers at an undervalue

9.14.1. Transfer to a connected person

A buys a leasehold flat for his daughter B to occupy while she is a trainee solicitor. When B qualifies, A transfers the flat to her as a gift. At that time the flat is worth £175,000. In accordance with the terms of the lease, B executes a direct covenant with the landlord that she will pay the rent and observe the lessee's covenants in the lease, and doing this releases A from ongoing liability for those matters.

Commentary:

The acquisition by A will be a standard transaction.

As A and B are individuals the deemed market value rule does not apply. The execution of the covenant by B is not chargeable consideration. The transaction is exempt as a transfer for no chargeable consideration.

Note: There will be no requirement for an SDLT1 but a self-certificate (SDLT60) will need to be completed.

9.14.2. Transfer at an undervalue

A buys a small house, with a mortgage, for his son B to occupy while he is a trainee accountant. When B qualifies, A transfers the house to B as a gift and B takes over the mortgage debt of £160,000. At that time the house is worth £230,000.

Commentary:

As A and B are individuals the deemed market value rules does not apply. The assumption of the mortgage debt by B is chargeable consideration.

Calculation of the SDLT:

The SDLT payable will be:

£160,000 x 1% = £1600

Completion of SDLT1 in relation to the transaction:

Box 12 of the SDLT1 (form of consideration) should show Code 31 (Debt).

9.14.3. Transfer at an undervalue

A and B own a house jointly, now worth £450,000. They have a joint mortgage of £300,000. A few months ago they made some home improvements at a cost of £15,000 which were paid for wholly by A. B is now emigrating to Australia and they transfer the house to A, upon A paying B £67,500 and taking over liability for the whole mortgage.

Commentary:
As in scenario 9.14.2 the assumption of the debt by A is chargeable consideration. The chargeable consideration will be increased by £150,000, being B's notional share of the mortgage debt. The cost of the home improvements paid for by A are ignored.

Calculation of the SDLT:
The SDLT payable will be:

£217,500 x 1% = £2175

Completion of SDLT1 in relation to the transaction:
Box 12 of the SDLT1 (form of consideration) should show Codes 30 (cash) and 31 (debt).

9.15. Transfers in matrimonial cases

9.15.1. Transfer pursuant to Court Order

Husband and wife are the joint owners of home valued at £540,000 subject to mortgage of £400,000. Pursuant to a Court Order Husband transfers his interest in the property to Wife, with Wife accepting liability for outstanding mortgage.

Commentary:

This transaction is exempt. A self-certificate (SDLT60) will need to be completed.

9.15.2. Transfer not fulfilling terms of exemption

Husband and wife live in a flat owned by an offshore company which is in turn owned by an offshore trust. Husband is ordered to use his best endeavours to secure the transfer of the flat to the wife in the most tax efficient manner. The flat is worth £2.5 million with no mortgage and is in due course transferred to the wife.

Commentary:

This will be a standard transaction as that land transaction will not be between the parties to a marriage. The fact that the transferor is an offshore company and is, presumably, a company which is ultimately owned or controlled by the husband does not affect matters. If there is no consideration the transaction will be exempt and a self-certificate (SDLT60) will need to be completed.

9.15.3. Transfer as part of divorce settlement

Husband is the sole owner of matrimonial home worth £1.2 million. Husband is to transfer to wife subject to mortgage as part of divorce settlement. Wife to indemnify husband against mortgage of £80,000 or discharge it.

Commentary:

This transaction is exempt. A self-certificate (SDLT60) will need to be completed.

9.16. Miscellaneous

9.16.1. Acquisition by a trust through an offshore company

Ms X, living in London, is within the class of beneficiaries of an offshore discretionary trust created by a family who were at the time resident and domiciled in South Africa. Ms X has found a flat that she wants the trust to buy for her to live in. The trust owns an offshore company and injects funds into the company to enable it to buy the flat for occupation by Miss X.

Commentary:

This is a standard transaction with the offshore company as the purchaser completing an SDLT4 as well as an SDLT1.

9.16.2. Purchase of a business: apportionment

A assigns his leasehold shop to B, together with the goodwill of his retail business, for £185,000, and also sells him his stock at valuation. The price fixed by valuation for the stock, on completion, is £25,000. A and B have not discussed how the sum of £185,000 is split between the lease and the goodwill.

Commentary:

The £185,000 will need to be apportioned on a fair and reasonable basis between the lease and any inherent goodwill so that the SDLT charge on the acquisition of the lease can be calculated. Goodwill which is not an inherent part of the land transaction does not count as chargeable consideration and this is likely to be the case here where there is a business sale. If it is the purchase of a business an SDLT4 will need to be filed.

9.16.3. Sale of business by a liquidator

The liquidator of A Ltd. sells the freehold of a small furniture factory to B for £230,000, the large fixed lathes and other fixed machinery in the factory for £25,000, the goodwill of the furniture business for £10,000 and the stock for £35,000.

Commentary:

This is a standard transaction with B as the purchaser. Goodwill which is not an inherent part of the land transaction does not count as chargeable consideration and this is likely to be the case here as there is a business sale. However, the value of the fixed machinery needs to be added to the value of the freehold. This brings the chargeable consideration to £255,000, and therefore the transaction falls in the second band (more than £250,000 and less than £500,000) and is charged at 3%.

Note: Where a company in liquidation is the purchaser, the liquidator as the proper officer of the company should sign the SDLT1. If it is the purchase of a business an SDLT4 will need to be filed.

9.16.4. Transfer by a liquidator (1)

A solvent company, S Limited, is voluntarily wound up and its sole property, worth £550,000, is transferred in specie by the liquidator to the only shareholder, B.

Commentary:

The acquisition by B would be exempt as a transfer for no chargeable consideration (see scenario 9.1.1).

Note: If B is a company, the deemed market value rule [985] will not apply (so as to disapply exemption). This is because although S Limited and B will be connected persons at the effective date of the transaction, the rule does not apply where the transaction is a distribution in specie by a liquidator (unless the interest transferred has been the subject of a group relief claim within the three years preceding the effective date).

9.16.5. Transfer by a liquidator (2)

A solvent company, S Limited, is voluntarily wound up and its sole property, worth £550,000, is to be transferred in specie by the liquidator to the two shareholders jointly. It is then suggested that the liquidator should transfer it to B only, who will pay £275,000 to the other shareholder. The transfer to B is completed on these terms.

Commentary:

This is a standard transaction. The chargeable consideration is £275,000.

Note: If B is a company, the deemed market value rule[986] may apply.

9.16.6. Transfer on reduction of capital

A solvent company, S Limited, resolves to reduce its capital by £400,000 and transfers a property worth £400,000, in specie to the shareholders.

Commentary

Provided that there is no chargeable consideration the transfer will be exempt (see scenario 9.1.1).

---

[985] Which substitutes a consideration of not less than the market value of the property transferred in certain cases where the purchaser is a company – see 1.7.2 above

[986] See footnote 985

PART FIVE
SDLT GLOSSARY

10. SDLT Glossary

(most terms are indexed in section 122, FA 2003)

Defined term	**Meaning**	**Location in FA 2003**
chargeable consideration	except where the deemed market value rule applies, any consideration in money or money's worth given for the 'subject matter' of the transaction	section 50 and Schedule 4
chargeable interest	any estate, interest, right or power in or over land situated in the UK, or the benefit of any obligation, restriction or condition affecting the value of such an estate, interest, right or power other than an 'exempt interest'	section 48(1)
chargeable transaction	any land transaction which is not 'exempt from charge'	section 49(1)
connected	**Section 839 Taxes Act 1988** **Connected persons** (1) For the purposes of, and subject to, the provisions of the Tax Acts which apply this section, any question whether a person is connected with another shall be determined in accordance with the following provisions of this section (any provision that one person is connected with another being taken to mean that they are connected with one another). (2) A person is connected with an individual if that person is the individual's spouse or civil partner, or is a relative, or the spouse or civil partner of a relative, of the individual or of the individual's spouse or civil partner. (3) A person, in his capacity as trustee of a settlement, is connected with— (*a*) any individual who in relation to the settlement is a settlor, (*b*) any person who is connected with such an individual, and (*c*) any body corporate which is connected with that settlement. In this subsection 'settlement' and 'settlor' have the same meaning as in Chapter 5 of Part 5 of ITTOIA 2005 (see section 620 of that Act) (3A) For the purpose of subsection (3) above a body corporate is connected with a settlement if-	section 108(1)

	(*a*) it is a close company (or only not a close company because it is not resident in the United Kingdom) and the participators include the trustees of the settlement; or (*b*) it is controlled (within the meaning of section 840) by a company falling within paragraph (*a*) above. (4) Except in relation to acquisitions or disposals of partnership assets pursuant to bona fide commercial arrangements, a person is connected with any person with whom he is in partnership, and with the spouse or civil partner or relative of any individual with whom he is in partnership. (5) A company is connected with another company— (*a*) if the same person has control of both, or a person has control of one and persons connected with him, or he and persons connected with him, have control of the other; or (*b*) if a group of two or more persons has control of each company, and the groups either consist of the same persons or could be regarded as consisting of the same persons by treating (in one or more cases) a member of either group as replaced by a person with whom he is connected. (6) A company is connected with another person if that person has control of it or if that person and persons connected with him together have control of it. (7) Any two or more persons acting together to secure or exercise control of a company shall be treated in relation to that company as connected with one another and with any person acting on the directions of any of them to secure or exercise control of the company. (8) In this section— 'company' includes any body corporate or unincorporated association, but does not include a partnership, and this section shall apply in relation to any unit trust scheme as if the scheme were a company and as if the rights of the unit holders were shares in the company; 'control' shall be construed in accordance with section 416; and 'relative' means brother, sister, ancestor or lineal	

	descendant.	
effective date	the date of completion unless section 44(4) (contract and conveyance: contract 'substantially performed' without having been completed) or section 46(3) (options and rights of pre-emption) applies	section 119
exempt interest	any 'security interest', licence to occupy land, tenancy at will, advowson, 'franchise' or manor	section 48(2)-(5)
exempt from charge	Schedule 3 provides that certain land transactions are exempt from charge subject to conditions. There are also reliefs which provide for exemption from charge[987]	section 49(2) and Schedule 3
implementation date	The 'implementation date' appointed by the Stamp Duty Land Tax (Appointment of the Implementation Date) Order 2003 (SI 2003/2899). This date was 1st December 2003	paragraph 2(2) Schedule 19
land	'land' includes buildings and structures and land covered by water	section 121
land transaction	any acquisition of a 'chargeable interest'	section 2(1)
land transaction return	Form SDLT1 and any supplementary forms	section 76 (1) and section 78
linked transactions	transactions forming part of a single scheme, arrangement or series of transactions between the same vendor and purchaser or persons 'connected' with them	section 108(1)
main subject matter	the 'chargeable interest' acquired	section 43 (6)
major interest	in England and Wales, a fee simple or term of years absolute	section 117(2)
market value	the price which might reasonably be achieved on a sale in the open market	section 118 applying sections 272-274 TCGA 1992
non-residential property	Any property that is not 'residential'	section 116
notifiable transaction	(i) The grant of a lease: (a) for a term of seven years or more for chargeable consideration ; or (b) for a term of less than seven years and either:	section 77

[987] See Chapter 3 above

	the chargeable consideration consists of or includes a premium in respect of which SDLT is chargeable at a rate of 1% or more (or would be but for a relief) or the chargeable consideration consists of or includes rent in respect of which SDLT is chargeable at a rate of 1% or more (or would be but for a relief) (ii) The assignment of a lease is notifiable if: (a) The grant of the lease, if occurring at the time of the assignment, would be notifiable; or (b) There is consideration for the assignment that is chargeable at the rate of 1% or higher, or would be so chargeable but for a relief. Any other acquisition of a 'major interest' in land is notifiable unless the transaction is exempt under Schedule 3 or the land consists of residential property and the chargeable consideration for the acquisition, together with that for any linked transaction, is less than £1,000. Any other acquisition of a chargeable interest is notifiable if SDLT is chargeable at the rate of 1% or more, or would be so chargeable but for the claiming of a relief. (iii) A land transaction that a person is treated as entering into by virtue of section 44A(3) (contract and conveyance to third party) is notifiable (iv) A lease to which paragraph 3 of Schedule 17A applies (leases that continue after a fixed term) is notifiable whatever its fixed term.	
purchaser	the person acquiring subject-matter of the transaction who is a party to the transaction or has given consideration for it.	section 43(4)-(5)
rate of tax	the percentage determined under section 55	section 55(7)
relevant consideration	the 'chargeable consideration' for the transaction, subject to the rules for linked transactions and to the provisions of section 74 (collective enfranchisement by leaseholders) and section 75 (crofting community right to buy)	section 55(3)-(5)
relevant land	the land an interest in which is the 'main subject-matter' of the transaction	section 55(3)
residential property	(*a*) a building that is 'used or suitable for use as a dwelling', or is in the process of being constructed	section 116

	or adapted for such use, and (*b*) land that is or forms part of the garden or grounds of a building within paragraph (*a*) (including any building or structure on such land), or (*c*) an interest in or right over land that subsists for the benefit of a building within paragraph (*a*) or of land within paragraph (*b*); *Note:* Where six or more separate dwellings are the subject of a single transaction involving the transfer of a major interest in, or the grant of a lease over, them, then, for the purposes of this Part as it applies in relation to that transaction, those dwellings are treated as not being residential property.	section 116(7)
relevant rental value (RRV)	The net present value of the rent payable over the term of a lease	paragraph 2(4) Schedule 5
Revenue certificate	a certificate by HMRC that a land transaction return has been delivered in respect of a land transaction	section 79(3)(a)
security interest	any interest or right (other than a rentcharge) held for the purpose of securing the payment of money or the performance of any other obligation	section 48(3)
self certificate	a certificate by the purchaser that no land transaction return is required in respect of a land transaction	section 79(3)(b)
subject matter	the 'main subject matter' together with any interest or right appurtenant or pertaining to it that is acquired with it	section 43(6)
substantial performance	the purchaser 'taking possession' of the whole or substantially the whole of the subject-matter of the contract or the 'payment or provision of a substantial amount of the consideration'	section 44(5)-(7)
used as a dwelling	A building used for any of the following purposes is used as a dwelling: (a) residential accommodation for school pupils; (b) residential accommodation for students, other than accommodation falling with subsection (3)(b); (c) residential accommodation for members of the armed forces; (d) an institution that is the sole or main residence of at least 90% of its residents and does not fall within any of paragraphs (a) to (f) of subsection (3). A building used for any of the following purposes	section 116(2)

	is not used as a dwelling: (a) a home or other institution providing residential accommodation for children; (b) a hall of residence for students in further or higher education; (c) a home or other institution providing residential accommodation with personal care for persons in need of personal care by reason of old age, disablement, past or present dependence on alcohol or drugs or past or present mental disorder; (d) a hospital or hospice; (e) a prison or similar establishment; (f) a hotel or inn or similar establishment.	section 116(3)
	Where a building is used for a purpose specified in subsection (3), no account shall be taken for the purposes of subsection (1)(*a*) of its suitability for any other use.	section 116(4)
	Where a building that is not in use is suitable for use for at least one of the purposes specified in subsection (2) and at least one of those specified in subsection (3): • if there is one such use for which it is most suitable, or if the uses for which it is most suitable are all specified in the same sub-paragraph, no account shall be taken of its suitability for any other use, • otherwise, the building shall be treated for those purposes as suitable for use as a dwelling.	section 116(5)
vendor	the person disposing of the subject-matter of the transaction	section 43(4)

PART SIX

SDLT FORMS

Land Transaction Return (SDLT1)

HM Revenue & Customs

Land Transaction Return

For official use only

Your transaction return

How to fill in this return

The guidance notes that come with this return will help you answer the questions.

- Write inside the boxes. Use black ink and CAPITAL letters.
- If you make a mistake, please cross it out and write the correct information underneath.
- **Leave blank any boxes that don't apply to you** – please don't strike through anything irrelevant.
- Show amounts in whole pounds only, rounded down to the nearest pound. Ignore the pence.
- Fill out the payslip on page 7.
- Do not fold the return. Send it back to us unfolded in the envelope provided.
- **Photocopies are not acceptable.**

If you need help with any part of this return or with anything in the guidance notes, please phone the Stamp Taxes enquiry line on **0845 603 0135**, open 8:30am to 5:00pm Monday to Friday, except Bank Holidays. You can get further copies of this return and any supplementary returns from the Orderline on **0845 302 1472**.

Starting your return

ABOUT THE TRANSACTION

1 **Type of property**

Enter code from the guidance notes

2 **Description of transaction**

Enter code from the guidance notes

3 **Interest transferred or created**

Enter code from the guidance notes

4 **Effective date of transaction**

D D M M Y Y Y Y

5 **Any restrictions, covenants or conditions affecting the value of the interest transferred or granted?** Put 'X' in one box

Yes No

If 'yes' please provide details

6 **Date of contract or conclusion of missives**

D D M M Y Y Y Y

7 **Is any land exchanged or part-exchanged?** Put 'X' in one box

Yes No

If 'yes' please complete address of location

Postcode

House or building number

Rest of address, including house name, building name or flat number

8 **Is the transaction pursuant to a previous option agreement?** Put 'X' in one box

Yes No

SDLT 1 PG 1 IMS6/05

ABOUT THE TAX CALCULATION

9 **Are you claiming relief?** Put 'X' in one box

Yes No

If 'yes' please show the reason

Enter code from the guidance notes

Enter the charity's registered number, if available, or the company's CIS number

For relief claimed on part of the property only, please enter the amount remaining chargeable

£ . 0 0

10 **What is the total consideration in money or money's worth, including any VAT actually payable for the transaction notified?**

£ . 0 0

11 **If the total consideration for the transaction includes VAT, please state the amount**

£ . 0 0

12 **What form does the consideration take?**
Enter the relevant codes from the guidance notes

13 **Is this transaction linked to any other(s)?**
Put 'X' in one box

Yes No

Total consideration or value in money or money's worth, including VAT paid for all of the linked transactions

£ . 0 0

14 **Total amount of tax due for this transaction**

£ . 0 0

15 **Total amount paid or enclosed with this notification**

£ . 0 0

Does the amount paid include payment of any penalties and any interest due? Put 'X' in one box

Yes No

ABOUT LEASES

If this doesn't apply, go straight to box 26 on page 3

16 **Type of lease**

Enter code from the guidance notes

17 **Start date as specified in lease**

D D M M Y Y Y Y

18 **End date as specified in lease**

D D M M Y Y Y Y

19 **Rent-free period**
Number of months

20 **Annual starting rent inclusive of VAT (actually) payable**

£ . 0 0

End date for starting rent

D D M M Y Y Y Y

Later rent known? Put 'X' in one box

Yes No

21 **What is the amount of VAT, if any?**

£ . 0 0

22 **Total premium payable**

£ . 0 0

23 **Net present value upon which tax is calculated**

£ . 0 0

24 **Total amount of tax due – premium**

£ . 0 0

25 **Total amount of tax due – NPV**

£ . 0 0

Check the guidance notes to see if you will need to complete supplementary return 'Additional details about the transaction, including leases', SDLT4.

SDLT 1 PG 2

+

ABOUT THE LAND including buildings

Where more than one piece of land is being sold or you cannot complete the address field in the space provided, please complete the supplementary return 'Additional details about the land', SDLT3.

26 **Number of properties included**

27 **Where more than one property is involved, do you want a certificate for each property?** Put 'X' in one box

Yes No

28 **Address or situation of land**
Postcode

House or building number

Rest of address, including house name, building name or flat number

Is the rest of the address on the supplementary return 'Additional details about the land', SDLT3?
Put 'X' in one box

Yes No

29 **Local authority number**

30 **Title number, if any**

31 **NLPG UPRN**

32 **If agricultural or development land, what is the area (if known)?** Put 'X' in one box

Hectares Square metres

Area

.

33 **Is a plan attached?** Please note that the form reference number should be written/displayed on map. Put 'X' in one box

Yes No

+

ABOUT THE VENDOR including transferor, lessor

34 **Number of vendors included** (Note: if more than one vendor, complete boxes 45 to 48)

35 **Title** Enter MR, MRS, MISS, MS or other title
Note: only complete for an individual

36 **Vendor (1) surname or company name**

37 **Vendor (1) first name(s)** Note: only complete for an individual

38 **Vendor (1) address**
Postcode

House or building number

Rest of address, including house name, building name or flat number

SDLT 1 PG 3

+

ABOUT THE VENDOR CONTINUED

39 **Agent's name**

40 **Agent's address**
Postcode

Building number

Rest of address, including building name

41 **Agent's DX number and exchange**

42 **Agent's e-mail address**

43 **Agent's reference**

44 **Agent's telephone number**

ADDITIONAL VENDOR

Details of other people involved (including transferor, lessor), other than vendor (1). If more than one additional vendor please complete supplementary return 'Land Transaction Return – Additional vendor/purchaser details', SDLT2.

+

45 **Title** Enter MR, MRS, MISS, MS or other title
Note: only complete for an individual

46 **Vendor (2) surname or company name**

47 **Vendor (2) first name(s)**
Note: only complete for an individual

48 **Vendor (2) address**

Put 'X' in this box if the same as box 38.

If not, please give address below
Postcode

House or building number

Rest of address, including house name, building name or flat number

SDLT 1 PG 4

ABOUT THE PURCHASER including transferee, lessee

49 **Number of purchasers included** (Note: if more than one purchaser is involved, complete boxes 65 to 69)

50 **National Insurance number (purchaser 1), if you have one.** Note: only complete for an individual

51 **Title** Enter MR, MRS, MISS, MS or other title
Note: only complete for an individual

52 **Purchaser (1) surname or company name**

53 **Purchaser (1) first name(s)**
Note: only complete for an individual

54 **Purchaser (1) address**

Put 'X' in this box if the same address as box 28.

If not, please give address below

Postcode

House or building number

Rest of address, including house name, building name or flat number

55 **Is the purchaser acting as a trustee?** Put 'X' in one box

Yes No

56 **Please give a daytime telephone number** - this will help us if we need to contact you about your return

57 **Are the purchaser and vendor connected?**
Put 'X' in one box

Yes No

58 **To which address shall we send the certificate?**
Put 'X' in one box

Property (box 28) Purchaser's (box 54)

Agent's (box 61)

59 **I authorise my agent to handle correspondence on my behalf.** Put 'X' in one box

Yes No

60 **Agent's name**

61 **Agent's address**
Postcode

Building number

Rest of address, including building name

62 **Agent's DX number and exchange**

63 **Agent's reference**

64 **Agent's telephone number**

SDLT 1 PG 5

+

ADDITIONAL PURCHASER

Details of other people involved (including transferee, lessee), other than purchaser (1). If more than one additional purchaser, please complete supplementary return 'Land Transaction Return – Additional vendor/purchaser details', SDLT2.

65 **Title** Enter MR, MRS, MISS, MS or other title
Note: only complete for an individual

66 **Purchaser (2) surname or company name**

67 **Purchaser (2) first name(s)**
Note: only complete for an individual

68 **Purchaser (2) address**

Put 'X' in this box if the same as purchaser (1) (box 54).
If not, please give address below
Postcode

House or building number

Rest of address, including house name, building name or flat number

69 **Is purchaser (2) acting as a trustee?** Put 'X' in one box

Yes No

+

ADDITIONAL SUPPLEMENTARY RETURNS

70 **How many supplementary returns have you enclosed with this return?** Write the number in each box. If none, please put '0'.

Additional vendor/purchaser details, SDLT2

Additional details about the land, SDLT3

Additional details about the transaction, including leases, SDLT4

DECLARATION

71 **The purchaser(s) must sign this return.** Read the guidance notes in booklet SDLT6, in particular the section headed *'Who should complete and sign the Land Transaction Return?'*.

If you give false information, you may face financial penalties and prosecution.
The information I have given on this return is correct and complete to the best of my knowledge and belief.

Signature of purchaser 1

Signature of purchaser 2

Please keep a copy of this return and a note of the unique transaction reference number, which is in the 'Reference' box on the payslip.

Finally, please send your completed return to:
HM Revenue & Customs, Stamp Taxes/SDLT, Comben House, Farriers Way, NETHERTON, Merseyside, Great Britain, L30 4RN, or the DX address is: Rapid Data Capture Centre, DX725593, Bootle 9

Please don't fold it - keep it flat and use the envelope provided. Fill out the payslip on the next page and pay in accordance with the 'How to pay' instructions.

SDLT 1 PG 6

How to pay

Please allow enough time for payment to reach us by the due date. We suggest you allow at least 3 working days for this.

MOST SECURE AND EFFICIENT

We recommend the following payment methods. These are the most secure and efficient.

1. Direct Payment
Use the Internet or telephone to make payment. Provide your bank or building society with the following information

- payment account
- sort code 10-50-41
- account number 23456000
- your reference as shown on the payslip.

2. BillPay
You can pay by Debit Card over the Internet. Visit **www.billpayment.co.uk/hmrc** and follow the guidance.

3. At your bank
Take this form with payment to **your** bank and where possible to **your own** branch. Other banks may refuse to accept payment. If paying by cheque, make your cheque payable to 'HM REVENUE & CUSTOMS ONLY'.

4. At a Post Office
Take this form with your payment to any Post Office. If paying by cheque, make your cheque payable to 'POST OFFICE LTD'. The Post Office also accept payment by Debit Card.

5. Alliance & Leicester Commercial Bank Account
Alliance & Leicester Commercial Bank customers can instruct their bank to arrange payment.

OTHER PAYMENT METHODS

By post
If you use this method

- Make your cheque payable to 'HM REVENUE & CUSTOMS ONLY'.
- Write your payslip reference after 'HM REVENUE & CUSTOMS ONLY'.
- Send the payslip and your cheque, **both unfolded**, in the envelope provided to
  HM Revenue & Customs SDLT
  Netherton
  Merseyside
  L30 4RN

By DX
As above, but send to
Rapid Data Capture Centre
DX725593
Bootle 9

FURTHER PAYMENT INFORMATION

You can find further payment information at **www.hmrc.gov.uk/howtopay**

Sample

Alliance & Leicester COMMERCIAL BANK Transcash
Bootle Merseyside GIR 0AA

Payslip HM Revenue & Customs

bank giro credit

159
209
24

Reference

Credit account number 610 5041

£ Amount due
(not fee payable at PO counter)
CHEQUE ACCEPTABLE

By transfer from Alliance & Leicester account number

For official use only

Name

Cashier's stamp and initials

Signature __________ Date __________

CASH

CHEQUE

BANK OF ENGLAND
HEAD OFFICE COLLECTION A/C
HM REVENUE & CUSTOMS

£

10-50-41

SDLT1/P

Please do not fold this payslip or write or mark below this line

Sample Sample

Land Transaction Return (additional vendor/purchaser details) (SDLT2)

Inland Revenue

Land Transaction Return

Additional vendor/purchaser details

When to fill in this return

You must fill in this return for each additional vendor and/or purchaser. The guidance notes will help you answer the questions.

If you need help with any part of this return or with anything in the guidance notes, please phone the Stamp Taxes enquiry line on **0845 603 0135**, open 8:30am to 5:00pm Monday to Friday, except Bank Holidays. Calls are charged at local rates. You can get further copies of this return from the Orderline on **0845 302 1472**.

REFERENCE

Insert the reference number from the payslip on page 7 of the Land Transaction Return, SDLT1, here.

For official use only

sample

VENDOR OR PURCHASER

1 **Please indicate if this return is for an additional vendor or an additional purchaser.** Put 'X' in one box

Vendor Complete section below only

Purchaser Complete section below and the section over the page

COMPLETE IN ALL CASES

2 **Title** Enter MR, MRS, MISS, MS or other title
Note: only complete for an individual

3 **Surname or company name**

4 **First name(s)**
Note: only complete for an individual

5 **Address**
Postcode

House or building number

Rest of address, including house name, building name or flat number

Please turn over for additional purchaser details

SDLT 2 PG 1 BS09/03

+

ADDITIONAL PURCHASER DETAILS

Only complete this section if this return is for an additional purchaser.

6 **Are the purchaser and vendor connected?**
Put 'X' in one box

☐ Yes ☐ No

7 **Is the purchaser acting as a trustee?** Put 'X' in one box

☐ Yes ☐ No

8 **Declaration**

The purchaser(s) must sign this return.
Read the notes in Section 1 of the guidance notes, SDLT6 'Who should complete the Land Transaction Return?'

If you give false information, you may face financial penalties and prosecution.

The information I have given on this form is correct and complete to the best of my knowledge and belief.

Signature of purchaser

+

SDLT 2 PG 2

Land Transaction Return (additional details about the land) (SDLT3)

Inland Revenue

Land Transaction Return

Additional details about the land

When to fill in this return
Fill in this return when you cannot fit all the details on the main Land Transaction Return, SDLT1. The guidance notes will help you answer the questions.

If you need help with any part of this return or with anything in the guidance notes, please phone the Stamp Taxes enquiry line on **0845 603 0135**, open 8:30am to 5:00pm Monday to Friday, except Bank Holidays. Calls are charged at local rates. You can get further copies of this return from the Orderline on **0845 302 1472**.

REFERENCE

Insert the reference number from the payslip on page 7 of the Land Transaction Return, SDLT1, here.

For official use only

sample

ABOUT THE LAND

1 **Type of property**

Enter code from the guidance notes

2 **Local authority number**

3 **Title number, if any**

4 **NLPG UPRN**

5 **Address or situation of land**
Postcode

House or building number

Rest of address, including house name, building name, flat number or continuation from the SDLT1

Please turn over

SDLT 3 PG 1 BS09/03)

+

ABOUT THE LAND CONTINUED

6 **If agricultural or development land, what is the area (if known)?**

☐ Hectares ☐ Square metres

Area

☐☐☐☐☐☐☐☐☐☐ . ☐☐☐

7 **If there are any minerals or mineral rights reserved enter the code below**

☐☐ Enter code from the guidance notes

8 **Is a plan attached?** Please note that the form reference number should be written/displayed on map. Put 'X' in one box

☐ Yes ☐ No

9 **Interest transferred or created**

☐☐ Enter code from the guidance notes

+

SDLT 3 PG 2

Land Transaction Return (additional details about the transaction, including leases) (SDLT4)

Inland Revenue

Land Transaction Return

Additional details about the transaction, including leases

When to fill in this return

You must fill in this return where additional information about the transaction and/or lease can be provided.
The guidance notes will help you answer the questions.

If you need help with any part of this return or with anything in the guidance notes, please phone the Stamp Taxes enquiry line on **0845 603 0135**, open 8:30am to 5:00pm Monday to Friday, except Bank Holidays. Calls are charged at local rates. You can get further copies of this return from the Orderline on **0845 302 1472**.

REFERENCE

Insert the reference number from the payslip on page 7 of the Land Transaction Return, SDLT1, here.

For official use only

sample

ABOUT THE TRANSACTION

1 **If this transaction is part of the sale of business, please say if the sale includes** Put 'X' in relevant boxes

Stock
Goodwill
Other
Chattels and moveables

What is the total amount of the consideration for the sale of the business apportioned to these items?

£ . 0 0

2 **If the property is for commercial use, what is it?** Put 'X' in the appropriate box(es)

Office
Hotel
Shop
Warehouse
Factory
Other
Other industrial unit

3 **Have you applied for and received a post transaction ruling in accordance with Code of Practice 10, or asked us for advice on the application of the law to this transaction?** Put 'X' in one box

Yes
No

If 'yes' have you followed it when completing this return? Put 'X' in one box

Yes
No
Ruling not received

4 **Is any part of the consideration contingent or dependent on uncertain future events?**

Yes
No

5 **Have you agreed with the Inland Revenue that you will pay on a deferred basis?**

Yes
No

6 **If there are any minerals or mineral rights reserved enter the code below**

Enter code from the guidance notes

7 **If the purchaser is VAT registered, give their VAT reference number**

8 **If the purchaser is a company please give the following details**

Tax reference number

Company registration number

If registered abroad, give its place of registration

Please turn over

SDLT4 V2 PG 1 BS11/04

ABOUT THE TRANSACTION CONTINUED

9 **Give a description of the purchaser**
Enter code from the guidance notes

ABOUT LEASES

Complete if the transaction notified on SDLT1 is for the grant of more than one lease

10 **Type of property**

Enter code from the guidance notes

11 **Address or situation of land**

Put 'X' in this box if the same as box 28 on SDLT1

If not, please give address below

Postcode

House or building number

Rest of address, including house name, building name, flat number or continuation from the SDLT1

continued at the top of the next column

12 **Local authority number**

13 **Title number, if any**

14 **NLPG UPRN**

15 **If the transaction is for land, what is the unit and area of measurement?** Put 'X' in one box

Hectares　　Square metres

Area

16 **Is a plan attached? Please note that the form reference number should be written/displayed on the map.**
Put X in one box

Yes　　No

17 **Interest transferred or created**

Enter code from the guidance notes

18 **Type of lease**

Enter code from the guidance notes

SDLT 4 V2　　PG 2

+

ABOUT LEASES CONTINUED

19 Start date as specified in lease

D D M M Y Y Y Y

20 End date as specified in lease

D D M M Y Y Y Y

21 Rent free period
Number of months

22 Annual starting rent inclusive of VAT (actually) payable

£ . 0 0

End date for starting rent

D D M M Y Y Y Y

Later rent known? Put 'X' in one box

Yes No

23 What is the amount of VAT, if any?

£ . 0 0

24 Total premium payable

£ . 0 0

25 Net present value upon which tax is calculated

£ . 0 0

26 Total amount of tax due - premium

£ . 0 0

27 Total amount of tax due - NPV

£ . 0 0

28 Any terms surrendered

29 Break clause type Put 'X' in one box

Landlord Tenant only

Either

30 What is the date of the break clause?

D D M M Y Y Y Y

31 Which of the following relate to this lease?
Put 'X' in relevant boxes. If none, leave blank

Option to renew

Market rent

Turnover rent

Unascertainable rent

Contingent reserved rent

32 Rent review frequency

33 Date of first review

D D M M Y Y Y Y

34 Rent review clause (type) Put 'X' in one box

Open market RPI

Other

35 If Schedule 17A para 7FA 2003 has been used in calculating the NPV, what is the date of the rent change?

D D M M Y Y Y Y

+

Please turn over

+

ABOUT LEASES CONTINUED

36 **Service charge amount if known**

£ . 0 0

37 **Service charge frequency** Put 'X' in one box

Monthly

Annually

Quarterly

Other

38 **Other consideration – tenant to landlord**
(for example, services, building works)
Enter the relevant codes from the guidance notes

39 **Other consideration – landlord to tenant**
(for example, services, building works)
Enter the relevant codes from the guidance notes

+

SDLT 4 V2 PG 4

Land Transaction Return Guidance notes (SDLT6)
As SDLT6 is now updated regularly online by HMRC, we have not reproduced this as an appendix. Before undertaking any new transaction, the reader is advised to consult the HMRC website at:

http://www.hmrc.gov.uk/so/sdlt6.pdf, for a printable pdf, or
http://www.hmrc.gov.uk/sdlt6/index.htm, for the html version.

Certificate that no Land Transaction Return is required for a land transaction (SDLT60)

HM Revenue & Customs

Stamp duty land tax

Certification that no Land Transaction Return is required for a land transaction

This is a self-certificate under Section 79(3) of Finance Act 2003

Effective date of transaction

/ /

Title number/folio number

Property or land address

Name and address of purchaser's solicitor/agent

Name(s) and address of purchaser

Name(s) and address of vendor

Please turn over

SDLT 60

HMRC 03/06

Reason no Land Transaction Return is required

√

- ☐ Transfer or conveyance of a freehold interest in land for no chargeable consideration.
- ☐ Grant of a lease in England & Wales or Northern Ireland for a term of seven years or more and for no chargeable consideration (that is, no premium and no rent of any monetary value).
- ☐ Transfer or assignment of a lease for no chargeable consideration.
- ☐ Grant of a lease where all the following are satisfied:
  - the term of the lease is less than seven years, and
  - the amount of any premium is not such as to attract a charge to SDLT at a rate of 1% or higher (ignoring the availability of any relief), and
  - the amount of any rent is not such as to attract a charge to SDLT at a rate of 1% or higher (ignoring the availability of any relief).
- ☐ Transfer or assignment of a lease where both the following are satisfied:
  - the term of the lease when granted was less than seven years, and
  - the amount of any consideration for the assignment is not such as to attract a charge to SDLT at a rate of 1% or higher (ignoring the availability of any relief).
- ☐ Land transaction (other than the transfer of a freehold interest in land, or grant or assignment of a lease) where the amount of the consideration is not such as to attract a charge to SDLT at a rate of 1% or higher (ignoring the availability of any relief).
- ☐ Land transaction exempt from SDLT under Schedule 3 paragraph 3 Finance Act 2003 (transactions in connection with divorce or dissolution of a civil partnership formed under the Civil Partnership Act 2004).
- ☐ Land transaction exempt from SDLT under Schedule 3 paragraph 4 Finance Act 2003 (variation of testamentary dispositions).
- ☐ Transfer or conveyance of a freehold interest in land consisting entirely of residential property where the chargeable consideration, together with that of any linked transaction(s), is less than £1,000.
- ☐ Acquisition by a beneficiary entitled under a will or on intestacy, where the only consideration given is the assumption of 'secured debt' as defined in paragraph 3A of Schedule 3 Finance Act 2003.
- ☐ Transfer of interest in a partnership for chargeable consideration not exceeding the zero rate threshold.

Note: in Scotland

- for 'a freehold interest in land' read 'ownership of land'
- 'a lease' includes missives of let constituting a lease
- for 'assignment of a lease' read 'assignation of a tenant's interest under a lease (including missives of let constituting a lease)'

Declaration

This certificate must be signed by the person acquiring the interest. Signature by an agent is not acceptable. Where there is more than one transferee all of them must sign the certificate, except in certain circumstances (please refer to guidance notes).

I certify that for the reason given (as ticked) I do not need to submit a Land Transaction Return to HM Revenue & Customs.

If you give false information in this certificate you may face financial penalties and prosecution.

I declare that the information I have given in this form is true and complete to the best of my knowledge and belief.

Signature of purchaser(s)

Name (printed)

Capacity in which signing

Date

/ /

Index